Praise for *The Slave Ship*

"With passion and power, Rediker presents four slave ship dramas. . . . Straight from the heart of darkness, he explores the legacies of race, class, and slavery through 'ghost ships sailing on the edges of modern consciousness.' "   —*The Baltimore Sun*

"[An] exquisite and grotesque narrative."   —*The New York Sun*

"Marcus Rediker escapes the 'the violence of abstraction' in this history of slave ships that richly mines the extant writings of captains, sailors, and slaves."   —*Chicago Tribune*

"The slave ship was a machine that manufactured modernity. As it moved across the Atlantic, the world changed. It joined Europe, Africa, and the Americas, creating enormous wealth and untold misery, and its hellish voyages continue to cast a shadow over our lives. Marcus Rediker, a preeminent historian of the maritime Atlantic, unravels its history with unmatched knowledge of the material changes and moral ruptures its created. *Slave Ship* is the best of histories, deeply researched, brilliantly formulated, and morally informed."   —Ira Berlin, distinguished university professor, University of Maryland, and author of Bancroft Prize–winner *Many Thousands Gone*, *Slaves Without Masters*, and *Generations of Captivity*

"I admire this book more than I can easily say. At the heart of it is the slave ship, engine of wood and hemp and canvas, instrument of terror. From this dark heart Marcus Rediker ranges outward over four centuries and three continents. He brings to his task a combination of dedicated research, deep human concern, and narrative power of a high order. By insisting on the realities of individual experience, he counteracts our human tendency to take refuge from horror in comforting abstractions. We are all indebted to him for this. In range and scope and in the humanity of its treatment, this account of the Atlantic slave trade is unlikely ever to be superceded."
                                        —Barry Unsworth, author of *Sacred Hunger*

"I was hardly prepared for the profound emotional impact of *The Slave Ship: A Human History*. Reading it established a transformative and never to be severed bond with my African ancestors who were cargo in slave ships over a period of four centuries. Their courage, intelligence, and self-respect;

their fierce efforts to free themselves (and, though cruelly bound, to create community) moved me so deeply that, for several days, I took to my bed. There I pondered the madness of greed, the sadism of wielding absolute power over any creature in chains, the violence of attempting to dominate and possess what is innately free. For all Americans and indeed all those who live in the Western world who have profited by, or suffered from, the endless brutality of the slave trade, during all its centuries and into the present, this book is *homework* of the most insistent order. There is no rebalancing of our wrecked planet without sitting with, and absorbing, the horrifying reality of what was done, by whites, by the West, by the wealthy, to our beloved ancestors, the Africans, who endured and sometimes survived 'the middle passage' to bring their radiance and their indomitable spirits into the New World. What, now, is to be done? That is the question that can only have a collective answer." —Alice Walker, author of *The Color Purple*

"*The Slave Ship* is a book, like *Bury My Heart at Wounded Knee*, that will change the way we see history and ourselves. In this brilliant work, Marcus Rediker achieves the impossible: he enables us to imagine centuries of unimaginable cruelty. He also enables us to imagine the resistance to slavery that eventually brought it down, through the evocation of unforgettable characters: Olaudah Equiano, a slave who recorded the ordeal of the Middle Passage in his autobiography; James Field Stanfield, the anti-slavery sailor and poet; John Newton, the slave ship captain turned abolitionist who wrote 'Amazing Grace.' Rediker writes with the care of a scholar, the eye of a poet, and the heart of a rebel. He does justice to the story of a monstrous injustice."   —Martín Espada, author of *The Republic of Poetry*

"*The Slave Ship* is truly a magnificent and disturbing book—disturbing not only because it details the violence and barbarism of the free market in human beings, but it reminds us that all actors in this drama are human, including the ship's crew. *The Slave Ship* is not for the faint-hearted, but like the millions who took this voyage in the past, we have no choice. We have to come to terms with this history if we want to understand how this modern, racialized, and globalized economy based on exploitation came to be."
                    —Robin D. G. Kelley, author of *Freedom Dreams:*
                    The Black Radical Imagination

"*The Slave Ship* is a tour de force that conveys the reality of the slave trade more vividly and convincingly than ever before. I am sure that it will continue to be read as long as people want to understand a crucial episode in the birth of the modern world."
——Robin Blackburn, author of *The Making of New World Slavery*

"This beautifully written and exhaustively researched book gives us unforgettable portraits of the captives, captains, and crewmen who came together in that particular kind of hell known as the slave ship. This is Atlantic history at its best." ——Robert Harms, author of *The Diligent*

"Marcus Rediker is one of the most distinguished historians of the eighteenth-century Atlantic world, and he brings to the slave ship both an unrivaled knowledge of maritime labor and a deep theoretical perspective on the slave trade's role in the rise of capitalism."
——Steven Hahn, author of the Pulitzer Prize–winning *A Nation Under Our Feet*

"This Atlantic epic brilliantly reveals the slave ship as a 'vast machine,' transforming its human cargo into slaves—and portrays precisely the variety of Africans, free and captive, in their choices and desperate struggles."
——Patrick Manning, author of *Slavery and African Life*

"Marcus Rediker, like the incomparable Herman Melville, understands both the immediate human drama and the sweeping global context of life aboard a cramped ocean vessel in the age of sail. He uses his unique gifts to take us belowdecks, giving a human face to the inhuman ordeal of the Middle Passage." ——Peter H. Wood, author of *Strange New Land: Africans in Colonial America*

"The Atlantic's foremost historian from below has written a masterpiece; we hear the shrieks of pain, the groans of loss, and uproar of rebellion. In the end, with ex-slaves offering amazing graces to discarded sailors, the cry rises up from this magnificent book for justice and for reparation."
——Peter Linebaugh, author of *The London Hanged*

PENGUIN BOOKS

THE SLAVE SHIP

Marcus Rediker is a professor of history at the University of Pittsburgh. He is the author of *The Amistad Rebellion; The Slave Ship: A Human History*, winner of the George Washington Book Prize and the Merle Curti Award; and (with Peter Linebaugh) *The Many-Headed Hydra: Sailors, Slaves, Commoners, and the Hidden History of the Revolutionary Atlantic.*

Visit www.MarcusRediker.com.

The

SLAVE SHIP

A Human History

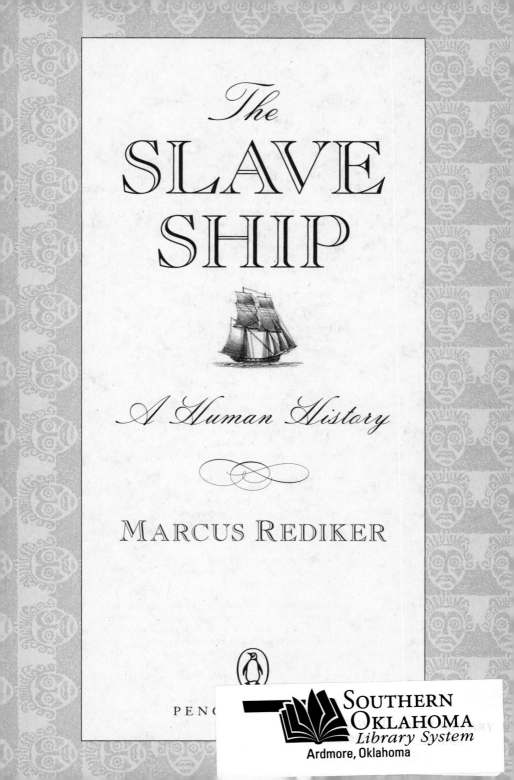

MARCUS REDIKER

PENG

PENGUIN BOOKS
Published by the Penguin Group
Penguin Group (USA) Inc., 375 Hudson Street, New York, New York 10014, U.S.A.
Penguin Group (Canada), 90 Eglinton Avenue East, Suite 700, Toronto,
Ontario, Canada M4P 2Y3 (a division of Pearson Penguin Canada Inc.)
Penguin Books Ltd, 80 Strand, London WC2R 0RL, England
Penguin Ireland, 25 St Stephen's Green, Dublin 2, Ireland (a division of Penguin Books Ltd)
Penguin Group (Australia), 250 Camberwell Road, Camberwell,
Victoria 3124, Australia (a division of Pearson Australia Group Pty Ltd)
Penguin Books India Pvt Ltd, 11 Community Centre, Panchsheel Park, New Delhi – 110 017, India
Penguin Group (NZ), 67 Apollo Drive, Rosedale, North Shore 0632,
New Zealand (a division of Pearson New Zealand Ltd)
Penguin Books (South Africa) (Pty) Ltd, 24 Sturdee Avenue,
Rosebank, Johannesburg 2196, South Africa

Penguin Books Ltd, Registered Offices:
80 Strand, London WC2R 0RL, England

First published in the United States of America by Viking Penguin,
a member of Penguin Group (USA) Inc. 2007
Published in Penguin Books 2008

14 15 16 17 18 19 20

THE LIBRARY OF CONGRESS HAS CATALOGED THE HARDCOVER EDITION AS FOLLOWS:
Rediker, Marcus Buford.
Slave ship : a human history / Marcus Rediker.
p.   cm.
Includes bibliographical references and index.
ISBN 978-0-670-01823-9 (hc.)
ISBN 978-0-14-311425-3 (pbk.)
1. Slave trade—Africa—History.   2.   Slaves. 3.   Merchant mariners. 4.   Race relations. I.   Title.
HT1322.R42 2007
306.3'62096—dc22   2007018081

Printed in the United States of America
Designed by Carla Bolte • Set in Granjon
Maps by Jeffrey L. Ward

To Wendy, Zeke, and Eva

with love and hope

———∞∞∞———

CONTENTS

SLAVE SHIP

Introduction

Lying in the bottom of the canoe in three or four inches of dirty water with a woven mat thrown over her travel-weary body, the woman could feel the rhythmic pull of the paddles by the Bonny canoemen, but could not see where they were taking her. She had traveled three moons from the interior, much of it by canoe down the rivers and through the swamps. Several times along the way, she had been sold. In the canoe-house barracoon where she and dozens of others had been held for several days, she learned that this leg of the journey was nearing its end. Now she wiggled upward against the wet torso of another prostrate captive, then against the side of the canoe, so she could raise her head and peer above the bow. Ahead lay the *owba coocoo,* the dreaded ship, made to cross the "big water." She had heard about it in the most heated threats made in the village, where to be sold to the white men and taken aboard the *owba coocoo* was the worst punishment imaginable.[1]

Again and again the canoe pitched up and down on the foamy surf, and each time the nose dipped, she could glimpse the ship like an oddly shaped island on the horizon. As they came closer, it seemed more like a huge wooden box with three tall spikes ascending. The wind picked up, and she caught a peculiar but not unfamiliar odor of sweat, the pungency of fear with a sour trail of sickness. A shudder rippled through her body.

To the left of the canoe, she saw a sandbar and made a decision. The paddles plashed gently in the water, two, three, four times, and she jumped over the side, swimming furiously to escape her captors. She heard splashes as a couple of the canoemen jumped in after her. No sooner had they hit the water than she heard a new commotion, looked over her shoulder, and saw them pulling themselves back into the canoe. As she waded onto the edge of the sandbar, she saw a large, stocky gray shark, about eight feet long, with a blunt, rounded snout and small eyes, gliding alongside the canoe as it came directly at her. Cursing, the men clubbed the shark with their paddles, beached the watercraft, jumped out, and waded, then loped after her. She had nowhere to run on the sandbar, and the shark made it impossible to return to the water. She fought, to no avail. The men lashed rough vine around her wrists and legs and threw her back into the bottom of the canoe. They resumed paddling and soon began to sing. After a while she could hear, at first faintly, then with increasing clarity, other sounds—the waves slapping the hull of the big ship, its timbers creaking. Then came muffled screaming in a strange language.

The ship grew larger and more terrifying with every vigorous stroke of the paddles. The smells grew stronger and the sounds louder—crying and wailing from one quarter and low, plaintive singing from another; the anarchic noise of children given an underbeat by hands drumming on wood; the odd comprehensible word or two wafting through: someone asking for *menney,* water, another laying a curse, appealing to *myabecca,* spirits. As the canoemen maneuvered their vessel up alongside, she saw dark faces, framed by small holes in the side of the ship above the waterline, staring intently. Above her, dozens of black women and children and a few red-faced men peered over the rail. They had seen the attempted escape on the sandbar. The men had cutlasses and barked orders in harsh, raspy voices. She had arrived at the slave ship.

The canoemen untied the lashing and pushed the woman toward a rope ladder, which she ascended with fifteen others from her canoe, everyone naked. Several of the men climbed up with them, as did the black trader in a gold-laced hat who had escorted them from the canoe house to the *owba coocoo*. Most of the people in her group, herself included, were amazed by what they saw, but a couple of the male captives seemed strangely at ease, even speaking to the white men in their own tongue. Here was a world unto itself, with tall, shaved, limbless trees; strange instruments; and a high-reaching system of ropes. Pigs, goats, and fowl milled around the main deck. One of the white men had a local parrot, another a monkey. The *owba coocoo* was so big it even had its own *ewba wanta* (small boat) on board. Another white man, filthy in his person, leered at her, made a lewd gesture, and tried to grope her. She lunged at the man, digging her fingernails into his face, bringing blood in several places before he disentangled himself from her and lashed her sharply three times with a small whip he was carrying. The black trader intervened and hustled her away.

As she recovered her composure, she surveyed the faces of the other prisoners on the main deck. All of them were young, some of them children. In her village she was considered middling in age, but here she was one of the oldest. She had been purchased only because the clever black trader had sold a large group in a lot, leaving the captain no choice but to take what he was offered, all or none. On the ship she would be an elder.

Many of the people on deck seemed to speak her language, Igbo, although many of them differently from herself. She recognized a couple of other groups of people from her home region, the simple Appas and the darker, more robust Ottams. Many of the captives, she would learn later, had been on board the ship for months. The first two had been named Adam and Eve by the sailors. Three or four were sweeping the deck; many were washing up. Sailors handed out small wooden bowls for the afternoon meal. The ship's cook served beef and bread to some, the more familiar yams with palm oil to others.

The main deck bustled with noisy activity. A white man with black skin, a sailor, screamed *"Domona!"* (quiet) against the din. Two other white men seemed to be especially important to everything that happened. The big man on board was the captain, whose words caused the other white men to jump. He and the doctor busily checked the newcomers—head, eyes, teeth, limbs, and belly. They inspected a family—a husband, wife, and child—who had come aboard together from her canoe. The man was taken, with tears in his eyes, through the barricado door into the forward part of the ship. From beyond the barrier, she heard the cries of another man getting *pem pem,* a beating. She recognized his anguished intonation as Ibibio.

Soon after she had been examined, a white man barked at her, "Get below! Now! Hurry!" and pushed her toward a big square hole in the deck. A young woman standing nearby feared that she did not understand the order and whispered urgently, *"Gemalla! Geyen gwango!"* As she descended the rungs of a ladder into the lower deck, a horrific stench assaulted her nostrils and suddenly made her dizzy, weak, queasy. She knew it as the smell of *awawo,* death. It emanated from two sick women lying alone in a dark corner, unattended, near the *athasa,* or "mess-tub," as the white men called it. The women died the following day, their bodies thrown overboard. Almost instantaneously the surrounding waters broke, swirled, and reddened. The shark that had followed her canoe had its meal at last.

* * *

The story of this woman was one act in what the great African-American scholar-activist W. E. B. DuBois called the "most magnificent drama in the last thousand years of human history"—"the transportation of ten million human beings out of the dark beauty of their mother continent into the new-found Eldorado of the West. They descended into Hell." Expropriated from her native land, the woman was forced aboard a slave ship to be transported to a new world of work and exploitation, where she would likely produce sugar, tobacco, or rice and make her owner wealthy. This book follows her, and others like her, onto the tall ships, those strange and powerful European machines that made it all possible.[2]

The epic drama unfolded in countless settings over a long span of time, centering not on an individual but rather a cast of millions.

Over the almost four hundred years of the slave trade, from the late fifteenth to the late nineteenth century, 12.4 million souls were loaded onto slave ships and carried through a "Middle Passage" across the Atlantic to hundreds of delivery points stretched over thousands of miles. Along the dreadful way, 1.8 million of them died, their bodies cast overboard to the sharks that followed the ships. Most of the 10.6 million who survived were thrown into the bloody maw of a killing plantation system, which they would in turn resist in all ways imaginable.[3]

Yet even these extraordinary numbers do not convey the magnitude of the drama. Many people captured in Africa died as they marched in bands and coffles (human trains) to the slave ships, although the lack of records makes it impossible to know their precise numbers. Scholars now estimate that, depending on time and place, some portion between a tenth and a half of the captives perished between the point of enslavement and the boarding of the slave ship. A conservative estimate of 15 percent—which would include those who died in transit and while being held in barracoons and factories on the coast—suggests another 1.8 million deaths in Africa. Another 15 percent (or more, depending on region), a million and a half, would expire during the first year of laboring life in the New World. From stage to stage—expropriation in Africa, the Middle Passage, initial exploitation in America—roughly 5 million men, women, and children died. Another way to look at the loss of life would be to say that an estimated 14 million people were enslaved to produce a "yield" of 9 million longer-surviving enslaved Atlantic workers. DuBois's "most magnificent drama" was a tragedy.[4]

The so-called golden age of the drama was the period 1700–1808, when more captives were transported than any other, roughly two-thirds of the total. More than 40 percent of these, or 3 million altogether, were shipped in British and American ships. This era, these ships, their crews, and their captives are the subjects of this book. During this time the mortality rate on the ships was falling, but the sheer number of deaths remains staggering: nearly a million died throughout the slave trade, a little less than half of these in the commerce organized from

British and American ports. The numbers are more chilling because those who organized the human commerce knew the death rates and carried on anyway. Human "wastage" was simply part of the business, something to be calculated into all planning. This would be denounced as murder pure and simple by the African writer Ottobah Cugoano, himself a veteran of the Middle Passage, and others who built a transatlantic movement to abolish the slave trade in the 1780s.[5]

Where did the souls caught up in the drama come from, and where did they go? Between 1700 and 1808, British and American merchants sent ships to gather slaves in six basic regions of Africa: Senegambia, Sierra Leone/the Windward Coast, the Gold Coast, the Bight of Benin, the Bight of Biafra, and West Central Africa (Kongo, Angola). Ships carried the captives primarily to the British sugar islands (where more than 70 percent of all slaves were purchased, almost half of these at Jamaica), but sizable numbers were also sent to French and Spanish buyers as a result of special treaty arrangements called the Asiento. About one in ten was shipped to North American destinations. The largest share of these went to South Carolina and Georgia, with substantial numbers also to the Chesapeake. The drama would continue in a new act after the captives stumbled off the ships.[6]

On the rolling decks of the slave ship, four distinct but related human dramas were staged, again and again, over the course of the long eighteenth century. Each was meaningful in its own day and again in ours. The players in these dramas were the ship captain, the motley crew, the multiethnic enslaved, and, toward the end of the period, middle-class abolitionists and the metropolitan reading public to whom they appealed in both Britain and America.

The first drama centered on the relations between the slave-ship captain and his crew, men who in the language of the day must have neither "dainty fingers nor dainty noses," as theirs was a filthy business in almost every conceivable sense.[7] Captains of slavers were tough, hard-driving men, known for their concentrated power, ready resort to the lash, and ability to control large numbers of people. Violent command applied almost as much to the rough crews of the slavers as to the hundreds of captives they shipped. Discipline was often brutal, and many a sailor was lashed to fatality. Moreover, for sailors in the slave trade, rations were poor, wages were usually low, and the mortality rate was high—as high as that of the enslaved, modern scholarship has shown. Sailors captured this deadly truth in a saying:

> Beware and take care
> Of the Bight of Benin;
> For the one that comes out,
> There are forty go in.

Many died, some went blind, and countless others suffered lasting disability. Captains and crews therefore repeatedly clashed, as could be suggested even by names: Samuel Pain was a violent slave-ship captain; Arthur Fuse was a sailor and mutineer. How did captains recruit sailors to this deadly trade in the first place, and how did these relations play out? How did relations between captain and crew change once the enslaved came aboard?[8]

The relationship between sailors and slaves—predicated on vicious forced feedings, whippings, casual violence of all kinds, and the rape of women captives—constituted the second drama. The captain presided over this interaction, but the sailors carried out his orders to bring the enslaved on board, to stow them belowdecks, to feed them, compel them to exercise ("dance"), maintain their health, discipline and punish them—in short, slowly transform them into commodities for the international labor market. This drama also witnessed endlessly creative resistance from those being transported, from hunger strikes to suicide to outright insurrection, but also selective appropriations of culture from the captors, especially language and technical knowledge, as, for example, about the workings of the ship.

A third and simultaneous drama grew from conflict and cooperation among the enslaved themselves as people of different classes, ethnicities, and genders were thrown together down in the horror-filled lower deck of the slave ship. How would this "multitude of black people, of every description chained together" communicate? They found ways to exchange valuable information about all aspects of their predicament, where they were going, and what their fate would be. Amid the brutal imprisonment, terror, and premature death, they managed a creative, life-affirming response: they fashioned new languages, new cultural practices, new bonds, and a nascent community among themselves aboard the ship. They called each other "shipmate," the equivalent of brother and sister, and thereby inaugurated a "fictive" but very real kinship to replace what had been destroyed by their abduction and enslavement in Africa. Their creativity and resistance made them collectively indestructible, and herein lay the greatest magnificence of the drama.[9]

The fourth and final drama emerged, not on the ship but in civil society in Britain and America as abolitionists drew one horrifying portrait after another of the Middle Passage for a metropolitan reading public. This drama centered on the image of the slave ship. Thomas Clarkson went down to the docks of Bristol and Liverpool to gather information about the slave trade. But once his antislavery sentiments became known, slave-trading merchants and ship captains shunned him. The young Cambridge-educated gentleman began to interview sailors, who had firsthand experience of the trade, complaints to register, stories to tell. Clarkson gathered this evidence and used it to battle merchants, plantation owners, bankers, and government officials—in short, all who had a vested interest in the slave trade and the larger institution of slavery. The success of the abolitionist movement lay in making real for people in Britain and America the slave ship's pervasive and utterly instrumental terror, which was indeed its defining feature. The "most magnificent drama" had a powerful final act: the shipbuilder's diagram of the slave ship *Brooks,* which showed 482 "tight-packed" slaves distributed around the decks of the vessel, eventually helped the movement abolish the slave trade.

The year 1700 was a symbolic beginning of the drama in both Britain and America. Although merchants and sailors had long been involved in the trade, this was the year of the first recorded slaving voyage from Rhode Island, which would be the center of the American slave trade, and from Liverpool, which would be its British center and, by the end of the century, the center of the entire Atlantic trade. At the end of May 1700, the *Eliza,* Captain John Dunn, set sail from Liverpool for an unspecified destination in Africa and again to Barbados, where he delivered 180 slaves. In August, Nicholas Hilgrove captained the *Thomas and John* on a voyage from Newport, Rhode Island, to an unspecified destination in Africa and then to Barbados, where he and his sailors unloaded from their small vessel 71 captives. Hundreds of slavers would follow from these ports and from others in the coming century.[10]

Despite shifts in the numbers of people shipped, as well as their sources and destinations, the slave ship itself changed relatively little between 1700 and 1808. Slaving vessels grew somewhat larger in size over time, and they grew more efficient, employing smaller crews in relation to the number of the enslaved shipped. They certainly grew in number, to handle the greater volume of bodies to be transported. And their atmosphere grew healthier: the death rate, for sailors and for slaves, declined, especially in the late eighteenth century. Yet the essentials of running a slave ship, from the sailing to the stowing, feeding, and exercising of the human cargo, remained roughly the same over time. To put the matter another way, a captain, a sailor, or an African captive who had experienced a slave ship in 1700 would have found most everything familiar a century later.[11]

What each of them found in the slave ship was a strange and potent combination of war machine, mobile prison, and factory. Loaded with cannon and possessed of extraordinary destructive power, the ship's war-making capacity could be turned against other European vessels, forts, and ports in a traditional war of nations, or it could be turned to and sometimes against non-European vessels and ports in imperial trade or conquest. The slave ship also contained a war within, as the crew (now prison guards) battled slaves (prisoners), the one training its guns on the others, who plotted escape and insurrection. Sailors also "produced" slaves within the ship as factory, doubling their economic value as they moved them from a market on the eastern Atlantic to one on the west and helping to create the labor power that animated a growing world economy in the eighteenth century and after. In producing workers for the plantation, the ship-factory also produced "race." At the beginning of the voyage, captains hired a motley crew of sailors, who would, on the coast of Africa, become "white men." At the beginning of the Middle Passage, captains loaded on board the vessel a multiethnic collection of Africans, who would, in the American port, become "black people" or a "negro race." The voyage thus transformed those who made it. War making, imprisonment, and the factory production of labor power and race all depended on violence.

After many voyages and stalwart service to the Atlantic economy, the slave ship finally hit stormy seas. The opponents of the slave trade launched an intensive transatlantic agitation and finally forced the slavers to stop sailing—or at least, after new laws were passed by the British and American governments in 1807 and 1808 respectively, to stop sailing legally. The traffic continued illegally for many years, but a decisive moment in human history had been reached. Abolition, coupled with its profound coeval event, the Haitian Revolution, marked the beginning of the end of slavery.

* * *

Curiously, many of the poignant tales within the great drama have never been told, and the slave ship itself has been a neglected topic within a rich historical literature on the Atlantic slave trade. Excellent research has been conducted on the origins, timing, scale, flows, and profits of the slave trade, but there exists no broad study of the vessel that made the world-transforming commerce possible. There exists no account of the mechanism for history's greatest forced migration, which was in many ways the key to an entire phase of globalization. There exists no analysis of the instrument that facilitated Europe's "commercial revolution," its building of plantations and global empires, its development of capitalism, and eventually its industrialization. In short, the slave ship and its social relations have shaped the modern world, but their history remains in many ways unknown.[12]

Scholarship on the slave ship may be limited, but scholarship on the slave trade is, like the Atlantic, vast and deep. Highlights include

Philip Curtin's landmark study *The African Slave Trade: A Census* (1969); Joseph Miller's classic *Way of Death: Merchant Capitalism and the Angolan Slave Trade, 1730–1830* (1988), which explores the Portuguese slave trade from the seventeenth to the nineteenth century; Hugh Thomas's grand synthesis *The Slave Trade: The Story of the African Slave Trade, 1440–1870* (1999); and Robert Harms's elegant microhistory of a single voyage of the *Diligent* from France to Whydah to Martinique in 1734–35. The publication of *The Trans-Atlantic Slave Trade: A Database,* compiled, edited, and introduced by David Eltis, Stephen D. Behrendt, David Richardson, and Herbert S. Klein, represents an extraordinary scholarly achievement.[13] Other important studies of the slave trade have been literary, by writers such as Toni Morrison, Charles Johnson, Barry Unsworth, Fred D'Aguiar, Caryl Phillips, and Manu Herbstein.[14]

What follows is not a new history of the slave trade. It is, rather, something more modest, an account that uses both the abundant scholarship on the subject and new material to look at the subject from a different vantage, from the decks of a slave ship. Nor is it an exhaustive survey of its subject. A broader history that compares and connects the slave ships of all the Atlantic powers—not only Britain and the American colonies but also Portugal, France, the Netherlands, Spain, Denmark, and Sweden—remains to be written. More attention also needs to be trained on the connecting links between, on the eastern Atlantic, African societies and the slave ship and, on the western, the slave ship and plantation societies of the Americas. There is still much to be learned about the "most magnificent drama of the last thousand years of human history."[15]

The shift of focus to the slave ship expands the number and variety of actors in the drama and makes the drama itself, from prologue to epilogue, more complex. If heretofore the main actors have been relatively small but powerful groups of merchants, planters, politicians, and abolitionists, now the cast includes captains in their thousands, sailors in their hundreds of thousands, and slaves in their millions. Indeed the enslaved now appear as the first and primary abolitionists as they battle the conditions of enslavement aboard the ships on a daily basis and as they win allies over time among metropolitan activists and dissident sailors, middle-class saints and proletarian sinners. Other important players were African rulers and merchants, as well as workers in England and America, who joined the cause of abolition and indeed turned it into a successful mass movement.[16]

Why a human history? Barry Unsworth captured one of the reasons in his epic novel *Sacred Hunger*. Liverpool merchant William Kemp is talking with his son Erasmus about his slave ship, which, he has just learned by correspondence, has taken on board its human cargo in West Africa and set sail for the New World.

> In that quiet room, with its oak wainscotting and Turkey carpet, its shelves of ledgers and almanacks, it would have been difficult for those two to form any true picture of the ship's circumstances or the nature of trading on the Guinea coast, even if they had been inclined to try. Difficult, and in any case superfluous. To function efficiently—to function at all—we must concentrate our effects. Picturing things is bad for business, it is undynamic. It can choke the mind with horror if persisted in. We have graphs and tables and balance sheets and statements of corporate philosophy to help us remain busily and safely in the realm of the abstract and comfort us with a sense of lawful endeavour and lawful profit. And we have maps.[17]

Unsworth describes a "violence of abstraction" that has plagued the study of the slave trade from its beginning. It is as if the use of ledgers, almanacs, balance sheets, graphs, and tables—the merchants' comforting methods—has rendered abstract, and thereby dehumanized, a reality that must, for moral and political reasons, be understood concretely. An ethnography of the slave ship helps to demonstrate not only the cruel truth of what one group of people (or several) was willing to do to others for money—or, better, capital—but also how they managed in crucial respects to hide the reality and consequences of their actions from themselves and from posterity. Numbers can occlude the pervasive torture and terror, but European, African, and American societies still live with their consequences, the multiple legacies of race, class, and slavery. The slaver is a ghost ship sailing on the edges of modern consciousness.[18]

To conclude on a personal note, this has been a painful book to write, and if I have done any justice to the subject, it will be a painful book to read. There is no way around this, nor should there be. I offer this study with the greatest reverence for those who suffered almost unthinkable violence, terror, and death, in the firm belief that we must remember that such horrors have always been, and remain, central to the making of global capitalism.

—⚉—

CHAPTER I

Life, Death, and Terror in the Slave Trade

A voyage into this peculiar hell begins with the human seascape, stories of the people whose lives were shaped by the slave trade. Some grew prosperous and powerful, others poor and weak. An overwhelming majority suffered extreme terror, and many died in horrific circumstances. People of all kinds—men, women, and children, black, white, and all shades in between, from Africa, Europe, and the Americas—were swept into the trade's surreal, swirling vortex. They included, at the bottom, a vast and lowly proletariat, hundreds of thousands of sailors, who, in their tarred breeches, scuttled up and down the ratlines of a slave ship, and millions of slaves, who, in their nakedness, crouched on the lower deck. They included, at the top, a small, high, and mighty Atlantic ruling class of merchants, planters, and political leaders, who, in ruffles and finery, sat in the American Continental Congress and British Parliament. The "most magnificent drama" of human commerce also featured in its dramatis personae pirates and warriors, petty traders and hunger strikers, murderers and visionaries. They were frequently surrounded by sharks.

Captain Tomba

Among a gang of dejected prisoners in a holding pen, facing purchase by a slaver, one man stood out. He was "of a tall, strong Make, and bold, stern aspect." He saw a group of white men observing the barracoon, with "a design to buy," he thought. When his fellow captives submitted their bodies for examination by prospective buyers, he expressed contempt. John Leadstine, "Old Cracker," the head of the slave factory, or shipping point, on Bance Island, Sierra Leone, ordered the man to rise and "stretch out his Limbs." He refused. For his insolence he got a ferocious whipping with a "cutting *Manatea Strap*." He took the lashing with fortitude, shrinking little from the blows. An observer noted that he shed "a Tear or two, which he endeavoured to hide as tho' ashamed of."[1]

This tall, strong, defiant man was Captain Tomba, explained Leadstine to the visitors, who were impressed by his courage and eager to know his history, how he had been captured. He had been a headman of a group of villages, probably Baga, around the Rio Nuñez. They opposed the slave trade. Captain Tomba led his fellow villagers in burning huts and killing neighbors who cooperated with Leadstine and other slave traders. Determined to break his resistance, Leadstine in turn organized a midnight expedition to capture this dangerous leader, who killed two of his attackers but was finally taken.

Captain Tomba was eventually purchased by Captain Richard Harding and taken aboard the *Robert* of Bristol. Chained and thrown into the lower deck, he immediately plotted his escape. He combined with "three or four of the stoutest of his Country-men" and an enslaved woman who had freer range about the ship and hence better knowledge of when the plan might be put into action. One night the unnamed woman found only five white men on deck, all asleep. Through the gratings she slipped Captain Tomba a hammer, to pound off the fetters, and "all the Weapons she could find."

Captain Tomba encouraged the men belowdecks "with the Prospect of Liberty," but only one and the woman above were willing to join him. When he came upon three sleeping sailors, he killed two of them instantly with "single Strokes upon the Temples." In killing the third, he made commotion that awoke the two others on watch as well as the rest of the crew, sleeping elsewhere. Captain Harding himself picked up a handspike, flailed at Tomba, knocked him out, and "laid him at length flat upon the Deck." The crew locked up all three rebels in irons.

When the time came for punishment, Captain Harding weighed "the Stoutness and Worth" of the two male rebels and decided it was in his economic interest to "whip and scarify them only." He then selected three others only marginally involved in the conspiracy—but also less valuable—and used them to create terror among the rest of the enslaved aboard the vessel. These he sentenced to "cruel Deaths." He killed one immediately and made the others eat his heart and liver. The woman "he hoisted up by the Thumbs, whipp'd, and slashed her with Knives, before the other Slaves till she died." Captain Tomba was apparently delivered at Kingston, Jamaica, with 189 other enslaved people and sold at a high price. His subsequent fate is unknown.[2]

"The Boatswain"

Leadership among the captives arose from belowdecks during the Middle Passage. A sailor aboard the *Nightingale* told the story of a captive woman whose real name is lost to posterity but who came to be known on board the ship as "the boatswain"—because she kept order among her fellow enslaved women, probably with a fierce determination that they should all survive the ordeal of oceanic crossing. She "used to keep them quiet when in the rooms, and when they were on deck likewise."

One day in early 1769, her own self-constituted authority clashed with that of the ship's officers. She "disobliged" the second mate, who gave her "a cut or two" with a cat-o'-nine-tails. She flew into a rage at this treatment and fought back, attacking the mate. He in turn pushed her away and lashed her smartly three or four more times. Finding herself overmatched and frustrated that she could not "have her revenge of him," she instantly "sprung two or three feet on the deck, and dropped down dead." Her body was thrown overboard about half an hour later, and torn to pieces by sharks.[3]

Name Unknown

The man came aboard the slave ship *Brooks* in late 1783 or early 1784 with his entire family—his wife, two daughters, and mother—all convicted of witchcraft. The man had been a trader, perhaps in slaves; he was from a village called Saltpan, on the Gold Coast. He was probably Fante. He knew English, and even though he apparently disdained to talk to the captain, he spoke to members of the crew and explained how he came to be enslaved. He had quarreled with the village chief, or "caboceer," who took revenge by accusing him of witchcraft, getting him and his family convicted and sold to the ship. They were now bound for Kingston, Jamaica.[4]

When the family came on board, noted the physician of the ship, Thomas Trotter, the man "had every symptom of a sullen melancholy." He was sad, depressed, in shock. The rest of the family exhibited "every sign of affliction." Despondency, despair, and even "torpid insensibility" were common among the enslaved when they first came aboard a slave ship. The crew would have expected the spirits of the man and his family to improve as time passed and the strange new wooden world grew more familiar.

The man immediately refused all sustenance. From the beginning of his captivity aboard the ship, he simply would not eat. This reaction, too, was commonplace, but he went further. Early one morning, when sailors went below to check on the captives, they found the man a bloody mess. They urgently called the doctor. The man had attempted to cut his own throat and had succeeded in "dividing only the external jugular vein." He had lost more than a pint of blood. Trotter stitched up the wound and apparently considered force-feeding the man. The throat wound, however, "put it out of our power to use any compulsory means," which were of course common on slavers. He referred to the *speculum oris,* the long, thin mechanical contraption used to force open unwilling throats to receive gruel and hence sustenance.

The following night the man made a second attempt on his own life. He tore out the sutures and cut his throat on the other side. Summoned to handle a new emergency, Trotter was cleaning up the bloody wound when the man began to talk to him. He declared simply and straightforwardly that "he would never go with white men." He then "looked wistfully at the skies" and uttered several sentences Trotter could not understand. He had decided for death over slavery.

The young doctor tended to him as best he could and ordered a "diligent search" of the apartment of the enslaved men for the instrument he had used to cut his throat. The sailors found nothing. Looking more closely at the man and finding blood on his fingertips and "ragged edges" around the wound, Trotter concluded that he had ripped open his throat with his own fingernails.

Yet the man survived. His hands were secured "to prevent any further attempt," but all the efforts came to naught against the will of the nameless man. Trotter later explained that "he still however adhered to his resolution, refused all sustenance, and died in about a week or ten days afterwards of mere want of food." The captain of the ship had also been informed of the situation. Captain Clement Noble said the man "stormed and made a great noise, worked with his hands, and threw himself about in an extraordinary manner, and shewed every sign of being mad."

When Thomas Trotter told the man's story in 1790 to a parliamentary committee investigating the slave trade, it set off a flurry of questions and indeed something of a debate. Members of Parliament with proslavery sentiments sided with Captain Noble and tried to discredit Trotter, denying that willful suicidal resistance could be the moral of the story, while antislavery MPs supported Trotter and attacked Noble. An MP asked Trotter, "Do you suppose that the man who attempted to cut his throat with his nails was insane?" Of this Trotter had no doubt: he answered, "By no means insane; I believe a degree of delirium might [have] come on before he perished, but at the time when he came on board, I believe that he was perfectly in his senses." The man's decision to use his own fingernails to rip open his throat was an entirely rational response to landing on a slave ship. And now the most powerful people in the world were debating the meaning of his resistance.

"Sarah"

When the young woman came aboard the Liverpool slave ship the *Hudibras* in Old Calabar in 1785, she instantly captured everyone's attention. She had beauty, grace, and charisma: "Sprightliness was in her every gesture, and good nature beamed in her eyes." When the African musicians and instruments came out on the main deck twice a day for "dancing," the exercising of the enslaved, she "appeared to great advantage, as she bounded over the quarter-deck, to the rude strains of African melody," observed a smitten sailor named William Butterworth. She was the best dancer and the best singer on the ship. "Ever lively! ever gay!" seemed to sum up her aura, even under the extreme pressure of enslavement and exile.[5]

Other sailors joined Butterworth in admiration, and indeed so did Captain Jenkin Evans, who selected this young woman and one other as his "favourites," to whom he therefore "showed greater favours than the rest," likely as small recompense for coerced sexual services. Slave-ship sailors like Butterworth usually detested the captain's favorites, as they were required to be snitches. But for the nimble singer and dancer, the sailors had the highest esteem. She was "universally respected by the ship's company."

Captain Evans gave her the name Sarah. He chose a biblical name, linking the enslaved woman, who was likely an Igbo speaker, to a princess, the beautiful wife of Abraham. Perhaps the captain hoped that she would share other traits with the biblical Sarah, who remained submissive and obedient to her husband during a long journey to Canaan.

Soon the enslaved men on the *Hudibras* erupted in insurrection. The goal was to "massacre the ship's company, and take possession of the vessel." The rising was suppressed, bloody punishments dispensed. Afterward Captain Evans and other officers suspected that Sarah and her mother (who was also on board) were somehow involved, even though the women had not joined the men in the actual revolt. When questioned closely, with violence looming, they denied having any knowledge, but "fear, or guilt, was strongly marked in their countenances." Later that night, as male and female captives angrily shouted recriminations around the ship in the aftermath of defeat, it became clear that both Sarah and her mother not only knew about the plot, they had indeed been involved in it. Sarah had likely used her privileged position as a favorite, and her great freedom of movement that this entailed, to help with planning and perhaps even to pass tools to the men, allowing them to hack off their shackles and manacles.

Sarah survived the Middle Passage and whatever punishment she may have gotten for her involvement in the insurrection. She was sold at Grenada, with almost three hundred others, in 1787. She was allowed to stay on the vessel longer than most, probably with the special permission of Captain Evans. When she went ashore, she carried African traditions of dance, song, and resistance with her.[6]

Cabin Boy Samuel Robinson

Samuel Robinson was about thirteen years old when he boarded the *Lady Neilson* in 1801, to sail with his uncle, Captain Alexander Cowan, and a motley crew of thirty-five from Liverpool to the Gold Coast, to Demerara. The stout Scottish lad made a second voyage with his uncle, in the *Crescent,* to the Gold Coast and Jamaica in 1802. He kept journals of his voyages and used them when he decided, in the 1860s, to write a memoir. His declared purpose was to counter the abolitionist propaganda of his times. He admitted that the slave trade was wrong, even indefensible, but he had heard "so many gross mis-statements respecting West Indian slavery, and the horrors of the 'Middle Passage,'" he wanted "to disabuse the minds of well-meaning people, who may have seen only one side of this question." By the time he finished the account of his life, he could boast, "I am the only man alive who served an apprenticeship to the slave trade."[7]

Robinson grew up in Garlieston, a coastal village of southwest Scotland, where he heard an older local boy spin yarns about a voyage to the West Indies. Robinson was spellbound. He described his path to the slave ship: "an irresistible desire for a seafaring life so completely carried me away, that it became a matter of perfect indifference to me where the ship went, if not to the bottom, provided I was aboard her—or in what trade engaged, if not a pirate." Since any ship would do, his uncle's involvement in the slave trade closed the deal.

Robinson's experience aboard the slaver seems to have been typical for a ship's boy. He got seasick, he got laughed at and picked on by the old salts, he got into fights with the other boys. One day when sent up to the tops, he found himself "swinging sixty or seventy feet one way by the roll of the ship, and again as far again in an opposite direction." At that moment, he recalled, "I certainly thought myself far from home." He was terrified by the sharks that circled the slave ship, and when the *Lady Neilson* arrived at the Rio Sestos near Sierra Leone, he stood amazed by the sight of a large fleet of canoes manned by naked African men: "I gazed on this wonderful spectacle in a state of perfect bewilderment. It was a scene worth coming all the way to look upon." When the enslaved were brought on board his vessel, he seems to have shown little interest, even in the boys his own age. One of his most significant encounters was with drunken and tyrannical Captain John Ward of the slaver *Expedition,* on which Robinson was forced to work his homeward passage after his ship was condemned in Demerara. One day Ward thought the boy was not working hard enough, or moving fast enough, so he decided to "freshen his way" by lashing him with a two-inch rope. To escape his wrath, Robinson jumped from the mizzen shrouds to the main deck and severely injured his ankle, which in the long term proved his undoing as a sailor.

When Robinson looked back on his original motivations to go to sea, he reflected, "The ocean paradise which loomed so brightly in my imagination, now appears considerably shorn of its beams." He cited the "brutal tyranny" of the officers (including his uncle), the "beggarly" quality of food and water, and the isolation from "moral or religious training or good example." Having gone to sea as a buirdly boy, he asked, at the end of his second slaving voyage, "What am I now? A poor sallow skeleton, needing a staff to enable me to crawl along the street; my hopes of following the profession of my choice blasted in the bud, and my future prospects dark indeed."

Sailor and Pirate Bartholomew Roberts

Bartholomew Roberts was a young Welshman who sailed as second mate aboard the *Princess,* a 140-ton Guineaman, as a slave ship was called, out of London for Sierra Leone. He had apparently worked in the slave trade for a while. He knew navigation, as the mates of slavers had to be ready to assume command in the not-uncommon event of the captain's death. The *Princess* was captured in June 1719 by Howell Davis and a rowdy gang of pirates, who asked Roberts and his mates on the prize vessel if any of them wished to join "the brotherhood." Roberts hesitated at first, knowing that the British government had in recent years left the corpses of executed pirates dangling at the entrance of one Atlantic port city after another. But soon he decided that he would indeed sail under the black flag.[8]

It was a fateful decision. When Davis was killed by Portuguese slave traders not long afterward, "Black Bart," as he would be called, was elected captain of his ship and soon became the most successful sea robber of his age. He commanded a small flotilla of ships and several hundred men who captured more than four hundred merchant vessels over three years, the peak of "the golden age of piracy." Roberts was widely known and just as widely feared. Naval officers on patrol spotted him and sailed in the opposite direction. Royal officials fortified their coasts against the man they called "the great pirate Roberts." He acted the part by strolling the decks of his ship dressed as a dandy, in a lush damask waistcoat, a red feather in his hat, and a golden toothpick in his mouth. His motto as a pirate was "A Merry Life and Short One."

Roberts terrorized the African coast, sending the traders there "into a panick." He so despised the brutal ways of slave-trading captains that he and his crew enacted a bloody ritual called the "distribution of justice," dispensing a fearful lashing to any captured captain whose sailors complained of his usage. Indeed Roberts gave some of these drubbings himself. Slave-trading merchants responded to this threat to their profits by persuading Parliament to intensify naval patrols on the coast of West Africa. HMS *Swallow* found and engaged Roberts in February 1722. Roberts stayed upon deck to lead the battle and encourage his men but took a fatal volley of grapeshot in the throat. His mates honored a long-standing pledge and dumped his still-armed body overboard. The naval vessel defeated the pirates, captured the survivors, and took them to the slave-trading fortress at Cape Coast Castle, where they were tried and hanged en masse. Captain Challoner Ogle then distributed corpses up and down the African coast so local slave traders could hang them up as a message to sailors. Ogle made it a special point to visit the king of Whydah, who had promised him fifty-six pounds of gold dust "if he should secure that rascal *Roberts,* who had long infested his coast."

Sailor and Petty Slave Trader Nicholas Owen

Nicholas Owen was a real-life Robinson Crusoe, a picaresque Irish sailor who went to sea after his spendthrift father had squandered the family fortune. He crossed the Atlantic five times, three times on slavers, twice with calamitous ends. One voyage culminated in mutiny when Owen and four of his mates, tired of "sevare usage" by their captain, seized what Owen called "that liberty which every Europain is intitle to." Near Cape Mount south of Sierra Leone, the sailors made an armed escape and lived for months on the run, subsisting on wild rice, oysters, and the hospitality of the indigenous people. The second disaster came a year or so later, when other Africans proved not so friendly, cutting off Owen's ship in revenge for a recent kidnapping by a Dutch slave ship. His ship plundered and he taken prisoner, Owen lost everything—four years' wages, all in gold, and trade goods he had planned to sell to augment his pay. The natives knew their captives to be English rather than Dutch and therefore spared their lives. They eventually released them to a Mr. Hall, a local white slave trader, for whom Owen went to work. Soon Owen set up on his own, settling into the ruins of a small slave-trading fortress on York Island in the Sherbro River and working as a middleman, connecting local African groups to European traders.[9]

Owen began to keep a journal in order to "lay open to the world the many dangers of a seafareing life." He was his own best example. He had suffered natural dangers while he lived and worked "upon that angery element." This he could tolerate, because the sea had "no respect to persons"—it could kill a prince as easily as a common jack-tar. The deeper problem was that "a saylor that has no other means to satisfy the nececereys of this life then sailing the sais [seas] for wages." He depended entirely on money for subsistence. Owen made the point through comparison: "I look upon him to be more miserable then a poor farmer who lives upon his labour, who can rest at night upon a bed of straw in obscurity, then a saylor who comforts himself in the main top by blowing of his fingers in a frostey night." He railed against "scrapeing the world for money, the uneversal god of mankind, untill death overtakes us."

Owen sought to escape wage slavery by becoming a petty slave trader. He could have gone back to sea, even back to live "among Cristians and my native people." He decided instead to live among what he called "a barbarous people that nous [knows] neither God or a good quality in man." And he acknowledged that it was a choice: "Some people may think it strange that we should stay so long among people of the above charetar, when we have so many opertuniteys of going of[f] the coast home." He worried that if he went home, tongues would wag and he would be called "the Mallato [mulatto] just come from Guinea." So he opted instead for what he himself saw as an idle, indolent life at the edge of empire, subordinating others to the ruthless rule of the "uneversal god of mankind." The choice resulted in failure, as Owen well understood and his miserable journal makes clear. He died of a fever in 1759, penniless and alone. He had long been "much inclin'd to melloncholy."

Captain William Snelgrave

Captain William Snelgrave was gathering a cargo of Africans on the
"Slave Coast" of Benin to transport to Antigua when, to his surprise,
he was invited by the king of Ardra (also called Allada) to visit. This
presented a dilemma. On the one hand, Snelgrave dared not refuse if
he wanted to curry favor for future supplies of slaves. But, on the other
hand, he considered the king and his people to be "fierce brutish Cannibals." The captain resolved the dilemma by deciding to visit and to
take with him a guard of ten sailors "well armed with Musquets and
Pistols, which those savage People I knew were much afraid of."[10]

Canoed by escorts a quarter mile upriver, Snelgrave found on his arrival the king "sitting on a Stool, under some shady Trees," with about
fifty courtiers and a large troop of warriors nearby. The latter were
armed with bows and arrows, swords, and barbed lances. The armed
sailors took a guarded position "opposite to them, at the distance of
about twenty paces" as Snelgrave presented gifts to a delighted king.

Snelgrave soon noticed "a little Negroe-Child tied by the Leg to a
Stake driven in the Ground." Two African priests stood nearby. The
child was "a fine Boy about 18 Months old," but he was in distress, his
body covered with flies and vermin. Agitated, the slave captain asked
the king, "What is the reason of the Child's being tied in that manner?" The king replied that "it was to be sacrificed that night to his
God *Egbo,* for his prosperity." Upset by the answer, Snelgrave quickly
ordered one of his sailors "to take the Child from the Ground, in order
to preserve him." As he did so, one of the king's guards ran at the sailor,
brandishing his lance, whereupon Snelgrave stood up and drew a pistol,
halting the man in his tracks and sending the king into a fright and the
entire gathering into a tumult.

When order was restored, Snelgrave complained to the king about
the threatening action of the guard. The king replied that Snelgrave
himself "had not done well" in ordering the sailor to seize the child,
"it being his Property." The captain excused himself by explaining
that his religion "expressly forbids so horrid a Thing, as the putting of

a poor innocent Child to death." He added the golden rule: "the grand Law of human Nature was, To do to others as we desir'd to be done unto." The conflict was ultimately resolved not through theology but the cash nexus, as Snelgrave offered to buy the child. He offered "a bunch of sky coloured beads, worth about half a Crown Sterling." The king accepted the offer. Snelgrave was surprised that the price was so cheap, as traders such as the king were usually "very ready, on any extraordinary occasion, to make their Advantage of us."

The rest of the meeting consisted of eating and drinking the European food and liquor Snelgrave had brought for the king. African palm wine was also on offer, but Snelgrave refused to drink it, as the wisdom among slave-ship captains was that it could be "artfully poison[ed]." The sailors had no such worries and drank avidly. Upon parting, the king declared himself "well pleased" with the visit, which meant that more slaves would be forthcoming. As the Europeans canoed back to the ship, Snelgrave turned to a member of his crew and said that they "should pitch on some motherly Woman [among the enslaved already on board] to take care of this poor Child." The sailor answered that "he had already one in his Eye." The woman "had much Milk in her Breasts."

As soon as Snelgrave and the sailors came aboard, the very woman they had been discussing saw them with the little boy and ran "with great eagerness, and snatched him from out of the white Man's Arms that held him." It was the woman's own child. Captain Snelgrave had already bought her without realizing the connection. Snelgrave observed, "I think there never was a more moving sight than on this occasion, between the Mother and her little Son."

The ship's linguist then told the woman what had happened, that, as Snelgrave wrote, "I had saved her Child from being sacrificed." The story made its way around the ship, through the more than three hundred captives on board, who soon "expressed their Thankfulness to me, by clapping their Hands, and singing a song in my praise." Nor did the gratitude end there, as Snelgrave noted: "This affair proved of great service to us, for it gave them a good notion of White Men; so that we had no Mutiny in our Ship, during the whole Voyage." Snelgrave's benevolence continued upon arrival in Antigua. As soon as he told the story of child and mother to a Mr. Studely, a slave owner, "he bought the Mother and her Son, and was a kind Master to them."

William Snelgrave could thus think of Africans as "fierce brutish Cannibals" and think of himself as an ethical, civilized redeemer, a good Christian with qualities that even savages would have to recognize and applaud. He could think of himself as the savior of families as he destroyed them. He could imagine a humane outcome for two as he delivered hundreds to a plantation fate of endless toil and premature death. His justifications in place, he could even invoke the golden rule, which would soon become a central saying of the antislavery movement.

Captain William Watkins

As the *Africa,* a Bristol Guineaman captained by William Watkins, lay at anchor in Old Calabar River in the late 1760s, its prisoners were busy down in the hold of the vessel, hacking off their chains as quietly as they could. A large number of them managed to get free of the fetters, lift off the gratings, and climb onto the main deck. They sought to get to the gun room aft and the weapons they might use to recover their lost freedom. It was not unusual, explained sailor Henry Ellison, for the enslaved to rise, whether because of a "love of liberty," "ill treatment," or "a spirit of vengeance."[11]

The crewmen of the *Africa* were taken entirely by surprise; they seemed to have no idea that an insurrection was afoot, literally beneath their very feet. But just as the mutineers "were forcing open the barricado door," Ellison and seven of his crewmates, "well armed with pistols and cutlasses," boarded from a neighboring slave ship, the *Nightingale.* They saw what was happening, mounted the barricado, and fired above the heads of the rebels, hoping to scare them into submission. The shots did not deter them, so the sailors lowered their aim and fired into the mass of insurgents, killing one. The captives made a second attempt to open the barricado door, but the sailors held firm, forcing them to retreat forward, giving chase as they went. As the armed seamen pressed forward, a few of the rebels jumped overboard, some ran below, and others stayed on deck to fight. The sailors fired again and killed two more.

Once the crew had regained control of the situation, Captain Watkins reimposed order. He selected eight of the mutineers "for an example." They were tied up, and each sailor—the regular crew of the *Africa,* plus the eight from the *Nightingale*—was ordered to take a turn with the whip. The seamen "flogged them until from weariness they could flog no more." Captain Watkins then turned to an instrument called "the tormentor," a combination of the cook's tongs and a surgeon's instrument for spreading plasters. He had it heated white hot and used it to burn the flesh of the eight rebels. "This operation being over," Ellison explained, "they were confined and taken below." Apparently all survived.

Yet the torture was not over. Captain Watkins suspected that one of his own sailors was involved in the plot, that he had "encouraged the slaves to rise." He accused an unnamed black seaman, the ship's cook, of assisting the revolt, "of having furnished them with the cooper's tools, in order that they might knock themselves out of irons." Ellison doubted this, calling it "supposition only, and without any proof of the fact."

Captain Watkins nonetheless ordered an iron collar—usually reserved for the most rebellious slaves—fastened around the neck of the black seaman. He then had him "chained to the main masthead," where he would remain night and day, indefinitely. He was to be given "only one plantain and one pint of water per day." His clothes were nothing more than a pair of long trousers, which were little "to shield him from the inclemency of the night." The shackled seaman remained in the foretop of the ship for three weeks, slowly starving.

When the *Africa* had gathered its full cargo of 310 slaves and the crew prepared to sail away from the Bight of Biafra, Captain Watkins decided that the cook's punishment should continue, so he made arrangements with Captain Joseph Carter to send him aboard the *Nightingale,* where he was once again chained to the main top and given the same meager allowance of food and water. After ten more days, the black seaman had grown delirious. "Hunger and oppression," said Ellison, "had reduced him to a skeleton." For three days he struggled madly to free himself from the fetters, causing the chains to rub "the skin from several parts of his body." The neck collar "found its way to the bone." The "unfortunate man," said Ellison, had become "a most shocking spectacle." After five weeks in the two vessels, "having experienced inconceivable misery in both, he was relieved by death." Ellison was one of the sailors charged to throw his body from the foretop into the river. The minimal remains of the black seaman were "immediately devoured by the sharks."

Captain James Fraser

When Thomas Clarkson visited the slave-trading port of Bristol in July 1787 to gather evidence for the abolitionist movement, he sought the advice of a man named Richard Burges, an attorney opposed to the commerce in human beings. Their conversation turned to the captains of slave ships, which prompted an impatient Burges to howl that all of them deserved "long ago to be hanged"—except one. That one was Captain James Fraser of Bristol, a man who spent twenty years in the slave trade, voyaging five times to Bonny, four times to Angola, and once each to Calabar, the Windward Coast, and the Gold Coast. Nor was Burges the only abolitionist to praise Fraser. Alexander Falconbridge, the physician who penned a searing indictment of the slave trade, sailed with Fraser, knew him well, and said, "I believe him to be one of the best men in the trade." Clarkson, too, eventually joined in the chorus of praise.[12]

Captain Fraser ran an orderly ship with a minimum of coercion, or so he claimed when he testified before a parliamentary committee in 1790: "The Angola slaves being very peaceable, it is seldom necessary to confine them in irons; and they are allowed to go down between the decks, and come up on deck, as they find the weather warm or cold."

They were, as a result, "cheerful" on board. He added that he treated the Bonny and Calabar slaves differently, as they were more "vicious" and inclined to insurrection. But here, too, he was moderate by the standards of the day: "As soon as the ship is out of sight of land I usually took away their handcuffs, and soon after their leg-irons—I never had the Slaves in irons during Middle Passage, not even from the Gold and Windward Coast, excepting a few offenders, that were troublesome in the ship, and endeavouring to persuade the Slaves to destroy the White Men." He always provided the enslaved with clean apartments, exercise, and "frequent amusements peculiar to their own country." He offered abundant food to which they were accustomed in their native land. For those who refused to eat, Fraser explained, "I have always used persuasions—force is always ineffectual." The slaves who sickened got a special hospital berth, and "the surgeons always had orders, as well as free leave, to give them any thing that was in the ship."

Perhaps the most unusual statement he made to the parliamentary committee was the following: "we generally appoint the most humane and best disposed of the ship's company to attend to the Slaves, and serve their provisions." He would not tolerate abuse: "I have, with my own hands, punished sailors for maltreating the negroes." It followed logically from these practices that mortality for sailors and slaves on his ships was modest (with one exception of an epidemic). He insisted that he always treated his sailors with "humanity and tenderness." He cited as proof of this their reenlistment on subsequent voyages, some three or four times as he recalled. Indeed Falconbridge sailed with him on three voyages.[13]

Falconbridge contradicted Fraser's testimony in several key respects: he thought a greater proportion of the enslaved were kidnapped than Fraser was willing to admit and that Fraser himself would buy the kidnapped without asking questions. The material conditions on the ship were worse than the captain suggested, and the enslaved were not cheerful or peaceful, as proved by numerous suicides. He added, however, that Captain Fraser "always recommended to the planters never to part relations or friends." And Fraser did as he said regarding the crew: he treated them "exceedingly well; he always allowed them a dram in the morning, and grog in the evening; when any of them were sick, he always sent them victuals from his own table, and inquired every day after their health."

Captain and Merchant Robert Norris

Robert Norris was a man of many talents. He was an experienced and successful Liverpool slave-ship captain who made enough money to retire from the sea and carry on as a successful merchant in the slave trade. He was also a writer, a polemicist on behalf of the slave trade, and something of a historian. In 1788 he wrote and published anonymously *A Short Account of the African Slave Trade, Collected from Local Knowledge.* The following year he produced a history of a region of West Africa based on his personal knowledge: *Memoirs of the Reign of Bossa Ahádee, King of Dahomy, an Inland Country of Guiney.* In the latter he bemoaned the existence of so little historical writing about Africa, then offered his own explanation: "the stupidity of the natives is an insuperable barrier against the inquirer's information." Norris represented the Liverpool interest in the parliamentary hearings held between 1788 and 1791. He was one of the slave trade's very best public defenders.[14]

As the first to testify before the Committee of the Whole of the House of Commons in June 1788, Norris described the Middle Passage in detail. The slaves had good living quarters belowdecks, he explained, which sailors cleaned thoroughly and regularly. Air ports and windsails ventilated their apartments and admitted "a free Circulation of fresh Air." The enslaved had more than enough room. They slept on "clean boards," which were more wholesome than "Beds or Hammacks." They ate plentiful, high-quality food. The men and boys played musical instruments, danced, and sang, while the women and girls "amuse[d] themselves with arranging fanciful Ornaments for their Persons with Beads, which they are plentifully supplied with." The slaves were given the "Luxuries of Pipes and

Tobacco" and occasionally even a dram of brandy, especially when the weather was cold. Such good treatment, explained Norris, was in the captain's self-interest, as he stood to make a 6 percent commission over and above his salary on the slaves delivered healthy and alive on the western side of the Atlantic. Norris explained to the members of Parliament that "Interest" and "Humanity" were perfectly united in the slave trade.

And yet the one surviving document Norris wrote that was not intended for publication tells a different, rather less-idyllic story. Norris kept a captain's log for his voyage in the *Unity* from Liverpool to Whydah, to Jamaica, and back to Liverpool between 1769 and 1771. A week after weighing anchor at Whydah and setting sail to cross the Atlantic, Norris noted that "the Slaves made an Insurrection, which was soon quelled with ye Loss [of] two Women." Two weeks later the enslaved rose again, the women once more in the lead and therefore singled out for special punishment: Norris "gave ye women concerned 24 lashes each." Three days later they made a third effort after several "got off their Handcuffs," but Norris and crew soon managed to get them back into their irons. And the following morning they tried for a fourth time: "the Slaves attempted to force up ye Gratings in the Night, with a design to murder ye whites or drown themselves." He added that they "confessed their intentions and that ye women as well as ye men were determin'd if disapointed of cutting off ye whites, to jump over board but in case of being prevented by their Irons were resolved as their last attempt to burn the ship." So great was their determination that in the event of failure they planned a mass suicide by drowning or self-incineration. "Their obstinacy," wrote Norris, "put me under ye Necessity of shooting ye Ringleader." But even this did not end the matter. A man Norris called "No. 3" and a woman he called "No. 4," both of whom had been on the ship a long time, continued to resist and died in fits of madness. "They had frequently attempted to drown themselves, since their Views were disapointed in ye Insurrection."

Merchant Humphry Morice

On board Humphry Morice's ship the *Katherine,* the enslaved died of many causes, noted Captain John Dagge in 1727–28. A man and a woman jumped overboard and drowned, one on the African coast, one during the Middle Passage. A woman perished of "Palsey and lost the use of Limbs." A man expired "Sullen and Mallancholy," another "Sullen (and a Foole)." "Sullen" usually meant that the cat-o'-nine-tails did not work on the person so described. Others died suddenly, with a fever, with "Swelling and Pains in his Limbs," with lethargy and flux, with dropsy, with consumption. One grew emaciated ("Meager") and passed away. Another nineteen died, mostly of dysentery. One boy managed to "Run away wh[en] the Doihmes Came." Perhaps the Dahomeys were his own group.[15]

All of these nameless people, plus the extraordinary number of 678 delivered alive by Captain Dagge to Antigua, belonged to Humphry Morice, scion of a leading merchant family in London, Member of Parliament, friend and close associate of Prime Minister Robert Walpole, and governor (first officer) of the Bank of England. He was involved at the highest level of global trade, finance capital, and the economy of the British Empire. He owned a sumptuous family estate in the Cornish countryside and a magnificent home in London. Servants attended the gentleman's every wish. Through marriage he had forged strategic connections to other powerful merchant families. He was a member of the ruling class.

Morice was, moreover, one of the free traders who led the attack against the chartered monopoly of the Royal African Company in the early years of the eighteenth century. He was the employer of slave-trade captain William Snelgrave. He was the main influence in persuading Parliament to dispatch HMS *Swallow,* which defeated the pirate Bartholomew Roberts on the coast of Africa in February 1722. Morice traded to Europe (especially Holland), Russia, the West Indies, and North America, but the heart of his trading empire lay in Africa. He was London's leading slave trader in the early eighteenth century.

The *Katherine* was one of a small fleet of slave ships owned by Morice and named for his wife and daughters. (One wonders how wife Katherine or daughter Sarah felt in knowing, if they knew, that the enslaved aboard the ships named for them had the letter *K* or *S* branded on their buttocks.) Morice's ships represented almost 10 percent of London's slave-trading capacity at a time when the city owned almost as many Guineamen as Bristol and more than Liverpool. They made sixty-two voyages, carried between £6,000 and £12,000 worth of well-sorted cargo to Africa, and transported almost twenty thousand people to New World plantations. This number does not include the many his captains sold for gold to Portuguese ships on the African coast. Gold, Morice liked to say, did not suffer mortality in the Middle Passage.

Morice was an engaged merchant and shipowner. He made it his business to learn the details of the trade, which he expressed in careful instructions to his team of captains. He explained how trading practices varied from one African port to the next. He knew that staying on the coast too long gathering a cargo risked higher mortality, so he worked out cooperative practices among his ships to evacuate the slaves quickly. He instructed his captains to buy slaves between the ages of twelve and twenty-five, two males to a female, "Good & healthy, and not blind Lame or Blemished." He no doubt followed the advice of his Jamaican factors about the "Defects to be carefully avoided":

Dwarfish, or Gigantick Size wch are equaly disagreeable
Ugly faces
Long Tripeish Breasts wch ye Spaniards mortally hate
Yellowish Skins
Livid Spots in ye Skin wch turns to an incureable Evil
Films in ye Eyes
Loss of Fingers, Toes, or Teeth
Navells sticking out
Ruptures wch ye Gambia Slaves are very Subject to
Bandy legs

Sharp Shins
Lunaticks
Idiots
Lethargicks[16]

He also explained how the slaves should be fed, how their food should be prepared. He demanded that both sailors and slaves be treated well. He put surgeons and limes (to combat scurvy) on his vessels before it was a common practice to do either. He told his captains to be sure to "get your negroes shaved and made clean to look well and strike a good impression on the Planters and buyers."

It is impossible to know precisely how much of Morice's great wealth in estate, land, ships, stocks, and funds derived from the slave trade, although it is possible to know that whatever the profits, he thought them inadequate to sustain his style of life. He took to defrauding the Bank of England (of approximately £29,000 total; almost $7.5 million in 2007 currency) by making up false bills of foreign exchange and to mismanaging funds of which he was trustee. When Morice died in disgrace on November 16, 1731, he was in a far different situation from those who died aboard the *Katherine* or any of his other ships. But the death of this fabled slave trader was horrible in its own way. People whispered, "'Tis supposed he took Poyson."

Merchant Henry Laurens

In April 1769, Henry Laurens, one of early America's wealthiest merchants, wrote to Captain Hinson Todd, who was seeking a cargo in Jamaica to carry to Charleston, South Carolina. Laurens was an experienced slave trader and he was worried that Todd was not. He therefore cautioned that if the Jamaica merchant "should Ship Negroes on board your Sloop, be very careful to guard against insurrection. Never put your Life in their power a moment. For a moment is sufficient to deprive you of it & make way for the destruction of all your Men & yet you may treat such Negroes with great Humanity." It was an odd but revealing statement. Laurens instructed the captain to treat with "great humanity" the very people who would, given a split-second chance, annihilate him and his entire crew. Such were the contradictions Laurens faced, and not he alone. He knew the brutal realities of the slave trade and the resistance it always engendered, and yet he tried to put a human face on the situation. Perhaps he feared that he had scared the captain, who might then overreact and damage his dangerous but valuable property.[17]

Laurens had by this time already built a fortune through booming Atlantic commerce, the slave trade in particular. In 1749, at the youthful age of twenty-five, he had formed a mercantile partnership, Austin & Laurens, which expanded to include a new partner, George Appleby, ten years later. More than half of the slaves imported into the American colonies/United States came through Charleston, which served as a distribution point for the entire lower South. His firm played a leading part, and Laurens himself grew knowledgeable about the various African ethnicities who arrived aboard the slave ships. He expressed a strong preference for Gambian and Gold Coast peoples as plantation workers and a decided distaste for Igbo and Angolans.[18]

Like Humphry Morice a generation earlier, Laurens organized the importation of about sixty cargoes of slaves. Unlike Morice, who was usually a sole owner and investor in his voyages, Laurens spread the risk by pooling money through partnerships. He wrote, "The Africa Trade is more liable to such Accidents than any other we know of, so it highly concerns such as become adventurers in that branch to fortify themselves against every disappointment that the trade is incident to." The trade was hazardous, as he cautioned Captain Todd, but it was also lucrative, "gainful," or, as he once put it, "the most profitable." By 1760, Laurens was one of the richest merchants not only in South Carolina but throughout the American colonies.

Laurens made a conscious decision to withdraw much of his business from the slave trade around 1763, although he remained involved by taking numerous slave cargoes on consignment, as suggested by his letter to Captain Todd. He had lost both a partner and a wealthy backer, which may have limited his ability to hedge the risk. Or perhaps the wealthy merchant simply no longer wished to be an "adventurer." In any case he turned his attention—and his slave-trade profits—to becoming a planter, a land speculator, and a politician. He accumulated vast tracts of land and over time he acquired six plantations. Two, Broughton Island and New Hope, were in Georgia, and four were in South Carolina: Wambaw, Wrights Savannah, Mount Tacitus, and Mepkin. The last of these, his main residence, was 3,143 acres, on which several hundred slaves produced rice and other commodities for export, which were then shipped thirty miles down the Cooper River to Charleston and from there pumped into the Atlantic economy.

Laurens turned his economic power into political power. He was elected to office seventeen times, serving in the South Carolina assembly and the Continental Congress, ascending after a short time to the presidency of the latter. He helped to negotiate the Treaty of Paris, which gave the American colonies their independence, and he was selected to represent South Carolina in the Constitutional Convention of 1787 (although he declined to serve). This man who had counseled Captain Todd never to put his life under the power of enslaved Africans owed his wealth, standing, and genteel life to his own decision to keep hundreds, indeed thousands, of lives under his own power, as a planter and a slave-trade merchant.

"The Greedy Robbers"

Sharks began to follow slave ships when they reached the Guinea coast. From Senegambia along the Windward, Gold, and Slave coasts, to Kongo and Angola, sailors spotted them when their vessels were anchored or moving slowly, and most clearly in a dead calm.[19] What attracted the sharks (as well as other fish) was the human waste, offal, and rubbish that was continually thrown overboard. Like a "greedy robber," the shark "attends the ships, in expectation of what may drop over-board. A man, who unfortunately falls into the sea at such a time, is sure to perish, without mercy." Young Samuel Robinson recalled the chill of the voracious predator: "The very sight of him slowly moving round the ship, with his black fin two feet above the water, his broad snout and small eyes, and the altogether villainous look of the fellow, make one shiver, even when at a safe distance." Sharks were especially dangerous when trade was carried on in boats and canoes, in high surf, between the slavers anchored offshore and the trading forts or villages on land. They swarmed around the smaller craft, occasionally lunging out of the water to bite an oar in half, hoping all the while, as one nervous trader noted, "to see the Bottom of our Canoe turn'd upwards." Sharks were known as the "dread of sailors."[20]

Sharks became an even greater dread as members of the crew began to die. Captains sometimes made efforts to bury deceased sailors ashore, as, for example, in Bonny, where corpses were interred in shallow graves on a sandy point about a quarter mile from the main trading town. But when the tidal river rose, the current sometimes washed the sand away from the bodies, causing a noxious stench and inviting hungry sharks. On most stretches of the coast, slavers had no burial rights, which resulted in what Silas Told saw happen to the cadaver of a former comrade in the harbor of São Tomé around 1735: "the first [shark] seized one of his hind-quarters, and wrenched it off at the first shake; a second attacked the hind-quarter, and took that away likewise; when a third furiously attacked the remainder of the body, and greedily devoured the whole thereof." Crews tried to outsmart the sharks by sewing a dead sailor into his hammock or an old canvas sail and enclosing a cannonball to pull the body to the bottom, hopefully uneaten. This strategy often failed, as a sea surgeon noted: "I have seen [sharks] frequently seize a Corpse, as soon as it was committed to the Sea; tearing and devouring that, and the Hammock that shrouded it, without suffering it once to sink, tho' a great Weight of Ballast in it."[21]

If the shark was the dread of sailors, it was the outright terror of the enslaved. No effort was made to protect or bury the bodies of African captives who died on the slave ships. One commentator after another reiterated what Alexander Falconbridge said of Bonny, where sharks swarmed "in almost incredible numbers about the slave ships, devouring with great dispatch the dead bodies of the negroes as they are thrown overboard."[22] The Dutch merchant Willem Bosman described a feeding frenzy in which four or five sharks consumed a body without leaving a trace. Late-arriving sharks would attack the others with blows so furious as to "make the sea around to tremble." The destruction of corpses by sharks was a public spectacle and part of the degradation of enslavement.[23]

Sharks followed the slavers all the way across the Atlantic into American ports, as suggested by a notice from Kingston, Jamaica, that appeared in various newspapers in 1785: "The many Guineamen lately arrived here have introduced such a number of overgrown sharks, (The constant attendants on the vessels from the coasts) that bathing in the river is become extremely dangerous, even above town. A very large one was taken on Sunday, along side the Hibberts, Capt. Boyd." Abolitionists would do much to publicize the terror of sharks in the slave trade, but this evidence comes from a slave society, before the rise of the abolitionist movement. More came from Captain Hugh Crow, who made ten slaving voyages and wrote from personal observation that sharks "have been known to follow vessels across the ocean, that they might devour the bodies of the dead when thrown overboard."[24]

Slaving captains consciously used sharks to create terror throughout the voyage. They counted on sharks to prevent the desertion of their seamen and the escape of their slaves during the long stays on the coast of Africa required to gather a human "cargo." Naval officers used the fear of sharks, too. In the late 1780s, an African sailor from Cape Coast, who had been brought to Jamaica by a Liverpool Guineaman and somehow managed to escape slavery and find a berth on a man-of-war, killed a shark that had made it dangerous for sailors to swim or bathe around the vessel. He might have been a hero to his mates, but the commanding officer took a different view. As it happened, that shark had "prevented a number of desertions," so the African sailor "got a merciless flogging" for killing it. Naval officers were even said to feed sharks to keep them around their vessels.[25]

So well known was the conscious use of terror by the slave captain to create social discipline that when Oliver Goldsmith came to write the natural history of sharks in 1774, he drew heavily on the lore of the slave trade. The histories of terrorism and zoology intersected. Goldsmith recounted two instances:

> The master of a Guinea-ship, finding a rage for suicide among his slaves, from a notion the unhappy creatures had, that after death they should be restored again to their families, friends, and country; to convince them at least that some disgrace should attend them here, he immediately ordered one of their dead bodies to be tied by the heels to a rope, and so let down into the sea; and, though it was drawn up again with great swiftness, yet in that short space, the sharks had bit off all but the feet.

A second case was even more gruesome. Another captain facing a "rage for suicide" seized upon a woman "as a proper example to the rest." He ordered the woman tied with a rope under her armpits and lowered into the water: "When the poor creature was thus plunged in, and about half way down, she was heard to give a terrible shriek, which at first was ascribed to her fears of drowning; but soon after, the water appearing red all around her, she was drawn up, and it was found that a shark, which had followed the ship, had bit her off from the middle." Other slave-ship captains practiced a kind of sporting terror, using human remains to troll for sharks: "Our way to entice them was by Towing overboard a dead Negro, which they would follow till they had eaten him up."[26]

CHAPTER 2

The Evolution of the Slave Ship

Thomas Gordon introduced his book *Principles of Naval Architecture* (1784) with a sweeping statement: "As a Ship is undoubtedly the noblest, and one of the most useful machines that ever was invented, every attempt to improve it becomes a matter of importance, and merits the consideration of mankind." He captured, as a naval architect should, the tall ship's combination of grandeur and utility as he suggested the importance of its technical refinement and specialization. He noted that the progress of naval architecture could not be confined to this or that nation but belonged properly to all of mankind, whom the ship had helped to connect around the globe. Perhaps most important, he saw the ship as a machine, one of the most useful ever invented. He knew, of course, that the European deep-sea sailing ship—of which the slave ship was a variant—had helped to transform the world from the era of Christopher Columbus to his own time. It was the historic vessel for the emergence of capitalism, a new and unprecedented social and economic system that remade large parts of the world beginning in the late sixteenth century. It was also the material setting, the stage, for the enactment of the high human drama of the slave trade.[1]

The origins and genesis of the slave ship as a world-changing machine go back to the late fifteenth century, when the Portuguese made their historic voyages to the west coast of Africa, where they bought gold, ivory, and human beings. These early "explorations" marked the beginning of the Atlantic slave trade. They were made possible by a new evolution of the sailing ship, the full-rigged, three-masted carrack, the forerunner of the vessels that would eventually carry Europeans to all parts of the earth, then carry millions of Europeans and Africans to the New World, and finally earn Thomas Gordon's admiration.[2]

As Carlo Cipolla explained in his classic work *Guns, Sails, and Empires*, the ruling classes of Western European states were able to conquer the world between 1400 and 1700 because of two distinct and soon powerfully combined technological developments. First, English craftsmen forged cast-iron cannon, which were rapidly disseminated to military forces all around Europe. Second, the deep-sea sailing "round ship" of Northern Europe slowly eclipsed the oared "long ship," or galley, of the Mediterranean. European leaders with maritime ambitions had their shipwrights cut ports into the hulls of these rugged, seaworthy ships for huge, heavy cannon. Naval warfare changed as they added sails and guns and replaced oarsmen and warriors with smaller, more efficient crews. They substituted sail power for human energy and thereby created a machine that harnessed unparalleled mobility, speed, and destructive power. Thus when the full-rigged ship equipped with muzzle-loading cannon showed up on the coasts of Africa, Asia, and America, it was by all accounts a marvel if not a terror. The noise of the cannon alone was terrifying. Indeed it was enough, one empire builder explained, to induce non-Europeans to worship Jesus Christ.[3]

European rulers would use this revolutionary technology, this new maritime machine, to sail, explore, and master the high seas in order to trade, to fight, to seize new lands, to plunder, and to build empires. In so doing they battled each other as fiercely as they battled peoples outside Europe. Thanks in large part to the carrack, the galleon, and finally the full-rigged, three-masted, cannon-carrying ship, they established a new capitalist order. They rapidly became masters of the planet, a point that was not lost on the African king Holiday of Bonny, who explained to slave-ship captain Hugh Crow, "God make you sabby book and make big ship."[4]

The ship was thus central to a profound, interrelated set of economic changes essential to the rise of capitalism: the seizure of new lands, the expropriation of millions of people and their redeployment in growing market-oriented sectors of the economy; the mining of gold and silver, the cultivating of tobacco and sugar; the concomitant rise of long-distance commerce; and finally a planned accumulation of wealth and capital beyond anything the world had ever witnessed. Slowly, fitfully, unevenly, but with undoubted power, a world market and an international capitalist system emerged. Each phase of the process, from exploration to settlement to production to trade and the construction of a new economic order, required massive fleets of ships and their capacity to transport both expropriated laborers and the new commodities. The Guineaman was a linchpin of the system.

The specific importance of the slave ship was bound up with the other foundational institution of modern slavery, the plantation, a form of economic organization that began in the medieval Mediterranean, spread to the eastern Atlantic islands (the Azores, Madeiras, Canaries, and Cape Verde), and emerged in revolutionary form in the New World, especially Brazil, the Caribbean, and North America during the seventeenth century.[5] The spread of sugar production in the 1650s unleashed a monstrous hunger for labor power. For the next two centuries, ship after ship disgorged its human cargo, originally in many places European indentured servants and then vastly larger numbers of African slaves, who were purchased by planters, assembled in large units of production, and forced, under close and violent supervision, to mass-produce commodities for the world market. Indeed, as C. L. R. James wrote of laborers in San Domingue (modern Haiti), "working and living together in gangs of hundreds on the huge sugar-factories which covered North Plain, they were closer to a modern proletariat than any group of workers in existence at the time." By 1713 the slave plantation had emerged as "the most distinctive product of European capitalism, colonialism, and maritime power."[6]

One machine served another. A West Indian planter wrote in 1773 that the plantation should be a "well constructed machine, compounded of various wheels, turning different ways, and yet all contributing to the great end proposed."[7] Those turning the wheels were Africans, and the "great end" was the unprecedented accumulation of capital on a world scale. As an essential part of the "plantation complex," the slave ship helped Northern European states, Britain in particular, to break out of national economic limits and, in Robin Blackburn's words, "to discover an industrial and global future."[8]

The wide-ranging, well-armed slave ship was a powerful sailing machine, and yet it was also something more, something sui generis, as Thomas Gordon and his contemporaries knew. It was also a factory and a prison, and in this combination lay its genius and its horror. The word "factory" came into usage in the late sixteenth century as global trade expanded. Its root word was "factor," a synonym at the time for "merchant." A factory was therefore "an establishment for traders carrying on business in a foreign country." It was a merchant's trading station.[9]

The fortresses and trading houses built on the coast of West Africa, like Cape Coast Castle on the Gold Coast and Fort James on Bance Island in Sierra Leone, were thus "factories" but so, too, were ships themselves, as they were often permanently anchored near shore in other, less-developed areas of trade and used as places of business. The decks of the ship were the nexus for exchange of Africa-bound cargo such as textiles and firearms, Europe-bound cargo such as gold and ivory, and America-bound cargo such as slaves. Seaman James Field Stanfield sailed in 1774 from Liverpool to Benin aboard the slave ship Eagle, which was to be "left on the coast as a floating factory."[10]

The ship was a factory in the original meaning of the term, but it was also a factory in the modern sense. The eighteenth-century deep-sea sailing ship was a historic workplace, where merchant capitalists assembled and enclosed large numbers of propertyless workers and used foremen (captains and mates) to organize, indeed synchronize, their cooperation. The sailors employed mechanical equipment in concert, under harsh discipline and close supervision, all in exchange for a money wage earned in an international labor market. As Emma Christopher has shown, sailors not only worked in a global market, they produced for it, helping to create the commodity called "slave" to be sold in American plantation societies.[11]

The slave ship was also a mobile, seagoing prison at a time when the modern prison had not yet been established on land. This truth was expressed in various ways at the time, not least because incarceration (in barracoons, fortresses, jails) was crucial to the slave trade. The ship itself was simply one link in a chain of enslavement. Stanfield called it a "floating dungeon," while an anonymous defender of the slave trade aptly called it a "portable prison." Liverpool sailors frequently noted that when they were sent to jail by tavern keepers for debt and from there bailed out by ship captains who paid their bills and took their labor, they simply exchanged one prison for another. And if the slave ship seemed a prison to a sailor, imagine how it seemed to a slave locked belowdecks for sixteen hours a day and more. As it happened, the noble and useful machine described by Thomas Gordon benefited certain parts of mankind more than others.[12]

Malachy Postlethwayt: The Political Arithmetic of the Slave Trade, 1745

Malachy Postlethwayt was a British merchant and a lobbyist for the Royal African Company. Striving in the mid-1740s to persuade Parliament to subsidize the slave trade by paying for the upkeep of the fortresses and factories in West Africa, he asserted the centrality of the slave trade to the British Empire. His own position and economic interests perhaps made him exaggerate his claims on behalf of the trade, but, when viewed from the longer perspective of the eighteenth century, after the slave trade expanded dramatically beyond what he could have foreseen, some of his thoughts would become basic ruling-class wisdom about the trade and its place in a larger "political arithmetic" of empire.[13]

Postlethwayt stated his main argument in the title of his first pamphlet, *The African Trade, the Great Pillar and Support of the British Plantation Trade in America,* published in London in 1745. He began with the claim that "our *West Indian* and *African Trades* are the most nationally beneficial of any we carry on." He knew that the plantation revolution had transformed the empire and that both depended on the shipment of labor power. As for the plantation and slave ship, "the one cannot subsist without the other." He also pointed out that the slave trade was important to Britain's rising capitalist manufactures: a slave ship's "Cargo rightly sorted for Africa, consists of about Seven-Eights *British* Manufactures and Produce; and they return us not inconsiderable profit." He repeated a long-standing argument that would become controversial in debates in the 1780s: the slave trade created a "great Brood of Seamen" and was therefore a "formidable Nursery of Naval Power." The slave ship thus produced both slave and seafaring labor power.

Postlethwayt mounted his defense of what he politely called the "Africa Trade" because he knew that some people, even as early as the 1740s, had already turned against what they angrily denounced as the "slave trade": "Many are prepossessed against this Trade, thinking it a *barbarous, inhuman,* and *unlawful Traffic for a Christian Country to trade in Blacks.*" But, like all slave traders, he had convinced himself that Africans would be better off "living in a civilized Christian Country" than among "Savages." In any case, humanitarian concerns were trumped by national economic and military interest: the slave trade represented "an inexhaustible Fund of Wealth and Naval Power to this Nation." By promoting the Africa trade, Parliament would promote "*the Happiness and Prosperity of the Kingdom in General.*" Britain's Atlantic system depended on the resources, labor, and wealth of Africa and America. In so saying he anticipated William Blake's famous illustration half a century later, *Europe Supported by Africa & America.*[14]

Postlethwayt's view of a "triangular trade," in which the ships proceeded from a European (or American) port with a cargo of manufactured goods to West Africa, where they traded for slaves, to America, where they traded for plantation produce such as sugar, tobacco, or rice, became the dominant way of viewing the slave trade for the next two and a half centuries. Recently scholars have discovered that the trade was not strictly triangular, because many slave ships could not get a return cargo in the West Indies or North America. Yet the notion of a triangular trade remains valuable, because it permits a visualization of the three essential corners and components of the trade—British or American capital and manufactures, West African labor power, and American commodities (sometimes raw materials).

By the time Postlethwayt wrote, around 4 million Africans had already been delivered by slave ships to ports of the western Atlantic. Like almost all other European maritime states, Britain played an important role in the early phases of the slave trade, chartering and subsidizing Postlethwayt's own employer, the Royal African Company, a trading monopoly, in 1672. Slave trading was so expensive and demanded such a concentration of resources that private capital alone could not originally finance it. Beginning in the early eighteenth century, the so-called free traders finally triumphed over the regulated monopolies, but only after the state had helped to build the infrastructure for the trade. Indeed this is what moved Postlethwayt to petition for compensation and support in a deregulated age.[15]

British and American merchants took their chances in a trade that had high entry costs and enormous risks. In earlier days small investors, the middling sort, including artisans, might make money by buying a partial share or putting a little cargo in a Guinea ship, but by the eighteenth century the trade was firmly in the hands of merchants who had huge sums of capital and in most cases carefully acquired experience and knowledge of the trade. As John Lord Sheffield wrote in 1790, this meant that the trade was carried on by "men of capital, and transient adventurers will be discouraged from engaging in it." Profits for these big merchants could be extraordinary, as much as 100 percent on investment if everything went right, but the losses could also be immense, because of the dangers of disease, insurrection, shipwreck, and capture

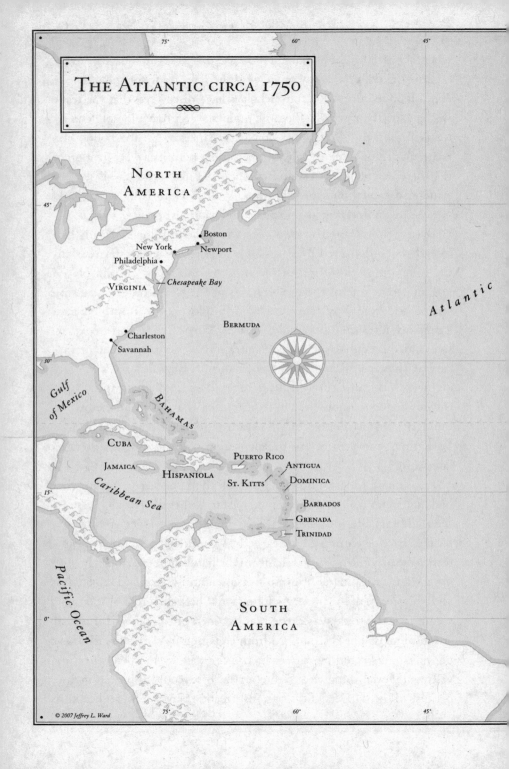

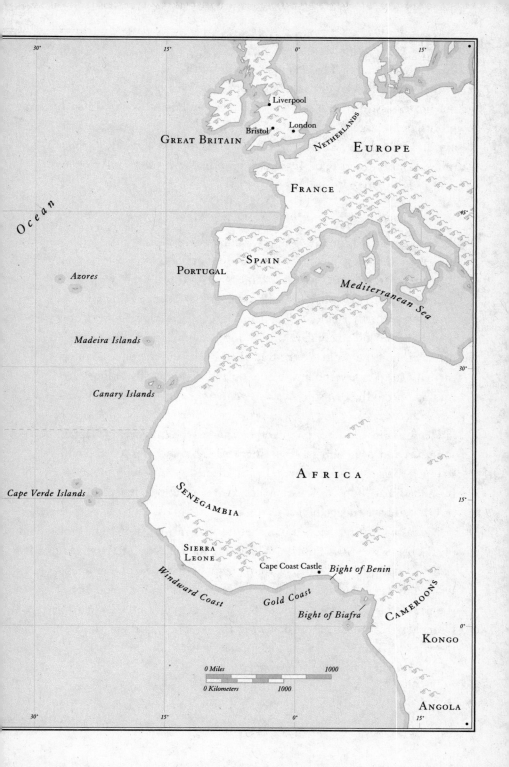

30°   15°   0°   15°

Liverpool

Bristol   London

GREAT BRITAIN

NETHERLANDS   EUROPE

FRANCE

Ocean

PORTUGAL   SPAIN

45°

Azores   *Mediterranean Sea*

Madeira Islands

30°

Canary Islands

AFRICA

Cape Verde Islands

SENEGAMBIA

15°

SIERRA
LEONE

Cape Coast Castle   *Bight of Benin*

Windward Coast   *Gold Coast*

CAMEROONS

Bight of Biafra

0°

KONGO

0 Miles   1000

0 Kilometers   1000

ANGOLA

30°   15°   0°   15°

by enemy privateers. The average rate of profit for slave-trade investors in the eighteenth century was 9 to 10 percent, which was considerable but not excessive by the standards of the day. Postlethwayt had such profits and a larger imperial system in mind when he noted that Britain, and indeed all the maritime powers of Europe, was raising "a magnificent Superstructure of *American Commerce and Naval Power* on an *African Foundation.*"[16]

Joseph Manesty: A Slave Ship Built, 1745

Liverpool merchant Joseph Manesty wanted two ships "for the Affrica trade," and he knew just how he wanted them built. He wrote to John Bannister of Newport, Rhode Island, on August 2, 1745, to place a transatlantic order. It was a perilous moment for traders, as England was at war with both France and Spain, and indeed Manesty had only months before lost a new slave ship, the aptly named *Chance,* to a French privateer. Still the profits of the trade beckoned, and men like Manesty carried a surging Liverpool past London and Bristol as the leading slave-trading port in the British Atlantic.[17] Manesty traded vigorously to West Africa between 1745 and 1758, as primary owner of at least nine vessels (and a minority owner of several others) and as the employer of Captain John Newton.[18] He wrote to Bannister that "no trade [was] push'd with so much spirit as the Affrican and with great Reason"—high profits!—but added that "ships are so scarce here that none is to be had at any rate or I should have engaged one this spring."[19]

Manesty's first instruction was that his prison ships were to be built of "the best white Oak Timber." The woodlands of New England were rich in high-quality, relatively rot-resistant white oak, and Manesty wanted to use it. He also demanded careful attention to the quality of the masts. He wrote five weeks later, "as both Ships are design'd for Guinea a great regard must be had to the goodness of their Masts on the whole." A broken mast was not easily replaced on the coast of Africa and could spell ruin for a voyage.[20]

The vessels, Manesty wrote in fine detail, were to be "Square stern'd," 58 feet in length, 22 feet in width, and 10 feet deep in the hold, with a height of "5 feet twixt Decks" for the incarceration of the enslaved. The main mast was to be 60 feet long, the main yard 44 feet, the main topmast 30 feet; "all the other Masts and Yards in proportion." Vessels in the slave trade needed to be sturdy and durable, so Manesty insisted that both vessels be built with heavy "2½ and 3 Inch plank with good substantial bends or Whales" (wales, thick wooden joints bolted on the side of the vessel). He wanted the bulkheads to be a "Solid beam," and he demanded that "the Gun Wall on the Main Deck [be] 14 Inches Solid." The vessels would be well armed to defend themselves against privateers, although the number of cannon was not specified. In a postscript to the letter, Manesty added, "2 Gun Ports Stern."[21]

Manesty requested that the hulls of the slavers be "middling," that is, "sharp" enough for speed, to reduce the duration of the Middle Passage and hence mortality among the enslaved, and "full" enough for stability and carrying capacity, for armaments and the sometimes-bulky commodities to be carried to the African coast and from American plantations back to Europe. He wanted a full-bodied vessel that would not pitch a lot, to reduce the effects of excessive motion on the human cargo. He wanted the sides of the vessels flared "for the more commodious stowing [of] Negroes twixt Decks." Another characteristic he desired was "rounding in the Top as the other Decks, for Messing [feeding] Negroes on lower deck laid fore and aft." The ribs or timbers were to be "left high enough to Support Rails all round the Vessel," probably in part to facilitate the addition of netting designed to prevent suicidal slaves from jumping overboard. Finally he wanted sheathing to protect against the worms that would bore through the hulls in Africa's tropical waters. He ordered an extra lining of deal boards coated, as was standard, with tar and horsehair, to be tacked on while the vessels were still in the stocks. Vessels would later be sheathed in copper.[22]

Probably because of the war and the dangers of capture, Manesty wrote that he "wou'd have as little money laid out on the Vessels as possible." He wanted "Plain sterns," no quarter windows, and little or no work to be done by joiners in the captain's cabin. He wanted every-thing done in a "frugal Suitable manner." It is not known how much money Manesty paid for the vessels, but Elizabeth Donnan notes that in 1747 a Rhode Island vessel could be bought at £24 old tenor per ton.[23] By 1752 the price had risen to £27 per ton for a sloop, £34 per ton for a "double decker." Prices were about one-fifth less in Swansea, in nearby Massachusetts, where the vessel might have been built. Assum-ing that seven pounds old tenor equaled one pound sterling, and esti-mating that Manesty's two-deck vessels were to be around a hundred tons carrying capacity, each would have cost a little over £500 (about $130,000 in 2007). Larger ships would run to £700 ($182,000) and some to well over £1,000 ($260,000), but ship costs were nonetheless modest in relation to the value of the cargoes to be shipped in them.[24]

Manesty realized that certain essential items for the vessel were available more cheaply in Liverpool, so he arranged to send over "Cordage, Sails, Anchors, Nails" as well as a trading cargo. By June he had already dispatched some of the materials—"Sheating Nails and single Spikes"—and he hoped that the carpenters who were working on the vessels might be willing "to take Goods on acco't of these Ves-sels," no doubt because wages in the American colonies were relatively high. Manesty knew that it would take the shipwright about a year to finish the vessels, which meant launchings in August 1746. He would send a master for the first vessel in April of that year, to oversee the finishing details and to sail the vessel to Africa as soon as it was ready. In his eagerness to trade for slaves, he added, "shou'd it happen that a Vessel of or near the Dimentions of one of these order'd can be imme-diately bought Cheap with you or of any other size suitable for Affrica I shou'd choose to do it and build only one if that can be done."[25]

Manesty could have had his slave ships built in a variety of places, or he could simply have bought a vessel or two that were built for other trades and had them converted for slaving. This latter would have been the preferred solution for most merchants, as the vast ma-jority of vessels employed in the slave trade had not been built specifi-cally for it. The types detailed below—sloops, schooners, brigs, snows, and ships—were all more or less standardized by the 1720s. Hull form, sail, and rigging would change relatively little over the next hundred years, although sharper, faster ships came to be preferred in the early nineteenth century.[26]

Had Manesty ordered his vessels a few years earlier, he might have gone to London or Bristol, the dominant slaving ports of the early eighteenth century. But by the time he wrote to Bannister, Liverpool was eclipsing both in the slave trade and in the building of slave ships. As timber grew scarce, some merchants turned to shipbuilders in the American colonies, where prices were lower. Increasingly, the ships that went into the African trade were, as English merchants described them, "plantation-built." They were constructed in New England, especially in Rhode Island and Massachusetts; in the upper South, Maryland and Virginia; and, after the 1760s, in the lower South, primarily South Carolina. Especially popular among slave-ship merchants was the Bermuda sloop, built with native red cedar that was light, strong, and rot-resistant. As the oak forests of northeastern America were slowly depleted over the course of the eighteenth century and the cost of bringing timber to the coast increased, a preferred source became southern pine, which meant that much of the wood for the slavers was hewn by slaves, many of whom had crossed the Atlantic on slave ships. Liverpool shipbuilders even imported pine from the slave-based colonies of Virginia and Carolina with which to build Guineamen in their own yards. This suggests one of the ways in which the slave trade helped to reproduce itself on an international scale. The ships brought the laborers and the laborers cut the wood to make more ships.[27]

The shipbuilders of Liverpool, soon to be the capital of the slave trade, began to custom-build slave ships around 1750. Shipbuilding had long been central to the commercial prosperity of the city, and as the city's merchants invested more and more heavily in the trade to Africa, they ordered ships from local builders. In 1792 there were nine yards for the construction of ships, another three for boats. Most ships were built in "the pool," the tidal inlet on the river Mersey. In the last two decades before abolition (1787–1808) Liverpool shipwrights built 469 vessels, on average 21 per year. (The shipbuilding firm that undoubtedly had the best—and, to merchants, most soothing—name was Humble and Hurry, named for shipwrights Michael Humble and William Hurry.) By the 1780s the abolitionist movement had managed to politicize shipbuilding in the slave trader's strongest base. William Rathbone, a leading Quaker merchant, refused to sell timber to any yard that made slavers. Nonetheless slave ships continued to be launched at Liverpool right up to the moment of abolition, after which they had to be converted to other purposes.[28]

Former seaman-turned-artist Nicholas Pocock drew an image of a Bristol shipyard, owned by master shipwright Sydenham Teast, in 1760. It is not clear if any of the vessels pictured were slave ships, but it is clear that Bristol was at this time deeply involved in the slave trade and that Teast himself was an investor. Based on his work, one can imagine how it took a small army of workers to build a slave ship, especially one of average size, two hundred tons. The master shipwright directed the complex effort, which involved dozens of workers and began with the laying of the keel and the attachment of the ribs. As the hull grew, staging was built around it, so that planking could be attached inside and out, and faired. Caulkers filled the seams between the planks with oakum (unraveled hemp). As soon as the hull was complete, new craftsmen arrived, and the scene grew even busier. Joiners built rails and finished the interior. Blacksmiths attended to the ironwork (and later brought on board the anchors). Masons laid the bricks that supported the galley (the slaver required a special furnace and hearth), while a tinman lined the scuppers and a glazier installed glass stern windows. Masts, blocks, and cordage required mast and spar makers, who worked with block makers and rope makers; then came the riggers to put their system in place. Sailmakers provided the canvas, and the boatbuilders brought aboard the yawl and the longboat, with sweeps carved by the oar maker. Coopers contributed the barrels for cargo, provisions, and water. Depending on how much decoration and luxury the person buying the ship wanted, then came the painters, wood-carvers, and finishers. Finally arrived the butchers, bakers, and brewers for victualing the vessel.[29]

Shipbuilding was an ancient craft, in which highly specialized knowledge was passed down over the centuries through a system of mastery. For most of the eighteenth century, shipwrights still built "by eye," or from models, which means that there are relatively few surviving scale drawings of the vessels of this era. Shipbuilders used published works, such as William Sutherland's *The Shipbuilder's Assistant* (1711) and *Britain's Glory; or, Ship-Building Unvail'd, being a General Director for Building and Compleating the said Machines* (1729), both influential. Other widely read authors included John Hardingham, Mungo Murray, Fredrik Henrik af Chapman, Marmaduke Stalkartt, William Hutchinson, David Steel, and Thomas Gordon.[30] Shipbuilding was a truly international craft, as shipwrights themselves moved around, much to the worry of governments. More tellingly still, the ships themselves moved around, making for a relatively easy transfer of craft, knowledge, and technology. Shipwrights routinely studied the vessels produced in other nations to assess the state of the art at any given moment. This helped to diffuse a general uniformity of design and production. Slave ships of all European nations were roughly similar in design and construction during the eighteenth century.[31]

And yet "science" was slowly entering and transforming the craft, as suggested by the entry "naval architecture" in the 1780 edition of William Falconer's *Universal Dictionary of the Marine* and by the formation in 1791 of the Society for the Improvement of Naval Architecture, to gather and disseminate scientific information across national boundaries on a variety of subjects. The society publicized works on subjects ranging from naval affairs and tactics and military defense to physics (fluids and matter) and mathematics (tables). It staged competitions and offered prizes for scientific proposals on how to compute the tonnage of ships, how to strengthen ship-body construction, how to get rid of bilge, how to proportion masts and yards, how to prevent and control fire on ships, how to save a sinking ship. It wanted to encourage thought on "the laws respecting bodies moving through the water with different velocities." The science also had its graphic manifestation, as the drawing of ships took on more careful proportion and greater perspective, as reflected in the image of the *Brooks*.[32]

Captain Anthony Fox: A Slave Ship's Crew, 1748

An unusual document surviving in the archive of the Society of Merchant Venturers in Bristol gives a well-rounded view of a slaving crew, the workers who would sail the machine named the *Peggy* to Africa on August 13, 1748. Captain Anthony Fox drew up "An Account of Men Belonging to the Snow Peggy" (a two-masted vessel), which gives abundant information about himself and his thirty-eight men. They ranged in age from fifteen to forty-two, Captain Fox and two other men being the oldest on board. The average age was twenty-six, and, for the common seaman, the age would have been even lower were we able to exclude the ages of the officers, who were usually older. (For all the information he recorded, Fox did not indicate which jobs the men performed.) Despite their relative youth, almost a third of the crew—twelve of thirty-nine—would come to a premature death on the voyage. Captain Fox also recorded "size," by which he meant height. Perhaps he was conscious of this because he was the tallest man on board at five feet ten inches. The average was five-six.[33]

The men on board the *Peggy* were well traveled. One of the columns in Captain Fox's account was "where borne" rather than the usual "place of abode." The crewmen of the *Peggy* were mainly from the port cities of Britain, but broadly so, from England, Wales, Scotland, and Ireland. A few came from overseas—there were four Swedes on the ship, and others from Holland, Genoa, and Guinea. Captain Fox himself was born in Montserrat. The crew members had sailed on various merchant and naval craft from Britain to Africa, the West Indies, North America, the East Indies, and the Mediterranean, Turkey in particular. Several men had been demobilized after the War of Austrian Succession in 1748. Their previous ships included men-of-war such as the HMS *Russell,* HMS *Devonshire,* HMS *Torbay,* and HMS *Launceston.* One man had served on the "*Salamander* Bomb."

The African sailor John Goodboy had sailed previously on the "Defiance Ship of War."

Captain Fox also recorded "complexion," probably in order to identify runaways should he need to do so at some point in the voyage. As it happened, the captain had only two categories for complexion—"browne" and "blacke." Most people were "browne," including the captain himself. Those he considered "blacke" included Robert Murray of Scotland, Peter Dunfry of Ireland, Perato Bartholomew of Genoa, and the African John Goodboy.

The division of labor on Fox's Guineaman would have been similar to what prevailed on all eighteenth-century deep-sea sailing ships, with a few special features. A typical slave ship had a captain, a first and second mate, a doctor, a carpenter, a boatswain, a gunner (or armorer), often a cooper (barrel maker), a cook, ten to twelve seamen, a handful of landsmen, and one or two ship's boys. Larger ships would have a third and even a fourth mate, mates for the doctor and the various skilled workers, especially the carpenter and gunner, and a few more seamen and landsmen. The unusual aspects were the number of mates, the necessity of a doctor, and the number of sailors and landsmen. These additional members of the crew reflected the special dangers of the slave trade, the need for larger numbers of people to guard the slaves and to withstand the mortality of the African coast and Middle Passage. The division of labor allocated responsibilities and structured working relations among the crew, forming a hierarchy of laboring roles and a corresponding scale of wages. A slave ship, like a man-of-war, required a wide variety of skills. It was "too big and unmanageable a machine" to be run by novices.[34]

The organization of labor on the slave ship began with the captain, the first person hired and the last to be discharged by the shipowner at voyage's end. He was the representative of the merchant and his capital throughout the voyage. His charge was "to manage the navigation and everything relating to [the ship's] cargo, voyage, sailors, &c." He hired the crew, procured the ship's provisions, oversaw the loading of the original cargo, and conducted all the business of the voyage, from the buying of the slaves in Africa to their sale in the Americas. He saw to the navigation of the vessel, tended the compasses, and gave the working orders. On the smaller ships, he ran one of the two watches. He was the monarch of his wooden world. He possessed near-absolute authority, and he used it however he saw fit to maintain social order aboard the ship.

Most slave ships had at least two mates, because the threat of mortality required that several people be on board who knew navigation. The chief mate was second in command, although much inferior in power to the captain. He commanded a watch and during the alternating time tended to the basic functioning of the ship. He managed the daily routine and set the crew to work. He minded the security of the vessel, making sure that the enslaved were under control. He also oversaw their feeding, exercise, and health. He often took responsibility for "stowing" the captives belowdecks. In those areas of Africa where the trade was carried on in boats, he took charge of one of them, which meant that he often conducted trade, bought slaves, and ferried them back to the ship.

Captain William Snelgrave touched upon most of these responsibilities in "Instructions for a first mate when in the road att Whydah," written for chief mate John Magnus in 1727. His main concern was security. He advised close control, especially of "ye strong rugged men Slaves." Check their chains closely; place sentries on guard and have them fire their arms at the evening meal (to prevent "insurrection"); make sure none hijack the ship's boat or jump overboard. Store the victuals safely and cleanly; boil well the slaves' "dab-a-dab" (a mash of horsebeans, rice, and corn) to avoid sickness; and give them water three times a day, tobacco once a week, and a dram of corn brandy on a cold morning. Divert them with music and dance in the evenings. He suggested that some of the enslaved be employed to clean between decks and that they get "a dram every day when they do their business well." If smallpox breaks out among the enslaved, isolate the sick person immediately to prevent contagion. If sailors get sick, give them special foods—sugar, butter, oatmeal. He added, "When any Slave dies lett Mr. Willson with some officer be present at the time of committing them to the water: noteing the day of the month and sickness which they died off." In the event of the death of a sailor, "take an Inventory of what he leaves; and naill the things up in his chest." The chief mate had many responsibilities, as did, in diminishing proportions, the second, third, and fourth mates after him.[35]

The doctor's difficult job was to keep the crew and the slaves alive from one side of the Atlantic to the other. He assisted in the purchase of slaves, carefully inspecting each one for signs of sickness or debility, knowing that the healthy would have the best chance of surviving the stay on the African coast and the Middle Passage and of fetching the highest prices in America. Once the slaves had come aboard, the doctor tended to them daily, attempted to answer their complaints, diagnosed illnesses, and prescribed medications. He also treated the crew, who themselves suffered a host of maladies once they crossed the pathogenic barrier reef into West Africa. Early in the eighteenth century, only the larger ships carried a doctor, and the smaller, faster American slave ships, most of them out of Rhode Island, rarely carried one throughout the century, taking instead a "recipe book" for medicines to be used by the captain. After the passage of the Dolben Act, or Slave Carrying Bill, of 1788, all British slave ships were required to have a doctor on board, and the doctor himself was required to keep records of sickness and death on the voyage.[36]

The carpenter, an important specialist in the wooden world, was responsible for the structural soundness of the ship and its various parts. He checked the hull regularly, forcing oakum and wooden plugs into the seams of planks to keep the vessel tight. He also repaired the masts, yards, and machinery. He gave the slave ship several of its distinctive characteristics. During the outward passage, he built the barricado on the main deck and the bulkheads and platforms on the lower deck, effectively transforming a generic merchant ship into a slaver. He paid special attention to the longboat and the yawl, especially when they were important to trade, as on the Windward Coast. The carpenter had learned his craft through apprenticeship and sometimes trained a mate on the ship.

The lesser officers and skilled workers included the boatswain, gunner, cooper, and cook. The boatswain, like the mate, was something of a foreman. He was responsible for the rigging, kept up the cables and anchors, and on some vessels took charge of the female slaves. The gunner, or armorer, was responsible for the firearms, the ammunition, and the artillery, as well as the locks and chains. He was crucial to an era in which trade itself was regarded by many as a form of warfare and to a vessel that was in effect a floating prison. The cooper built and repaired the casks and hogsheads in which many commodities (especially sugar and tobacco) were shipped and preserved, as well as food and especially water; he might also perform other woodworking tasks. On the slave ship as on other vessels, the cook was sometimes an older seaman who had seen better times and was now unable to go aloft or perform heavy physical labor. Or he might, alternatively, be an African-American, with the "black cook" emerging in the eighteenth century as a familiar figure on ships of all kinds, including slavers. His job was an arduous one, for he had to feed up to three or four hundred people twice a day. According to the crew and probably to the enslaved (if we had any evidence of their view), the cook would not have been considered a "skilled" worker.

The common seaman was a person trained to sail a ship—to "hand, reef, and steer," as the old phrase had it. He knew how to climb up and down the ratlines, how to set the sails, how to knot and splice the lines, and how to steer the ship. By 1700, seafaring labor was roughly the same everywhere. Sailors circulated from ship to ship and found the tasks performed and the skills required by each to be essentially the same. An "able seaman" knew how to do the work of the ship in all aspects. Slavers also had on board, at lower wages, "ordinary seamen," usually younger and less-experienced men who were still learning the mysteries of a dangerous occupation. The sailor on a slave ship was also a prison guard. He spent a lot of time supervising and guarding the enslaved as they washed, ate, danced, and sat on the main deck. This was the ship's reproductive or domestic labor.

Most slave ships, especially after 1750, had a number of landsmen on board. These were young, unskilled workers, sometimes from the countryside, sometimes from the city, who signed on to Guineamen when laboring jobs along the waterfront were hard to find, as they often were in peacetime. Their work consisted mainly of guarding the slaves, although they would also be deployed for any variety of unskilled manual labor aboard the ship or ashore. During the course of the voyage, they would learn the ship's work and after two or three voyages qualify as ordinary seamen. Until then they ranked only above the ship's boys in the working hierarchy. The boys, usually between the ages of eight and fourteen and one, two, or three in number, were being "bred up to the sea" by serving an apprenticeship, usually to the captain himself. Like Samuel Robinson, they performed odd jobs and were the object of no small amount of horseplay and even cruelty.

Thomas Clarkson: The Variety of Slaving Vessels, 1787

A vessel of almost any size could be a slave ship, as the abolitionist Thomas Clarkson discovered, to his utter astonishment, in June 1787. He had journeyed from London to Bristol to gather evidence about the slave trade. He was especially interested in the "construction and dimensions" of the ships and the packing of the bodies of would-be plantation workers. Having a few months earlier gone aboard Captain Colley's *Fly,* a more-or-less typical two-hundred-ton ship that lay at anchor in the Thames, Clarkson had a clear image of the slaver in mind. He was shocked to find at Bristol "two little sloops" that were fitting out for Africa. One was a vessel of only twenty-five tons; its master intended to pick up seventy slaves. The other was even smaller. It measured eleven tons and would take on board a mere thirty slaves. One of Clarkson's companions explained that vessels of this size sometimes served as tenders, going up and down West African coastal rivers, gathering three or four slaves at a time and delivering them to the big ships anchored off the coast and bound for the New World. But the tiny vessels discovered by Clarkson were said to be slavers in their own right and would transport their own captives to the West Indies.[37]

Clarkson did not believe it. He even wondered whether his informants were trying to trick him into making absurd statements about the slave trade that could be easily refuted and thereby "injure the great cause which I had undertaken." He learned that one of the vessels had been built as "a pleasure-boat for the accommodation of only six persons" on the Severn River and that one if not both were to be sold as pleasure craft after they delivered their slaves in the West Indies. Clarkson decided to measure both vessels and to ask one of his companions to find the builder of the vessels and get his measurements, too. The official information corresponded with Clarkson's own figures. In the larger vessel of the two, the area where the slaves would be incarcerated measured thirty-one feet in length by ten feet four inches in width, narrowing to five feet at the ends. Each slave, he calculated, would get about three square feet. In the smaller vessel, the slave room was twenty-two feet long, eight feet (tapering to four feet) wide. The height from keel to beam was five feet eight inches, but three feet were taken up by "ballast, cargo, and provisions," leaving for thirty slaves four square feet each and about two feet eight inches of vertical space. Still incredulous, Clarkson had four persons make separate inquiries to confirm that the vessels really were going to Africa. All four found the original declaration to be true, and indeed Clarkson himself soon confirmed the matter through official documents in the Bristol customshouse.[38]

Clarkson would have been even more astonished to learn that the eleven-ton vessel he found was not the smallest on record. A ten-ton vessel called the *Hesketh* sailed from Liverpool to the Windward Coast and carried thirty enslaved people on to St. Kitts in 1761, and vessels of the same size would deliver slaves to Cuba and Brazil in the middle of the nineteenth century. Two eleven-ton vessels, the *Sally* and the

Adventure, made voyages from Rhode Island to Africa in 1764 and 1770. As Clarkson learned, even the smallest vessel could be a slave ship.[39]

At the other end of the spectrum was the *Parr,* a 566-ton behemoth built by shipwright John Wright in Liverpool in 1797 and named for owners Thomas and John Parr, members of an eminent local slave-trading family. This was a square-sterned, double-decked ship, 127 feet long on deck and 32 feet broad, with three masts, quarter galleries, and a woman's figurehead on the prow. The ship was heavily armed, boasting twenty eighteen-pounders and twelve eighteen-pounder carronnades. A contemporary noted, "She is looked upon by judges to be a very beautiful vessel and the largest employed out of this port in the African trade for which she was designed." Built to accommodate seven hundred slaves and requiring a crew of one hundred sailors, the *Parr* proved to be not only the largest Liverpool slaver but the largest of the entire British Atlantic. Still, it came to a bad and sudden end not long after Wright and his gang of fellow shipyard workers launched it. In a trade infamous for human catastrophe, the *Parr* suffered one of the greatest of them all: in 1798, on her first voyage, to the Bight of Biafra, Bonny in particular, after Captain David Christian had reached the coast and taken on board about two hundred slaves, the ship exploded, killing everyone on board. The cause of the blast is unknown.[40]

If the diminutive eleven-ton sloop Clarkson found represented one end of the spectrum and the massive *Parr* the other, what were the most typical vessels in terms of design and size? Slave traders in Britain and America most commonly employed the sloop, schooner, brig, brigantine, snow, bark, and ship (which was both a specific type and a generic label for all vessels). Guineamen tended to be middling in size and carrying capacity: they were smaller than ships employed in the East and West Indies trades, about the same size as those that sailed to the Mediterranean, and larger than the craft involved in Northern European and coastal commerce. Like vessels in almost all trades in the eighteenth century they tended to increase in size over time, although this trend was more apparent in Bristol, London, and especially Liverpool than in the New World. American slave-ship merchants and captains preferred smaller vessels, especially sloops and schooners, which required smaller crews and carried smaller cargoes of enslaved Africans, who could be gathered more quickly on shorter stays on the African coast. British merchants preferred somewhat larger vessels, which required more logistical coordination but also promised greater profits while sharing some of the advantages of the smaller American vessels. Vessels built for one port might not work for others, as Liverpool slave-trade merchants made clear in 1774 when they said of the American slaver the *Deborah,* "though she was constructed in the usual manner for the Trade from Rhode Island to Africa," presumably to carry rum, "she would by no means suit for the Trade from Liverpool."[41]

The smallest vessel Clarkson saw was a sloop, which was not uncommon in the slave trade, especially out of American ports. The sloop usually ranged from 25 to 75 tons, had a single mast, fore-and-aft rigging, and a mainsail attached "to the mast on its foremost edge, and to a long boom below; by which it is occasionally shifted to either quarter." It was fast in the water and easily maneuvered, with shallow draft and light displacement. It required a modest crew of five to ten. An example of this kind of vessel appeared in the *Newport Mercury* (Rhode Island) on January 7, 1765. Offered for sale was "a SLOOP of about 50 Tons, compleatly fitted for a Guineaman, with all her Tackle. Likewise a few Negro Boys."[42] Captain William Shearer provided a more detailed description after his sloop the *Nancy* was seized by a mutinous crew on the river Gambia in April 1753. Built in Connecticut only nine months earlier and measuring 70 tons, the *Nancy* was square-sterned and deep-waisted, had six air ports cut into each side, carried four small cannon, and was steered by a wheel. Most of the exterior had been painted black. The stern was yellow, matching the curtains in the cabin and a small frieze nearby. Another frieze was painted the color of pearl, while the area around the ports and the roundhouse were streaked with vermilion. Captain Shearer added that the vessel "has no Register or Custom House Papers relating to the Cargo," perhaps because the crew had destroyed them. His final comment was that the *Nancy* "is an exceeding good going Vessel, and sails extremely well both upon a Wind and large."[43]

Two-masted vessels were common in the slave trade. The schooner, which emerged from American shipyards in the early eighteenth century, was exemplified by the *Betsey,* sold at public auction at Crafts North Wharf, Charleston, South Carolina, in 1796. It was described as "a good double decked vessel, well calculated for a Guineaman, about 90 tons burthen, and may be sent to sea immediately, being in good order." The brigantine, or brig, and the snow (snauw), which had the same hull form but different rigging, were especially popular in the slave trade, largely because of their intermediate size. They ranged from 30 to 150 tons, with the average slaver running to about 100 tons. Vessels of this size often had more actual deck and aerial space per ton than larger ones, as pointed out by Sir Jeremiah Fitzpatrick, M.D., in 1797.[44]

According to William Falconer, the compiler of one of the greatest maritime dictionaries of the eighteenth century, the ship was "the first rank of vessels which are navigated on the ocean." It was the largest of the vessels employed in the slave trade, combining good speed and spacious carrying capacity. It had three masts, each of which carried a lower mast, a topmast, and likely a topgallant mast. As a man-of-war, the ship was something of a "moveable fortress or citadel," carrying batteries of cannon and possessing huge destructive power. As a merchant ship, it was more variable in size, ranging from 100 tons up to a few at 500 tons or more, like the *Parr,* and capable of carrying seven hundred to eight hundred slaves. The average slave ship was the size of the first one Clarkson had seen, 200 tons like the *Fly.* Not far from typical was the *Eliza,* which was to be sold at public auction at the Carolina Coffee House in Charleston on May 7, 1800. Lying at Goyer's wharf, with "all her appurtenances," for any prospective buyer to see was the copper-bottomed ship of 230 tons, "fitted for carrying 12 guns, a remarkable fast sailer, well adapted for the West India or African trade, exceedingly well sound in stores, and may be sent to sea at an easy expense."[45]

As the slave trade grew and changed over the years, the Guinea-man evolved. Most slavers were typical sailing ships of their time, and most of them were not built specifically for the trade. Vessels of many sizes and types remained involved in the trade for the full duration of the period from 1700 to 1808, but a more specialized slaving vessel did emerge, especially from the shipyards of Liverpool, after 1750. It was larger and had more special features: air ports, copper bottoms, more room between decks. The ship underwent further modification in the late 1780s, as a result of pressures created by the abolitionist movement and the passage of reform legislation in Parliament to improve the health and treatment of both sailors and slaves. The slave ship, as Malachy Postlethwayt, Joseph Manesty, Abraham Fox, and Thomas Clarkson all from their varying vantage points knew, was one of the most important technologies of the day.

John Riland: A Slave Ship Described, 1801

John Riland read the letter from his father with rising horror. The year was 1801, and it was time for the young man to return to the family plantation in Jamaica after his studies at Christ Church, Oxford. His father gave him precise instructions: he would journey from Oxford to Liverpool, where he would take a berth as a passenger aboard a slave ship. From there he would sail to the Windward Coast of Africa, observe the purchase and loading of a "living cargo" of slaves, and travel with them across the Atlantic to Port Royal, Jamaica. Young Riland had been exposed to antislavery ideas and now had serious misgivings about the commerce in human flesh; he had, he noted, no desire to be "imprisoned in a floating lazar-house, with a crowd of diseased and wretched slaves." He took comfort from a classmate's comment that recent abolitionist accounts of the Middle Passage and the slave ship had been "villainously exaggerated."[46]

It so happened that the senior Riland, like the son, had begun to entertain doubts about slavery. His Christian conscience apparently told him that the young man who would inherit the family estate should see firsthand what the slave trade was all about. The dutiful son did as the patriarch commanded. He went to Liverpool and sailed as a privileged passenger with a "Captain Y——" aboard his ship, the *Liberty*. Riland used the experience to write one of the most detailed accounts of a slave ship ever penned.[47]

When Riland stepped aboard the vessel he would take to Africa and across the Atlantic, the captain apparently knew that he was no friend of the slave trade. The man in charge of the wooden world was determined, therefore, to present the ship and its practices in the best possible light. He tried, wrote Riland, to "soften the revolting circumstances which he saw would develop themselves on our landing [in Africa]; during also our stay on the coast, and in our subsequent voyage to Jamaica." He referred to the purchase of more than two hundred captives, the close crowding, the inevitable sickness and death. The captain also undertook to educate his young passenger. He sat with him night after night in the captain's cabin (where Riland slept and ate), conversing with him by the dim light of swaying lamps, explaining patiently how "the children of Ham" benefited by being sent to American plantations such as the one the senior Riland owned.

Soon after the captain had secured his "living cargo" on the African coast, he informed Riland that now he would see that "a slave-ship was a very different thing from what it had been represented." He referred to the abolitionist propaganda that had changed public opinion in England and abroad. Against all that he would show his passenger "the slaves rejoicing in their happy state." To illustrate the point, he approached the enslaved women on board and said a few words, "to which they replied with three cheers and a loud laugh." He then went forward on the main deck and "spoke the same words to the men, who made the same reply." Turning triumphantly to Riland, the captain said, "Now, are you not convinced that Mr. Wilberforce has conceived very improperly of slave-ships?" He referred to the parliamentary leader who had trumpeted the horrors of slave transportation. Riland was not convinced. But he was intrigued, and he was eager to learn whether the captain might be telling the truth. He therefore observed closely "the economy of this slave ship."[48]

In describing a medium-size vessel, apparently a bark or ship of approximately 140 tons, Riland began with the lower deck, the quarters where 240 enslaved people (170 males, 70 females) were incarcerated for sixteen hours a day and sometimes longer. Riland saw the vessel's dungeonlike qualities. The men, shackled together two by two at the wrists and ankles and roughly 140 in number, were stowed immediately below the main deck in an apartment that extended from the mainmast all the way forward. The distance between the lower deck and the beams above was four and a half feet, so most men would not have been able to stand up straight. Riland did not mention platforms, which were routinely built on the lower deck of slavers, from the edge of the ship inward about six feet, to increase the number of slaves to be carried. The vessel was probably stowed to its maximum number of slaves according to the Dolben Act of 1788, which permitted slave ships to carry five slaves per three tons of carrying capacity.

On the main deck above, a large wooden grating covered the entrance to the men's quarters, the open latticework designed to permit a "sufficiency of air" to enter. For the same purpose, two or three small scuttles, holes for admitting air, had been cut in the side of the vessel, although these were not always open. At the rear of the apartment was a "very strong bulk-head," constructed by the ship's carpenter in a way that would not obstruct the circulation of air through the lower deck. Still, Riland considered ventilation to be poor down below, which meant that men were subjected to a "most impure and stifling atmosphere." Worse, they had too little room: the space allotted was "far too small, either for comfort or health." Riland saw that the men, when brought up from below, looked "quite livid and ghastly as well as gloomy and dejected." Having been kept in darkness for many hours on end, they would emerge each morning blinking hard against the sunlight.[49]

The midsection of the lower deck, from near the mainmast back to the mizzenmast, was the women's apartment, for the *Liberty,* unlike most slavers, did not have a separate area for boys. To separate the men and women, therefore, a space of about ten feet was left between the men's and women's quarters as a passageway for the crew to get into the hold, where they stowed trading goods, naval stores, and provisions (food and water, probably in oversize "Guinea casks"). Fore and aft, the women's room was enclosed by sturdy bulkheads. The women, most of whom were not in irons, had more room and freedom of movement than the men, as only about forty-five of them slept here. The grating lay, boxlike, about three feet above the main deck and "admitted a good deal of air," thought Riland. Those down below might have begged to differ.[50]

Two additional apartments were created beneath the quarterdeck, which was raised about seven feet above the main deck and extended to the stern of the vessel. The aftermost of these was the cabin, where hung the cots of the captain and Riland himself. But even these two most privileged people shared their sleeping space as every night twenty-five little African girls gathered to sleep beneath them. The captain warned his cabinmate that "the smell would be unpleasant for a few days," but reassured him that "when we got into the trade winds it would no longer be perceived." Riland's gentlemanly sensibilities apparently never recovered, for he later wrote, "During the night I hung over a crowd of slaves huddled together on the floor, whose stench at times was almost beyond endurance."

The situation was similar in the other, adjacent room, which opened up onto the main deck. Here slept the surgeon and first mate, who also shared the space: beneath them each night lay twenty-nine boys. Other spaces on the main deck were reserved for the sick, especially those with dysentery, who were "kept separate from the others." Sick men were placed in the longboat, which had a tarpaulin thrown over it as an awning; sick women went under the half deck. Very little room was left for the sailors, who hung their hammocks under the longboat, near the sick, hoping that the awning would protect them from the elements, especially nightly dews on the African coast.

Riland emphasized another feature that was literally central to the social organization of the main deck—the barricado, a strong wooden barrier ten feet high that bisected the ship near the mainmast and extended about two feet over each side of the vessel. This structure, built to turn any vessel into a slaver, separated the bonded men from the women and served as a defensive barrier behind which the crew could retreat (to the women's side) in moments of slave insurrection, but it was also a military installation of sorts from which the crew guarded and controlled the enslaved people on board. Built into the barricade, noted Riland, was a small door, through which might pass only one person at a time, slowly. Whenever the men slaves were on the main deck, two armed sentinels protected the door while "four more were placed, with loaded blunderbusses in their hands, on top of the barricade, above the head of the slaves: and two cannons, loaded with small shot, were pointed toward the main-deck through holes cut in the barricade to receive them." The threat of insurrection was ever present. The captain assured a nervous Riland that he "kept such a guard on the slaves as would baffle all their efforts, should they attempt to rise." They had already tried once while on the coast of Africa and failed. When the slaves were brought above, the main deck became a closely guarded prison yard.

Riland noted the ship's longboat, where the sick men slaves were isolated, but he did not explain its significance to the ship and its business. This strong vessel, up to thirty feet in length, with a mast and often a swivel cannon, could be sailed or rowed and was capable of carrying a sizable burden. It could even be used to tow the ship when becalmed. Slavers also usually carried a second small craft called a yawl, which had a sail but was more commonly rowed by four to six sailors. These two vessels were critical to a slave ship, as almost all trading on the African coast was done at anchor, requiring an endless traffic back and forth to the shore, carrying manufactured goods in one direction and the enslaved in the other (in African canoes as well). Both boats usually had shallow hulls for easy beaching and for stability when carrying valuable cargo.[51]

Other features of the slave ship, on which Riland did not remark, were nonetheless important. The gun room, usually near the captain's cabin (as far away as possible from the apartment of the enslaved men), would have been presided over by the vessel's gunner and closely guarded. Special large iron or copper boilers would have been part of the cook's domain in the galley, so he could prepare food for some 270 people, both the enslaved and the crew. Netting, a fencelike assemblage of ropes, would be stretched by the crew around the ship to prevent slaves from jumping overboard.[52]

Because slave ships like the *Liberty* spent long periods of time on the coast of Africa gathering their human cargoes, they usually had another special feature, that is, copper-sheathed hulls, to protect them against boring tropical worms, or molluscs, a prime example of which was *Teredo navalis,* the shipworm. By 1800, copper sheathing was common, even though it was a relatively recent technical development. Early in the eighteenth century, the hulls of vessels bound to tropical waters were sheathed, usually with an extra layer of deal board, about half an inch in thickness, tacked to the hull (as Manesty had ordered). Beginning in 1761, the British Royal Navy, which patrolled regularly in the tropics, experimented in copper sheathing, with success. Within a few years, slavers were being sheathed, although experimentation continued, and by the 1780s the practice had become common, especially on larger vessels.[53] The 350-ton *Triumph,* formerly a slaver called the *Nelly,* was built in Liverpool and announced for sale by auction in Newport, Rhode Island, in 1809 as "coppered to the bends" and "copper fastened."[54] In the last quarter century of the slave trade, from 1783 to 1808, one of the features most commonly emphasized in the sale of any given slave ship was its copper bottom.[55]

By the time the *Liberty* sailed in 1801, some of the larger slave ships used windsails to enhance ventilation and improve the health of the enslaved belowdecks. The windsail was a funnel tube, made of canvas and open at the top, hooped at various descending sections, and attached to the hatches to "convey a stream of fresh air downward into the lower apartments of a ship." The windsail had been devised for use on men-of-war, to preserve the health of the sailors, and had now been applied to the slave trade, although inconsistently. One observer noted a few years earlier that only one in twenty slavers had windsails, and the *Liberty* was almost certainly among the vast majority without.[56]

Riland also noted the chains used to bind the men slaves aboard the *Liberty,* and here he touched upon another essential part of a prison ship: the hardware of bondage. These would have included manacles and shackles, neck irons, chains of various kinds, and perhaps a branding iron. Many slave ships carried thumbscrews, a medieval instrument of torture in which the thumbs of a rebellious slave would be inserted into a viselike contraption and slowly crushed, sometimes to force a confession. A sale on board the slave ship *John* announced by the *Connecticut Centinel* on August 2, 1804, featured "300 pair of well made Shackles" and "150 Iron Collars together with a number of Ring-Bolts Chains &c. In suitable order for the confinement of slaves."[57]

These distinctive characteristics made Guineamen easy to identify after a catastrophe, when, for example, a brig without masts was "driven ashore upon a reef" in Grand Caicos in the Bahama Islands in 1790. It was known to be "an old Guineaman, from the number of handcuffs found in her."[58] A few years later, in 1800, Captain Dalton of the *Mary-Ann* found another ghost ship on the coast of Florida. It was a large vessel lying on its side, without sails, full of water, with no crew members in sight. It turned out to be the *Greyhound,* of Portland, Maine, recognizable to the captain as a slaver "by the gratings fore and aft." John Riland suffered no such disaster, but he was well aware that he had boarded a peculiar sort of machine. Its capacity to incarcerate and transport African bodies had helped to bring into existence a new Atlantic world of labor, plantations, trade, empire, and capitalism.[59]

CHAPTER 3

African Paths to the Middle Passage

In late 1794, about a hundred miles up the Rio Pongas from the Windward Coast, two bands of hunters from rival Gola and Ibau kingdoms ventured into disputed territory in pursuit of game. An Ibau man speared the animal, or so one of his countrymen later insisted, but the Gola claimed the prize as rightfully their own. A fray ensued, in which a Gola man was killed and several Ibau severely wounded. The Gola took flight, and the Ibau brought the game home in triumph. But soon the outraged king of Gola raised an army and invaded the nearest Ibau lands, destroying a couple of villages and taking prisoners whom he promptly sold as slaves. Dizzy with success, he pressed on to his enemy's capital, Quappa, hoping to subjugate the entire kingdom. After several furious battles and at last a tactical miscalculation that allowed his warriors to be trapped, the king retreated and escaped but lost seven hundred of his best fighters to the Ibau. Once the captives were safely bound and confined, the king of the Ibau sent word down the rivers to the coast that he wished to trade with the "Sea Countries." He found a taker when the slave ship *Charleston* arrived on the coast. Captain James Connolly sent Joseph Hawkins with an African guide through the dense forest to purchase one hundred Gola warriors and march them to the coast.[1]

Meanwhile the "greatest warriors" of the Gola lay naked in their place of confinement, "bound indiscriminately together by the hands and legs, the cords being fastened to the ground by stakes." When Hawkins arrived, he was instructed by the king of the Ibau to select the ones he wanted. A troop of Ibau warriors would drive the coffle to the sea. They secured the prisoners to poles in rows, four feet apart, each with a wicker bandage around the neck, elbows pinioned back. As they commenced their march to the waterside, the countenances of the Gola prisoners turned to "sullen melancholy." They stopped, turned around, and looked back, their "eyes flowing with tears."[2]

After an uneventful six-day march, the coffle came to the river's edge and to a momentous transition—from land to water, from African to European ownership, from one technology of control to another. Waiting for them with iron manacles and shackles were the sailors of the *Charleston,* who had come upriver in a small shallop, then rowed two boats to the riverbank to take the prisoners. The prisoners' prospects for escape seemed to be at an end, all hopes dashed. The captives began to wail. The "change from the cordage to iron fetters," wrote Hawkins, "rent their hopes and hearts together."

As the Gola were moved from the boats to the shallop, two of them jumped overboard. One was captured by a sailor in a small boat astern, the other hit over the head with an oar. The rest, four of them unfettered on deck and others locked below, "set up a scream." Those free on the main deck tried to throw two of the sailors overboard, but the scream alerted the rest of the crew, who rushed on deck with guns and bayonets. Meanwhile five of the slaves in irons had managed to get loose and were struggling mightily to free the others. Those locked below reached up through the gratings, grabbing the legs of the sailors, encouraging their companions, and "shouting whenever those above did any thing that appeared likely to overcome one or [the] other of us." Eventually the sailors prevailed, with considerable bloodshed on both sides. One of the enslaved was killed, and nine were wounded. The rest were locked in double irons. Five sailors plus Hawkins (who lost a little finger) were injured, none of them mortally. The slaves were soon loaded from the shallop onto the *Charleston,* where they joined four hundred others, all bound for South Carolina. Little could the Gola warriors have known that a conflict over hunting rights could land them five thousand miles away, in Charleston, South Carolina. Now they had a different war to fight.[3]

For the Gola captives, like millions of others, enslavement began in the interior of Africa with separation from family, land, and place. Most people who ended up on slave ships were enslaved by force, against their wills, most commonly in one or another kind of "war," in capture, or through judicial punishments in their society of origin, as a sentence for a crime committed. A long Middle Passage thus contained two stages, as the case of the Gola reveals: the first was in Africa, a march on land and often travel by internal waterway (by shallop in this instance, but more commonly canoe) to the coast and the slave ship. Slave traders called this a "path," a reliable route for the movement of labor power out of Africa into the global economy. The second stage took place on the slaving vessel, in an oceanic Middle Passage from an African port to an American one. Together they connected expropriation on one side of the Atlantic to exploitation on the other. Paths and experiences varied from region to region in Africa, depending on the kinds of societies from which both slaves and slave traders came. Who the enslaved were, where they came from, and how they got to the slave ship would shape not only how they would respond once they got there but how those who ran the slave ships would attempt to control them. For almost all captives, save a few who might return as sailors, the passage out of Africa would be permanent. When the enslaved reached the ship, they reached the point of no return.[4]

The Slave Trade in Africa

In 1700, West and West-Central Africa had a population of about 25 million people, who lived in a complex range of kin-ordered and tributary societies along four thousand miles of coastline that stretched from Senegambia to Angola. The smallest were stateless, many more were of modest size but possessed some degree of internal stratification, and a few were big, class-based states that controlled extensive territory, lucrative trade, and mass armies. The last type frequently

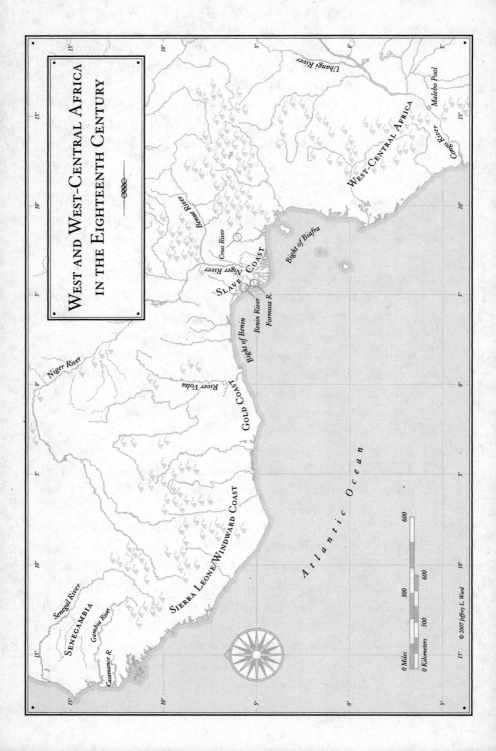

WEST AND WEST-CENTRAL AFRICA
IN THE EIGHTEENTH CENTURY

WEST-CENTRAL AFRICA

Ubangi River

Malebo Pool

Congo River

Benue River

Cross River

Niger River

SLAVE COAST

Bight of Biafra

Benin River

Formosa R.

Bight of Benin

GOLD COAST

River Volta

Niger River

SIERRA LEONE/WINDWARD COAST

SENEGAMBIA

Senegal River

Gambia River

Casamance R.

Atlantic Ocean

0 Miles   300   600

0 Kilometers   300   600

© 2007 Jeffrey L. Ward

dominated the others, forcing them to pay tribute and to defer in matters of commerce and war, while allowing them to retain local autonomy and control of land and labor.[5]

Slavery was an ancient and widely accepted institution throughout the larger societies of the region, usually reserved for war captives and criminals. Slave trading had gone on for centuries. From the seventh century to the nineteenth, more than nine million souls were carried northward in the trans-Saharan trade organized by Arab merchants in North Africa and their Islamic allies. These slaves were traded in highly developed commercial markets. In many areas, when European slave traders arrived on the coast, they simply entered preexisting circuits of exchange and did not immediately alter them.[6]

Yet as the historian Walter Rodney has pointed out, slaveholding and class differentiation developed most rapidly in those areas of West Africa where the Atlantic trade was most intensive. Partly this was because slave-ship captains wanted to deal with ruling groups and strong leaders, people who could command labor resources and deliver the "goods," and partly because wealth and powerful technologies (especially guns) accrued to these same people during the course of the trade. Smaller, more egalitarian societies could and did in some regions engage in the slave trade, but they were more likely to sell agricultural products for provisions. Larger groups who purchased guns and gunpowder often grew into stronger, centralized, militaristic states (Asante, Dahomey, Oyo, the Niger city-states, and Kongo, for example), using their firearms to subdue their neighbors, which of course produced the next coffle of slaves to be traded for the next crate of muskets. In the areas where slave trading was most extensive, a new division of labor grew up around slave catching, maintenance, and transport. Merchants became powerful as a class, controlling customs, taxes, prices, and the flow of captives. The number of slaves held and the importance of slavery as an institution in African societies expanded with the Atlantic slave trade.[7]

By the eighteenth century, the Portuguese, Swedish, Danish, Dutch, French, and English all had their spheres of influence and preferred ports of trade, but it was usually not in the interest of African merchants to let any European nation have a monopoly, even though they did make deals with different national groups from time to time. The trade on the African coast therefore remained relatively open and competitive, as British traders learned after the American Revolution when African merchants at Anomabu declared their right to continue to trade with the newly independent Americans. The trade also featured ebbs and flows—increases after major internal wars, decreases after a region's supply of slaves had been exhausted by intensive trading.[8]

The slave trade varied by region and trading partner, with two basic arrangements: in the "fort trade," ship captains bought slaves from other Europeans who resided in places like Cape Coast Castle on the Gold Coast (presently Ghana); in the "boat trade," carried out in the many areas where there were no forts, business was often conducted on the main deck of the slave ship after canoes, longboats, and yawls had ferried cargo to and from shore. This commerce was sometimes called the "black trade" because it was controlled largely by African merchants, some as representatives of big trading states, others on behalf of middling or even smaller groups, from region to region. Sometimes the two types of trade existed side by side.

Senegambia

The man the Malinke traders brought aboard was tall, five feet ten inches, and thin, in his late twenties, his head and beard close-shaved like a prisoner of war. Captain Stephen Pike of the *Arabella* bought him, but apparently without looking at his hands—to see if they were hard and rough, accustomed to labor. As it happened, they were not. The man's name was Hyuba, Boon Salumena, Boon Hibrahema, or "Job, son of Solomon, son of Abraham."[9] He was a "Mohametan," or Muslim, and moreover the son of the highest priest, or imam, of the town of Boonda near the Senegal River, in the kingdom of Futa Jallon. He had been captured while slave-trading himself, trying to sell "two Negroes," no doubt "pagans," to get money to buy paper for himself and his literate coreligionists. Once purchased, he somehow managed to explain his plight to Captain Pike, who offered to let his father redeem him, but the family residence was far away, and the ship soon departed. In Maryland he attracted the attention of a sympathetic attorney, who was impressed by his learning (he had memorized the Koran by age fifteen) and by his lofty social station: "we could perceive he was no common slave." He was sent to England, where a group of gentlemen contributed by subscription and bought his freedom. He became a cause célèbre; he met the king, the queen, and the Duke of Montague, among others. Less than three years after he first boarded the *Arabella,* the Royal African Company repatriated the African elite to James Fort on the Gambia, where he immediately bought a slave woman and two horses. When he returned to Boonda and his family, he was greeted by "raptures" and "floods of tears." He found that his father had died and one of his wives had taken up with another man, but all five of his children were alive and well. The Royal African Company had hoped that he would promote their interests once he had returned home. He did not disappoint them.[10]

As the part of West Africa closest to Europe, Job Ben Solomon's native Senegambia was the region where Atlantic slave trading had the longest history. Stretching from the Senegal River, southwest around Cape Verde, back southeast to the Gambia River, and farther south to the Casamance River, Senegambia featured, over a stretch of three hundred miles, three major hydrographic systems that linked the interior to the coast. Along the coast resided four main Wolof groups, including the Jolof (Solomon's), who controlled commerce between coast and interior. Most of the rulers of these groups were Muslim, but many commoners were not, at least until the late eighteenth or early nineteenth century. Farther inland were the Mande-speaking Malinke, also Muslim; beyond them, in the middle of the Senegal River basin, were the Fulbe (Muslim pastoralists); and, in the upper part of the river, the Serrakole. In the interior were the Bambara, who had been unified in the late seventeenth century by the warlord Kaladian Kulubali and transformed into a society of warrior-cultivators. In the

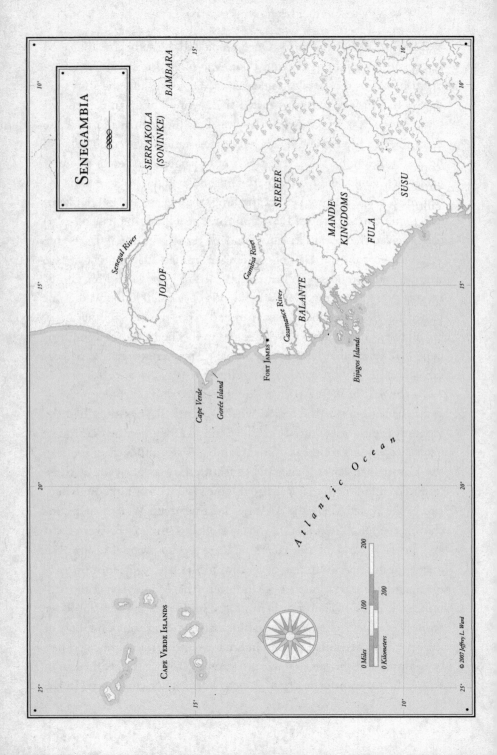

SENEGAMBIA

BAMBARA

SERRAKOLA
(SONINKE)

SEREER

MANDE
KINGDOMS

SUSU

FULA

Senegal River

JOLOF

Gambia River

BALANTE

Casamance River

FORT JAMES

Cape Verde

Gorée Island

Bijagos Islands

Atlantic Ocean

CAPE VERDE ISLANDS

0 Miles   100   200
0 Kilometers   200

© 2007 Jeffrey L. Ward

south-central part of the region were the Sereer and, farther south, various Malinke groups. Interspersed throughout, and especially along the coast, were small communal societies such as the Balante and, off the coast, the Bijagos Islanders.[11]

Islam had begun to spread through Senegambia in the ninth century and by the eighteenth century was a defining, although still-contested, reality of the region. With the expansion of the aristocratic, militaristic, horse-riding Malinke, many members of the smaller cultural groups were taken and sold to the slavers. Bijago men were known to commit suicide on capture. Jihad against non-Islamic groups (and merely nominal Islamic leaders) erupted in the 1720s and lasted through the 1740s, flaring up again in the 1780s and 1790s. As a result of the Futa Jallon jihad, slave exports spiked in both periods, although the process of enslavement remained uneven over time and space. Fula cattle herdsmen, for example, revolted against Susu rulers in the 1720s and managed to gain control of some land for themselves. Resistance to enslavement was fierce and would be carried onto the slave ships.

Other commoners gradually converted to Islam, not least to save themselves from being enslaved, especially in the area around the Gambia River. Meanwhile Islam continued to spread by commerce as Dyula merchants, classic mobile middlemen, traded, converted, and formed new settlements. The enslaved came from three catchment areas: the coast, the upper Senegal and Gambia River valleys, and the region around the middle and upper Niger. They were mostly cultivators and herdsmen, speakers of the related languages of the West Atlantic group. In Senegambia more than anywhere else in Guinea, Islamic/Saharan and European/Atlantic forces met, clashed, and cooperated, ultimately transforming the region. Over the course of the eighteenth century, about four hundred thousand enslaved people in this region were sold to the slave ships and sent to the New World, about half of them in British and American ships. Job Ben Solomon was, at the time of his enslavement, one of just two persons ever known to reverse the Middle Passage and return home.[12]

Sierra Leone and the Windward Coast

During the 1750s, Henry Tucker was one of the "big men" of the Sierra Leone coast—big in wealth, power, status, and physical stature. "He's a fat man and fair spoken," said petty white trader Nicholas Owen of his boss. Tucker was part of a multigenerational coastal trading clan that began with Peter Tucker, a Royal African Company agent on York Island in the 1680s, and his African wife. The bicultural mulatto merchant Henry had traveled to Spain, Portugal, and England. He lived "after the English style," furnishing his home with pewter plates and silverware. His wardrobe was colorful. He had acquired a vast fortune in the slave trade and built around himself an entire town, in which he lived with six or seven wives, many children, and many more slaves and laborers ("grumettoes"). Everyone, it seemed, owed him money, which meant that he could sell most anyone into slavery for debt at any time. He was therefore "esteem'd and feared by all who has the misfortune to be in his power." Owen added that Tucker "bears the charectar of a fair trader among the Europeans, but to the contrary among the blacks." Captain John Newton considered him the only honest trader on the Windward Coast. Tucker brought endless numbers of slaves on board the ships, where he was wined and dined by the captains. By the mid-1750s, his riches set him "above the Kings" of the region.[13]

Tucker's region, Sierra Leone and the Windward Coast, was sometimes called the Upper Guinea Coast, although specific subregions were sometimes denominated the Grain Coast, the Ivory Coast, and the Malaguetta Coast. The area stretched from the Casamance River, along a zone of rain forest and very few good harbors, to the port of Assini at the edge of the Gold Coast, encompassing by today's map Guinea-Bissau, Guinea, Sierra Leone, Liberia, and the Ivory Coast. In the eighteenth century, trade in this region was rather more varied than in other parts of the Guinea coast, involving slaves but also kola nuts, beeswax, camwood, gold, malaguetta peppers, and high-quality ivory. Slave-ship captains spent much time here buying rice as victuals for the Middle Passage.

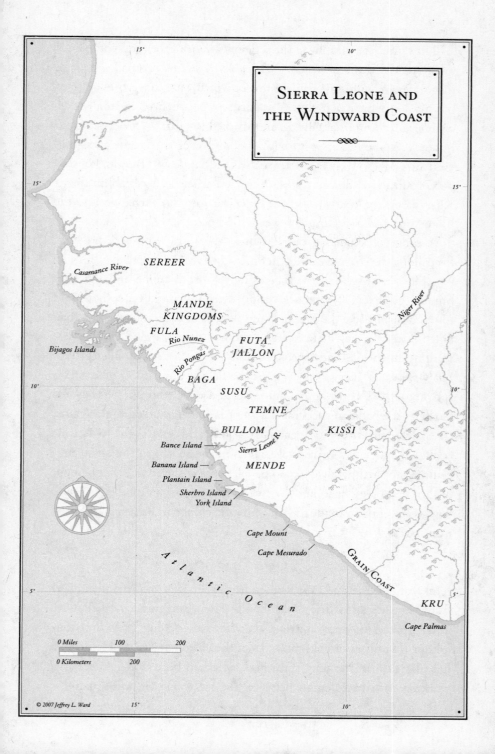

SIERRA LEONE AND
THE WINDWARD COAST

15°   10°

15°   15°

Casamance River   SEREER

                    MANDE
                    KINGDOMS
        FULA   Niger River
                Rio Nunez   FUTA
Bijagos Islands   JALLON
                Rio Pongas
                    BAGA
10°   SUSU   10°
                      TEMNE
                BULLOM   KISSI
Bance Island ──   Sierra Leone R.
Banana Island ──
Plantain Island ──   MENDE
    Sherbro Island /
    York Island

                    Cape Mount
                Cape Mesurado   GRAIN COAST

                                              5°
5°   Atlantic Ocean
                                        KRU

0 Miles   100   200   Cape Palmas

0 Kilometers   200

© 2007 Jeffrey L. Ward   15°   10°

The human geography of the region was one of the most complex of West Africa, as there existed few sizable states and a broad mosaic of ministates and cultural groups, some of which were converting to Islam but most of which were not. A majority of people lived in small-scale, egalitarian, communal villages and worked as farmers, fishermen, and hunters. Women seemed to have special power in certain areas and even took part in secret societies such as the Sande and Bundu. Political decentralization allowed traders like Henry Tucker to establish themselves along the coast, to organize production and exchange into the hinterland, and to accumulate wealth and power.

A range of smaller groups, such as the Baga, Bullom, and Kru, lived along the coast, while farther inland were the larger Susu, Temne, and Mende, as well as the increasingly Muslim Fulbe and Jallonke. Smaller groups in the interior included the Gola and Kissi (both said to be culturally like the Mende), and dozens of others such as the Ibau and Limba. In the Mane Wars of the late sixteenth and early seventeenth centuries, Mande speakers enslaved portions of smaller groups but were then themselves overrun by the Susu and the Fulbe. Islam spread beyond Senegambia into Sierra Leone and the Windward Coast as the Muslim theocracy of Futa Jallon conducted raids against those who practiced indigenous religions and sold them to Islamic traders in the north or coastal traders in the south. In the eighteenth century, approximately 460,000 people were enslaved and shipped out of this broad region, about 6.5 percent of the century's total. More than 80 percent of them made the transatlantic voyage in British and American slavers.[14]

Gold Coast

John Kabes came into Fort Komenda "bawling" at the African traders from the interior of the Gold Coast. They were fools, he bellowed. They wanted too much for the slaves they were selling. How dare they ask for six ounces of gold rather than the customary four? He drove a hard bargain in the year 1714, just as he had been doing since 1683, working as a middleman between the African state of Eguafo, or

Grand Commany, and European slavers. The English, the Dutch, and the French alternately wooed and vilified him. Without Kabes "nothing will be done" said an English factor; he is a turncoat and an "arrant coward," snarled a Dutch one; we promise "high rewards," added a hopeful Frenchman. He worked mostly with the English, for many years as an employee of the Royal African Company but not, in the parlance of the day, as its servant. He was a shrewd operator on his own behalf. He got three company agents fired because they could not work with him. "If we lose him our interest here is lost," wrote one official to company authorities at Cape Coast Castle, fifteen miles away. Indeed it was Kabes who mobilized the labor that *built* Fort Komenda, the men who quarried the stone and cut the wood for the hulking imperial edifice. The Dutch, ensconced nearby at Fort Vredenburg, opposed the construction of the fortress, so Kabes led several military expeditions against them to encourage their assent. He subsequently built up a sizable town around the fortress. But most important of all, he traded slaves. Through the gates of Fort Komenda passed thousands of captives to one slave ship after another. By the time he died in 1722, Kabes had become a sovereign power in his own right, a merchant-prince who possessed his own "stool," the ultimate symbol of political power among the Akan.[15]

The people of the Gold Coast had long traded with Europeans, originally, as the name signified, for the gleaming precious metal that spawned greed and massive fortresses, the first of which, at El Mina, was built by the Portuguese in 1482 to protect their golden hoard against Dutch, French, and English rivals. Eventually other European maritime powers, assisted by men like Kabes, came to build or seize forts of their own, which resulted in a string of fortifications along the five-hundred-mile coastline, from the port of Assini in the west to the river Volta in the east, the eastern portion of present-day Ivory Coast and most all of Ghana.

The English operated forts and trading establishments at Dixcove, Sekondi, Komenda, Anomabu, Accra, and Tantum; the seat of their operations was Cape Coast Castle. From these outposts traders loaded

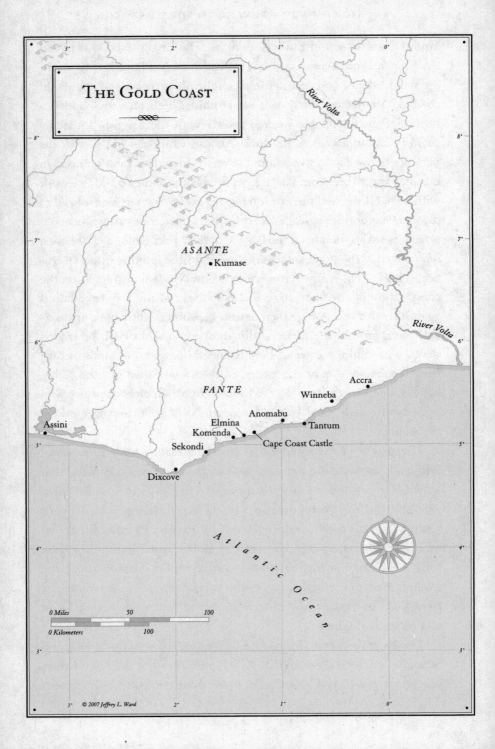

THE GOLD COAST

© 2007 Jeffrey L. Ward

Kumase

ASANTE

FANTE

Accra

Winneba

Anomabu

Elmina
Komenda
Cape Coast Castle
Tantum

Assini

Sekondi

Dixcove

River Volta

Atlantic Ocean

0 Miles   50   100
0 Kilometers   100

prisoners—black gold—into the lower decks of the ships. The building of the forts gave rise to ministates with *abirempon,* "big men" such
as Kabes and John Konny. Many people who lived in the Gold Coast
region in 1700 belonged to the broad cultural group the Akan (others
were the Guan, the Etsi, and the Ga). The Akan were themselves divided into competitive, often antagonistic states, as Denkyira, Ak-
wamu, and Akyem rose to prominence along the coast early in the
century, with the assistance of European firearms. The new elite were
called *awurafam,* "masters of firepower." Political power grew out of
the barrel of a gun.

The mightiest group in the region was the Asante, whose rise after
1680 resulted in one of the strongest stratified and centralized states of
West Africa. Osei Tutu built a regional alliance of "big men," slowly
incorporating various cultural groups under his central authority as
asantehene, or ultimate leader, symbolized by the golden stool, *sika
dwa.* The new Asante lords had brought several of the coastal ministates to heel by 1717 (adding Accra and Adangme in 1742) and continued their expansion in the north conquering smaller groups there,
sending slaves northward with Hausa merchants and southward to
the coast and the waiting slave ships. The Asante were skilled at war,
as their very name, derived from *osa nit,* "because of war," implied.
"Real" Asantes, it was said, would not be sold into slavery. The powerful Asante army consisted in 1780 of eighty thousand men, half of
them musketeers. Their slave trading over the course of the eighteenth
century was a consequence of their war making and state building
rather than a primary cause. Nonetheless it soon grew more profitable
to catch slaves than to mine gold, and the Asante, despite their independence, became reliable players and valuable partners to the Europeans
in the slave trade.[16]

Another major player were the coastal Fante, whose confederation
of nineteen independent polities developed as a reaction against the
Asante. The Fante at times signed treaties with the British but continued to trade with slavers of several flags. They served the slave
trade in myriad ways, selling people from inland regions and hiring

out their own to work for wages on the slavers. Built from matrilineal clans, the Fante used their formidable military prowess to protect local autonomy, all within a highly commercialized orbit. They acted as middlemen, connecting the Asante in the interior to the English slavers on the coast. They would remain independent until conquered by the Asante in 1807, the year of abolition. Over the course of the eighteenth century, the Gold Coast produced more than a million slaves, about 15 percent of the total shipped from West Africa as a whole. Roughly two-thirds of the total were carried by British and American ships.[17]

Bight of Benin

The fishing village at the mouth of the Formosa River usually bustled with activity, but on this day in 1763 it was eerily quiet. Three people in a small canoe had come from far away and did not know the danger they were in. They might have wondered at the big ship, a brigantine, that lay at anchor a distance out in the Gulf of Benin, surrounded by ten war canoes. The *Briton* had come from even farther away. It belonged to Messrs. John Welch (or Welsh) and Edward Parr, merchants of Liverpool, and was captained by William Bagshaw. The war canoes, some of them large enough to have mounted six to eight swivel guns (small cannon), had come from upriver and belonged to a man named Captain Lemma Lemma, "a kind of pirate admiral" who traded in slaves. The people who lived on the lower river considered Lemma Lemma to be "a robber or stealer of men"; everyone was "exceedingly afraid of venturing out whenever any of his war canoes were in sight." He was an important supplier of slaves to European Guineamen, which is why Captain Bagshaw had been entertaining him for ten days with food, drink, hospitality, and *dashee,* gifts to encourage sales.

From the main deck of the slaver, Lemma Lemma spied the strangers paddling by and ordered a group of his canoemen to capture them. They deftly took to the water, seized the three—an old man, a young man, and a young woman—and brought them aboard, offering them

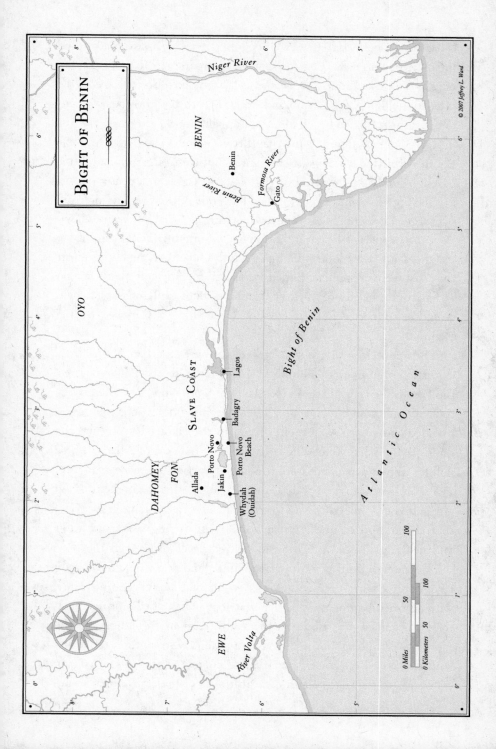

for sale to Captain Bagshaw, who bought the younger two but refused the older one. Lemma Lemma sent the old man back to one of his canoes and gave an order: "his head was laid on one of the thwarts of the boat, and chopped off," head and body then thrown overboard. Captain Bagshaw carried his children to Rappahannock, Virginia.[18]

The Bight of Benin, which lay between the Volta River and the Benin River (today's Togo, Benin, and southwest Nigeria), had a turbulent history as a slave-trading region in the eighteenth century. During the previous century, Benin had been one of the first kingdoms to get large shipments of European firearms. Unlike the Asante, however, the peoples of Benin did not have the organizational capacity to use them, and they soon went into decline. Once-thriving regions near the coast were depopulated, their lands left uncultivated. Benin would remain the nucleus of various tributary states and societies, which would be connected to the slave ships by the likes of Captain Lemma Lemma.

The main cultural groups of the region were the Ewe to the west, consisting of more than a hundred small, autonomous village societies, the Fon in the central region (originally inland), and the more powerful and numerous Yoruba to the eastern interior, where they commanded the great Oyo Empire. Early in the eighteenth century, the main slaving ports were Whydah and Jakin, the port of Allada. These polities were independent until conquered by the Fon in the 1720s and 1730s and incorporated into Dahomey. Now that Dahomey's King Agaja had eliminated the middlemen, he and his heirs built a strong, centralized, and relatively efficient state, organizing systematic raids and bending judicial processes to deliver slaves directly to the slave ships, although from a circumscribed hinterland that would in the long term limit slaving capacity. Dahomey maintained a standing army, with a storied regiment of women warriors, but the Dahomeans nonetheless began to pay tribute in the 1730s (regularly after 1747) to the more powerful neighboring Oyo, whose military strength in the heartland was based on horses, cavalry, and control of the savanna. Long connected to the north-south caravan routes of the trans-Sahara slave trade, the Yoruba had by 1770 gained control of the ports of Porto Novo, Badagry, and, later in the eighteenth century, Lagos, although supplies to all would diminish with their own decline beginning in the 1790s. Altogether the Bight of Benin exported almost 1.4 million slaves in the eighteenth century, nearly a fifth of the total trade, but only about 15 percent of the total from the region were shipped by British and American slave vessels, which called increasingly to ports farther east.[19]

Bight of Biafra

Antera Duke was a leading Efik trader at Old Calabar in the Bight of Biafra during the late eighteenth century. He lived at Duke Town, about twenty miles from the Calabar River estuary. Over time he prospered and became a member of the local Ekpe (Leopard) Society, which wielded enormous power in the slave trade and the broader affairs of the town. He participated in what he called "plays," communal occasions of music, singing, and dancing. He arranged funerals, which for men of standing like himself included the ritual sacrifice of slaves, who were decapitated to accompany the master into the spirit world. He settled "bobs" and "palavers," small disputes and big debates. He even oversaw the burial of a slave-ship captain, Edward Aspinall, "with much ceremony." He entertained an endless procession of captains in his home, sometimes five or six at a time, drinking *mimbo* (palm wine) and feasting into the late hours of the night. Captains in turn sent their carpenters and joiners to work on his big house.[20]

Antera Duke listened for the roar of cannon at Seven Fathoms Point, which meant that a slave ship, or its tender, was headed upriver to trade. One "fine morning," he noted in his diary, "wee have 9 ship in River." He and other Efik traders "dressed as white men" and routinely went aboard the vessels, drinking tea and conducting business; taking customs and *dashee;* negotiating credit or "trust"; leaving and ransoming pawns; trading for iron bars, coppers, and gunpowder; and selling yams as provisions for the Middle Passage. He sold slaves, and sometimes he caught them himself: "wee & Tom Aqua and John Aqua be join Catch men." On another occasion he settled an old score with a

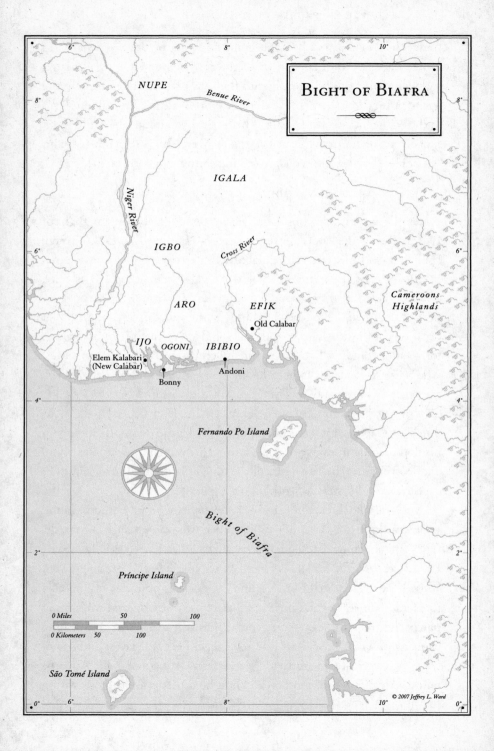

BIGHT OF BIAFRA

NUPE

Benue River

IGALA

Niger River

IGBO

Cross River

ARO

EFIK

Old Calabar

IJO   OGONI   IBIBIO

Elem Kalabari
(New Calabar)

Andoni

Bonny

Cameroons
Highlands

Fernando Po Island

Bight of Biafra

Príncipe Island

0 Miles   50   100

0 Kilometers   50   100

São Tomé Island

© 2007 Jeffrey L. Ward

Bakassey merchant, seizing him and two of his slaves and personally carrying them aboard a slaver, he noted proudly in his diary. At other times he bought slaves from traders of outlying regions. During the three years he kept his diary (1785–88), he noted the departure of twenty vessels he had helped to "slave." Every last one of them was from Liverpool. They carried almost seven thousand men, women, and children to New World plantations. He recorded a typical entry on June 27, 1785: "Captin Tatum go way with 395 slaves."[21]

The Bight of Biafra stretched along a coastline of mangrove swamp from the Benin River through and across the Niger River delta to the Cross River and beyond in the west. Because of merchants like Antera Duke, it was a major source of slaves and indeed one of the most important to British and American traders by the end of the eighteenth century. The region, consisting of what is, by today's map, eastern Nigeria and western Cameroon, had no major territorial states. The traffic in slaves was handled by three large, competitive, sometimes warring city-states, which were themselves made up of "canoe houses": New Calabar (also called Elem Kalabari), Bonny, and Duke's own Old Calabar. The first two were "monarchies" of sorts, the last more a republic, in which founding Efik families used the Ekpe Society to integrate strangers and slaves into a system of extended fictive kinship and commercial labor. ("Fathers" like Duke incorporated "sons" and "daughters.") Leaders of the canoe houses grew rich and powerful by dealing with European traders. In so doing they were perhaps more affected by European ways, especially in dress and culture, than were people in any other area of West Africa. Traders like Duke boarded the slave ships dressed in gold-laced hats, waistcoats, and breeches, speaking English and cursing up a storm, and at the end of the day returned to European-style homes.[22]

The main cultural groups of the Bight of Biafra were the Ibibio, dominant around the port of Andoni, and the more populous and decentralized Igbo, the latter representing a broad geographic culture from which a large majority of the enslaved originated. Other significant groups were the Igala (in the northern interior), the Ijo (along the coast to the west), and the Ogoni (around the Cross River delta). The primary form of social organization of the peoples of the region was the autonomous village. Some class differentiation was known, but local notables were usually first among equals. Slavery was not unknown, but it was mild in nature and limited. Most commoners were yam cultivators. One of the best descriptions of the Igbo way of life has been summed up in the phrase "village democracy."

The landmass along the Bight of Biafra was densely populated on the coast and for hundreds of miles inland. The Igbo in particular had experienced intensive population growth in the seventeenth century, partly because of productive yam cultivation. Coastal and riverine peoples tended to fish. Rivers broad and deep penetrated far into the interior, which made canoes central to travel, communication, and the movement of the enslaved. The regions surrounding the Niger, Benue, and Cross rivers represented the main catchment area for captives, although some were also brought westward from the Cameroon Highlands. Most of the enslaved were taken in small raids, as large-scale wars were uncommon in the region. By the middle of the eighteenth century, much of the slaving and internal shipment was handled by a relatively new cultural group, the Aro, who used their access to European firearms and other manufactures to build a trading network that linked the canoe houses to the interior. In the course of the eighteenth century, especially after the 1730s, the traders of the Bight of Biafra exported more than a million people, mostly Igbo, 86 percent of the total in British and American vessels. Many went to Virginia between 1730 and 1770, the majority to the British West Indies.[23]

West-Central Africa

According to their own origin story, the Bobangi began as fishermen, branching off from other groups along the Ubangi River in the Kongo region of West-Central Africa. Over time they occupied higher ground and expanded into agriculture (plantains and especially cassava) and limited manufacturing, and from there to local and regional waterborne trade. Yet they remained primarily fishermen until the eighteenth century, when they began to trade in slaves. They sent captives south-west by canoe to Malebo Pool, a major nexus for trade to the coast, where the slave ships lay at anchor like hungry beasts with empty bellies. The Bobangi made a distinction between two types of slaves they traded: A *montamba* was a person sold by his or her kin group, usually after conviction for a crime or in some cases because of famine or economic hardship. Second and perhaps more numerous as the eighteenth century progressed was the *montange,* a person made a slave in one of three ways—by formal warfare, an informal raid, or kidnapping. As prices for slaves went up, Bobangi merchants gathered more and more captives and began to march them overland by several routes to the coast, to Loango, Boma, and Ambriz. These middleman traders rose to regional prominence and ended up supplying a substantial minority of the slaves traded out of Loango in the eighteenth century. Their language became the trading lingua franca up and down the Ubangi River and its numerous tributaries.[24]

West-Central Africa consisted of a vast expanse of coast with two main slaving regions, Kongo and Angola, and within them hundreds of cultural groups. It was one of the most important regions of trade as the eighteenth century wore on, and it became the single most significant in the 1790s. Slave ships called with increasing frequency along a coastline of some twelve hundred miles, beginning around the island of Fernando Po and extending southward to Benguela and Cape Negro. By today's map the area begins in Cameroon and extends southward to include Equatorial Guinea, Gabon, the Republic of the Congo, a small coastal bit of the Democratic Republic of Congo, and most of Angola. West-Central Africa was historically a place of Portuguese colonization and influence, both on the coast and deep inland. In the seventeenth century, the influence included a mass conversion to Christianity in the kingdom of Kongo, one of the main client states in the slave trade. British and American traders began to make inroads, with lasting success, in the middle of the eighteenth century.

The main engine of enslavement in the region was the expansion of the Lunda Empire in the interior of Angola. Most of the enslaved were

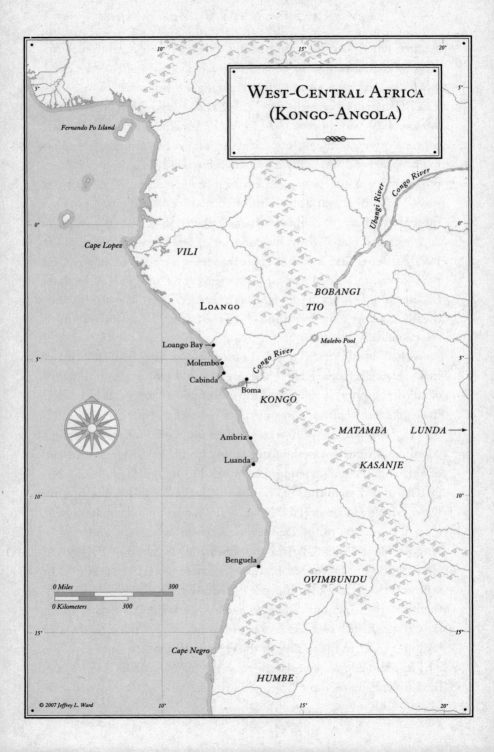

WEST-CENTRAL AFRICA
(KONGO-ANGOLA)

Fernando Po Island

Cape Lopez

VILI

Ubangi River

Congo River

BOBANGI

LOANGO

TIO

Loango Bay

Malebo Pool

Molembo

Congo River

Cabinda

Boma

KONGO

Ambriz

MATAMBA

LUNDA

KASANJE

Luanda

Benguela

OVIMBUNDU

0 Miles   300

0 Kilometers   300

Cape Negro

HUMBE

© 2007 Jeffrey L. Ward

captured in wars of conquest, after formal battle and in quick-strike raids. A substantial number of slaves came as tribute the Lunda collected from the various groups and states they ruled. The Lunda deployed a highly effective administrative system and used middle-size intermediary states such as Kasanje and Matamba to facilitate the movement of their slaves to the ships on the coast. Other active parties in West-Central Africa's far-reaching human commerce, in addition to the Bobangi, were Vili merchants, who in the seventeenth century linked the northern inland regions to the Kongo coast. Southern states such as Humbe and Ovimbundu also served as middlemen in an extensive, lucrative trade.

West-Central Africa was an area of extraordinary cultural diversity and dozens of languages, although all of them were Bantu in origin, and this would serve as a commonality for the peoples in diaspora. Political organization also spanned a broad spectrum, ranging from small autonomous villages to huge kingdoms, most important the Kongo, Loango, and Tio, and the Portuguese colonial state based in Luanda.The lifeways of the commoners who were most likely to be enslaved varied by ecological zone. Those from the coast, rivers, and swamps necessarily made their livings by water, usually fishing, while those from the forest and savanna zones tended to combine farming, usually the domain of women, and hunting, done by the men. Many communities were organized along matrilineal lines. Because of the frequency of warfare, many of the men had military experience of one kind or another. As the tentacles of the slave trade grew, many communities stratified internally, and *kumu*, "big men," emerged to facilitate the commerce. The main ports of the region, from north to south, were Loango, Cabinda, Ambriz, Luanda, and Benguela, the last built by the Portuguese for the slave trade. Between 1700 and 1807, traders funneled a million souls through Loango and growing numbers after 1750 to Molembo and Cabinda, the Kongo estuary ports. In the eighteenth century alone, more than 2.7 million slaves were delivered. They constituted 38 percent of the century's total, making West-Central Africa the most important region of the slave trade by a considerable margin.[25]

A Social Portrait of the Captives

As the summaries of the six main slaving regions suggest, most people who found themselves on slave ships did so in the aftermath of war, especially during historic moments when one or another group, the Fon or the Asante, for example, was extending its political dominance over its neighbors. What one observer called the "eternal wars" among smaller groups were another major source of slaves. Like the conflict between the Gola and the Ibau, these wars had their own geopolitical logic and causes, and were not always influenced by the slave trade. Indeed, as slave-trade merchant and historian Robert Norris noted, wars had gone on in Africa long before the arrival of the Europeans, with the same causes that motivated conflict in all times and places: "Ambition, Avarice, Resentment, &c." Advocates and opponents of the slave trade agreed that war was a major source of slaves in West Africa.[26]

Yet they disagreed vehemently about what constituted a war. Most advocates of the trade agreed that "war" was simply whatever African traders said it was. But they had to admit that the term covered a multitude of activities. "Depredations . . . are denominated wars!" exclaimed a Liverpool trader in 1784. John Matthews, a fierce defender of human commerce, noted that in Sierra Leone every "petty quarrel" was called a war. Sea surgeon John Atkins observed that war in West Africa was just another name for "robbery of inland, defenceless creatures." Those opposed to the trade went even further, insisting that "wars" were nothing more than "pyratical expeditions," and they even found a witness to prove it: British seaman Isaac Parker had participated in such marauding raids out of New Town in Old Calabar in the 1760s. Abolitionists contended that what was called "war" was for the most part simply kidnapping. Moreover, "wars" often commenced when a slave ship appeared on the coast, whereupon the local traders (with the help—and guns—of the slave-ship captain) would equip war parties (usually canoes) to head inland to wage war and gather slaves, who would then be sold to the captain who had helped to finance the expedition in the first place. Otherwise, as one African explained to a member of a slaving crew, "Suppose ship no come, massa, no takee slavee." War was a euphemism for the organized theft of human beings.[27]

Second to war as a source of slaves were the judicial processes in and through which African societies convicted people of crimes ranging from murder to theft, adultery, witchcraft, and debt; condemned them to slavery; and sold them to African traders or directly to the slave-ship captains. This was not unlike the transportation of convicted English felons to the American colonies until 1776 and to Botany Bay, Australia, beginning in 1786. Many Africans and (abolitionist) Europeans felt that judicial processes in West Africa had been corrupted and that thousands had been falsely accused and convicted in order to produce as many tradeworthy bodies as possible. Royal African Company official Francis Moore noted that for those found guilty of crime around 1730 in the Gambia region, "All Punishments are chang'd into Slavery." Walter Rodney observed that on the Upper Guinea Coast local ruling groups made law "into the handmaid of the slave trade."[28]

A third major source was the purchase of slaves at markets and fairs located in the interior, some distance from the coast, often linked to the Islamic slave-trade circuits to the north, east, and west. The purchase of these people (the vast majority of whom had been free, but enslaved farther inland) was especially common in Senegambia, the Gold Coast, and the Bight of Benin. By the 1780s many of the slaves sold at New Calabar, Bonny, and Old Calabar had been bought a hundred miles or more inland, and for other ports the catchment area was even deeper. Slave-ship captains assumed that the people they purchased had become slaves by war or judicial process, but in truth they did not know—and did not care—how their "cargo" had been enslaved. That was not their business, testified one after another in parliamentary hearings between 1788 and 1791.[29]

In the seventeenth century, most captives seem to have come from within fifty miles of the coast. But in the early eighteenth century, especially after the European deregulation of the slave trade (the eclipse of chartered companies by private traders), both the trade and catchment areas expanded, in some cases several hundred miles into the interior. Most commentators thought that somewhere between a tenth and a third of the enslaved came from coastal regions, the rest from the interior. The "bulk" of the slaves, wrote John Atkins of his experience of the early 1720s, were "country People," whose wits, in his condescending view, grew dimmer the farther from the coast they had come. The "coast-Negroes," on the other hand, were sharp, even roguish, more likely to speak English, and more knowledgeable about slave ships and the trade. Those who came from the waterside had likely been enslaved through judicial process, while those from the country were more likely taken in one or another kind of "war." By the end of the century, more and more slaves were arriving from "a very great distance," traveling "many moons," and having been sold numerous times along the way. The captain of the *Sandown* was sure that five men he purchased in October 1793 had traveled a thousand miles.[30]

Enslavement produced immediate and spontaneous resistance, especially when the mode was raiding or kidnapping. People fought back, fled, did whatever they could to escape the enslavers. Once they had been captured and organized into coffles, the main form of resistance was running away, which the captors tried to prevent by armed vigilance and various technologies of control. The newly enslaved, especially the men, were sometimes individually bound, using vines, cords, or chains, then strapped by the neck in groups of two and four, and finally tied to other groups of the same size. African captors sometimes attached to the men a long, heavy log to burden their movements, tire them out, and discourage resistance. Every member of the coffle would be required to labor as a porter—that is, carry food and merchandise, sometimes large tusks of ivory. One clever group of raiders devised and attached a contraption to the mouth of the prisoners to prevent them from crying out to gain the attention and perhaps assistance of sympathetic folk during the long march. Other forms of resistance included a refusal to eat and, occasionally, coordinated insurrection. The enslaved might even escape into the forest to form a kind of maroon community. All these forms of resistance would be carried onto the slave ships and, upon the completion of the voyage, into the plantation societies of the New World.[31]

The overwhelming majority of those enslaved were commoners—agriculturalists of one kind or another, though a few were nomadic pastoralists and hunter-gatherers. From the larger societies came artisans, domestic slaves, and waged workers. Two-thirds of those sent overseas were male, mostly young men, many of whom had been soldiers and were therefore trained in the ways of war. Roughly a third were female and a quarter children, the portion of each increasing in the late eighteenth century. Very few Africans of high station and authority found themselves enslaved and thrown aboard a slave ship. African military elites frequently executed their leading adversaries after battle to prevent their encouragement of resistance to new rulers. Moreover, the slave raiders usually chose "the roughest and most hardy" and avoided the privileged "smooth negroes" (like Job Ben Solomon), who had a harder time adjusting to the ship and slavery. And in any case, the slave trader's preference for the young also excluded most of those who were the older, wiser, natural leaders in many African cultures.[32]

As a result of this process of selection, enslavement and shipment created a deep and enduring rupture between African commoners and ruling groups, which in turn had enormous implications for cultural and political practice in the diaspora. Those many unfairly convicted and enslaved lost respect for rulers and their institutions, and the absence of a dominant class in diaspora meant that the commoners would, of necessity, do things their own way, more freely and creatively, on the slave ship and in the New World. More egalitarian relations and practices would be the order of the day, as Hugh Crow saw among the Igbo on his own ships: "I have seen them, when their allowance happened to be short, divide the last morsel of meat amongst each other thread by thread."[33]

Grand Pillage: Louis Asa-Asa

One of the main ways of making slaves was what the French called "grand pillage"—a sudden, organized raid upon a village, usually in the middle of the night. The marauders burned homes and captured the terrified villagers as they fled, then marched them to the coast in coffles and sold them. A man named Louis Asa-Asa experienced enslavement by "grand pillage" when he was a boy, thirteen years old. He described the trauma, and his own path to the ship, in detail.[34]

Asa-Asa lived with his parents and five brothers and sisters "in a country called Bycla, near Egie, a large town" located inland, "some way from the sea." His family was respectable. His father, who had land and a horse, was not one of the "great men" of the village, but his uncle was, for he had a lot of land and cattle and "could make men come and work for him." His father worked with his oldest son on their land, making charcoal, but Asa-Asa was "too little" to join them as they worked. The strongest memory of his African family and life before slavery was simple and telling: "we were all very happy."[35]

The happiness soon went up in flames, as "some thousands" of Adinyé warriors converged on Egie one morning before daybreak, setting fire to the huts, creating chaos, killing some, and over two days capturing many others. They bound the captives by the feet until it was time to tie them into coffles and march them toward the coast, whereupon "they let them loose; but if they offered to run away, they would shoot them"—with European guns. The Adinyés were expert, even professional marauders: "They burnt all the country wherever they found villages." They took any and all, "brothers, and sisters, and husbands, and wives; they did not care about this." Those taken in the initial raid included about a dozen people Asa-Asa counted as "friends and relations." Everyone carried away was sold as a slave to the Europeans, some for "cloth or gunpowder," others for "salt or guns." Sometimes "they got four or five guns for a man." Asa-Asa knew these to be "English guns."[36]

Asa-Asa and his family saw their home set afire, but they escaped by running from the village, keeping together, and living for two days in the woods. When the Adinyés left, they returned home "and found every thing burnt." They also found "several of our neighbours lying about wounded; they had been shot." Asa-Asa himself "saw the bodies of four or five little children whom they had killed with blows on the head. They had carried away their fathers and mothers, but the children were too small for slaves, so they killed them. They had killed several others, but these were all that I saw. I saw them lying in the street like dead dogs."

The family built a "little shed" for their shelter and slowly began "to get comfortable again," but a week later the Adinyés returned, torching the sheds and any houses that they had missed the first time. Asa-Asa and his family, uncle included, ran again to the woods, but the next day the warriors came after them, forcing them deeper into the forest, where they stayed "about four days and nights." They subsisted on "a few potatoes" and were "half starved." The Adinyés soon found them. Asa-Asa recalled the moment: "They called my uncle to go to them; but he refused, and they shot him immediately: they killed him." The rest ran in terror, but Asa-Asa, the youngest of the group, fell behind. He climbed a tree in an effort to elude his pursuers, but in vain as they spotted and caught him, tying his feet. He recalled sadly, "I do not know if they found my father and mother, and brothers and sisters: they had run faster than me, and were half a mile farther when I got up into the tree: I have never seen them since." Asa-Asa also remembered a man who had climbed the tree with him: "I believe they shot him, for I never saw him again."

Young Asa-Asa joined twenty others in a march to the sea, each person carrying a load, part of it the food they would eat along the way. The newly enslaved were not beaten, he noted, but one man, formerly a neighbor, was killed. He was ill and too weak to carry his load, so "they ran him through the body with a sword." He was the only one who died along the way.

Soon began a series of sales, each one bringing Asa-Asa and the others closer to the slave ship. The thirteen-year-old was "sold six

times over, sometimes for money, sometimes for cloth, and sometimes for a gun." Even after he and his coffle-mates reached the
coast, they continued to be sold: "We were taken in a boat from place
to place, and sold at every place we stopped at." It took about six
months after his capture to reach the "white people" and their "very
large ship."[37]

Kidnapping: Ukawsaw Gronniosaw

A less-common but still-important means of enslavement was trick-
ery, which was used by slave traders to prey upon the naive and unsuspecting. Among European sailors and indentured servants, the
wily labor agent was called a "spirit," the process itself "spiriting" or
alternatively trepanning or kidnapping. In this instance a path to the
ship began with a degree of consent and evolved into coercion, as discovered by a boy named Ukawsaw Gronniosaw in 1725.[38]

The merchant had traveled far to reach the village of Borno, near
Lake Chad in today's northeastern Nigeria, and when he arrived, he
told a magical tale. He spoke of a place by the sea where "houses with
wings upon them . . . walk on water." He also spoke of peculiar "white
folks" aboard the winged, waterborne abodes. These words mesmer-
ized the teenage Gronniosaw, the youngest of six children and the
grandson of the king of Zaara. Gronniosaw later recalled, "I was highly
pleased with the account of this strange place, and was very desirous of
going." His family agreed to let him go. He traveled a thousand miles
with the merchant, whose demeanor changed once he had gotten the
boy away from his parents and village. Gronniosaw grew "unhappy
and discontented," fearful that he would be killed. When he arrived on
the Gold Coast, he found himself "without a friend or any means to
procure one." He was enslaved.

The coastal king announced that Gronniosaw was a spy and
should be killed, but the boy spoke up in protest: "I came . . . there to
see houses walk upon the water with wings to them, and the white
folks." The king relented and allowed Gronniosaw to have his wish,
but with a wicked twist: he would be sold to the white master of one

of those winged houses. The boy was offered to a French captain, who refused to buy him because he was too small. Taken aboard a Dutch Guineaman, and terrified that he would be killed if he were once again rejected, Gronniosaw threw himself on the captain and begged to be taken. The captain obliged, trading "two yards of check" (cloth) for him. During the Middle Passage, Gronniosaw "was exceedingly sea-sick at first; but when I became more accustomed to the sea, it wore off." He noted that he was treated well by the captain until they arrived in Barbados, where he was sold for "fifty dollars."

The slave ship—or the "house with wings," as Gronniosaw called it—would be astonishing to anyone who had never seen one. The explorer Mungo Park relayed another such reaction in 1797, when he and his guide, Karfa, ended their travels into the interior of West Africa by arriving at the river Gambia, where they saw a schooner lying at anchor. "This was," wrote Park, "the most surprising object which Karfa had yet seen." The inland African surveyed the deep-sea vessel carefully. He wondered about the "manner of fastening together the different planks which composed the vessel, and filling up the seams so as to exclude the water." He was fascinated by "the use of masts, sails, and rigging." Most of all he marveled about how "it was possible, by any sort of contrivance, to make so large a body move forwards by the common force of the wind." All of this, wrote Park, "was perfectly new to him." Park concluded that "the schooner with her cable and her anchor, kept Karfa in deep meditation the greater part of the day."[39]

In stark contrast to Gronniosaw and Karfa stood the Africans who traded on the coast as described by Captain John Newton: "they are so quick at distinguishing our little local differences of language, and customs in a ship, that before they have been in a ship five minutes, and often before they come on board, they know, with certainty, whether she be from Bristol, Liverpool, or London." A great many Africans, especially among the Fante on the Gold Coast, worked on canoes and some actually on board the slave ships for extended periods, so they knew them intimately, not only by national differences but by local ones. A few had actually worked transatlantic voyages, so they knew perfectly how to make these big machines "move forward" through the water. But whether the path to the ship ended in wonder or familiarity, the feeling would soon turn to terror.[40]

The Point of No Return

For captives the process of expropriation in Africa shattered the life-governing institutions of family and kinship, village, and in some cases nation and state. Many experienced dispossession from their native land as theft. As Africans repeatedly explained to one slave-ship sailor during his voyages of the 1760s, they were "all stolen," although in many ways. Ukawsaw Gronniosaw went through an individual enslavement that began in free choice. Louis Asa-Asa chronicled the experience of family and village through violent pillage as seen through the eyes of a thirteen-year-old boy. The Gola warriors followed a collective, military, and national path to the ship. The latter two experienced the coffle, an odd and ever-changing social body. It might exist for several months, during which time members died and were sold, as others were added along the journey to the coast. All were subjected to violent discipline and the threat of death, and indeed a lot of people died along the way. The captives fought back—against Africans, to remain in Africa—but rarely with success. They were the vanquished, the wretched of the earth.[41]

Things could get worse and did. To board the sinister ship was, as the Gola warriors discovered, a terrifying moment of transition, from African to European control. Much of what the captives had known would now be left behind. Africans and African-Americans have come to express the wrenching departure through the symbol of the "door of no return," one famous example of which exists in the House of Slaves on Goree Island, Senegal, another at Cape Coast Castle in Ghana. Once the enslaved were taken beyond the point of no return, transition turned to transformation. Shackled and trapped in the bowels of a slaver, unable to go home again, the captives would now have no choice but to live in the struggle, a fierce, many-sided, never-ending fight to survive, to live, of necessity, in a new way. The old had been destroyed, and suffering was at hand. Yet within the desolation lay new, broader possibilities of identification, association, and action.[42]

CHAPTER 4

Olaudah Equiano: Astonishment and Terror

When Olaudah Equiano first laid a child's eyes on the slave ship that would carry him across the Atlantic, he was filled "with astonishment, which was soon converted into terror." Born in Igbo land (in present-day Nigeria), he would slave in the Americas, gain his freedom working as a deep-sea sailor, and in the end become a leading figure in the movement to abolish the slave trade in England. The astonishment and terror of the slave ship, he wrote in his autobiography of 1789, "I am yet at a loss to describe." But the slave ship was central to his life story, as to millions of others', so he described it as best he could.[1]

Carried aboard the vessel by African traders in early 1754, the eleven-year-old boy was immediately grabbed by members of the crew, "white men with horrible looks, red faces, and long hair," who tossed him about to see if he was sound of body. He thought they were "bad spirits" rather than human beings. When they put him down, he looked around the main deck and saw first a huge copper boiling pot and then nearby "a multitude of black people of every description chained together, every one of their countenances expressing dejection and sorrow." Fearing that he had fallen into the hungry, grasping hands of cannibals, he was "overpowered with horror and anguish." He fainted.

When Equiano came to, he was filled with dread, but he would soon discover that the parade of horrors had only just begun. He was taken down to the lower deck, where a loathsome stench promptly made him ill. When two members of the crew offered food, he weakly refused. They hauled him back up to the main deck, tied him to the windlass, and flogged him. As the pain coursed through his small body, his first thought was to try to escape by flying over the side of the ship, even though he could not swim. He then discovered that the slave ship was equipped with nettings to prevent precisely such desperate rebellion. Thus the original experience of the slave ship and the ensuing memory of it were suffused with violence, terror, and resistance.

Equiano, better known in his own day as Gustavus Vassa, was the first person to write extensively about the slave trade from the perspective of the enslaved. He penned what was at the time perhaps the greatest literary work of the abolitionist movement and what has in recent years become history's most famous description of the slave ship and the Middle Passage. But now a controversy surrounds his birthplace and hence the authenticity of his voice. Was he born in Africa as he claimed? Or was he born in South Carolina, as suggested by the literary scholar Vincent Carretta, and then later in life invented for himself African origins in order to oppose the slave trade with greater moral authority?[2]

The matter will continue to be debated, but for present purposes it does not matter. If Equiano was born in West Africa, he is telling the truth—as he remembered it, modified by subsequent experience—about his enslavement and voyage on the slave ship. If he was born in South Carolina, he could have known what he knew only by gathering the lore and experience of people who had been born in Africa and made the dreaded Middle Passage aboard the slave ship. He thus becomes the oral historian, the keeper of the common story, the griot of sorts, of the slave trade, which means that his account is no less faithful to the original experience, only different in its sources and genesis. All who have studied Equiano—on both sides of the debate—agree that he spoke for millions. He wrote his autobiography, and within it his account of the astonishment and terror of the slave ship, in the "interest of humanity." He was "the voice of the voiceless."[3]

Equiano's Home

Equiano wrote that he was born "in the year 1745, in a charming fruit-ful vale, named Essaka," which was possibly Isseke, near Orlu in the Nri-Awka/Isuama region, in central Nigeria.[4] He was his family's youn-gest of seven children who "lived to grow up." His father was a man of consequence, some combination of lineage head (*okpala*), wealthy man (*ogaranya*), respected elder (*ndichie*), and member of the council (*ama ala*) that made decisions for the village as a whole. Equiano was to fol-low in his father's footsteps and, with some dread, to receive the marks of distinction: the *ichi* scarification on the forehead. He was especially attached to his mother, who helped to train him in the arts of agricul-ture and war (gun and spear, which he called "javelin"), and to his sis-ter, with whom he would share the tragedy of enslavement. Equiano indicated the prosperity and standing of the family by noting that his father had "many slaves." (He hastened to add that this slavery, in which slaves lived with and were treated like family, was nothing like the cruel system of the same name to be found in the Americas.) His village was located so far from the coast that "I had never heard of white men or Europeans, nor of the sea."[5]

Equiano was born during a time of crisis, when change swept through his homeland and indeed swept up the young boy himself. The first half of the eighteenth century witnessed drought and famine in Igbo land and, even more seriously for the long term, the slow col-lapse of the Nri civilization, of which Equiano and his village were a part. This helped to open the way for the expansion into the region of the Aro, warlord traders from the south who called themselves *umu-chukwu*, "children of god," who used marriage, alliance, intimidation, and warfare to build an expansive trading network. They funneled thousands of slaves down the three riverine systems—the Niger, the Imo, and the Cross—to the mercantile city-states of Old Calabar, Bonny, and New Calabar. Over the years 1700–1807 more than a mil-lion would be enslaved throughout the broader region, the Bight of Biafra. Some would be sold locally; many would die on the way to the coast. Almost nine hundred thousand were packed onto mostly British ships, and after Middle Passage mortality more than three-quarters of a million were delivered to New World ports. Somewhere between a third and three-fourths of those enslaved and shipped out of the region (the proportion is in dispute) were from Igbo land. Of the hundreds of thousands, Equiano would be one.[6]

Equiano came from a society in which lands were owned and worked in common. Nature was fruitful and benevolent: the soil was rich, he explained; agriculture was productive. Manners were simple and luxuries few, but they had more than enough food and, moreover, "no beggars." In his village, men and women worked "in a body" in the common fields and in other work—building houses, for example. Using hoes, axes, shovels, picks (which Equiano called "beaks"), they cultivated numerous crops, most important among them the yam, which was boiled, pounded, and made into *fufu,* their staple foodstuff. According to the historian John Oriji, the Igbo were in this period the "world's most enthusiastic yam cultivators." They also produced and consumed cocoyams, plantains, peppers, beans and squashes of various kinds, Indian corn, black-eyed peas, watermelon, and fruit. They cultivated cotton and tobacco, raised livestock (bullocks, goats, and poultry), and practiced manufacture. Women spun and wove cotton, making garments, and as ceramic potters they fashioned pipes and "earthen vessels." Blacksmiths forged implements for war and husbandry, while other metalworking specialists crafted delicate ornaments and jewelry. Most produce was consumed locally, where trade was by barter and money was "of little use." Yet the economy was not isolated or autarkic, as goods, mostly agricultural, were traded around the region.[7]

Equiano's family and extended kin were, like all others, organized as a patrilineal clan (*umunne*), governed by a male head of household and collectively by a council of elders. Because land was communally owned and farmed, class divisions were limited, but the village did feature a clear division of labor and distinctions of status, as exemplified by Equiano's own father. Equiano also referred to various kinds of specialists—the priest, the magician, the wise man, the doctor, and the healer, who sometimes were all the same person, the *dibia,* a medium of the spirit world and object of respect and fear in Igbo society. At the other end of the social order were slaves, those captured in war or found guilty of crimes (he mentions kidnapping and adultery). In the end, distinctions were minor and a rough equality prevailed. The village also had a great deal of autonomy, and indeed it—not class, nation, or ethnicity—was the primary source of identity for all its members. Equiano recalled that "our subjection to the king of Benin was little more than nominal"; in truth there was probably no subjection at all, to the king of Benin or anyone else. The people of his region prided themselves on a fierce localism and resistance to political centralization. They would long be known for the proverb *"Igbo enwegh eze,"* which means "The Igbo have no king."[8]

Of his people Equiano wrote, "We are almost a nation of dancers, musicians, and poets." Ritual occasions were marked by elaborate ceremonies of artistic and religious performance, often to summon and gratify ancestral spirits. The Igbo believed that the line between the worlds of humans and spirits, or the living and the dead, was thin and porous. Indeed spirits both good and evil, although invisible, were always present in Igbo society, promising to help or threatening to hinder, depending on how they were treated. Feeding the spirit through sacrifice (*aja*) was essential to good fortune. The *dibia* communicated directly with the spirits, linking the two worlds. The Igbo also believed that premature death was caused by malevolent spirits and that the spirits of the dead would wander and haunt until properly buried. These beliefs would have serious implications aboard the slave ship.[9]

By the time Equiano was eleven years old, slave trading and raiding in his native part of Igbo land had already grown extensive, as his autobiography reveals, in ways numerous and subtle. When the adults of the village went to work on the common, they took arms in case of an attack. They also made special arrangements for the children they left behind, bringing them together in a single place, with instructions that they keep a lookout. Wandering strangers inspired fear, especially if they were traders called the Oye-Eboe, whose name meant "red men living at a distance." These were the Aro, "stout, mahogany-coloured men" from the south. They carried on legitimate, consensual trade, and indeed Equiano noted that his own village sometimes offered them slaves in exchange for European trade goods—firearms, gunpowder, hats, and beads. Such traders encouraged raids of "one little state or district on the other." A local chief who wanted European wares therefore "falls on his neighbours, and a desperate battle ensues," after which those taken prisoner would be sold. The Aro also seized people on their own. Their main business, Equiano found in retrospect but apparently did not fully understand as a child, was to "trepan our people." Ominously, they carried "great sacks" with them wherever they went. Equiano would soon see one of them from the inside.[10]

Kidnapped

"One day, when all our people were gone out to their works as usual," Equiano and his sister were left alone to mind the house. For reasons unknown the adults did not take the usual precautions. Two men and a woman soon climbed over the earthen walls of the family compound and "in a moment seized us both." It happened so suddenly that the children had no opportunity "to cry out, or make resistance." The raiders covered their mouths and "ran off with us into the nearest wood," where they tied their hands and hurried as far from the village as they could before nightfall. Equiano did not say who his attackers were, but he implied that they were Aro. Eventually they came to "a small house, where the robbers halted for refreshment, and spent the night." The bindings of the children were removed, but they were apparently too upset to eat. Soon, "overpowered by fatigue and grief, our only relief was some sleep, which allayed our misfortune for a short time." The long, arduous, traumatic passage to the coast had begun.[11]

The next day the small band traveled through the woods to avoid human traffic, emerging eventually onto a road Equiano thought familiar. As people passed by, the boy "began to cry out for their assistance." But to no avail: "my cries had no other effect than to make them tie me faster, and stop my mouth, and then they put me into a large sack. They also stopped my sister's mouth, and tied her hands; and in this manner we proceeded till we were out of the sight of these people." At the end of another fatiguing day of travel, Equiano and his sister were offered food but refused to eat, thereby employing a form of resistance that would be commonplace on the slave ship. Violently disconnected from his village, most of his family, and almost all he held dear, Equiano took deep solace in the companionship of his sister. The "only comfort we had," he wrote, "was in being in one another's arms all that night, and bathing each other with our tears."

The following day the trauma deepened. It would prove to be "a day of greater sorrow than I had yet experienced." Equiano's captors pulled him and his sister apart "while we lay clasped in each other's arms." The children begged not to be parted, but in vain: "she was torn from me, and immediately carried away, while I was left in a state of distraction not to be described." For some time Equiano "cried and grieved continually." For several days he "did not eat anything but what they forced into my mouth." The comfort of shared misery, "weeping together" with the last remaining family member, was now lost. His alienation from kin and village was complete.

As if to emphasize the point, now began the endless buying and selling of the young boy. Equiano was soon sold to "a chieftain," a blacksmith who lived "in a very pleasant country." Brought into the family in the African style, Equiano was treated well. He took comfort in realizing that even though "I was a great many days journey from my father's house, yet these people spoke exactly the same language with us." He slowly gained freedom of movement in his new circumstances, which he used to gather knowledge about how he might run away and get back to his village. "Oppressed and weighed down by grief after my mother and friends," he took his bearings and imagined his home "towards the rising of the sun." Then one day he accidentally killed a villager's chicken and, fearing punishment, hid out in the bushes as a prelude to running away. He overheard people who were searching for him say that he had probably headed homeward but that his village was too far away and he would never reach it. This sent the boy into "a violent panic," which was followed by despair at the prospect of never being able to return home. He went back to his master and was soon sold again. "I was now carried to the left of the sun's rising, through many dreary wastes and dismal woods, amidst the hideous roarings of wild beasts." Here slaving operations seemed commonplace. He noticed that the people "always go well armed."

Then, amid all the calamity, came a joyous surprise. As he continued his trek toward the coast, Equiano spied his sister once more. Judging by what he wrote here and elsewhere in his autobiography, it was one of the most emotional moments of his life: "As soon as she saw me she gave a loud shriek, and ran into my arms.—I was quite overpowered: neither of us could speak; but, for a considerable time, clung to each other in mutual embraces, unable to do anything but weep." The tearful embrace seemed to move all who saw it, including the man Equiano considered to be their joint owner. The man allowed each of them to sleep at his side, during which time they "held one another by the hands across his breast all night; and thus for a while we forgot our misfortunes in the joy of being together." But then dawned the "fatal morning" on which they were separated again, this time forever. Equiano wrote, "I was now more miserable, if possible, than before." He agonized about his sister's fate. "Your image," he tenderly wrote to her years later, "has been always rivetted in my heart."

The passage to the coast resumed. Equiano was carried and sold hither and yon, eventually to a wealthy merchant in the beautiful city of Tinmah, which was likely in the Niger delta. Here he tasted coconuts and sugarcane for the first time and also observed money he called "core" (*akori*). He befriended the son of a neighboring wealthy widow, a boy about his own age, and the woman bought him from the merchant. He was now treated so well that he forgot he was a slave. He ate at the master's table, was served by other slaves, and played with bows and arrows and other boys "as I had been used to do at home." Over the next two months, he slowly connected to his new family "and was beginning to be reconciled to my situation, and to forget by degrees my misfortunes." He was rudely awakened early one morning and rushed out of the house and back onto the road toward the seacoast. He had the "fresh sorrow" of a new dispossession.

To this point almost all of the peoples Equiano had met in his journey were culturally familiar to him. They had roughly the same "manners, customs, and language"; they were, or would become in time, Igbo. But he finally arrived in a place where the cultural familiarity vanished. Indeed he was shocked by the culture of the coastal Ibibio, who, he observed, were not circumcised, did not wash as he was accustomed to do, used European pots and weapons, and "fought with their fists amongst themselves." The women of the group he considered immodest, as they "ate, and drank, and slept, with their men." They ornamented themselves with strange scars and filed their teeth sharp. Most startling, they made no proper sacrifices or offerings to the gods.

When Equiano came to the banks of a large river, possibly the Bonny, his astonishment grew. Canoes were everywhere, and the people seemed to live on them with "household utensils and provisions of all kinds." The boy had never seen such a large body of water, much less people who lived and worked in this way. His amazement turned to fear when he was put into a canoe by his captors and paddled along the river, around and through the swamps and mangrove forests. Every night they dragged their canoes ashore, built fires, set up tents or small houses, cooked a meal, and slept, arising the next morning and eating again before getting back into the canoes and continuing downriver. He noted how easy the people were, swimming and diving in the water. The travels resumed, now by land and again by water, through "different countries, and various nations." Six or seven months after he had been kidnapped, "I arrived at the sea coast" and likely the big, bustling slave-trading port of Bonny.

On the Magical Ship

The slave ship that inspired horrified awe in Equiano when he first arrived on the coast was a snow, probably between sixty and seventy feet long, with a mainmast of about sixty feet and a main topmast of thirty. The *Ogden,* with eight cannon and a crew of thirty-two, was riding at anchor and "waiting for its cargo," of which the boy himself, he suddenly realized, would be a part.[12] The African traders would have carried him to the vessel by canoe and brought him, and probably several others, up the side of the vessel by a rope ladder, over the rail, and onto the main deck. Here Equiano saw the terrifying sailors, whose language "was very different from any I had ever heard." He saw the copper boiling pot and the melancholy captives, and, fearing cannibalism, he fainted. The black traders who had brought him on board revived him and tried to cheer him up, "but all in vain." He asked if the horrible-looking white men would eat him; they answered no. Then a member of the crew brought Equiano a shot of liquor to revive his spirits, but the small boy was afraid of him and would not take it. One of the black traders took it and gave it to him. He drank it, but it had the opposite effect from what the sailor intended. Having never tasted anything like it, the boy fell "into the greatest consternation." Soon things got even worse. Once the black traders were paid off, they left the ship, and Equiano despaired at their departure: "I now saw myself deprived of all chance of returning to my native country, or even the least glimpse of hope of gaining the shore." After experiencing the stench of the lower deck and a flogging for refusing food, he longed to trade places with "the meanest slave in my own country." Finally he wished in utter despair "for the last friend, Death, to relieve me."[13]

The slave trade always brought together unusual agglomerations of people and to some extent leveled the cultural differences among them. Equiano did not immediately find his "own countrymen," and indeed he had to search for them. In addition to the Igbo, those most likely to have been aboard were Nupe, Igala, Idoma, Tiv, and Agatu, from north of Equiano's own village; the Ijo from the southwest; and from the east a whole host: Ibibio, Anang, Efik (all Efik speakers), Ododop, Ekoi, Eajagham, Ekrikuk, Umon, and Enyong. Many of these people would have been multilingual, and quite a few, maybe most, would likely have spoken or understood Igbo, which was important to trade throughout the region, on the coast and in the interior. Some would have spoken pidgin languages, English, and perhaps a few words of Portuguese. Communication would be complicated aboard the snow, but many means were available.[14]

On the slave ship, Equiano and many others began to discover that they were Igbo. In Equiano's village and indeed throughout the interior, the term "Igbo" was not a term of self-understanding or identity. Rather, according to the famous Nigerian/Igbo writer Chinua Achebe, "Igbo" was originally "a word of abuse; they were the 'other' people, down in the bush." "Igbo" was an insult, a designation that someone was an outsider to the village. Equiano himself suggested this contemptuous meaning when he called the Aro "Oye-Eboe." But on the slave ship, everyone was outside the village, and broader similarities suddenly began to outweigh local differences. Cultural commonalities, especially language, would obviously be crucial to cooperation and community. Igbo, like other African ethnicities, was in many ways a product of the slave trade. In other words, ethnogenesis was happening on the ship.[15]

Equiano soon noticed the systematic use of terror aboard the slaver. The whites "looked and acted, as I thought, in so savage a manner; for I had never seen among any people such instances of brutal cruelty" as occurred regularly aboard the ship. The "poor Africans" who dared to resist, who refused to eat or tried to jump overboard, were whipped and cut. Equiano himself was lashed several times for rejecting food. He also noted that the terror was not confined to the enslaved. One day while he and others were on the main deck, the captain had a white sailor "flogged so unmercifully with a large rope near the foremast, that he died in consequence of it; and they tossed him over the side as they would have done a brute." It was no accident that this was a public event. The use of violence against the crew multiplied the terror: "This made me fear these people the more; and I expected nothing less than to be treated in the same manner."

One of the most valuable parts of Equiano's account of his time on the slave ship is his summary of conversations that took place on the lower deck. As a child and as someone who came from many miles inland, he was among the least knowledgeable on board about the Europeans and their ways. Continuing the struggle to communicate among a group of people from a variety of cultures, he searched for and found people of "his own nation" among "the poor chained men." Because of his fears of cannibalism, his most urgent question was, "what was to be done with us?" Some of the men slaves "gave me to understand we were to be carried to these white people's country to work for them." This answer gave Equiano comfort, as he explained: "if it were no worse than working, my situation was not so desperate."

Still, the fears about the savage Europeans lingered and brought forth new questions. Equiano asked the men "if these people had no country, but lived in this hollow place," the ship? The answer was, "they did not, but came from a distant one." Still puzzled, the young boy asked, "how comes it in all our country we never heard of them?" It was because they "lived so very far off." Where were their women, Equiano then demanded; "had they any like themselves?" They replied, they did, but "they were left behind."

Then came questions about the ship itself, the source of astonishment and terror. Still dazzled by what he had seen, Equiano asked how the vessel could go. Here the men ran out of certain answers but showed that they had been studying the ship in an effort to understand it: "They told me they could not tell; but that there were cloths put upon the masts by the help of the ropes I saw, and then the vessel went on; and the white men had some spell or magic they put in the water when they liked in order to stop the vessel." Equiano declared, "I was exceedingly amazed at this account, and really thought they were spirits." The wonder caused by the ship intensified when one day upon deck Equiano saw a vessel bearing toward them under full sail. He and everyone else who saw it stood amazed, "the more so as the vessel appeared larger by approaching nearer." When the approaching ship eventually dropped anchor, "I and my countrymen who saw it were lost in astonishment to observe the vessel stop; and were now convinced it was done by magic."

Middle Passage

Equiano's Middle Passage proved to be a pageant of cruelty, degradation, and death.[16] It began, crucially, with all of the enslaved locked belowdecks "so that we could not see how they managed the vessel." Many of the things he complained about while the vessel was anchored on the coast suddenly worsened. Now that everyone was confined together belowdecks, the apartments were "so crowded that each had scarcely room to turn himself." The enslaved were spooned together in close quarters, each with about as much room as a corpse in a coffin. The "galling of the chains" rubbed raw the soft flesh of wrists, ankles, and necks. The enslaved suffered extreme heat and poor ventilation, "copious perspirations," and seasickness. The stench, which was already "loathsome," became "absolutely pestilential" as the sweat, the vomit, the blood, and the "necessary tubs" full of excrement "almost suffocated us." The shrieks of the terrified mingled in cacophony with the groans of the dying.[17]

Kept belowdecks, probably because of bad weather, for days at a time, Equiano watched as his shipmates expired, "thus falling victims to the improvident avarice, as I may call it, of their purchasers." The ship was filling up with the troubled spirits of the deceased, whom the living could neither bury properly nor provide with offerings. Conditions had "carried off many," most of them probably by the "bloody flux," or dysentery. The Bight of Biafra had one of the highest mortality rates of any slaving area, and the eight months it took the *Ogden* to gather its enslaved "cargo" only made matters worse. Equiano himself soon grew sick and expected to die. Indeed his death wish returned as he hoped "to put an end to my miseries." Of the dead thrown overboard, he mused, "Often did I think many of the inhabitants of the deep much more happy than myself. I envied them the freedom they enjoyed, and as often wished I could change my condition for theirs." Equiano considered those who had committed suicide by jumping overboard to be still alive, happy and free, and apparently still in touch with people on the ship.[18]

Against the horror and the death wish stood stubborn, resistant life. Equiano continued to communicate with his fellow enslaved for the sake of survival. This he owed in part to enslaved women, who may or may not have been Igbo, and who washed him and showed maternal care for him. Because he was a child, he went unfettered, and because he was sickly, he was kept "almost continually on deck," where he witnessed an increasingly fierce dialectic of discipline and resistance. The crew grew more cruel as the enslaved resolved to use whatever means available to them to fight back. Equiano saw several of his hungry countrymen take some fish to eat and then get flogged viciously for it. Not long after, on a day "when we had a smooth sea, and moderate wind," he witnessed at close range three captives break from the crew, jump over the side of the ship, elude the nettings, and splash into the water below. The crew snapped into action, putting everyone belowdecks to prevent the attempted suicide from escalating (as Equiano was convinced it would have done), then lowered the boat to recover those who had gone overboard. There "was such a noise and confusion amongst the people of the ship as I never heard before." Despite the crew's efforts, two of the rebels successfully completed their self-destruction by drowning. The third was recaptured, brought back on deck, and whipped ferociously for "attempting to prefer death to slavery." Equiano thus noted a culture of resistance forming among the enslaved.

One part of Equiano's own strategy of resistance was to learn all he could from the sailors about how the ship worked. This would, in the long run, prove to be his own path to liberation, since he would work as a sailor, collect his wages, and buy his freedom at age twenty-four. He described himself as one of the people on board who was "most active," which in eighteenth-century maritime parlance meant most vigorous in doing the work of the ship. As he watched the sailors toil, he grew fascinated and at the same time mystified by their use of the quadrant: "I had often with astonishment seen the mariners make observations with it, and I could not think what it meant." The sailors noted the bright boy's curiosity, and one of them decided one day to gratify it. He let Equiano peer through the lens. "This heightened my wonder; and I was now more persuaded than ever that I was in another world, and that every thing about me was magic." It *was* another world, a seafaring society unto itself, and it had a magic that could be learned. Equiano had made a beginning.[19]

Barbados

Yet another world soon appeared on the horizon. Upon sighting land, the crew "gave a great shout" and made "many signs of joy." But Equiano and the rest of the captives did not share in the excitement. They did not know what to think. Before them lay Barbados, epicenter of the historic sugar revolution, crown jewel of the British colonial system, and one of the most fully realized—and therefore most brutal—slave societies to be found anywhere in the world. The plantations of the small island would be the destination of most of the captives aboard the ship.[20]

As the snow came to anchor in the busy harbor of Bridgetown, nestling among a forest of ship masts, a new set of fears gripped Equiano and his fellows of the lower deck. In the darkness of night, strange new people came aboard, and all the enslaved were herded up to the main deck for inspection. Merchants and planters, prospective buyers of the enslaved, began immediately to examine Equiano and his shipmates carefully. "They also made us jump," Equiano recalled, "and pointed to the land, signifying we were to go there." They organized the captives into "separate parcels" for sale.

All the while Equiano and apparently others "thought by this we should be eaten by these ugly men, as they appeared to us." Soon everyone was put back belowdecks, but new horror had taken root, as Equiano explained: "there was much dread and trembling among us, and nothing but bitter cries to be heard all the night from these apprehensions." How long the cries went on is not clear, but eventually the white visitors responded by summoning "some old slaves from the land to pacify us." These veterans of Barbados plantation society "told us we were not to be eaten, but to work, and were soon to go on land, where we should see many of our country people." The tactic seemed to work: "This report eased us much; and sure enough, soon after we were landed, there came to us Africans of all languages."

Presently Equiano and the others were taken ashore, to the "merchant's yard," as he called it, a place where "we were all pent up together like so many sheep in a fold, without regard to sex or age," which would have seemed odd after experiencing the gender and age separations of the ship. Despite the harrowing uncertainty of the new situation, the sights of Bridgetown filled Equiano with fresh wonder. He noticed that the houses were built high, with stories, unlike any he had known in Africa. "I was still more astonished," he noted, "on seeing people on horseback. I did not know what this could mean; and indeed I thought these people were full of nothing but magical arts."[21] Other shipmates, however, were not surprised. Some "fellow prisoners" from a distant part of Africa, no doubt the northern savanna, observed that the horses "were the same kind they had in their country." This was confirmed by others, who added that their own horses were "larger than those I then saw."[22]

A few days later came the sale, by "scramble." The merchants arrayed the human commodities in the yard, then sounded a signal, the beating of a drum, whereupon buyers frantically rushed in to pick those they wanted to purchase. The "noise and clamour" of the moment terrified the Africans and made them think that the greedy buyers would be the agents of their doom. Some still feared cannibalism. The fear was justified, as most of those purchased would indeed be eaten alive—by the deadly work of making sugar in Barbados.

A third separation was now at hand, which illuminates the connections made on the ship while anchored on the coast of Africa and during its Middle Passage. Equiano noted that at this moment, without scruple, "relations and friends separated, most of them never to see each other again." He recalled the sad fate of several brothers who had been confined together in the men's apartment of his vessel, who were now sold in separate lots to different masters. He wrote that "it was very moving on this occasion to see and hear their cries at parting." Husbands were separated from wives, parents from children, brothers from sisters.

Yet it was not only blood kin who shrieked and grieved at the prospect of separation. It was "dearest friends and relations," people who had already been separated once from their kindred, who had now mingled "their sufferings and sorrows" aboard the ship. Some of these people had been together on the ship for as long as eight months *before* the Middle Passage. They had cheered each other amid the "gloom of slavery." They had what Equiano called "the small comfort of being together," crying together, resisting together, trying to survive together. The new community that had been formed aboard the ship was being ripped asunder as the captives would all be forced to go "different ways." Equiano noted with deep sadness that "every tender feeling" that had developed aboard the ship would now be sacrificed to avarice, luxury, and the "lust of gain."[23]

Long Passage

For Equiano and several of his shipmates, the Middle Passage did not end in Barbados. These few "were not saleable amongst the rest, from very much fretting." The traumatic passage had apparently made them unhealthy—emaciated, diseased, melancholy, or all of these. The buyers must have doubted their survival and declined to purchase them. They became "refuse slaves." They stayed on the island for a few days and were then carried to a smaller vessel, a sloop, perhaps the *Nancy,* Richard Wallis master, bound for the York River in Virginia. The second passage was easier than the first. Compared to the slave ship, the number of the enslaved on board now was much smaller, the atmosphere was less tense and violent, and the food was better, as the captain wanted to fatten them up for sale farther north. Equiano wrote, "On the passage we were better treated than when we were coming from Africa, and we had plenty of rice and fat pork." But all was not well, as Equiano felt the loss of his shipmates who were sold in Barbados: "I now totally lost the small remains of comfort I had enjoyed in conversing with my countrymen; the women too, who used to wash and take care of me, were all gone different ways, and I never saw one of them afterwards." Had he seen one or more of them, the bond of the shipboard experience would have been activated and re-newed.[24]

The boy apparently formed new bonds with his fellow Africans aboard the sloop, even though they did not speak his language. But then these bonds, too, were shattered upon landing in Virginia, as "at last all my companions were distributed different ways, and only my-self was left." Disconnected yet again, and envying even those who were sold in lots, he explained, "I was now exceedingly miserable, and thought myself worse off than any of the rest of my companions; for they could talk to each other, but I had no person to speak to that I could understand." In this situation his death wish returned: "I was constantly grieving and pining, and wishing for death, rather than anything else."

Equiano continued in his lonely, forlorn state until a former naval officer and now merchant ship captain, Michael Henry Pascal, bought the boy as a gift for someone in England. Equiano was taken aboard the *Industrious Bee,* "a fine large ship, loaded with tobacco, &c. and just ready to sail." The Middle Passage must have seemed like endless pas-sage, but at least now he was on a deep-sea ship whose purpose was not to transport slaves. The conditions of life improved accordingly: "I had sails to lie on, and plenty of good victuals to eat; and every body on board," at least at first, "used me very kindly, quite contrary to what I had seen of any white people before." Maybe they were not bad spirits after all, and in any case the all-encompassing, terror-filled category "white people" began slowly to change: "I therefore began to think that they were not all of the same disposition." He also began to speak English, talked with members of the crew, and continued to learn the workings of a ship.

Perhaps the most important thing to happen to Equiano on this voyage was his discovery of a new shipmate, a boy of about fifteen named Richard Baker. Son of an American slaveholder (and indeed the owner of slaves himself), well educated, and possessed of a "most amiable temper" and a "mind superior to prejudice," Baker befriended the African boy, who explained, "he shewed me a great deal of partiality and attention, and in return I grew extremely fond of him." The two became inseparable, Baker translating for Equiano and teaching him many useful things.

As a privileged passenger on the voyage, Baker ate at the captain's table, and as the voyage dragged on and provisions grew scarce, Captain Pascal cruelly joked at mealtime that they might have to kill Equiano and eat him. At other times he would say the same thing to Equiano himself but then add that "black people were not good to eat," so they might have to kill Baker first "and afterwards me." Pascal also asked Equiano if his own people in Africa were cannibals, to which the panicked boy replied no.

These exchanges reignited the terror of the slaving voyage in Equiano, especially after the captain put everyone on board to short allowance, a rationing of food. "Towards the last," remembered Equiano, "we had only one pound and a half of bread per week, and about the same quantity of meat, and one quart of water a day." They caught fish to supplement their victuals, but food remained scarce. The joking grew more ominous: "I thought them in earnest, and was depressed beyond measure, expecting every moment to be my last." He was also alarmed for his friend and shipmate Baker. Whenever Baker was called by captain or mate, Equiano "would peep and watch to see if they were going to kill him."

Believing as he did in the power of supernatural spirits to rule the natural world, Equiano was especially frightened when the waves around him began to churn and run high. He thought that "the Ruler of the seas was angry, and I expected to be offered up to appease him." Later, at dusk one evening, members of the crew spotted some grampuses near the ship. Equiano thought they were the spirits of the seas and that he might be sacrificed to them. During the latter stages of the passage, his mind was filled with agony. He appeared before the captain "crying and trembling." At last, after thirteen weeks, the sailors of the *Industrious Bee* sighted land. "Every heart on board seemed gladdened on our reaching the shore," recalled Equiano, "and none more than mine." The terror of the slave ship had persisted from the original

Middle Passage until Equiano finally left his third vessel in Falmouth, England.

Terror in Black and White

Equiano understood the passage from expropriation in Africa to exploitation in America. Millions like himself and his sister fell "victims to the violence of the African trader, the pestilential stench of a Guinea ship, the seasoning in the European colonies, or the lash and lust of a brutal and unrelenting overseer." He went through a jarring series of separations. What remains to be emphasized is how he responded to his dispossession, how he cooperated with and connected to others. The process began on the internal passage in Africa from village to seacoast, and it continued on the slave ships, on the coast and in his long, segmented Middle Passage.[25]

During his grueling trek to the coast, Equiano remained attached for part of the way to his sister, the last link to his family and village. He twice joined African families, first that of the chieftain-blacksmith for a month, then that of the wealthy widow and her son in Tinmah for two months. On the way to each and again after he was sold, he apparently formed no meaningful ties with the numerous African traders with whom he traveled, nor with any other enslaved people besides his sister. Indeed how could he while being endlessly bought and sold along the route? He was radically individualized as a commodity, a slave.

Still he was not yet culturally alienated, as he remained part of an Igbo speech community on the way to the coast. He noted that "a great many days journey" after his kidnapping, he found the "same language" being spoken among the people around him. The same was true in Tinmah. In fact, he explained that "from the time I left my own nation I always found somebody that understood me till I came to the sea coast." There were variations in dialects, which he found he easily learned. He added that on his way to the coast, "I acquired two or three different tongues." Even though Equiano suffered "the violence of the African trader," he emphasized that his treatment during the passage to the coast was not cruel. He felt compelled to explain to his readers, "in honour of those sable destroyers of human rights, that I never met with any ill treatment, or saw any offered to their slaves, except tying them, when necessary, to keep them from running away."

Entry into the astonishing, terrifying slave ship meant, in Equiano's case as in many others, a traumatic transition from African to European control. This was the moment of his most extreme alienation, and the height of his death wish, which would come and go but remain with him for a long while. The ship seems to have induced a stark, polar, racialized way of thinking and understanding. The seamen appeared to the young Equiano as evil spirits and horrible-looking "white people." More tellingly, the African traders who brought him aboard the ship were "black people," with whom, suddenly, he had newly discovered sympathies. It was they who tried to comfort him when he fainted on the main deck, and it was they who represented the only surviving link to his home. When they left the ship, they "left me abandoned to despair," without a means of "returning to my native country." At the point of no return, he wished for the familiarity and comfort of African slavery, as he identified with "black people." At least they would not eat him.

For the rest of his time on the ship, Equiano employed the monolithic category "white people," which was, in his mind, more or less synonymous with mysterious and oppressive terror. The conversations he recorded with his countrymen concerned the strange "white people," where they came from, why he did not know of them, did they have women, and what this thing was that they arrived on, the ship. Most of his observations about the crew referred to disciplinary violence, usually flogging and suicide prevention. The most common word he used to describe them was "cruel." Equiano never mentioned the captain of the slave ship, nor did he mention any officers, and indeed he showed a consciousness of hierarchy or division among the crew on only one occasion—when the white sailor was beaten with a rope, died, and was unceremoniously thrown overboard "like a brute," or animal.

There were, however, a few moments in the narrative where relations with the Europeans were not marked by violence and cruelty. He notes the offer of liquor by a sailor, to cheer his spirits (even though the result was greater agitation). On another occasion sailors from a different slave ship came aboard his own: "Several of the strangers also shook hands with us black people, and made motions with their hands, signifying I suppose we were to go to their country; but we did not understand them." Another sailor indulged his curiosity about the quadrant. It was, however, not until Equiano got on board the nonslaver *Industrious Bee* that his monolithic view of the "white people" began to break down. His early impressions were very much at odds with the radical, antiracializing phrase from the Bible he used to introduce his book, that all people were "of one blood."

The process of dispossession and reconnection was reflected in Equiano's use—and nonuse—of personal names as he tried to make his way in a world of nameless strangers. In recounting his history starting at the moment he was taken from his home until after he arrived in Virginia, a trek by land and water that lasted sixteen months, he names no one, neither African nor European, thereby emphasizing his own lonely and total alienation. He does not mention even the names of his father, mother, or sister. This was not accidental, for he also showed an awareness of naming as an act of power. Just as the loss of a name was part of the culture stripping of dispossession, the assignment of a new name could be an act of aggression and domination. It was on the slave ship that his given name, Olaudah Equiano, was taken from him and lost until he reclaimed it thirty-five years later. He wrote, "on board the African snow I was called Michael." On the next vessel, the sloop to Virginia, he was named again, this time Jacob. Finally, aboard the *Industrious Bee,* his new master, Captain Pascal, gave him a fourth name, Gustavus Vassa. Equiano recalled, with some pride, that he "refused to be called so, and told him as well as I could that I would be called Jacob." (Why he preferred this name, he does not say.) But Captain Pascal insisted on the new name, to which the young boy "refused to answer." The resistance, Equiano wrote, "gained me many a cuff; so at length I submitted." He thus lost his original name to violence and gained a new one in the same way.[26]

Equiano saw that his fellow enslaved—the "multitude of black people, of every description chained together"—were themselves a motley crew of different classes, ethnicities, and genders who had been jumbled together aboard the slave ship. He saw the struggle to communicate and to be understood, for the sake of survival. For Equiano this began with the black traders who had brought him aboard the ship. He then found his "own countrymen" in the men's apartment on the lower deck. He also discovered Igbo speakers, indeed "Africans of all languages," in Barbados, sent by the slave owners to pacify the newly arrived "salt water negroes" as they were called. Equiano lamented the loss of his countrymen and fellow Igbo speakers during his voyage to Virginia; there was "no one to talk to me." But at the same time, he communicated with people who did not speak his own original language. He noted that he was able to talk with someone "from a distant part of Africa," and he noted also his own acquisition of English, learned mostly from sailors aboard his various ships. This, too, would have helped his communication with other Africans, especially those from coastal regions. Additionally, Equiano witnessed the formation of a new language—of resistance manifested in action, as, for example, when the three slaves defied the crew and jumped over the side of the ship. This, too, could contribute to a sense of solidarity and a community aboard the slave ship.

Out of the fragile bonds grew a new kinship among people who called themselves "shipmates."[27] Although Equiano does not use the word, he did articulate clearly its basic bonding principle. And he did so in a rather surprising way, referring not to a fellow African but rather to his American shipmate Richard Baker, a teenager like himself with whom he grew very close. They lived together in cramped quarters, sharing the intimate difficulties of life in a ship: "he and I have gone through many sufferings together on shipboard; and we have many nights lain in each other's bosoms when we were in great distress." It was precisely so for the hundreds on board each slave ship.

In this way dispossessed Africans formed themselves into informal mutual-aid societies, in some cases even "nations," on the lower deck of a slave ship. Like his many "countrymen," Equiano would slowly come to understand a new meaning of the Igbo proverb *Igwe bu ke*— "Multitude is strength."[28]

CHAPTER 5

James Field Stanfield and the
Floating Dungeon

Few people in the eighteenth century were better equipped to capture the drama of the slave trade than was James Field Stanfield. He had made a slaving voyage, and a gruesome one it was, from Liverpool to Benin and Jamaica and back during the years 1774–76, and he had lived for eight months at a slave-trading factory in the interior of the Slave Coast. An educated man, he was a writer who would over the course of his lifetime acquire something of a literary reputation. And he was, perhaps most tellingly, an actor, a strolling player, whose work in the theater probed the triumphs and tragedies of humanity. So in the late 1780s, when Stanfield, encouraged by a nascent abolitionist movement, decided to write about the horrors of the slave trade, he had a unique combination of talents and experience at hand.[1]

Stanfield was one of the earliest to write a first-person exposé of the slave trade. His *Observations on a Guinea Voyage, in a Series of Letters Addressed to the Rev. Thomas Clarkson* was published by the Society for Effecting the Abolition of the Slave Trade in London in May 1788.[2] Later that year the pamphlet was serialized in seven installments and published in America, appearing in the *Providence Gazette and Country Journal,* placed there, no doubt, by local abolitionists.[3] The following year Stanfield drew on his experience of the slave ship again, writing *The Guinea Voyage, A Poem in Three Books.*[4] In 1795 he published a shorter poem, without a formal title, under the inscription

"Written on the Coast of Africa in the year 1776," in the *Freemason's Magazine, or General Complete Library*.[5] Taken together, these works represent a dramatic rendering of his experience aboard the slave ship. The decks were a stage, and the theater was the Atlantic for the "performance of a Guinea voyage."[6] A reviewer in the *Gentleman's Magazine* in 1789 noted that *The Guinea Voyage* was, like the previous *Observations,* an "addition to the stage machinery of the abolition of the slave trade."[7] The metaphor was apt.

Stanfield was also the first to write about the slave trade from the perspective of the common sailor. This he himself considered to be of the first importance. He was angry that an "impenetrable veil . . . has been thrown over this traffic for such a number of years" and that important information has "been withheld from the publick eye by every effort that interest, ingenuity, and influence, could devise." With bitter sarcasm he asked:

> From whom is it expected that this information should be derived? Who are the persons qualified to produce the authentic evidence? Will the merciful slave-merchant step forward, and give up the long catalogue of rapacity, murder, and destruction, his own avarice has framed? Will the humane Guinea-Captain produce his fatal muster-roll,—and for once impelled by justice, change that *useful* disease,—*flux, flux, flux,* which has hitherto so conveniently masked the death-list of his devoted [doomed] crew, to the real, the mortal causes, that have thinned his ship? Will petty officers, bravely despising all thoughts of preferment, disregarding the thoughts of owners and agents, and nobly resolving to pass their lives in labour, wretchedness, and servile dependence—will they disclose the horrid scenes they have been witnesses to—the barbarities they have seen practised, and the cruelties, of which, they themselves have been, perhaps, the unwilling instruments?

No, Stanfield answered, those with a material interest in the trade could never be trusted to tell the truth about it. The only person who could "give the truth in plain, unbiassed information" was the common sailor, who, like the others, knew the slave trade firsthand. The problem was, there were "few meagre survivors" to tell the tale, as many sailors on slaving voyages were lost to death and desertion. Stanfield would thus take it upon himself to represent the dead and the missing as he wrote his accounts, which were organized and narrated to "connect the whole round of a GUINEA VOYAGE," to tell the dramatic truths of the slave trade and the experience of the common sailor within it. Among the dozens who wrote poems about the commerce in human flesh, he was one of only a handful who had actually traveled through what he called "the dark mazes of th' *inhuman Trade*." Stanfield's descriptions of the ship and the trade were among the very best ever written by a working sailor.[8]

What an English Tar Should Be

Stanfield became a sailor, it seems, through an act of rebellion. Born in Dublin, Ireland, in 1749 or 1750, he was ensconced in studies for the priesthood, apparently in France during the late 1760s, when he underwent a secular awakening. As he described it, "Science first open'd my views."[9] He searched for the joys and beauties of nature and philosophy. He was a man of feeling, a romantic before his time. Young, vigorous, free, and mobile, he went to sea, choosing an occupation that was in almost every way the very antithesis of priest. Among sailors, irreverence, free thought, sensuality, and action trumped piety, doctrine, celibacy, and contemplation. He sailed to many parts of the world, and his experience as a sailor would remain a defining part of his identity for the rest of his life. A fellow actor noted in 1795 that Stanfield "was bred a sailor, and is what an English tar should be, a man of bravery, and that aided by marks of strong genius and good understanding." At the end of his life, Stanfield wore a sailor's jersey beneath his waistcoat when his more famous and revealingly named son, the artist Clarkson Stanfield (after abolitionist Thomas Clarkson), painted his portrait.[10]

Stanfield's career as an actor seems to have begun in Manchester in 1777, soon after he left the sea. Like many actors of the era, Stanfield was indigent much of the time, as income was modest and intermittent.

Moreover, he would eventually have ten children by two wives to care for, which added to a life of "chronic financial hardship." Stanfield was nonetheless a man of cheerful disposition. He was known for his spirited intelligence, independent mind, and distinctive looks (he was considered unhandsome in the extreme). The Scottish painter David Roberts, who befriended him in his later life, called him "an enthusiastic warm-hearted Irishman." Combining the Irish and seafaring backgrounds, he was an entertaining storyteller and a gleeful singer of songs, some of which he wrote himself.[11]

By the time he took his slaving voyage, Stanfield was already an experienced sailor and a knowledgeable one. He had for several years lived "a seafaring life" and sailed "to almost all parts of Europe, the West Indies and North America." Along the way and afterward, he talked to other sailors and compared his own experience aboard the Guineaman to theirs. He concluded that the conduct of the officers and the workings of the trade were roughly the same on most voyages. A few sailors found better treatment, a few worse: "I never heard but of *one* Guinea vessel, in which the usage and conduct were in any degree of moderation."[12]

Stanfield was a common seaman but not a typical one. Compared to other seamen, he was better educated (he knew Latin) and he was apparently better off (he was lodging in a coffeehouse while in Liverpool). But he was not an officer aboard the ship. He did not eat at the captain's table. By the end of the Atlantic crossing, he had, by force of mortality, become a mate and an unqualified substitute surgeon, but his perspective remained steadfastly that of the common sailor. He was trusted and respected by his brother tars, who asked him to keep track of their "small accounts"—money and expenses—during the voyage, to protect against the chicanery of the captain. On his ship's muster list, his name appears like the other common tars', with no special rank or skill alongside.[13]

Stanfield departed Liverpool for Benin on September 7, 1774, working for Captain David Wilson aboard an old, leaky vessel called the *Eagle,* which was to be "left on the coast as a floating factory," a place for slave trading.[14] Almost as soon as the vessel arrived, in November 1774, the sailors of the *Eagle* began to sicken and die, but Stanfield escaped by going inland to "Gatoe [Gato], many miles from the sea, in the heart of the country," where he resided at a slave-trading fortress for eight months, until late June 1775.[15] Eventually a "fresh ship," the *True Blue,* arrived. Its captain, John Webster, went ashore to conduct business on behalf of the merchant Samuel Sandys, who owned both vessels. Wilson then took command of the *True Blue,* hired a new crew of fifteen, including Stanfield, brought aboard a cargo of captives, and set sail for Jamaica. On the Middle Passage more than half (eight) of the crew died. In December, Captain Wilson sold 190 slaves in Jamaica before heading back to Liverpool, where he arrived on April 12, 1776. Stanfield probably helped to unload the ship, as his last day of wages was April 15, 1776. Along with Captain Wilson, carpenter Henry Fousha, and seaman Robert Woodward, he was one of four members of the *Eagle* who made it back to the port of origin.[16]

Forging the Chain

For Stanfield the drama of the Guinea voyage began not on the coast of Africa, not even on the slave ship, but rather in the gentlemanly setting of the merchant's exchange or coffeehouse. It began, in short, with slave traders and their money—the pooling of capital to buy a ship and cargo and to hire a captain and crew. Stanfield saw this as the forging of the first link of a chain that would reach from Liverpool to West Africa to the West Indies, a metaphor that runs throughout his writing:

> At length harden'd merchants close combine,
> And midnight Council broods the black design;
> Strikes the first link of the tremend'ous chain,
> Whose motion vibrates thro' the realms of pain.

He ascribed the hard, conspiratorial impulse to the "insatiate thirst of av'rice" and a host of secondary causes: fancy, vice, intemperance, folly, and pride. He insisted, from the beginning, on the causal relationship between the greed of the few in the port city and the manifold misery of the many around the Atlantic.[17]

Stanfield saw that the merchants' capital set labor of many kinds in motion, that workers on the Liverpool waterfront hammered new links of the chain into place: "The sounding anvil shakes the distant main, / Forging with pond'rous strokes th' accursed chain." As the ship was repaired and serviced and the trading cargo gathered amid the tumult, the merchant, captain, and officers searched for a group of "Neptune's sons" to sail the ship to Africa. "Nothing is more difficult," wrote Stanfield, "than to procure a sufficient number of hands for a Guinea voyage."

James Stanfield knew sailors. He had lived and worked among them for years, so he knew their ways of thinking and acting, their ideas and customs, their characteristics good, bad, and quirky. He knew that they did not like the slave trade. He also knew that many of them were "jolly" and often "heedless," given to dancing, drinking, and carousing along the waterfront, especially if they had recently returned to port from long voyages and their many privations. With money in their pockets, they were the "Lords of Six Weeks" and often less. They crowded the waterfront taverns, spending their hard-earned wages lavishly and often recklessly amid wild merriment. This reflected the "unsuspecting, thoughtless, dissipated propensity that marks the character of an English sailor." Stanfield also knew that Guinea merchants and ship captains saw in these riotous scenes their opportunity to get sailors aboard their vessels. He illuminated the methods of the employers and the workings of the waterfront labor market for the slave trade. His retelling carries a lantern from the dingy waterfront tavern to the city jail to the Guineaman anchored offshore.

Whenever a slaver was fitting out, Stanfield explained, merchants and their captains, clerks, and crimps (unscrupulous labor agents) prowled the streets of Liverpool "without intermission." They relentlessly hurried one sailor after another into taverns whose proprietors were under their influence and where sailors found music, prostitutes, and drink. Stanfield himself had been "dragged into houses three times" as he tried to walk down a single street. Once inside, the hustle began, with professions of sympathy and friendship and endless offers of rum or gin. The goal was to drive the sailors to intoxication and debt, both of which were essential means of manning a slave ship.

Many a drunken sailor—perhaps Stanfield himself—signed "articles of agreement," a wage contract, with a Guinea merchant or captain after a long, rakish binge. Many who did so were young and inexperienced, but some were old hands who should have known better. Stanfield declared, "I have known many seamen, who fancied themselves cunning enough to evade these practices, go with the crimps to some of their houses, boasting that they would cheat the Merchant out of a night's merriment, and firmly resolved to oppose every artifice that could be offered." But, once drunk, they "signed articles with the very men, whose purposes they were aware of, and have been plunged into a situation, of which they had known the horrors." It was a dangerous game. Sailors who played and lost often paid with their lives.

As the festivities carried on deep into the night and the following morning, the landlord drew strokes on the wall with chalk to indicate a sailor's rising debt: "Four chalks for one shilling" was the saying in Liverpool. As the sailors got drunker, the accounting got more creative, and soon the debts, real and fictitious, multiplied. Those who had refused to sign articles now faced a different situation. The landlord would offer inebriated, indebted sailors a deal. If they would agree to go on board a slaver, they could use their advance pay to settle their debts. If the sailors refused the deal, the landlord would call the constable and have them committed to jail. Stanfield captured this process in verse: the merchants, he wrote,

With specious arts subdue th' unwary mind,
Then close their web, and fast their victims bind.
At length with debts fictitious charge their case,
And make a *dungeon* stare them in the face.

Some sailors took the deal and went on board the ship; others took the dungeon. But when they got there, they discovered that "from that place, no other vessel will engage him; ships in every other employ find seamen willing to *offer* their services: and the Captains of these have a natural objection to what they call *jail-birds*." The sailor was

> Shut now from comfort, agoniz'd with grief,
> Hopeless alike of justice, or relief—
> Only one portal opes the gloomy road;
> One dire condition bursts the drear abode.
> *Slav'ry*'s dark genius heaves the iron door,
> And, grinning ghastly, points to *Guinea*'s shore—

As the wretch left the prison gate, wrote Stanfield, he felt "with horror his approaching fate." The wily merchant had attached the chain to his leg.

By hook and by crook, a variety of people were lured aboard the ships. Some were drunk and indebted, forced to exchange a landed dungeon for a floating one. These included "restless youth" and those of "unwary mind," as well as those who thought they could outwit the crimp and ended up outwitting themselves. "Some few," wrote Stanfield, "the voluntary woe embrace." Some of these were smarting from "false friends"; some were fleeing "undeserv'd disgrace"; some were no doubt in trouble with the law. Others had suffered misfortune of one kind or another, were "weary of griefs no patience can endure." Some had lost at love and were "of hopeless passion torn." Stanfield exemplified this last in the poem by a friend he called Russel, a "harmless spirit—gentlest of thy kind, / Was ne'er to savage cruelty inclin'd." To the slave ship he was "by the winds and fiercer passions blown." Headed to the tropics, he now "tries the ardours of the flaming zone." Slave-trade sailors were similar to those who sailed in other trades, but were perhaps a little more naive, down and out, and desperate. Stanfield gave clues as to his own motivations in the poem "Written on the Coast of Africa in 1776" (actually 1775). He refers to his "rash youth," his "youthful ardours," how "I rush'd on the shore with the throng." These might refer to actions that put him in a crimp's snare. But at the same time he suggests a positive interest in Africa: the "rich scenr'y," the "beauty of Nature," and an interest in "observation." He sought "stores intellectual" and "treasures of wisdom" in "these far-favour'd regions of day!"[18]

A crew of thirty-two had come aboard the *Eagle,* and the time to sail had arrived. Friends and family members of some of the sailors gathered on the dock to say good-bye. The occasion was supposed to be festive, but, as Stanfield wrote, "The bending deck receives the parting crowd; / And shades of sorrow ev'ry face o'ercloud." Not all of the sailors had someone to see them off. Those who had been taken from the jail would have had no opportunity to explain where they were going. But even those who had an opportunity, thought Stanfield, had not "sent their friends the smallest account of their destination." Some were apparently ashamed of making a Guinea voyage and did not want anyone to know about it. In any case the time for parting had arrived. From those on shore, "Three soul-expanding shouts the skies divides." The sailors answered and "Three wild, responsive cheers re-echo wide."

Once at sea, the sailors turned their attention to the ship and its work:

> Firm in their stations, ply th' obedient crowd,
> Trim the directing lines, and strain the shroud;
> Tug at the beating sheets with sinew'd force,
> And give the vast machine its steady course.

The "vast machine" was now under way toward the Gold Coast and the Bight of Benin, and despite the shenanigans and mistreatments that made it all possible, the ship was at this moment a thing of beauty, with new sails and fresh paint, with colors flying and banners streaming in the sea breeze, all of which, to Stanfield, concealed a deeper malaise:

See o'er the glossy wave the vessel skim,
In swelling garments proud, and neatest trim,
Glitt'ring in streamers, deck'd in painted guile
Cov'ring the latent bane with spacious smile,
In shining colours, splendidly array'd,
Assume the honours of an *honest trade,*
And hide, beneath a prostituted glare,
Thy poison'd purpose, and th' insidious snare.

Savage Rigour

The voyage began normally enough, thought Stanfield: "the usage of
the seamen is moderate, and their allowance of provisions sufficient: in
short, the conduct of the Captain and officers appears like that which is
the continual practice in every other employ." Stanfield had sailed in
several trades and could make the comparison. But he noticed a subtle
change once the ship had sailed beyond the sight of land, to a place
where "there is no moral possibility of desertion, or application for justice." The captain and officers began to talk of flogging. No one was
actually flogged, because, Stanfield believed, the old ship was leaky and
might have to put in at Lisbon for repairs. This had a moderating effect
on the officers.[19]

Once it became clear that repairs in port would not be necessary, and
once the ship was well south of Lisbon, everything changed. The sailors were soon put to short allowance of food and water. "A quart of
water in the torrid zone!" protested Stanfield, and this while eating salt
provisions and performing heavy physical labor from morning to night.
Sailors were reduced to licking droplets of their own sweat. When
Stanfield discovered that dew collected atop the ship's hen coops overnight, he sucked up the moisture every morning until others found his
"delicious secret." Some men were so thirsty they drank their entire
daily portion of water as soon as they got it and remained in a state of
"raging thirst" for the next twenty-four hours. All the while the captain
had abundant wine, beer, and water.

One reason for the scarcity of water, Stanfield explained, was "the vessel's being stowed so full of goods for the trade, that room for necessaries is made but a secondary consideration." It was a classic case of profits over people. Every "corner and cranny [of the ship] is crammed with articles of traffic; to this consideration is bent every exertion of labour and ingenuity; and the healths and lives of the seamen, as of no value, have but little weight in the estimation." What Stanfield called the "avaricious accumulation of cargo" also meant that the sailors had no room to sling their hammocks and bedding. They were forced to "lie rough," on chests and cables. When they got to the tropics, they slept upon deck, exposed to "the malignity of the heavy and unwholesome dews."

Then came the beatings, floggings, and torture. They began not far from the Canary Islands. Stanfield overheard the following "barbarous charge" given by the captain to the other officers: "You are now in a Guinea ship—no seaman, though you speak harshly, must dare to give you a saucy answer—*that* is out of the question; but if they LOOK to displease you, knock them down." The violence soon "spread like a contagion." Stanfield recounted one instance of cruelty practiced against the ship's cooper, "a most harmless, hard-working, worthy creature." He answered the mate in a humorous way and was knocked down for it. As he tried to crawl to the captain's cabin to complain, he was knocked down a second, third, and fourth time, until "some of the sailors rushed between [him and the mate], and hurried him away." The smallest error in work brought forth a lashing, and occasionally three sailors at once were bound together to the shrouds. After the floggings the officers sometimes literally added salt to the wound—they applied a briny solution called "pickle" to the deep, dark red furrows made by the cat-o'-nine tails, the infamous whip. The violence was inflicted without remorse and "without fear of being answerable for the abuse of authority." As the voyage went on, Stanfield wrote, "the dark pow'r / Of savage rigour ripens ev'ry hour."[20]

The Demon Cruelty

Arrival on the African coast signaled another set of transformations chronicled by Stanfield—in the ship, the crew, the captain, and the

African societies with whom the trade was carried out. The ship itself was physically altered as the sailors "built house" on the main deck, constructing a thatched-roof awning from the stem of the ship to near the mainmast to protect all on board from the tropical sun and to provide security against escape of the ever-growing number of purchased slaves. Building house required the sailors to work in the water on the riverside, bare-chested and exposed to the burning sun, cutting wood and bamboo with which to make the awning: "They are immersed up to the waist in mud and slime; pestered by snakes, worms, and venomous reptiles; tormented by muskitoes, and a thousand assailing insects; their feet slip from under them at every stroke, and their relentless officers do not allow a moment's intermission from the painful task." Stanfield thought that this work contributed to the high mortality of the sailors, but so in his opinion did the awning itself, which, with the various bulkheads built belowdecks to separate the slaves, obstructed the proper circulation of air through the ship and damaged the health of everyone on board.[21]

The declining health of the sailors moved Stanfield's captain to make another important change in the working order of the ship. On the Gold Coast, he hired Fante workers, who were "sturdy, animated, laborious, and full of courage"—and accustomed to both the climate and disease environment. "Many of this nation," wrote Stanfield, "are reared from their childhood, in the European vessels that frequent the coast; they learn their languages, and are practiced in all the habits of seamanship; and more especially all that relate to the business of *slaving*." This was common practice. Captains engaged Fante workers after entering into a written agreement with their king and the English governor at Cape Coast Castle or another factory. Stanfield believed that such arrangements were essential to the slave trade: "When the poor sailors fall off [sick], these hardy natives, who have every indulgence the captain can allow them, carry on the business with a vigour and activity, of which the British seamen from their ill usage and scanty fare are incapable." A motley crew did the work of the ship from the moment it arrived on the

African coast until it departed, and occasionally all the way across the Atlantic.

Once they got to the African coast, the biggest change, in Stanfield's view, took place in the slave-ship captain. He put the matter this way: "It is unaccountable, but it is certainly true, that the moment a Guinea captain comes in sight of this shore, the Demon cruelty seems to fix his residence within him." Stanfield made the same point in the poem, allegorically, as the Demon Cruelty dispatched a devil to the ship: "Fly, says the night-born chief, without delay, / To where yon vessel rides the wat'ry way." Off he flies,

> And to the *master* turns his stedfast eyes;
> Down, like the lightning's fury, rushes prone,
> And on his heart erects his bloody throne.

If the captain seemed barbarous on the outward passage, he was now positively demonic, his heart colonized by cruelty. Stanfield did not lack for concrete examples to illustrate the transformation. He spoke of a visitor aboard his own ship, a Guineaman captain who was legendary for his brutality: he flogged his own sailors for no good reason; he tormented his cabin boy; his "whole delight was in giving pain."

In "Proud Benin"

Most of Stanfield's pamphlet concerned the experience of the common sailor in the slave trade, but he did offer reflections on Africa, on the traders, and on the enslaved who came aboard the ship, and these thoughts he expanded considerably in his poem. His observations had a firm basis in experience, and not only aboard the ship, for Stanfield lived ashore at one of the slave-trading fortresses in Benin for eight months. His most basic conclusion sharply contradicted the then-prevalent proslavery propaganda about Africa and its peoples: "I never saw a happier race of people than those in the kingdom of BENIN." These people were "seated in ease and luxury" and engaged in extensive manufacturing, especially of cloth. The slave trade excepted, everything in their society "bore the appearance of friendship, tranquility, and primitive independence."[22]

Stanfield saw the slave trade as a destructive force, and indeed one of the most unusual features of his poem was his effort to understand it from an African perspective. Once the Guineaman arrived on the coast of Africa, the poet's point of view shifted from the ship to the "primeval forests" and the Niger River, where the continent's guardian empress surveyed the unfolding scene. Now that the enslaving chain had arrived from Liverpool, Stanfield asked,

> Say, can ye longer brook the savage hand,
> That, with rapacious av'rice, thins the land?
> Can ye restless see the ruthless chain
> Still spread its horrors o'er th' unpeopled plain?

Endless war, enslavement, forced migrations across the Atlantic, and fearful free migrations toward the interior had depopulated some areas of the West African coast, as Stanfield could see. The guardian empress watched as the slave traders poured in "savage swarms upon the blood-stain'd shore," toting "all their store of chains." The tables had been turned. The Europeans were now the savages, swarming ashore, chains in hand, to bind the peoples of Africa. This required Stanfield to recognize the dual role of the sailor—and presumably himself—who up to this point in the poem has been a victim of the slave trade but now must of necessity appear as a victimizer. He speaks frankly about "the miseries occasioned by European visitors." He notes that "*Europe's* pail sons direct the bar'brous prow, / And bring their stores and instruments of woe." He identifies the "pallid robbers," the "traffickers in human blood," and the "tyrant-whites." He mentions the "sad purchase": the "wan traders pay *the price of blood*." The sailor shares in the tyranny.

Soon "av'rice, busting ev'ry tender band, / Sweeps, like a deluge, thro' the hapless land." Traders white and black expropriate the Africans, rip them from their families and communities, and attach the telltale chains:

Our realms, alas! abandon'd to despair,
Supinely sunk, the slavish shackles wear.

How did they come to wear the shackles? How did they get caught in the "accursed chain"? Stanfield was convinced that most of the enslaved who came aboard the ship had been kidnapped, taken by "fraud and violence." They were not "prisoners of war" as advocates of the slave trade had always maintained. In Benin he "made continual inquiries but never heard of any wars." The enslaved were conveyed to the ships by the likes of the "Joe-men," led by King Badjeka, a nomadic, independent group of raiders who "pitched their temporary huts where they considered it to be most opportune for their depredations." They bought no slaves, but they sold multitudes of them to the slavers. Of a man soon to be on board the slaver, the sailor-poet wrote, "The hind returning from his daily care, / Seiz'd in the thicket, feels the ruffian's snare."

In an effort to make real for readers the human consequences of the slave trade in Africa, Stanfield included in his poem a life story of an African woman named Abyeda—how she was "torn from all kindred ties" and marched to the ship. It is unknown whether she was real or fictitious or some combination of the two. In any case, by writing about her, Stanfield helped to identify and publicize an emerging theme within the abolitionist movement: the special mistreatments and sufferings of enslaved women aboard the ship.[23]

Abyeda has been captured and brought on the slaver when Stanfield recounts her life in idyllic terms. She is a beautiful and "happy maid," in love with "youthful *Quam'no*," who protected her from the "treach'rous Whites" who traded in slaves. On their long-planned wedding day, she was seized:

In rush the spoilers with detested cry,
Seize with rapacious force the trembling prey;
And to the shore the hapless maid convey.

Quam'no tries to save her but is killed in the struggle. Devastated, Abyeda is carried aboard the ship, where she is chained to the mast and lashed (for what reason Stanfield does not say). As she groans with each stroke of the lash, the other women aboard the ship, her "sad associates," join in sympathy, and in a variation on traditional African call-and-response, cry out in cadence. Soon, "o'er her wan face the deadly jaundice steals," and the end finally comes: "Convulsive throbs expel the final breath, / And o'er the fatal close sits ghastly death." Stanfield's description suggests a real death, and maybe several, he had seen.[24]

Meanwhile, as the stay on the coast of Africa drags on, the miseries of the crew deepen. Having been off the ship for a time, Stanfield returned to find the second mate "lying on his back on the medicine-chest; his head hanging down over one end of it, his hair sweeping the deck, and clotted with the filth that was collected there." He soon died, unnoticed. Matters were even more shocking on the poop deck, where several members of the ship's crew were stretched out "in the last stage of their sickness, without comfort, without refreshment, without attendance. There they lay, straining their weak voices with the most lamentable cries for a little water, and not a soul to afford them the smallest relief." Stanfield then "passed a night of misery with them," after which he was convinced that another night would have meant his doom. One of these deaths may have belonged to his friend ("Russel"), who in the poem developed "sallow skin," "putrid sores," "palsied limbs," and expired amid the "filth and blood." Russel's last words concern his beloved, Maria. His body was dumped into a "fluid grave," "his honour'd corse in awful form dispos'd."

Stanfield also attempted to capture what Equiano called the astonishment and terror felt by "each agitated guest" when he or she came aboard the huge, seemingly magical slave ship:

Torn as his bosom is, still wonder grows,
As o'er the vast machine the victim goes,
Wonder, commix'd with anguish, shakes his frame
At the strange sight his language cannot name.

For all that meets his eye, above, below,
Seem but to him the instruments of woe.

One by one, the captives were "compressive stow'd" in the floating dungeon, immersed in the "putrid smell" and "deadly gloom" of the lower deck. Finally the ship "hoists the sail full, and quits the wasted shore."

Middle Passage

Stanfield and the other survivors from the *Eagle* now boarded the *True Blue,* bound for Jamaica, their lower deck packed with "shackled sufferers." Hence began the notorious Middle Passage, which the sailor-poet strove to describe in its "true colours." The ship over the next several weeks became an even more macabre chamber of horrors. Stanfield introduced his account by saying, "This horrid portion of the voyage was but one continued scene of barbarity, unremitting labour, mortality, and disease. Flogging, as in the outward passage, was a principal amusement in this."[25]

Captain Wilson was sick during the Middle Passage, but this seemed to Stanfield only to increase his tyranny. In his weakened state, the monarch of the wooden world made the crew carry him around bodily, all the while keeping "trade knives" close at hand to throw at people who incurred his displeasure. One after another member of the crew was cut down. The new second mate died not long after the captain had knocked him to the deck and severely gashed his head. The cook earned the captain's wrath by burning some dinner meat and was soon "beaten most violently with the spit." He crawled away and died within a day or two.

Seamen were also forced to work when sick, sometimes with fatal consequences. The boatswain, who was ill and unable to stand, was propped up on one of the mess-tubs from the lower deck and made to steer the vessel, which, in truth, he was too weak to do. He soon died, and his "body was, as usual, thrown overboard, without any covering but the shirt." The next day "his corps was discovered floating alongside, and kept close to us for some hours—it was a horrid spectacle, and seemed to give us an idea of the body of a victim calling out to heaven for vengeance on our barbarity!" Another sick sailor crawled out of his hammock and collapsed on the gratings. Describing what he found the following morning, Stanfield wrote, "I shudder at the bare recollection." The man "was still alive, but covered with blood—the hogs has picked his toes to the bones, and his body was otherwise mangled by them in a manner too shocking to relate."

Most of the manglings were man-made, and indeed the captain seemed to take a special delight in observing them. Because of his debility, he ordered anyone to be flogged tied to his bedpost so he could see the victims face-to-face, "enjoying their agonizing screams, while their flesh was lacerated without mercy: this was a frequent and a favourite mode of punishment." The captain's violence now had a broader object, the crew and the enslaved, who in Stanfield's view were trapped in the same system of terror.

> *Pallid* or *black*—the *free* or *fetter'd* band,
> Fall undistinguish'd by his ruffian hand.
> Nor age's awe, nor sex's softness charm;
> Nor law, nor feeling, stop his blood-steep'd arm.

This was true for both sailors and slaves: "Flogging, that favourite exercise, was in continual use with the poor Negroes as well as the seamen." It operated without regard to race, age, gender, law, or humanity.

Like many sailors, Stanfield thought that the slaves were in certain respects better off than the crew. At least the captain had an economic incentive to feed them and keep them alive during the Middle Passage. He wrote, "The slaves, with regard to attention paid to their health and diet, claim, from the purpose of the voyage, a condition superior to the seamen." But he was quick to qualify the statement: "when the capricious and irascible passions of their general tyrant were once set afloat, I never could see any difference in the cruelty of their treatment." He also argued against the standard proslavery refrain that "interest" would cause the captain to treat the "cargo" well. The "internal passions, that seem to be nourished in the very vitals of this employ, bid defiance to every power of controul." The Demon Cruelty routinely battered and bested rational concerns.

The ship was now full of its "sad freight." Stanfield offered a powerful view of the enslaved jammed belowdecks at night:

> Pack'd in close misery, the reeking crowd,
> Sweltering in chains, pollute the hot abode.
> In painful rows with studious art comprest,
> Smoking they lie, and breathe the humid pest:
> Moisten'd with gore, on the hard platform ground,
> The bare-rub'd joint soon bursts the painful bound;
> Sinks in the obdurate plank with racking force,
> And ploughs,—dire talk, its agonizing course!

Stanfield was conscious of the sounds of the slave ship—the "long groan," "strain of anguish," cries, death songs, "shrieks of woe and howlings of despair!" All in this instance were heard in the midnight hour. Sickness was a big part of the experience. Breathing "infected air" amid "green contagion," the fevered lie "strew'd o'er the filthy deck." Stanfield followed abolitionist surgeon Alexander Falconbridge in saying that the slave ship was "like a slaughterhouse. Blood, filth, misery, and disease."

Stanfield noted individual responses among the enslaved to this grim reality, which ranged from sad defeat to fiery indignation:

> Look at yon wretch (a melancholy case!)
> Grief in his eye, despair upon his face;
> His fellow—see—from orbs of blood-shot ire
> On his pale tyrants dart the indignant fire!

Stanfield chronicled another horror of the Middle Passage, the opening, in the morning, of the grates and the emergence of the enslaved from sixteen hours of darkness belowdecks. Stanfield imagined the aperture as a "noisome cave," even a monster's mouth: from belowdecks the "rank maw, belched up in morbid steam, / The hot mist thickens in a side-long beam." In "fetter'd pairs" the "drooping crowd" emerged. He described two men in particular who were "close united by the fest'ring chain." They had to be lifted up from below. One had died overnight; one was still living. Once unshackled, the dead man would be "to the sea consign'd"; the corpse the "briny monsters seize with savage force." Sharks, Stanfield understood, were part of the ship's terror.

The daily routine began, and "a joyless meal the tyrant-whites prepare." For those who refused to eat, "stripe follows stripe, in boundless, brutal rage." The pain of the whip caused some to faint. For those who were lashed and still refused to eat, the dreaded *speculum oris* was brought on deck:

> Then: See the vile engines in the hateful cause
> Are plied relentless in the straining jaws
> The wrenching instruments with barbarous force
> Shew the detested food th' unwilling course.

Two women, who were among "the finest slaves on the ship," watched the violence and took rebellious action. They poignantly folded themselves in each other's arms and "plunged over the poop of the vessel into the sea." As they drowned, the other women "cried out in a most affecting manner, and many of them were preparing to follow their companions." They were locked belowdecks immediately to prevent mass suicide.

Stanfield recalled a night when the slaves on the lower deck were already "packed together to a degree of pain" and then required to make room for another boatload of captives brought on board. This resulted in "much noise" as the quarters grew even more cramped. In the women's room, one of the new captives threw over one of the mess-tubs. The next morning she was tied to the captain's bedpost, "with her face close to his," and ordered to be whipped. When the "unwilling executioner" (whether a sailor or slave, Stanfield does not say) took pity on the woman and did not whip her as hard as the captain commanded, he in turn was tied up and given a "violent lashing." Soon after, the flogging of the woman resumed. Stanfield, who had inherited the medicine chest after the death of the doctor even though he was not qualified for the practice, dressed her wounds.

Finally, Stanfield mentioned, but refused to describe, what must have been the rape of a small girl by the captain. He made reference only to something "practised by the captain on an unfortunate female slave, of the age of eight or nine." Although he could not bring himself to name the crime—"I cannot express it in any words"—he nonetheless insisted that it was "too atrocious and bloody to be passed over in silence." He considered the act to be an example of the daily "barbarity and despotism" of the slave trade.

As the dark ship plowed the waves toward the plantations of the Caribbean, the sailors continued to weaken and die, which required yet another recomposition of the ship's working order. Stanfield explained, "As the crew fell off, an accumulated weight of labour pressed upon the few survivors—and, towards the end of the middle passage, all idea of keeping the slaves in chains was given up." The captain ordered many of the enslaved men unchained, brought up on deck, and taught how to work the ship, because "there was not strength enough left among the white men, to pull a single rope with effect." The enslaved "pulled and hawled" the ropes and sails as directed from the deck by the debilitated sailors. The slave ship was thus brought to its destination by people who would soon be sold there.

One Dreadful Shriek

When the ship reached its New World destination, it underwent yet another transformation, this one associated with a practice called the "scramble," by which the enslaved were sold on board the vessel. The main deck was enclosed and darkened, tentlike, by the hanging of canvas sails and tarred curtains all around: "Now o'er the gloomy ship, in villain guise, / The shrouding canvas drawn, shuts out the skies." The enslaved had been cleaned up—shaved, oiled, sores disguised—and were now arrayed on deck but apparently did not understand what was to happen next. They were in the dark, both literally and figuratively, arranged in rows, trembling, "dumb and almost lifeless." Once the signal had been given, prospective buyers rushed aboard in a mad, disorderly way, throwing cords—the transatlantic chain—around the slaves they wished to purchase:

> With cords now furnish'd, and the impious chain,
> And all the hangman-garniture of pain,
> Rush the dread fiends, and with impetuous sway,
> Fasten rapacious on the shudd'ring prey.

The enslaved were terrified, as indeed they were meant to be, during this second sale aboard the ship. Shrieks pierced the skies, and tears flowed from "wounded eyes." Several of the panicked slaves found openings in the canvas enclosure and threw themselves into the water, and another died of fright:

> Struck with dismay, see yonder fainting heap!
> Yon rushing group plunge headlong in the deep!
> (With the fierce blast extinct the vital fires)
> Yon falling maid, shrieks—shivers—and expires.

The next stage was the dispersion of the ship's enslaved population, as the newly purchased were crowded into small boats and carried away one load after another. Stanfield was conscious that this was yet one more moment of rupture, this time of the bonds that had been formed among the enslaved on the ship, during the stay on the coast and the Middle Passage. As the cords tightened and pulled them away, the enslaved tried to hold fast to their family members, friends, and comrades, without success. The tumult of screaming and crying did not weaken, it only grew louder:

> One dreadful shriek assaults th' affrighted sky,
> As to their friends the parted victims cry.
> With imprecating screams of horror wild,
> The frantick mother calls her sever'd child.

One universal tumult raves around;
From boat to ship responds the frantick sound.

The enslaved were once again "separated from their connexions," their shipmates. The slaving voyage ends amid the "frantick sound" of "horror wild."[26]

Real Enlightenment

James Field Stanfield's account of the slave trade was in many ways more detailed, more gruesome, and, in a word, more dramatic, than anything that had yet appeared in print by May 1788. His eye for the "horrid scene"—the fiery eyes of the man in chains brought up from the lower deck, the sick mate's long hair clotted in filth—gave his accounts evocative power. A critic at the *Monthly Review* noted that in *The Guinea Voyage* Stanfield "dwells on every minute circumstance in this tale of cruelty, and obliges us to witness every pang of complicated misery!" Such was Stanfield's dramatic strategy, to make the slave ship and its people and their sufferings real.[27]

Stanfield presented the ship itself, the material setting of the drama, in a variety of ways, depending on its function at a given moment of the voyage and from whose perspective it was observed. It was at first a thing of beauty, then a "vast machine" to its workers, and finally a "floating dungeon" to sailors and especially the enslaved. Almost everyone was a captive in one way or another and subject to an institutionalized system of terror and death. The transatlantic chain encompassed all, whether the path to the slave ship originated in a walk with a constable from the Liverpool jail or a coffle march with raiders from the interior of Africa. But of course the ship was worst for the enslaved, for whom it appeared as a collection of "instruments of woe"—shackles, manacles, neck rings, locks, chains, the cat-o'-nine tails, the *speculum oris*. The lower deck was a "floating cave," the hatchway a belching, monstrous mouth. The carceral slave ship ate people alive.

The characters in Stanfield's drama included the "merciful" slave merchant, whose avarice produced rapacity, destruction, and murder.

Indeed the killing was planned, as he calculated how many would go on the "dead list" in order to make his profits. Next came the "humane" Guinea captain, the keeper of the floating dungeon. A torturer, rapist, and killer, he was variously barbarous, tyrannical, fiendish, despotic, and at the deepest level demonic. He possessed the "dark pow'r / Of savage rigour." The ship's officers, potentially noble and brave, were agents of violence on the one hand, and victims of violence on the other. They died without care or comfort. Stanfield generously considered some of them the "unwilling instruments" of barbarity and cruelty.

The sailor, according to Stanfield, was the almost stereotypical jolly jack-tar—heedless, thoughtless, often drunken, but also truthful, hardworking, and virtuous. The crew, many of them having been forced from landed dungeon to floating dungeon, were less responsible than those above them for the horrors of the slave trade, but they were certainly complicit as prison guards, as wielders of the cruel "instruments of woe," and ultimately as "white men." Wagering that the reading public would sympathize with the sailor, protector of the realm and a symbol of British pride, Stanfield joined Clarkson and other abolitionists in playing a racial and national trump card.

Stanfield depicted Africans in a variety of ways. Black slave traders such as the Joe-men were pictured straightforwardly as ruthless predators, like their white counterparts. The Fante, who worked aboard the ship and were no less central to the slave trade, were strong and courageous, perhaps ennobled by the dignity of seafaring labor as opposed to body snatching. Based on his experience in Benin, Stanfield depicted free Africans as full of "friendship, tranquility, primitive independence." Abyeda was a "happy maid" until captured. Such people lived more or less as "noble savages" in an Edenic state until European barbarians intruded, destroyed, and enslaved. The "fetter'd crowd," taken aboard the ship, appeared primarily as victims, with an occasional act of resistance. Belowdecks they did nothing but suffer. On the main deck, other possibilities appeared, as for example when the collective power of the enslaved women reared its head on several occasions. At the point of sale in Jamaica, everyone was wretched, terrified, and lifeless.

Stanfield says nothing to suggest that he actually got to know any of the African people on his voyage (unless perhaps Abyeda), nor does it appear that he tried to free anyone. He apparently considered himself powerless in the "floating dungeon," at the time and in retrospect. He might have shown compassion to various individuals, as for example when he dressed the wounds of the slave woman lashed by Captain Wilson. He certainly showed compassion after he left the ship, suggesting that while he experienced revulsion at his experience in the slave trade, it took a social movement to agitate and activate him in purposeful opposition. He also resisted the vulgar racist stereotypes of the day and wrote about the slave trade with an antiracializing rhetoric. All people were, for instance, "of one blood."

In the end, Stanfield appealed to the immediate, visceral experience of the slave ship, over and against abstract knowledge about the slave trade, as decisive to abolition, and indeed he helped to make it so. He explained, "One *real* view—one MINUTE absolutely spent in the slave rooms on the middle passage, would do more for the cause of humanity, than the pen of a *Robertson,* or the whole collective eloquence of the British senate." Real enlightenment began not with a Scottish philosopher or a member of Parliament, but rather in the meeting of a sailor and a slave amid the "instruments of woe" on board the "vast machine," the slave ship.[28]

CHAPTER 6

John Newton and the
Peaceful Kingdom

The eighteenth-century sea captain was a figure of almost unlimited power, as John Newton wrote to his wife, Mary, early in his first voyage as master of a slaver:

My condition when abroad, and even in Guinea, might be envied by multitudes who stay at home. I am as absolute in my small dominions (life and death excepted) as any potentate in Europe. If I say to one, Come, he comes; if to another, Go, he flies. If I order one person to do something, perhaps three or four will be ambitious for a share in the service. Not a man in the ship must eat his dinner till I please to give him leave; nay, nobody dares to say it is 12 or 8 o'clock, in my hearing, till I think it is proper to say so first. There is a mighty business of attendance when I leave the ship, and strict watch kept while I am absent, lest I should return unawares, and not be received in due form. And should I stay out till midnight, (which for that reason, I never do without necessity) nobody must presume to shut their eyes, till they have had the honour of seeing me again. I would have you judge from my manner of relating these ceremonials, that I do not value them highly for their own sake; but they are old established customs, and necessary to be kept up; for, without a strict discipline, the common sailors would be unmanageable.

In the sovereign space of the ship, captains commanded labor, subsistence, even the reckoning of time. The captain of a slaver wielded the greatest power of all, for he had to manage not only dozens of common sailors but hundreds of captive Africans.[1]

John Newton has long been the best-known captain in the history of the African slave trade. He made four voyages, one as mate and three as captain, between 1748 and 1754, but his fame derives from his subsequent career, in which he became an active, visible minister of evangelical bent in the Church of England, wrote numerous hymns, most famously "Amazing Grace," and finally toward the end of his life publicly rejected his own past and embraced the cause of abolition. He wrote a vivid pamphlet about the horrors of the trade in 1788, entitled *Thoughts upon the African Slave Trade,* and he testified in similar fashion before committees of the House of Commons in 1789 and 1790. He declared himself a sinner who had seen the error of his ways.[2]

Newton left a uniquely rich documentary record of his involvement in the slave trade, as a sailor, as a "slave" himself, as a mate, and finally as a captain. He was a prolific writer. Like most masters he kept logs of his voyages, detailing the daily business of work, winds, and weather, but he went further. He was an avid correspondent: he wrote 127 letters to Mary during his slaving travels and a series of letters to the Anglican divine David Jennings. He also kept a spiritual diary during the last two voyages. Later, as an introspective Christian minister, he reflected on his life to draw from it the proper moral lessons—in 1763, when he penned a series of letters in spiritual autobiography, and in the late 1780s, when he joined the rising abolitionist movement. Newton may have written more from the decks of a slave ship—and more about what transpired on the decks of a slave ship—than has any other captain in the almost four centuries of the trade.[3]

John Newton wielded absolute power in his wooden world, in his management of the daily routines of the slave ship and in his control over the likes of Olaudah Equiano and James Field Stanfield. He would assert "strict discipline" over both sailors and slaves, who would in turn resist. He would respond in various ways, often with violence, to maintain and reassert his control. His power and position were such that what appeared to Equiano as terror, and to Stanfield as horror, appeared to the captain as good order. By recording his hopes and fears, his contemplations and actions, and his many social relationships in careful, introspective detail, Newton provides unparalleled insight into the life of a slave-ship captain.

From Rebel Sailor to Christian Captain

John Newton was in many ways fated to be a ship captain. His father was a captain (in the Mediterranean trade), and he carried a shipboard demeanor into domestic life, as his son recalled: "he always observed an air of distance and severity of carriage, which overawed and discouraged my spirit." The elder Newton groomed his son for command at sea from an early age. Young Newton was, in the eighteenth-century phrase, "bred to the sea"—that is, placed aboard a ship at the age of eleven as an apprentice so he could learn the work, acquire the experience, and rise through the ranks. He made several voyages between 1736 and 1742 and was in 1743 impressed aboard HMS *Harwich,* whereupon his father got the lad of eighteen a preferment to midshipman. Now a member of the Royal Navy, he gained the patronage of a captain and seemed to be on his way up in the maritime world.[4]

But young Newton proved rather wild and refractory, and his path to the captain's cabin would be a crooked one. Having lived and worked at sea, he was, he later recalled, "exposed to the company and ill example of the common sailors," whose oppositional values and practices he soon imbibed. He became a freethinker, a libertine, and a rebel. Looking back on this period, Newton recalled his egalitarian and antiauthoritarian impulses: "I was once so proud that I acknowledged no superior."[5]

So when he was sent ashore by his captain, in a boatload of sailors to prevent their desertion, Newton himself deserted, but not for long. He was quickly captured, jailed for two days, sent back aboard the ship, kept in irons, "then publicly stripped and whipped." He was also busted back from midshipman to common seaman. "I was now in my turn brought down to a level with the lowest, and exposed to the insults of all," he wrote. (He was reviled because he had borne his midshipman's authority rather too haughtily.) His spurned and now-vindictive naval captain planned to place the turbulent sailor aboard an East India ship for a five-year voyage. When he learned of this, Newton first contemplated suicide but decided instead to murder the captain. "I actually formed designs against his life," Newton confessed later.

The captain's life might have been saved by the chance appearance of a slave ship on the horizon. The master of the slaver apparently had some mutinous men on board and wanted, as was common, to put them on board the man-of-war in exchange for a few naval sailors. Newton enthusiastically volunteered for the exchange to escape the threatened East India voyage. The naval captain let him go and probably thought good riddance. Newton thus got into the slave trade by a combination of his own rebelliousness and an accidental meeting of ships at sea.

It so happened that the slave-ship captain knew Newton's father, but neither this connection nor the fresh start caused Newton to change his ways: "I had a little of that unlucky wit, which can do little more than multiply troubles and enemies of its possessor; and, upon some imagined affront, I made a song, in which I ridiculed his [the captain's] ship, his designs, and his person, and soon taught it to the whole ship's company." The captain would not have been amused as Newton and his brother tars ridiculed him in song, but no matter, as he soon died. What did matter was that the chief mate who ascended to command liked Newton no better and promptly threatened to put him back aboard a man-of-war at the first opportunity. Horrified by the thought, Newton took again to his fast feet and deserted the ship, with nothing more than the clothes on his back. He got ashore on Plantain Island at the mouth of the Sherbro River on the coast of Sierra Leone.

Newton went to work for a local white trader, who acted as a middleman between African merchants and the slave ships. Newton then got into trouble with his new boss and found himself mistreated and abused. He made a bad situation worse by falling afoul of the trader's black wife, who essentially got him enslaved. He was chained, starved, beaten, and mocked. His almost-naked body was blistered by the tropical sun, but this did not keep him from studying Euclid and "drawing diagrams with a long stick upon the sand." Over the course of an endless year, he survived on raw roots and on food given to him "by strangers; nay, even by the slaves in the chain, who have secretly brought me victuals (for they durst not be seen to do it) from their own slender pittance." Would he remember this kindness? He later quoted chapter 16 of the book of Ezekiel to describe himself as "an outcast lying in my blood." His treatment, he wrote, "broke my constitution and my spirits." Newton considered himself a "slave," someone "depressed to the lowest degree of human wretchedness."[6]

Newton eventually escaped this trader and went to work for another at Kittam. His situation improved, and indeed he became happy, primarily by adapting to African culture. He explained the transformation this way:

> There is a significant phrase frequently used in those parts, That such a white man is grown black. It does not intend an alteration of complexion, but disposition. I have known several, who, settling in Africa after the age of thirty or forty, have, at that time of life, been gradually assimilated to the tempers, customs, and ceremonies, of the natives, so far as to prefer that country to England: they have even become dupes to all the pretended charms, necromancies, amulets, and divinations of the blinded negroes, and put more trust in such things than the wiser sort among the natives. A part of this spirit of infatuation was growing upon me, (in time perhaps I might have yielded to the whole); I entered into closer engagements with the inhabitants; and should have lived and died a wretch among them, if the Lord had not watched over me for good.

Newton's "closer engagements" probably means that he took an African "wife," maybe more than one. But the situation was transitory. The white man who had grown black soon reverted.

After he went to work for yet a third slave merchant, he one day in February 1747 encountered a vessel called the *Greyhound,* whose captain came ashore and asked a startling question: had anyone at this trading post seen a man named John Newton? The captain, it turned out, was yet another friend of Newton's ubiquitous father. Perhaps in fear of the distant, severe patriarch, Newton did not want to return to Liverpool, but the captain would not be denied. He devised a stratagem, announcing that Newton had just inherited money and must return to England to claim it. This Newton was willing to do, but once aboard the ship he fell back into his oppositional ways, delighting in mischief, inventing new oaths, ridiculing "gospel-history," and glorying in "impiety and profaneness." The captain took to calling him Jonah, the source of all problems on the voyage.

During the homeward passage, Newton "was awaked from a sound sleep by the force of a violent sea, which broke on board us." Wet and astonished, he heard the cry from above that the ship was sinking. As Newton scrambled up to the main deck, one of his shipmates was swept overboard. The sea had torn away the upper timbers on one side, allowing torrents of water to gush in. The force of the waves splintered casks and carried livestock over the side. Newton and several other crewmen took to the pump, while others bailed with buckets and pails and stuffed their clothes and bedding as plugs into the weeping seams of the ship. Fortunately, the vessel had only a light cargo, beeswax and wood, both lighter than water, but at the moment this seemed no saving grace. Newton pumped furiously and tried to inspire his mates, but discouragement rose with the water in the hold. After several hours Newton went to the captain and said, "If this will not do, the Lord have mercy upon us." He surprised himself with these words and went back to the pump, where everyone now secured himself with ropes to keep from being washed away. After nine hours of backbreaking work, Newton collapsed into his bed, "uncertain, and almost indifferent, whether I should rise again." He slowly began to pray; the moment of his religious conversion was at hand. The winds and waves finally abated, and Newton considered his survival to be "an immediate and almost miraculous interposition of Divine Power." The remaining crew got ashore in Ireland and eventually back to Liverpool, where Newton arrived with no money, no friends, and no prospect of employment, but with a new faith and a resolution never to return to Africa.[7]

His resolve would soon be tested. The merchant Joseph Manesty, yet another friend of his father's, offered him command of a slave ship. Having never made a proper slaving voyage, Newton was reluctant to accept the lucrative offer, thinking that he lacked knowledge and experience. He therefore agreed to go on one voyage as a mate, with Captain Richard Jackson in the *Brownlow*. Newton kept a journal of the voyage, but, unlike his other personal accounts, it has not survived. Nonetheless it is clear from other evidence that he must have had a trying time. As mate, his main responsibility on the African coast was "to sail from place to place in the long-boat to purchase slaves." During the rainy season, he spent five or six days at a time in the boat, "without, as we say, a dry thread around me, sleeping or waking." He saw several sailors poisoned while ashore, "and in my own boat I buried six or seven people with fevers." More than once he was thrown out of his vessel by the violence of the surf and "brought to land half-dead, (for I could not swim)." Others drowned. Then a major slave insurrection broke out aboard the ship, resulting in significant loss of life, and a large portion of the enslaved died before the ship got to Charleston, South Carolina: 62 of 218 perished, a high mortality rate of 28.4 percent. Newton, however, was apparently undeterred, for after the *Brownlow* docked in Liverpool on December 1, 1749, he began preparations to assume command of Manesty's *Duke of Argyle,* in which he would take his first voyage as a master. He was only twenty-four years old, but he had the sea in his blood and he now had hard-won experience in the slave trade.[8]

First Voyage, 1750–51

Having made an arrangement with Mr. Manesty and begun to secure a cargo, Newton hired his crew. He wrote a list of their names but said little about them as individuals. He did, however, provide something of a collective portrait. He wrote that a few of them had, like himself, been "bred to it young" but added that "as of late years people in cred- itable life have too much disdain'd bringing up their Children this way." Most of his sailors were therefore not young men of respectable backgrounds who were learning the trade in order eventually to rise to a position of authority. They were rather what Newton called "the re- fuse and dregs of the Nation," the poor and the dispossessed. Many of them of them were jailbirds and runaways of various kinds, from the army, navy, workshops, or parents. Others were down on their luck, "already ruin'd by some untimely vice," not least alcoholism. A few may have been landsmen who had no experience at sea. Almost none of them had "good principles." If any of the better sort signed on, Newton ruefully noted, they were driven away by the degenerate com- pany they were forced to keep aboard the slave ship. Controlling such a rough crew would occupy a great deal of the captain's time and thought.[9]

Newton hired twenty-nine men and boys to fill specific roles aboard the *Duke of Argyle:* a surgeon, three mates, a boatswain, carpenter, gunner, cooper, tailor, steward, and cook; eleven "able seamen," three less-skilled "ordinary seamen," and three boys, or apprentices. Newton also hired a fiddler, for entertainment, no doubt, but also to exercise the slaves in what was euphemistically called "dancing."

At noon on August 11, 1750, Newton gave the order to cast off, whereupon the *Duke of Argyle* began its voyage from Liverpool to the Windward Coast of Africa and from there to Antigua in the West In- dies. The vessel was a snow (or snauw), meaning a two-masted vessel, of modest size at a hundred tons, with ten mounted cannon and a siz- able crew of thirty. The vessel was old, built in 1729; this was appar- ently only its second adventure as a Guineaman. Merchant Manesty intended that Newton should buy and carry a large cargo for the smallish ship—250 slaves, or 2.5 to a ton. Knowing this, Newton would have im- mediately calculated crew size: with thirty sailors he would have nearly a one-to-eight ratio, crew to enslaved, which he would have considered favorable, better than the usual one to ten.[10]

During the outward passage, which would last ten weeks, the *Duke of Argyle* would be transformed into a proper slaver as the carpenter, gunner, and boatswain readied the essential technologies of control. Newton noted on September 25: "Carpenter begun to raise the gratings of the women's room." He also marked off the various rooms and commenced to build the bulkheads to separate them, enclosing the apartments to hold men, women, and boys. He constructed a washroom for the women near the main chains, then built platforms on the lower deck, extending six feet from each side of the ship to the interior, in each apartment. The space between decks on Newton's ship was about five feet, so the headroom for the enslaved above and below the platform would have been roughly two feet four inches. Newton noted on November 19, probably with some relief (because slaves had already begun to come on board), that "the carpenter has finished the barricado."

Meanwhile the gunner was busy preparing the ship's firepower, making cartridges for the carriage and swivel guns. He also cleaned and loaded the small arms, checking each one to be sure it worked properly. A few had to be condemned, "being absolutely good for nothing, the worst I ever saw in my life," complained Newton. The boatswain, for his part, attached the netting to prevent escape or suicide by the enslaved. On December 7 the carpenter and gunner joined forces: "This day fixed 4 swivel blunderbusses in the barricado, which with the 2 carriage guns we put upon the main deck, and will, I hope, be sufficient to intimidate the slaves from any thoughts of an insurrection." These guns were elevated in order to fire down on any who dared to rebel.[11]

Newton encountered his first major disciplinary problem with the crew on October 24, when he returned from visiting Captain Ellis aboard the *Halifax* to discover that the boatswain had, in his absence, "behaved very turbulently," abusing several other members of the crew, all of which was "to the hindrance of the ship's business." Newton promptly clapped the man "in irons, in terrorem, being apprehensive he might occasion disturbance, when we got the slaves on board."

Newton thus expressed for the first time a worry about the spread of resistance. Three days later the boatswain had had enough. "Upon his submission and promise of amendment," Newton let him out of his confinement. This was but the first of actions to be taken in terrorem.

A week later Newton found, to his dismay, that a boatload of his sailors did not return from the Banana Islands to the *Duke of Argyle* as they were supposed to have done but rather went on board a French schooner and got drunk. They then went ashore to fight and got stuck there because the ebb tide was strong and they were too inebriated to pull their oars properly. Newton was forced to send a boatload of sober sailors after them. The captain therefore "gave two of my gentlemen a good caning and put one (William Lees) in irons, both for his behaviour in the boat and likewise being very troublesome last night, refusing to keep his watch and threatening the boatswain." Lees got saucy and swore he would not serve Newton. He would rather remain in chains all the way to Antigua. After three days stapled to the deck, he changed his mind. He petitioned the captain for release and promised better behavior. Newton accepted his offer, but the drama with this unruly sailor was far from over.

As the *Duke of Argyle* prepared to depart from the Banana Islands, Lees tried to desert by hiding himself ashore. Newton eventually found him, drunk and belligerent again, and was forced to pay some of the local natives a gallon of brandy to secure him in irons and carry him aboard the ship. When a group of African traders came aboard the slaver a few days later, Lees saw among them one who had helped to capture him, so he picked up a carpenter's maul and swung it viciously at the man's head, narrowly missing and instead grazing his breast. Newton was forced to give the man a laced hat in apology. He cuffed Lees and chained him to the deck again, adding for good measure his insolent and aptly named comrades Tom Creed and Tom True. Newton ended up putting these three and another mutinous sailor, Owen Cavanagh, aboard HMS *Surprize,* taking four sailors from the naval ship in return.

The purchasing of slaves soon began. Because the Windward Coast had no fortresses where large numbers of slaves were held pending arrival of the slave ships, Newton used his own ship as a factory, bringing black traders on board as he dispatched his boat and yawl to fetch "cargo" from the shore. He got word early that his work would not be easy. On October 23 he met with Captain Duncan of the *Cornwall,* who had been on the coast for six months and had managed to buy only fifty slaves.

The hurry and bustle of the trade commenced as the boats and canoes began their endless coming and going, to and from the *Duke of Argyle.* Shoreside traders made large fires in the night to signal their desire to come aboard. Newton received dignitaries such as the king of Charra and Prince William Ansah Setarakoo, who, returning to the Gold Coast from a visit to England, spent an evening with the captain. It was all "very much to my satisfaction," Newton wrote, he "being master of a great deal of solid sense and a politeness of behaviour I seldom meet with in any of our own complexion hereabouts." Most visitors were traders with anglicized names, such as Samuel Skinner, "Yellow Will," or, most important of all, the mulatto merchant Henry Tucker, who would be feted as he spent nights on board and given large quantities of "iron bars" (a main trade currency) on credit in exchange for the promise of slaves to be delivered in the future. On one occasion, when he gave Tucker a large part of his trading cargo, Newton lamented, "I cannot properly call this lending him money, for I am, rather, obliged to him to take it." The main advantage in dealing with Tucker, compared to all of the others, Newton thought, was his honesty. He noted, "I believe them to be all villains to a man except him." Newton felt a keen dependency on these men, was forced to humor them, and he resented it. He wrote on March 27, "Our slow purchase and pressing season reduces me to court those whose behaviour I have reason to resent and despise." He also thought longer stays on the coast meant higher mortality, so he was frustrated when forced to "do business (if I do any) just as it suits the humour and convenience of the people on shoar who are seldom in a hurry." He added an exclamation: "Patience!"

The trade itself was suffused with tension; indeed it took place within what Newton called a "warlike peace." He continued, "We trade under arms; and they are furnished with long knives." Previous depredations made African traders wary, retaliations were common, and fraud was the order of the day on both sides. Newton may have been surprised when he accused a black trader of malpractice and got an indignant reply: "What! Do you think I am a white man?"[12]

Newton began to purchase his cargo, selectively at first as instructed by Mr. Manesty. He was shown seven people on Bance Island, but he took only three. He was offered a woman slave, "who I refused being long breasted." He soon rejected two more "fallen breasted women" and four more slaves he considered too old. But he soon saw the truth of Captain Duncan's experience. Trade was slow and prices were high. No slave ships lay at anchor from Sierra Leone south to Mana, "the whole country [being] in a flame of war." The war would eventually produce slaves, but it was not producing any at the moment. Newton was therefore forced to buy what he considered lower "quality." On January 7, 1751, he bought a woman "tho she had a very bad mouth." He began, with misgivings, to buy more children. Newton wrote little in his journal about how these people had come to be enslaved, but later in life he noted that some were prisoners of war, some were convicts, some were born slaves in Africa and had been sold, and some had simply been kidnapped. He was convinced that most of them had come great distances from the interior of the Windward Coast. Perhaps their bodies bore the marks of hard travel.

In early March an eerie opportunity presented itself. Newton was offered for purchase a surprisingly large number of prime slaves. He immediately—and rightly—suspected that these were the people who had recently risen up and "cut off" a French slaver not far away, killed the captain and crew, and escaped, only to be retaken by coastal traders and now resold. Would he take violent rebels aboard his own ship? Would he capitalize on the misfortunes of another slave captain? He would. Newton bought two large lots, including "the principals in taking the vessel." He was "sorry to reflect I owe it to another's misfortune, they being all the Frenchman's slaves." Yet he was "obliged to dissemble at present and say little" or else "hurt my own business without any advantage to the sufferers." He resolved to take as many of the slaves as he could get. Newton later took comfort in learning from Henry Tucker that the French captain was still alive; Tucker had redeemed him from local captors. Still, six members of the crew had been murdered and three more driven overboard. Newton now had the experience of an almost-successful insurrection aboard his vessel.

The work of guarding the ever-growing slave population aboard the ship became more important than ever, but so did the daily acts of buying and storing provisions, feeding the enslaved, and cleaning their quarters. Early on in the process of purchasing slaves, on December 18, Newton noted, "Having now 12 men slaves on board [out of 36] began this day with chains and sentrys." The slaves were brought on board as "enemies." Newton and crew assumed that they would do whatever they could to escape their bondage and regain their freedom. The men slaves would therefore be chained in the usual way, by twos, and armed guards would routinely pace the decks. Newton also initiated the regular firing of the small arms, often during mealtime when everyone was on deck, explicitly for the sake of intimidation and terror. The guns would then be cleaned and reloaded, readied for the next scheduled firing, or worse. Nettings were repaired to prevent escape, the barricado was respiked at the top, and the slave quarters were regularly searched for weapons. On the evening of May 6, wrote the captain, "The people found 2 knives and a bag of small stones in the men's room." The male captives were sullen, and many would remain so throughout the voyage. The "scorching days and damp foggy nights" were filling with tension.[13]

Newton incarcerated the enslaved on the lower deck, where they would breathe an almost-unbearable "hot and corrupted air." At night the captives had trouble making their way through the crowd and the darkness to the "necessary tubs," where the enslaved relieved themselves. Furious fights broke out between those chained to each other and between one who stepped on another. Sometimes, Newton noted, the tubs themselves turned over, making a horrific situation worse.

Meanwhile the bodies of the enslaved were rubbed raw by their chains and by being rolled around on the rough wooden planks of the lower deck as a result of the incessant tossing of the ship. On any given morning when the weather was good, after the gratings were lifted and the slaves brought up onto the main deck for "airing," feeding, and "dancing," Newton and crew might find a dead man shackled to a living one. The dead went over the side of the ship as the living were locked down by a chain reeved through their irons and attached to ringbolts fastened at intervals on the deck. Here they would be fed twice a day, their meals made of horse beans, peas, and rice with a little salt meat mixed in.[14]

Newton stockpiled food for the long, looming stay on the coast and the Middle Passage. He caught rainwater in barrels during storms and bought additional water at every opportunity. He purchased basket after basket of rice, tons of it, especially when it appeared, in April, that he would soon be leaving the coast. He moved the ship's furnace to midship to create more room and make it easier to feed his growing "cargo." He had the sailors clear the slave apartments and scrape them to remove the excrement and dirt. He then smoked the lower deck using "tar, tobacco and brimstone" to disinfect the living quarters and neutralize the stench.[15]

Before long a new shipboard enemy was discovered: the *Duke of Argyle* was teeming with rats. Newton wrote that "rats have done a great deal of damage [to the sails], we being quite over-run with them." He had brought cats with him out of Liverpool, but they had died, and now he could not get another one at any price. Newton set men to work mending the damaged sails but discovered that the rats destroyed them faster than they could be repaired. Soon the rats added a new horror to shipboard life: "We have so many on board they are ready to devour every thing." The ravenous creatures would nibble at the ship's cables "and actually bite the people when they catch them asleep."

The management of a disorderly crew remained a challenge. Will Lapworth, one of the sailors who came aboard from the HMS *Surprize* in exchange for Newton's mutinous four, broke into the stateroom and tapped a keg of brandy, thereby earning from the captain a stint in irons and "a smart dozen" from his cat-o'-nine-tails. Newton also learned that third mate John Hamilton was experienced in the slave trade in an unexpected way: he had "shot a man last trip somewhere below Cape Mount." The mate had just now taken a boat to the same area to trade, which caused Newton to fear revenge, something for which the natives of the region were known.

Newton exchanged information about sailors with other captains on the coast. He noted haunting news about the *Adlington,* his sister ship, also owned by Mr. Manesty. Its longboat had been "cut off" by Africans at Rio Sestos, "the mate and 1 more killed." He appealed to Captain Jasper of the *Prince Henry* "to see if I could get any hands." (Offered only an unskilled landsman at full wages, he declined.) He learned that Captains Pemberton, Freeman, and Wainwright had lost their yawls to deserting crews. He found it "odd that 3 successive vessels should all bring piratical crews." He did not pause to consider whether the conditions of work and life for seamen on the coast had anything to do with the oddness.

Even more worrisome than news of resistance by slaves and sailors was their health. The African tropics were deadly to Europeans, as everyone knew, which caused merchants like Manesty and captains like Newton to hire large crews, as they had done for the *Duke of Argyle.* Despite their cold calculations of premature death as they planned the voyage, the dangers of sickness remained a worry, as Newton himself would remark some years later. On most every voyage, the number and physical ability of seamen were declining just as the dangers of the trade were mounting, as more and more of the enslaved were being brought on board.

Members of the crew began to die on December 10, soon after the *Duke of Argyle* reached the coast. Edward Lawson expired of a fever and was buried quickly, "being extremely offensive." A month later a boatload of the crew returned to the ship in poor health after purchasing rice, ivory, camwood, and eleven slaves. One man was already dead and buried ashore, and four others were so sick they had to be rowed back to the ship by the women they had purchased. One soon died of a "nervous fever" as others, including the surgeon and several of the slaves, fell ill. Newton quickly secured the services of a physician from a nearby Guineaman, who came aboard and did what he could, which was nothing. Chief mate John Bridson soon died of what Newton called "the most violent fever I have ever seen." The few healthy members of the crew did what they could to bury the bodies.

The enslaved began to die on January 9, the first, according to Newton, "a fine woman slave, No. 11," of a "lethargick disorder, which they seldom recover from." (Dead crew members were called by name and buried, while dead Africans were noted only by the number assigned when they came on board the ship and thrown over the side to the waiting sharks.) Fearing an epidemic, Newton ordered the sailors to scrape the rooms, smoke the ship for two hours, and wash the decks with vinegar. Yet the march of death on the lower deck continued: a "man slave, No. 6"; a boy, "No. 27"; a man, "No. 33," all died of a flux that "has baffled all our medicines." As the stay on the coast dragged on and the rainy season threatened, a dozen more fell ill. Numbers 100, 79, and 92 died. The last of these, a young girl, Newton sent ashore to a black trader, not to help her recover but "to free the ship of a nuisance." Apparently she was not suffering in silence as the captain would have preferred. The *Duke of Argyle* now had "the melancholy appearance of a sickly ship," and soon things got so bad that Newton was forced to cancel religious services. But by early May the situation had stabilized. Newton wrote, "I believe my trade for this voyage is finished." Ten days later he would weigh anchor for Antigua, relieved that the most dangerous part of the voyage was over.

Soon after leaving the African coast, Newton may have regretted the decision to buy the slaves who had risen up on the French slaver. On the evening of May 26, a young man who had been "the whole voyage out of irons, first on account of a large ulcer, and since for this seeming good behaviour," passed a large marlinespike down the gratings to the men slaves, who used it to free themselves from their fetters. This they did quickly and quietly, it "being an instrument that made no noise," until "near 20 of them had broke their irons." The men had not been at it long before the intended plot was discovered. Newton noted that a sailor saw the young man pass the marlinespike down below (although why this went unreported for an hour remains a mystery). Newton immediately got all the rebels back into their irons. The following day he "punished 6 of the ringleaders of the insurrection," but he did not say how he did so. More than likely he whipped with the cat and tortured with the thumbscrews. He also had the carpenter repair the rear bulkhead the rebels had damaged belowdecks.

Newton considered it a "Favour of Providence" that he and his crew survived. "Their plot was exceedingly well laid," he wrote, "and had they been let alone an hour longer, must have occasioned us a good deal of trouble and damage." He also felt fortunate about the timing: "I have reason to be thankfull they did not make attempts on the coast when we often had 7 or 8 of our best men out of the ship at a time and the rest busy." He also knew that the resistance was not over. The slaves "still look very gloomy and sullen and have doubtless mischeif in their heads if they could find an opportunity to vent it." He hoped that the public punishments (whatever they were) and the firing of arms would, with "Divine Assistance," allow him and the crew "to fully overawe them now." In terrorem was the order of the day.

A couple of weeks later, Newton had another scare. It seemed that some of the men slaves "had found means to poison the water in the scuttle casks upon deck." They had managed to drop one of their "country fetishes" or "talismans" into a cask of water, no doubt with a malevolent curse attached. Newton thought it was meant to "kill all those who drank of it." His fear turned to derision as he mocked the superstitious pagans. He concluded, "if it please God thay make no worse attempts than to charm us to death, they will not much harm us, but it shews their intentions are not wanting."

The *Duke of Argyle* suffered several more deaths among sailors and slaves but completed the Middle Passage, arriving in Antigua on July

3, 1751. Newton said nothing in the journal about the sale of the 146 people he had transported alive to the Caribbean. He noted in businesslike fashion that he took on a new cargo and commenced the homeward passage to Liverpool "very full and lumbered." On the homeward passage, he suffered the death of his friend Dr. Robert Arthur, then a hurricane, which busied the sailors at the pump to keep the ship afloat. He arrived in Liverpool on October 7, 1751. His journal concludes, *"Soli Deo Gloria."*

The result of the voyage, to both owner and captain, was failure. Newton could count almost a quarter of his crew members dead (seven of thirty), and about one in six of the enslaved (28 of 164). The latter figure would no doubt have been larger had Newton been able to take on board the 250 slaves Mr. Manesty had wanted. The main goal of a slaver, Newton later explained, was "to be full." His was not, and the difference between the intended and actual cargo was a main reason the voyage was not profitable. Newton's career as a slave-ship captain was off to a shaky start.[16]

Second Voyage, 1752–53

John Newton first saw the *African,* his new vessel, "upon the sticks," meaning in the stocks of Fisher's dockyard in Liverpool as it was being built. He held himself back during the festivities when the ship was launched, thinking that a more serious frame of mind was called for. Newton's life had taken a deeper religious turn in the months between his first and second voyages, and he began to keep a spiritual diary, for three purposes: to "bring myself a deep sense of my past sins and follies"; to "enlarge my mind"; and to "compose my heart to a perfect peace & charity with all mankind." Fearful that he had been backsliding, he vowed to pray twice a day, to study the Bible, to observe the Sabbath to the fullest, to be an example to others, and to be "a good soldier under the banner of Jesus Christ." Conscious of his previous failure and now fearing "ruin," he prayed earnestly for the success of the voyage.[17]

The *African* left Liverpool on June 30, 1752. Like the *Duke of Argyle,* the new vessel was a snow of modest carrying capacity, a hundred tons. Mr. Manesty was apparently prospering in the slave trade despite Newton's less-than-profitable voyage. Once again the shipowner instructed the captain to pick up 250 slaves on the Windward Coast (Sierra Leone, Rio Nuñez, Cape Mesurado, Cape Pal) and to carry them this time to St. Kitts. The crew would be a little smaller at twenty-seven, but with the same division of labor. Only two members of the crew, steward Joseph Fellowes and apprentice Robert Cropper, reenlisted from the previous voyage.[18]

Except for a violent thunderstorm that shook the *African* on November 11 and stunned a couple of sailors with lightning, the outward passage was quiet and uneventful, Newton apparently paying more attention to his studies of the Bible, Latin, French, classics, and mathematics than to the business of the ship, which would prove to be a mistake. He wrote regularly and at length in his spiritual diary and carefully ordered his daily routine for devotional study, exercise, and rest. He thought life at sea was good for "an awakened mind," especially if one can "restrain gross irregularities in others." He wrote on Thursday, August 13, that he had arrived in Sierra Leone "with every body well, having not met with the least accident, & hardly the least inconvenience upon the passage." He called his vessel a "peaceful kingdom."[19]

Newton soon took a special interest in restraining the "gross irregularities" of his sailors, which is to say he became concerned with reforming their characters and saving their souls. He considered the "thoughtless ignorant & too often hardned condition of most Sailors," their debauchery, profaneness, and insensibility, and the many dangers they faced, especially in African voyages. He noted that "prosperous adventures" like the slave trade often cost many lives and souls. He decided to hold mandatory prayers twice each Sunday and to demand a rigorous observance of the holy day. His seamen, however, apparently did not welcome his ministry, for nowhere in his writings does the devout captain suggest that he got anywhere with any of them.[20]

"Gross irregularities" not only continued, they worsened. As the captain engaged in his devotional exercises, several of his sailors were organizing a mutiny against him. So much for Christian fellowship. On November 15, seaman William Cooney informed the captain that Richard Swain had attempted to get him to sign a round-robin, a seditious paper through which sailors swore each other to loyalty and secrecy in subversive action, in this case, it seems, to seize the ship and turn pirate. Newton was astonished: "I thought myself very secure from any danger of this kind, as every body has behaved very quiet the whole voyage and I do not remember the least complaint or grievance." Had he been too disengaged, too inattentive to the murmurings of the crew? Newton suddenly found himself in "ticklish times." He and the loyal part of the crew had to be continually "upon our guard against the slaves and the round robin gentlemen." It made matters worse that, as Newton explained, "I am not yet able to find out who are or are not in the gang."[21]

A second informer, seaman John Sadler, said that while working in the boat at Shebar, he had heard, at a distance, several sailors, including Swain and John Forrester, talking about the plot. One of them said that "somebody should pay for it, and the other that he was sure all the ship's company would [back?] him if he spoke the word." On another occasion Sadler heard Forrester say "in plain terms" that he "would kill Mr Welsh the doctor, or at least leave [him] only just alive." Sadler ended with his most damning evidence: a few days earlier, when he was on shore with the yawl, "Swain endeavoured to perswade him and the rest to go off with her."

Newton was saved, he thought, by illness: "I have reason to think this sickness we have had on board within these three days [beginning November 12] has prevented a black design when it was almost ripe for execution, and the unexpected stay of the boat brought it to light." Forrester and another seaman involved in the plot, Peter Mackdonald, fell ill, delaying the execution of the conspiracy, as did Swain's late return in the yawl, by which time Cooney had told Newton of the conspiracy. As soon as Swain returned, the captain clapped him into double irons. Forrester, once his health was restored, soon followed.

Mackdonald, who was "delirious & raving during his whole sickness," would have joined them, but he died.[22]

Newton was unsure how to punish the mutineers and reestablish his authority with the crew as a whole. He apparently decided not to whip Swain and Forrester, partly, it seems, because he worried about inflaming discontentment among their still-unidentified supporters on board the ship. He resolved not to treat the mutineers harshly, "but yet I do not think myself at liberty to dismiss the affair in silence lest encouragement should be thereby given to such attempts." So he now set about getting the leading mutineers off the ship. He appealed to Captain Daniel Thomson of the *Earl of Halifax,* who had "a large and clear ship" (i.e., no slaves), to take Swain and Forrester and to deliver them to the first man-of-war he should see. Thomson was not keen on the idea, but Newton finally persuaded him to take them.[23]

Newton concluded that he was saved by "a visible interposition of Divine Providence" and decided that he must "reflect upon my deliverance." He thanked God, indeed said a special prayer, for preserving him from this "mischeif of the blackest sort." The apocalypse had threatened, as he noted when he had finally gotten the situation in hand. Once he had removed Swain and Forrester, he wrote, "I am very glad to have them out of the ship, for tho I must say they behaved quietly in their confinement, I could not but be in constant alarms, as such a mark of division amongst us was a great encouragement to the slaves to be troublesome, and for ought I know, had it ever come to extremity, they might have joyned hands." One "black design" might lead to another or, worse yet, to a design that was both black and white.[24]

Not long after Swain and Forrester had been removed from the *African,* Newton found that his fears were warranted. Newton himself apparently went belowdecks and "Surprized 2 of them [slaves] attempting to get off their irons." He quickly organized a search of the men's room and an interrogation of several of the "boys" who had free range of the ship. He found among the men "some knives, stones, shot, etc., and a cold chissel." Newton then undertook a full investigation.

He suspected that several boys had passed the instruments to the men, so he clapped them in irons and began to torture them, "to urge them to a full confession." He put them in the thumbscrews and applied pressure "slightly." He finally identified eight men as the heart of the conspiracy and four boys who had supplied them with the "instruments." The following day he "examined" the men slaves, probably with the thumbscrews and rather more than "slightly." He punished six of them, probably with the cat, and "put 4 of them in collars," iron contraptions that made it difficult to move and almost impossible to rest. Worried now about being "weak-handed," with only twenty crew members, several of them young apprentices, to guard an increasing cargo of slaves that included many men, Newton decided to send the black ringleaders after the white ones—on board *Earl of Halifax*.

"Divine Providence" had interceded once again, and Newton offered thanks in a prayer he recorded in his spiritual diary:

> O my soul praise the Lord, thy always gracious preserver. Lord give the grace, still to set Thee always gracious & to be sensible that I only stand in Thee: & forasmuch as these accidents are so frequent & sudden, & have no other reason, than my long experience of thy distinguishing favour, to imagine I shall have a continual exemption from their consequences, enable me to hold myself in constant readiness, that if at any time Thou should see fit, by a stroke of casualty, to summons me before I'am aware to appear before Thee, I may be found in the course of my duty, & may not be greatly disconcerted, but thro grace empowering me to lay hold by faith on the mediation of my Redeemer, be willing with comfort to resign my spirit in thy merciful hands, & pass at once from death unto life eternal. Amen.

His prayer acknowledged the omnipresence of death in the slave trade. He did not ask God to change it, for it was in the nature of the business, but rather to help him be ready to meet it. Such was Newton's spiritual exercise in the aftermath of slave insurrection.

By the end of the year, Newton had reestablished shipboard order and confidence in his own command. On December 31 he noted in his spiritual journal his gratitude for good health and a "Chearful mind." Taking stock of the past on New Year's Day, he remembered his offenses against God, which were too many to be listed, and his blessings—health, friends, the goodwill of his employer, and his wife. Finally he recounted his deliverances. He "was particularly preserv'd from unseen evil, by the timely discovery of the plot my people were engag'd in, & afterwards of another amongst the Slaves." He wanted not only to note these but to have them "imprinted in my heart." That way "they may be always ready to excite my gratitude in times of safety, & to keep up my spirits & dependence when other dangers seem to threaten." He had "an easy and contented mind," but he knew it would not last. The dangers surrounding him were too great.[25]

On the afternoon of January 31, William Cooney, the informer against his fellow sailors, "seduced a slave down into the room and lay with her brutelike in view of the whole quarter deck." The woman who was raped, known only as Number 83, was pregnant. Newton put Cooney in irons, noting in his journal, "I hope this has been the first affair of the kind on board and I am determined to keep them quiet if possible." It is not clear what he meant by "keep them quiet." Did he mean that he wanted to keep these kinds of events quiet? Did he mean that he wanted to keep predatory seamen like Cooney quiet? Or did he mean that he anticipated loud protest from the enslaved once they learned what had happened? Newton's concluding conversation suggested his concern for property: "If anything happens to the woman I shall impute it to him, for she was big with child."

Soon after this event, Newton had a strange and disturbing dream. He was stung by a scorpion and was then given "oyl" by a stranger to ease the pain. The unknown person told him that the dream was "predictive of something that would happen shortly" but that Newton should not be afraid, as he would suffer no harm. What did the dream mean? Who was the scorpion, what was the sting, and who was the helpful healer? Was it the sailors, the mutiny, and the informer William Cooney? Was it the slaves, the plotted insurrection, and the boys who snitched? The captain decided that the sting came from a wealthy black slave trader named Bryan who had accused Newton of "laying with one of his women when he was on shoar." Newton now feared going ashore to conduct business, as he would find himself "amongst a mercenary enraged crew and who have poyson always in readiness where they dare not use more open methods of revenge." Newton drew up a declaration of his innocence in the presence of another captain, his mate, and his surgeon, and sent it to the trader on shore. He then sold his longboat for four tons of rice and sailed away.

Newton had spent a protracted eight and a half months on the coast gathering a human cargo. He had been plagued once again by sickness, though he was not as assiduous as on the first voyage about recording deaths. Perhaps he was getting used to them, or perhaps he did not want to leave a written record of mortality that his employer might inspect. In any case he felt he had done better trading than most captains who were then on the coast, and his fortunes improved with the health and mood of the enslaved men. Having for months been "continually alarmed with their almost desperate attempts to make insurrections upon us," and knowing that "when most quiet they were always watching for opportunity," Newton noticed that their disposition, even their "tempers," seemed to change. They began to behave "more like children in one family, than slaves in irons and chains and are really upon all accounts more observant, obliging and considerate than our white people." Newton was pleased, but not enough to alter his vigilant routine. He and his crew continued to guard them "as custom and prudence suggest," and he quoted the Bible to stress his own vulnerability: "except the Lord keep the city, the watchman waketh but in vain." This was true for any ship, he suggested, "and it is more observably true of a Guineaman."

As the *African* neared St. Kitts, Newton had the sailors prepare the human commodities for sale: they "shaved the slaves' fore heads." He feared that the market would be bad and that another passage, perhaps to Jamaica or Virginia, would be required. Noting his long stay on the coast and the longer-than-normal Middle Passage, he wrote on

June 3, "we have had the men slaves so long on board that their patience is just worn out, and I am certain they would drop fast had we another passage to make." As it happened, his worries were misplaced since he sold his entire cargo of 167 men, women, and children at St. Kitts. After a routine homeward passage, Newton arrived in Liverpool on August 29, 1753.

Once again Newton had not lived up to his owner's hopes, although he had done better than on the previous voyage. He had taken on board only 207 slaves rather than the 250 he was supposed to take, and his mortality rate was higher than on the first voyage. He lost 40 slaves, 19.3 percent of the total. He did better with the sailors, only one of whom (of twenty-seven) died. But this did not save Mr. Manesty any money. The four who deserted and the three he discharged early did save money, as he did not have to pay their wages back to Liverpool. Once again Newton complained that the slave trade on the Windward Coast was "so overdone."

Third Voyage, 1753–54

After a quick turnaround of only eight weeks, Newton departed Liverpool on October 23, 1753, on his third voyage as captain of a slaver. Mr. Manesty retained him to command the *African,* to sail once again to the Windward Coast and St. Kitts. Newton hired a few more sailors this voyage, thirty in all, as he had done on his first voyage, probably in memory of the sickness and threatened insurrection of the slaves. The division of labor remained the same, with one exception. Newton took on a friend, an old salt named Job Lewis, who, down on his luck, went as "Volunteer and Captain's Commander." Four crew members reenlisted from the previous voyage: chief mate Alexander Welsh, second mate James Billinge, and apprentices Robert Cropper and Jonathan Ireland. The first two had incentives, and the second two probably had no choice. It is revealing that none of the common sailors signed on again. Maybe it was the mandatory religious services.[26]

Once again Newton kept an ordered and methodical schedule, rising early, walking the deck, reading two or three chapters of the

Bible, taking his breakfast. On Sundays he held a devotional service for the crew at 11:00 A.M. He took tea at 4:00 P.M., followed by another "scripture lesson" and a walk. In between he attended to business, although his various writings make it clear that he was becoming steadily less interested in worldly affairs, more interested in his godly calling. He wrote more about his spiritual life, less about the daily transactions of the ship. Still, he remained optimistic about business. Early in the voyage, he noted, "we are all in good health and good spirits" and expressed his hope for a quick passage. He arrived on the African coast without a major incident, natural or man-made, on December 3, 1753.

Newton had to dispense discipline to the crew on several occasions, none of them as serious as the near mutiny he suffered on the previous voyage. On December 21 he found himself in a ticklish situation with the carpenter, who on the one hand had behaved mutinously, refused orders from other officers while Newton was off the ship, even "grossly abused" the second mate, but who on the other hand had not yet finished building the utterly necessary barricado. Newton gave him two dozen stripes with the cat but added, "I could not afford to put him in irons." Two days later he noted, "Carpenter at work on the barricado." Later in the stay on the coast, Newton had to deal with desertion. A member of his crew named Manuel Antonio, a Portuguese sailor who had shipped out of Liverpool, ran away when the boat on which he was working stopped at Cachugo. He had alleged ill usage, but every officer swore (perhaps less than truthfully) that "he never was struck by any one." Newton believed he deserted because he had been noticed while "stealing some knives and tobacco out of the boat."[27]

Soon after he arrived on the coast, Newton got the local news: the *Racehorse* had been "cut off," the *Adventure* was "totally lost" to insurrection, and the *Greyhound* had three members of its crew killed at Kittam. Trade was slow, and the "villainy" of the traders was great. Newton quickly grew weary of the "noise, heat, smoke, and business" of the trade. He clashed with Job Lewis, whose profane ways undermined his own hoped-for Christian influence among the crew. He apparently worried about attacks from both within the vessel and without, so he made a practical alliance with Captain Jackson, likely the man with whom he had sailed as mate. Newton also began to worry about "dirty money matters"—whether this voyage would be yet another failure. He wrote to his wife, Mary, to console himself: "Perhaps we may not be rich—no matter. We are rich in Love." Such reasoning would not impress Mr. Manesty.[28]

Newton determined once again to find advantage in disaster. On December 30 he bought the *Racehorse,* presumably from the Susu people who had taken and probably plundered it. It was a small vessel at forty-five tons, but it had new copper sheathing on its hull. Newton paid the modest sum of £130 and put his friend Job Lewis aboard as captain. The vessel had to be refitted, which took about three weeks. A major setback took place on February 21, when Captain Lewis died. Newton distributed his clothes to his officers and promoted to command chief mate Alexander Welsh. Newton hoped that the purchase of the *Racehorse* would serve Mr. Manesty's interest, but the plan was, at bottom, self-serving: he would send several of his seamen aboard and depart the coast of Africa early, after only four months, with a small cargo of only eighty-seven slaves, cutting short the dangerous stay on the coast, limiting his mortality, and leaving the *Racehorse* to gather the rest of the slaves.[29]

On April 8, 1754, the day after the *African* departed the coast of Africa, Newton reflected on the news and lore that circulated among captains, then on his own situation: "This has been a fatal season to many persons upon the coast. I think I never heard of so many dead, lost, or destroyed, in one year. But I have been kept in perfect health, and have Buried neither White, nor Black." (He regarded Lewis as a death on a separate ship and therefore not his responsibility.) Yet ten days later, early in the Middle Passage, he found that he had spoken too soon. Newton himself fell ill of a violent, debilitating fever. Racked by high temperature and sore eyes, he thought he was going to die. He was terrified at the prospect of perishing "in the midst of this pathless ocean, at a distance from every friend," but he nonetheless decided to "prepare for eternity." He prayed and wrote a farewell letter to Mary.

It turned out that Newton had not caught the "most dangerous species" of fever and did not suffer the pain and delirium he had seen so often in sailor and slave. He languished for eight to ten days and felt "rather faint and weak" for almost another month once the fever had passed, even after the ship had arrived in St. Kitts on May 21. One reason the recovery took so long, Newton thought, was that he had generously distributed his stock (food and drink) "among the sick seamen, before I was taken ill myself."

After an uneventful passage from St. Kitts, Newton arrived in Liverpool on August 7, 1754. His third voyage had proved the quickest, and in many ways the easiest he made, but it is impossible to know if it was successful in economic terms. Newton certainly had his doubts. Having made three consecutive voyages of uncertain profitability in a row, he appealed to a different measure of success. He had managed, he proudly announced, "an African voyage performed without any disaster." He went around from church to church in Liverpool to return thanks for their blessings, noting everywhere that he had lost neither sailor nor slave. "This was much noticed and spoken of in the town," he explained, "and I believe it is the first instance of its kind." He considered it, of course, to be a sign of "divine Providence."[30]

Whether doubtful, proud, or both, Newton was rehired by Mr. Manesty and soon took command of a new slave ship, the *Bee*. He was within two days of sailing when his career and life took a sudden and unexpected turn. As he wrote later, "it pleased God to stop me by illness." Newton suffered an apoplectic stroke, a "violent fit, which threatened immediate death, and left me no signs of life, but breathing, for about an hour." On the advice of physicians, he resigned command of the ship and left the slave trade altogether—not by his own choice, it must be noted. He eventually got a job as the tide surveyor of Liverpool. It would be years before he wrote a critical word about the slave trade, and it would be more than three decades before he would declare himself against it.

Lost and Found

John Newton considered his role as a slave-ship captain to be a godly calling. He was, he wrote, "upon the whole satisfied with it, as the appointment Providence had marked out for me." Occasionally, he prayed "that the Lord, in his own time, would be pleased to fix me in a more humane calling, and, if it might be, place me where I might have more frequent converse with his people and ordinances, and be freed from those long separations from home which very often were hard to bear." Yet among his misgivings the inhumane work of the slave ship ranked as only one of three reasons to prefer a different calling. Writing to David Jennings from the coast of Sierra Leone in August 1752, Newton noted that he once was lost, "a deprav'd unhappy apostate," but now, as Christian master of a slave ship, he was "found." It is a cruel twist on the lyrics of "Amazing Grace," which Newton would write twenty-one years later, in 1773.[31]

Newton's Christianity played a double role in his life aboard the slave ship. On the one hand, it served a prophylactic screen against recognition of the inhuman things he was actually doing. He could sit in his captain's cabin vowing to do "good to my fellow creatures" as he gave orders to guarantee their killing enslavement. On the other hand, his Christianity limited, but did not eliminate, the cruelty so common to slave ships. He admonished himself to remember his own experience as a sailor harshly punished aboard the *Harwich* and as a slave much abused on Plantain Island. He exhorted himself not to be cruel to the sailors who had organized a mutiny against his command on the second voyage. He brought a limited Christian paternalism to his dealings with sailors, but apparently not to his dealings with slaves. And even though Newton was probably less cruel than most eighteenth-century slave-ship captains, he nonetheless faced mutiny by his sailors and insurrection by his slaves. He responded with chains, whips, and thumbscrews—in short, with terror.[32]

As Newton sat in the captain's cabin writing by candlelight to his wife on July 13, 1753, he looked back over his life, particularly his own enslavement in 1745 by a trader on Plantain Island, where he lay "in an abject state of servitude and sickness." He had come a long way in eight short years. He was now married, a man of some property and standing, and a proud Christian. He explained that God "brought me, as I must say, out of the land of Egypt, out of the house of bondage; from slavery and famine on the coast of Africa to my present situation." His situation, at that very moment, was to share a small wooden world with eighty-seven men, women, and children whom he was carrying through the Middle Passage into ever deeper bondage. Newton may have escaped Egypt, but he now worked for Pharaoh. He was blind to the parallel.[33]

CHAPTER 7

The Captain's Own Hell

Family, friends, and loved ones gathered on the docks at Liverpool to say good-bye to the men aboard the slave ship *Brownlow,* including chief mate John Newton, as they set sail for the Windward Coast of Africa in early 1748. Liverpool's slave trade was booming, offering both opportunities and dangers to its denizens. "Farewells" were literal hopes. Merchants and captains sometimes posted notices of impending voyages in places of worship on a Sunday morning, asking congregations to mention the name of each person on board the ship as they prayed for a safe and successful voyage. Everyone therefore understood that the wave of the hand from the dock might be the final communication with any given member of the crew, from captain to cabin boy. Death at sea was "no respecter of persons" and could strike at any time, especially in the Guinea trade, by accident, disease, or human will. Such departures for long and perilous voyages always had an emotional charge.[1]

Captain Richard Jackson stood upon the quarterdeck of the *Brownlow,* apparently unaffected by the collective feeling of the occasion. He was, however, keenly conscious that deep changes were afoot the moment the ship pushed off from the pier. He and his men were taking leave of landed society for an extended period, a year or more, sailing to places where social institutions such as family, church, community, and government had little reach. "With a suitable expression of countenance,"

Newton recalled years later, and perhaps with disdain for the religious overtones of the occasion, Captain Jackson took leave of the people standing on the pier, and muttered to himself, "Now, I have a Hell of my own!"

Captains wielded such power because they occupied a strategic position in the rapidly expanding international capitalist economy. Their power derived from maritime custom, but also from law and social geography. The state licensed the captain to use corporal punishment to maintain "subordination and regularity" among his crew as he linked the markets of the world. Resistance to his authority could be construed in court as mutiny or insurrection, both punishable by hanging. The geographic isolation of the ship, far from the governing institutions of society, was both a source of and a justification for the captain's swollen powers.[2]

The captain of a slave ship, like Richard Jackson, was the most powerful example of this general type. Like other captains, he was something of a craftsman—a highly skilled, experienced master of a sophisticated machine. He possessed technical knowledge about the working of the ship, natural knowledge—of winds, tides, and currents, of lands, seas, and sky—and social knowledge about how to deal with a wide variety of people. He worked as a multicultural merchant in far-flung markets. He acted as a boss, a coordinator of a heterogeneous and often refractory crew of wage laborers. He served as a warden, jailer, and slave master to transport hundreds of prisoners from one continent, across a vast body of water, to another. To succeed in these many roles, the captain had to be able to "carry a command"—of himself, a ship, a vast sum of property, his workers, and his captives.[3]

The Path to the Ship

"CROW! MIND YOUR EYE!" ordered Liverpool merchant William Aspinall as he sent his one-eyed captain, Hugh Crow, off to Bonny to buy a big shipload of slaves in July 1798. Crow had already made five voyages to Africa and would go on to a long and successful career as a slave-ship captain, making five more voyages and one of the last before the trade was abolished in 1807. Crow left a memoir of his life in the slave trade, which was published posthumously by friends in 1830. In it he explained how he got from his birthplace to the captain's cabin of a Guineaman.[4]

Crow was born in 1765 in Ramsey, on the north coast of the Isle of Man, located in the Irish Sea about eighty miles northwest of Liverpool, well within the booming port city's gravitational pull. He was, from his youth, blind in his "starboard eye," yet nonetheless early on he wanted to go to sea. His father was a respectable craftsman who worked along the waterfront. "Being brought up in a sea-port town," he explained, "I naturally imbibed an inclination for a sea-faring life."

Apprenticed by his father to a boatbuilder in Whitehaven, Crow worked for two years and got a little education before he took his first voyage, at age seventeen, in the coal trade. He soon ranged far and wide, sailing over the next four years to Ireland, Barbados, Jamaica, Charleston, Newfoundland, and Norway, among other places. He experienced seasickness, backbreaking work at the pump, a hurricane, mistreatment at the hands of his fellow sailors, a near drowning (saved by his fellow sailors), and a mutiny (along with his fellow sailors) against a drunken, incompetent captain. After five voyages Crow had completed his apprenticeship and was now an able seaman. He kept his one eye peeled for the main chance. He studied navigation, bought a quadrant, and began to move up the maritime hierarchy.

From the start he had a "prejudice" against the slave trade, or so he claimed, but he was eventually enticed by an offer to go as chief mate aboard the *Prince* to the Gold Coast in October 1790. He made four more voyages to Africa as a mate, following which Aspinall offered him his first command. After sixteen years at sea, half of them in the slave trade, the thirty-three-year-old Crow took the helm of the *Mary,* a three-hundred-ton ship.[5]

The captain Aspinall hired in 1798 was fairly typical in his origins, if not in the number of his eyes or his ability to survive in a deadly line of work. Most, like Crow, became captains of Guineamen after making numerous small decisions rather than a single big one. They grew up along the waterfront, were "bred to the sea," got aboard a slaver one way or another (perhaps not by choice), survived a first voyage, slowly progressed up the ship's working ladder, acquired experience, built a reputation among captains and merchants, and finally achieved command of their own vessel. The historian Stephen Behrendt has found that 80 percent of the captains of British slavers, sailing mostly out of Liverpool and Bristol, between 1785 and 1807, came from commercial backgrounds. A few had fathers who were merchants, usually of modest means. Some, like John Newton, descended from ship captains, others from slave-ship captains, as in the Noble and Lace families in Liverpool and the D'Wolfs in Rhode Island. But most were, like Crow, the sons of waterfront artisans of one kind or another. Family connections often guided the way to the captain's cabin, but only after considerable experience at sea. On average, the first command of a slaver came at age thirty in Liverpool and thirty-one in Bristol. The path to the ship was similar among captains in the Rhode Island slave trade, although American masters were less likely to specialize in it. The historian Jay Coughtry found that captains made an average of only 2.2 African voyages, but within this group fifty captains made 5 voyages or more each. A writer who knew several families involved in the British trade observed that "such is the dangerous nature of the Slave Trade, that the generality of the Captains of the vessels employed in it think themselves fortunate in escaping with life and health after four voyages." And "fortunate" is precisely the right word, because a captain who survived four voyages or more would likely have made a small fortune, far beyond what most men of his original station in life could expect to achieve. It was a risky but lucrative line of work, freely chosen.[6]

Merchant Capital

The captain got his command from a merchant or group of merchants who owned the ship and financed the voyage. Once hired, he was an employee and business agent, responsible for substantial property in a trade that was complex, risky, potentially disastrous, and soon to be distant from the eyes and hence control of the investors. The reality was summed up by the Liverpool merchant David Tuohy, who wrote to Captain Henry Moore of the *Blayds* in 1782: you "have a large Capital under you," he explained, and it "behoves you to be very circumspect in all your proceedings, & very attentive to the minutest part of yr Conduct." Some slave ships and their cargoes were worth as much as £10,000 to £12,000, which would be roughly $1.6 to $2 million in today's currency. The captain's power depended first and foremost on a connection to capitalists.[7]

What captains offered in return was experience, essentially of two kinds. The more general was experience at sea, a personal knowledge of navigation and things maritime, and a personal history of commanding sailors and ships. More specific was experience of the slave trade itself. The former was necessary, the latter was not, although it was highly desirable, because what merchants themselves knew about the trade was variable. A few merchants, like David Tuohy, had served as slave-ship captains and had accumulated capital to move into the ranks of investors. They knew exactly what happened on these ships, and they brought a wealth of practical knowledge to their business. Most slave-trading merchants, however, had never sailed on a Guineaman, never been to Africa, never experienced the Middle Passage. They knew the potentials and the risks of the slave trade, and they knew something of the Atlantic markets they were entering, but many of them would not likely have had a clear sense of what actually happened aboard a slave ship. Newport merchants Jacob Rivera and Aaron Lopez declared their inexperience to Captain William English in 1772: "we have no opinion of the Windward Coast trade." Much of what needed to be known about the slave trade could be learned only through experience. The merchant Thomas Leyland wrote to Captain Charles Watt, veteran of five slaving voyages, "We trust your long experience in the Congo." Most slave-ship owners wanted a captain at the helm who was experienced and trustworthy, a "good husband" to the merchant's property.[8]

Merchants wrote revealing letters of instruction to the ship captains they employed. They spelled out how the captain was to proceed—when and where he was to sail and how he was to conduct business as the delegated agent of the merchant. These letters varied considerably, partly because of regionally specific ways of doing business and partly because of the different experiences and temperaments of the merchants who wrote them and the captains who received them. Merchants who had been slave-ship captains often wrote lengthy, elaborate letters, as did merchants who instructed a captain with limited experience. Merchants who had employed a captain in the past and trusted both his knowledge and behavior wrote shorter letters. What stands out over the long run is the similarity of the letters, which suggests a broad continuity in the way the slave trade was organized and its business conducted.[9]

The letters often summarized the general working knowledge of the slave trade and usually expressed the deepest fears of investors. They reiterated three things in particular that could "prove the utter Ruine & destruction of your Voyage"—namely, accidents, mutiny and insurrection by sailors and slaves, and most of all runaway mortality. Thomas Leyland warned Captain Caesar Lawson of the *Enterprize* in 1803 to beware "Insurrection, Mutiny, and Fire." Like other merchants he also worried about the "great mortality among both Blacks and Europeans" in the slave trade.[10]

Most letters specified an outward passage from an originating port—say, Bristol, England, or Bristol, Rhode Island—to one or more locations in Africa, a Middle Passage to a West Indian or North American port, and a homeward passage. Occasionally the merchant would specify an African or European trader from whom the captain was to buy slaves, the king of Barra or old man Plunkett of the Royal African Company. Sometimes the merchant provided the names of agents who would handle the sale of the "cargo" in Jamaica or Virginia. Contingencies were built into the understanding, as the captain had to be able to respond to shifting markets on both sides of the Atlantic. Much would be left, as one merchant wrote, to "your prudence and Discretion to do as you shall see Occassion."[11]

Traders to Africa dealt in a variety of commodities. They instructed captains to exchange textiles, metalwares (knives, hoes, brass pans), guns, and other manufactured items for ivory or "teeth," partly because, as one merchant put it, "there's no Mortality to be feard." A few wanted gold (especially earlier in the eighteenth century), camwood (for its dye), beeswax, palm oil, or malaguetta pepper. One captain was told to trade for various items, including "curiosities." But of course the main object of purchase throughout the eighteenth century was human beings.[12]

Most merchants instructed their captains to buy young people, and those who did not mention this specifically would have assumed it as a given. Humphry Morice wanted those between the ages of twelve and twenty-five, two males for every female, which was typical. Thomas Leyland wanted mostly males, but in a different calculus—one-half "Prime Men Negroes from 15 to 25 yrs old," three-eighths boys "10 to 15," and one-eighth women "10 to 18"—all to be "well made, full chested, vigorous and without bodily imperfection." James Laroche, on the other hand, preferred girls between the ages of ten and fourteen, "very black and handsome." An official of the South Sea Company made a chilling request in 1717 for "all Virgins." Strong, healthy young people were most likely to survive the stay on the coast and also to "bear the passage." Conversely, merchants sometimes told captains to avoid "old Men or fallen-breasted Women" and anyone with physical defects such as hernia or lameness.[13]

Instructions specified wages for officers but not for sailors, who all signed straightforward contracts, usually negotiated by the captain. Payment to mates, the doctor, and the captain himself were more complex, as they involved not only wages but commissions and perquisites. A detailed example of such arrangements appeared in a letter of instruction written by a group of merchants to Captain Thomas Baker of the snow *Africa* in 1776. Baker would get £5 per month plus a commission of the value of 4 slaves per 100 delivered and sold, at the average value of sale. He would also get 7 "privilege" slaves, to be bought with the merchants' capital and sold at his own benefit at the going market rate. The other officers were paid, in addition to their wages (usually about £4 per month), as follows: the chief mate, Mr. William Rendall, got 2 "privilege" slaves; the second mate, Mr. Peter Birch, got 1 "privilege" slave; and Dr. Thomas Stephens got 1 "privilege" slave plus "head money," one shilling for every African delivered alive in Tobago. This last was an "inducement to him to take care of them to the place of Sale."[14] As it happened, Baker's vessel was shipwrecked before taking slaves aboard, but if his voyage had gone as planned, he would have made £5 per month for twelve months, the equivalent of the value of 10 slaves (on 250 slaves, at £28 each), and another 7 slaves at the same value. He therefore would have made about £536 on the voyage, or the equivalent, in today's currency, of $100,000. The common sailor on the same ship would have made £24, or $4,500. On a larger ship (and likely a longer voyage), the captain would have made as much as £750 to £1,000, as did Robert Bostock in 1774 (£774) or Richard Chadwick (£993), earlier in 1754.[15] Captain James Penny lost fourteen sailors and 134 slaves on a voyage of 1783–84 but still made £1,940, or more than $342,000 today.[16]

Clearly, "privilege" and "adventure" (shipping a slave purchased with one's own money freight-free) resulted in vastly higher earnings and set the officers apart from the common sailors, which was, after all, the point.[17] The wage agreement tied the interest of the captain (and the top officers) to the voyage and hence to the investing merchant or, in other words, gave them all, especially the captain, a material stake in the voyage. By making the commander a risk-sharing partner, merchants imposed the hard discipline of self-interest. As Mathew Strong explained to Captain Richard Smyth in 1771, "it suits as much your interest as ours to bring a good & healthy cargo."[18]

The next big issue was the management of the voyage—how to maintain the ship and its social order. Here merchants gave general instructions about keeping the ship clean, repaired, and functional ("take care of your Vessells Bottom"), stocking the vessel with the proper provisions, and caring for and disciplining the sailors and slaves. Merchants also routinely commanded a captain to cooperate with other captains (those in their own employ) while on the coast of Africa and to write with an update at every opportunity.[19]

A few shipowners tried to micromanage the voyage. One was the Liverpool merchant James Clemens, who had made three voyages to Angola in the 1750s and had many self-certain opinions about how things should be done. He wrote detailed instructions to Captain William Speers, himself an experienced captain, as he prepared to take the *Ranger* to Angola and then Barbados in 1767. Clemens required that the ship be "cleaned" and "sweetened" a particular way so that the lower deck would be dry and therefore healthier for the enslaved. He had strong views on fresh air and ventilation, explaining to Speers not only why he must not position the boat and the yawl near the gratings lest they obstruct the airflow, but how to use a "topmast Steering Sail" to funnel wind down into the men's room below. Clemens wanted the slaves washed in the evenings; they were "to rub each other with a piece of Cloth every Morning that will promote Circulation & prevent Swellings." He wanted them fed a certain way, for Angola slaves were "accustomed to very little food in their own Country" and must therefore not be overfed. He wanted "a few White people under Arms constantly" to prevent insurrection, not only because an uprising would be dangerous but because if the men should try and fail, "they pine afterwards and are never Easie." Some would fall into melancholy and waste away, so much better to prevent a rising in the first place. Clemens also indicated that the crew should get a little brandy and tobacco now and then to "attach them (if prudently served out) both to you and the Ship." He warned Speers against having open fire near the casks of combustible brandy: "don't suffer any Lights to be carried into the Hould to draw off Brandy on any pretence whatever." After saying all this and more, he generously agreed to leave the rest to Speers's discretion.[20]

Merchants feared accidents of all kinds, especially shipwreck, but in their instructions they concentrated on what they considered to be the preventable ones. In a wooden ship, fire was especially dangerous. "Of all things," wrote Thomas Leyland, "be carefull of Fire, an idea of the consequences attending which is horrible in the extreme." Lit candles had to be used with care. David Tuohy wrote, "You'l be carefull of your Powder & Brandy as many fatal Accidents happen with both." Slave ships were known to blow up, accidentally or by the design of rebellious captives.[21]

The resistance waged by both sailors and slaves was a second big worry. Sailors were known to embezzle, desert, and mutiny. Captains were urged to keep a careful watch on the cargo, especially rum and brandy, to be sure that sailors did not help themselves to it. They also had to be careful in the assignment of tasks, as James Clemens made clear: "suffer no Mutinous, or troublesome drunken people to go in the Boats a Slaving." The fear was twofold. If sailors deserted with the longboat or the yawl, the captain lost not only labor but a vessel that was crucial to the slaving process. The final concern was outright mutiny, the capture of the vessel by the crew, which happened numerous times over the eighteenth century and was a potential worry to any merchant.[22]

Merchants feared suicide and especially insurrection among the enslaved. Isaac Hobhouse and his co-owners advised in 1725 that the enslaved must be constrained by netting and chains, "fearing their rising or leaping Overboard." Humphry Morice told Captain Jeremiah Pearce in 1730 that "it is adviseable for you to be provided for the Worst that can attend you during the Course of your intended voyage and perticularly to be allways upon your Guard and defence against the Insurrection of your Negroes." Owners constantly urged vigilance and the consistent, visible use of armed sentries. An unnamed New England owner wrote to Captain William Ellery in 1759, "As you have guns and men, I doubt not you'll make a good use of them if required."[23]

Maintaining proper discipline was the crux of the whole enterprise. Merchants assumed that the captain would govern the crew and the enslaved in an appropriate manner and that this would include exemplary violence, which was an established part of maritime life. They also knew that the violence could easily become cruelty and that it could lead to catastrophic results if it sparked reactions such as mutiny by sailors or insurrection by slaves. Merchants therefore tried to draw a line between order and abuse or, as Hugh Crow put it, severity and cruelty, encouraging the former and forbidding the latter. Humphry Morice routinely told his captains, "Be carefull of and kind to your Negroes and let them be well used by your officers & Seamen."[24]

The treatment of the slaves was a ticklish matter, and merchant after merchant described the awkward balance they hoped for: treat the slaves kindly, but not too kindly. Act with "as much lenity as safety will admit." Another added, "During the Purchase and Middle Passage you will no doubt see the Propriety of treating the Slaves with every Attention and indulgence that Humanity requires and Safety will permit." This clause was as close as the owners ever came to admitting that terror was essential to running a slave ship. The instruction admitted many interpretations.[25]

Only one merchant, Robert Bostock of Liverpool, it seems, ever threatened to punish a captain should he mistreat the enslaved. In 1791, after the abolitionist movement had grown throughout England and around the Atlantic, Bostock wrote to Captain James Fryer of the *Bess,* "It's my particular desire that you take care to use your slaves with the greatest Humanity and not beat them up [on] any acc't nor suffer your Officers or People to use them ill in the smallest degree as if proof can be made of yr using the Slaves ill or causing them to be ill used by yr Officers etc. you then in that case forfeit your privilege & Commissions." This was a serious threat, as income from commission and privilege represented the lion's share of the captain's pay. Yet there is no evidence that Bostock or any other merchant ever punished a captain for mistreatment of the enslaved.[26]

The merchant's greatest fear, by far, was mortality, which could come via accident, mutiny, or insurrection, but most commonly with the outbreak of disease. This chronic danger affected sailors and slaves as well as officers and even the captain himself. The Bristol owners of the snow *Africa* wrote to Captain George Merrick in 1774, "In case of your Mortality which [we] hope God will prevent your Chief Mate

Mr. John Matthews is to take the Command of our Ship & follow these our Orders & Instructions and so on in sucession." In the years 1801–7, about one in seven captains died on the voyage, which meant that merchants had to prepare a chain of command with one and sometimes two mates ready to take over. The very fragility of power aboard the ship may have increased its ruthlessness.[27]

It was widely known that West Africa was a "graveyard for sailors," hence merchants commented frequently on the need to provide for their health. They advised that sailors be kept sober, as intemperance in the tropics was believed to contribute to premature death. They also requested that the sailors be given proper care, "especially if sick and out of Order," and that they not be abused or overworked in the hot climate. Some merchants understood that the mortalities of sailors and slaves might be related: "We recommend to you the care of your White People for when your Crew is healthy they will be able to take care of the Negroes."[28]

The health of the enslaved mattered even more. Thomas Starke put it clearly when he wrote to Captain James Westmore in 1700, "the whole benefitt of the Voyage lyes in your care in Preserving negroes lives." Two American merchants, Joseph and Joshua Grafton, made the same point in 1785: "on the health of the slaves, almost your whole voyage depends." One group of merchants went so far as to tell the captain to be sure to keep sheep and goats on board in order to make "Mutton broth," which was to be fed to sick slaves, by hand, by the sailors. Over time, merchants grew increasingly conscious that longer stays on the coast often resulted in more deaths. Robert Bostock wrote to Captain Samuel Gamble in 1790 that short stays and passages rarely met with much mortality. Some merchants even advised their captains to leave the coast before the ship was fully slaved in order to reduce mortality: as a group of Bristol investors wrote in 1774, "when you are half slaved don't stay long if there is a possibility of getting off as the risque of Sickness & Mortality there become great."[29]

Try as they might to manage the details of their voyages, merchants knew that everything depended on the judgment and discretion of the captain. As Joseph and Joshua Grafton wrote in 1785, "we submit the conducting of the voyage to your good judgment and prudent management, not doubting of your best endeavours to serve our interest in all cases." This was necessary partly because maritime "custom," which gave the captain great authority at sea, shaped the agreement and partly because the African trade was unpredictable and transacted far away from European and American ports. The most elaborate trading plans might crash on the rocks of new and unanticipated developments. Merchant Morice, for example, had for years sent slave ships to trade in Whydah. But Captain Snelgrave wrote to say that the king of Dahomey had overrun and vanquished the previous traders in April 1727. What now? Or Snelgrave might write that he had suffered a mutiny at the hands of the crew or a bloody insurrection by the enslaved. What now? The captain would decide.[30]

"The Guinea Outfit"

Sea surgeon Thomas Boulton published *The Sailor's Farewell; Or, the Guinea Outfit, a Comedy in Three Acts* in 1768. He likely wrote from personal experience, as he would soon sail on the slave ship *Delight*, which departed Liverpool for Cape Mount in July 1769. Whatever may have seemed humorous about the endeavor in 1768 was no longer so in December 1769, when Boulton sat in the maintop of his ship and watched as slaves below rose up in fierce insurrection, killing nine of his shipmates. Thanks to the intervention of Captain Thomas Fisher of the *Squirrel*, Boulton survived to write a letter about the event, which was published in the *Newport Mercury* on July 9, 1770. His account was literally a "history from the top down."[31]

The Sailor's Farewell was a different sort of history from above, as Boulton explored, from an officer's perspective, how captains and mates gathered a crew for a slaving voyage. What Boulton did not discuss adequately is how the captain recruited his officers, especially his first mate, maybe a second mate and a surgeon (like Boulton himself), before all others. The small officer corps would be crucial, literally a social base, for the captain's power on board the ship. He sought for these posts experienced men who knew and respected the traditions of the sea in general, the ways of the slave trade in particular. He wanted people he could trust, often hiring those who had sailed with him previously and performed their work well. Loyalty was so important among the officers that he would sometimes enlist family members. These officers, once hired, might also assist him in the difficult task of signing on a crew. It is likely that Boulton himself took part in recruitment and that this experience was the basis of his play. In his comedy he captured essential truths about recruiting for a deadly trade.

The play begins with Captain Sharp, "Master of Vessel lying in the [Mersey] River," and Will Whiff, his mate, looking for a crew. Eight days has the snow been in the river, the captain fumed, "and not a man to be got." Whiff gives good news. He has been out recruiting since 5:00 A.M. and has found two stout fellows and maybe a third. He has a landlady, Mrs. Cobweb, taking care of three drunk sailors at his expense. The captain approves, saying it was a good day's work, but adds that he will have to "put fresh baits to your hooks, and have a second cast." He concludes with a little advice: "Shew a tar the bottle, glass, and salt water, and he immediately becomes amphibious." Grog, the "liquor of life and the soul of a sailor," was critical to manning slave ships.

Boulton depicts both the voluntary and the coercive sides of getting a crew, and, not surprisingly (for an officer), he puts both in the best possible light. He describes how captain and mate persuade the sailors to come aboard. The officers meet with them in the public house, they cajole them, they drink grog and sing with them. They play up their seafaring backgrounds. Whiff declares that he was "brought up to the sea" and was "always a seaman's friend." The only reason the vessel has not sailed already is that he and the captain cannot find humane enough officers: "No, no, my mates shall both of them be men that have humanity in them." There will be no "cane officers" (he refers to the boatswain's rattan) for his "brother sailors." Captain Sharp says, "I was brought up a sailor," and adds that he is a leveler, a plain dealer, no friend of hierarchy or privilege: "I'm none of your Mr. or your Captain; call me Jack Sharp, and a seaman, and dam'me if I want any other name—I'm the same thing sea or a shore." They are full of promises. Their vessel? It is "as fine a snow as ever swam the seas." They are bound to the "healthiest part of the coast," on a short voyage with good wages. Captain and mate even court the wives of the sailors, promising good treatment and safe returns for their men. One of them, Moll, notes with knowing irony, "Aye, if all the Guinea Captains were of as sweet a temper, they would not want [lack] men to go with them."

Captain and mate prey on the naive and the dim-witted. When the clownish Bob Bluff asks, "what sort of place is this Guiney?" Whiff answers that it is a place of gold and no work, much like the traditional utopia, the Land of Cokaygne—"no, no, nothing to do there, but to lay your head on the knee of a delicate soft wench, while she plays with your hair; and when we've got as much money as we want, away we go to Jamaica, and get mahogany to make chests to hold our money in; while rivers of rum, hills of sugar, and clusters of limes, makes drinks for emperors—who wouldn't go to Guiney." The promise of money and African women was part of the sell, and indeed most slave ships took a few landsmen, out of work and fresh from the countryside, who had no experience at sea and perhaps no knowledge of Guinea.

Boulton describes the coercive side of recruitment when two drunken sailors and friends, Peter Pipe and Joe Chissel, find themselves in prison, put there by their landlady, to whom they owe money. Neither has been to Africa, but they know that the only way to get out of jail is to sign on with a Guinea captain like Jack Sharp, who will pay their debts. Pipe declares himself ready to go. He vows to sober up in Africa, get as "dry as a stockfish." Chissel hesitates, thinking that a slaver would be worse than prison. He tells the story of poor Will Wedge, who called his slave captain a rascal and got his left eye gouged out for it. Soon Captain Sharp shows up, offering to bail them out. The scene is left unresolved, but they appear ready to accept the deal. In short order the crew is gathered aboard the snow and pushes off for Africa.

Two real sailors, Silas Told and William Butterworth, insisted that captains were not "the same thing sea or a shore." While recruiting in port, they were charming and accommodating. On his first slaving voyage, Told went aboard the *Loyal George,* captained by Timothy Tucker: "a greater villain, I firmly believe, never existed, although at home he assumed the character and temper of a saint." Butterworth had a similar experience with Captain Jenkin Evans of the *Hudibras.* He was "all condescension, politeness, and civility" while recruiting on shore, but once aboard the ship he turned "morose, peevish, and tyrannical." He was the "consummate hypocrite." The captain would change dramatically as he built a hell of his own.[32]

Bully

For several months before finally procuring his crew, some of whom came aboard at the last minute, sober or drunk, by hook or by crook, the captain worked diligently to prepare for sailing with one of the merchant-shipowners, who acted as the "ship's husband" on behalf of the full group of investors. The ship itself usually required repairs, which meant that the captain had to deal with a small army of craftsmen, from the shipwright to caulkers, joiners, blacksmiths, masons, glaziers, to mast, block, and rope makers, to sailmakers and riggers, boatbuilders, coopers, painters, and upholsterers. At the end of the day, he had to be sure that everything had been done properly. Then came the provisioners—butchers with their beef, bakers with their biscuit, brewers with their beer. Water was critical. The captain made sure that the surgeon had his medical instruments and supplies and that the gunner had the necessary pistols, muskets, and small cannon to overawe the enslaved. He saw to the hardware of bondage: manacles, shackles, neck rings, and chains, as well as the cat-o'-nine-tails, the *speculum oris,* and the thumbscrews, essential elements among the cargo being hoisted aboard and stored in the hold. The captain also had to set up accounts for each member of the crew, to note advance pay, to allocate a portion of wages to a wife or family member, and to keep track of items sailors would buy during the course of the voyage. Meanwhile the mates and crew readied the sails, rigging, tackle, and anchor, making all shipshape and ready for sailing. By the time the vessel put to sea, the captain would be in full control of all aspects of the ship—its technology, cargo, food and water supply—as well as its microeconomy and its social system. The world of the ship was his.[33]

As soon as the voyage began, the captain asserted his power over the ship's work routines and the people who performed them. He delegated authority to his officers, who oversaw the ship's various labor processes, but no one doubted who was in control. He also arranged and occupied the inner sanctum of power—the captain's cabin. Here he slept, ate his higher-quality and specially prepared food—usually with the surgeon and mates—planned the voyage, and kept his various accounts: his log, the ledger to track food and water consumed and replaced during the voyage, credit and debt with various traders, cargo bought and sold. No one entered the cabin without permission, and only the other officers could even approach it. The cabin would also be the place where the captain asserted his power over the bodies of enslaved women on board as he routinely took "wives" or "favorites" and forced them to stay in his chambers and provide for his sexual pleasure. Aboard the *Charleston,* for example, in 1795, the captain and indeed all the officers took three to four "wives" each and sold them for a "good price" once they reached the New World. What happened in the captain's cabin was always a bit of a mystery to the crew, and this was by design. Most captains culti- vated what would later be called "command isolation." Too much fa- miliarity with the crew or the enslaved would only diminish authority. Distance, formality, and severity of carriage would enhance it.[34]

Indeed establishing his authority was an urgent necessity for the captain. This was partly a matter of maritime tradition and partly a matter of experience and knowledge. Any captain who knew well the craft of sailing a ship would command respect, and this would have been enhanced had the captain sailed to the African coast previously. Other aspects of control consisted of the wage contract the sailor had signed, which promised obedience. Failure to comply would result in loss of wages and/or punishment, either by the captain or at the hands of the state. The captain's power aboard any deep-sea sailing ship in the eighteenth century was personal, violent, and arbitrary. He knew his sailors well, and he ruled a small social world. But Guinea ships and their captains were different, as everyone understood. Because the slave ship would be full of roiling, explosive social tensions, captains often went to extreme lengths to assert their power from the beginning. For the crew this process often began soon after they lost sight of land.

Many slave-ship captains adopted a domineering style of shipboard leadership that can be summed up in a word: "bully." They swaggered, they blustered, they hectored, they bullied. One of the best examples of the type was the legendary Thomas "Bully" Roberts, who captained nine voyages out of Liverpool between 1750 and 1768. According to "Dicky Sam," a Liverpool writer who used documents and local folklore to write a history in 1884 of his city's slave trade, Roberts was a "born bully." It was "part of his nature." But whatever he may have been at birth and by nature, he was made more brutal by the slave trade, all of whose captains were "fearless, bold, and hard-hearted." The nineteenth century would come up with the word "bucko" to describe this kind of style. A bucko captain or mate was a hard-driving man who always went far beyond the usual requirements of shipboard discipline. This, too, was by design.[35]

One of the chief ways the captain established his power was by bullying the crew either in whole or, more commonly, in part. Some captains decided early in the voyage for a raw display of power: they ordered all men (except the officers) to come on deck with their sea chests. They then smashed, staved, and burned the chests, usually on the pretense of looking for a stolen item but more usefully to make a symbolic assertion of control over all aspects of the sailors' lives.[36] Captains would also choose a marginal member of the crew for bullying, using that person as a medium to intimidate the crew as a whole. This was usually a ship's boy, a cook, or a black sailor.[37] If bullying sometimes led to murder (or suicide), it also led on occasion to the brutal murder of the captain in return, as, for example, Captain John Connor, who was slain by his crew in 1788. His conduct had been marked by continuous "barbarous severity."[38]

Even when an individual was not singled out for bullying, violent discipline was usually the order of the day on Guinea ships. The most important "instrument of correction" was the cat-o'-nine-tails, which easily became an instrument of torture. Sea surgeon Alexander Falconbridge described it as "a handle or stem, made of a rope three inches and a half in circumference, and about eighteen inches in length, at one of which are fastened nine branches, or tails, composed of log-line, with three or more knots upon each branch." The cat was employed during the course of daily work and social routine, for minor infractions and indiscipline, and in moments of spectacular punishment, on both sailors and slaves. (Some captains were reluctant to whip sailors in view of the slaves, while others did it deliberately, indeed occasionally ordered a slave to lash a sailor.) Some officers grew so attached to the cat that they slept with it. The purpose of the nine tails and the three knots on each (some had wire interwoven) was to lacerate the skin of the victim. But the cat was not the only tool of discipline. The ship was full of items that could be used by a captain or mate as a weapon at any moment: fishgigs, knives, forks, belaying pins, marlinespikes, and pump bolts. Captains also did not hesitate to clap mutinous seamen into irons and in extreme cases even to lock them into iron collars, usually reserved for the most rebellious slaves. The captain used an entire technology of terror to control the crew.[39]

Some captains asserted a different kind of power when they put the crew to what they called "short allowance" on the way to the African coast or during the Middle Passage. The rationale for this was that adverse sailing conditions might lengthen the voyage, provisions might be hard to replace, and it was therefore necessary to conserve. Or a captain might simply announce that he had not hired the men to "fatten them up." Sailors resented this bitterly, thinking that the captain pinched their provisions to save on costs and hence to pad profits for himself and the owners. Food for sailors was not high in quality to begin with, and of course it deteriorated over the course of the voyage. Beef in brine melted away, and biscuit became so infested with vermin that it moved by itself. Water was a special source of conflict, especially when the vessel was in the tropics. Numerous slave-ship captains used a bizarre custom to limit its consumption. In the maintop they put a barrel of water and a gun barrel, which was the designated drinking instrument. Sailors were forced to climb all the way up to take a single drink.[40]

Another important aspect of the captain's control of the internal economy lay in selling personal items such as "slops" (frocks, trousers, jackets, caps), knives, tobacco, brandy, and rum to the crew while at sea, usually at inflated prices. This, too, occasioned resentment among sailors, because high prices cut deeply into their wages. At the end of a long, dangerous voyage, some seamen had no pay owed to them, and a few made what they called a "Bristol voyage," returning to the home port owing the captain more for items purchased at sea than he owed them in wages. This in turn created a kind of debt peonage, which gave the captain ready labor for the next slaving voyage.[41]

Trader

As soon as the slaver reached the coast of Africa, the captain became even more of a merchant, buying and selling cargo with both European and African traders on the African coast. Knowledge and experience were required for both the "fort trade" and the "boat trade" but were especially valuable in the latter and indeed in any direct trade with Africans. Slave-ship captains who had previously traded in a particular area and with specific individuals had a big advantage. Throughout the eighteenth century, captains could find interpreters on almost any part of the coast, and of course many African traders spoke pidgin or creole English. Yet a captain who knew one or more African languages had greater trading options. This gave an advantage to those who had been "bred up" in the slave trade and thereby learned African languages early in life. Hugh Crow started later but made numerous voyages, as sailor, mate, and captain, to the Bight of

Biafra, and he prided himself on being able to speak Igbo. Crow's ebullient personality seems to have made him something of a favorite among the traders he dealt with, or so he sought to suggest in his memoir.

Establishing authority within trading relations was no easy matter, and occasionally slave-ship captains resorted to the superior force of the fearsome gunned ship they commanded. In those areas where the Guineamen could anchor close to shore, a captain might fire a cannon or two toward the trading village to "encourage" the local merchants to bring more slaves to market or to offer them at lower prices. Seaman Henry Ellison testified before Parliament that in the 1760s he saw seven or eight slave-ship captains in concert fire "red hot shot" upon a trading town on the Gambia River, setting several houses aflame in an effort to get traders to lower prices. In June 1793 something similar happened in Cameroon, when Captain James McGauley fired a cannon at a black trader's canoe, killing one and sending a message that the man was to sell slaves to no other ships until he, McGauley, had his full complement. Yet it must be emphasized that these were unusual cases. Most captains carefully cultivated their relationships with African traders, especially if they aspired to trade beyond a single voyage. Commerce depended largely on trust and consent.[42]

To inaugurate the trade, the captain ordered his sailors to hoist from belowdecks a varied and expensive cargo of manufactured goods, which would then be exchanged for a human cargo. As the main deck of the ship became a marketplace, the captain then assumed the role of "big man," trading as equals with another "big man," sometimes a local "king," to whom he paid duties. To both the paramount political leader and to lesser traders, he also gave *dashee* or *comey* to encourage them to bring slaves to the ship. He served food and liquor and often invited some of the more important merchants to sleep aboard the vessel. A complex, drawn-out process of deal making followed, which would slowly fill the lower deck with enslaved people to be shipped to the Americas. The captain's work as a business agent was described in astonishing detail in a document produced by William Jenkins of the *Molly* in 1759–60 during a voyage to Bonny.[43]

Jenkins first recorded the items his owners had stowed on board the ship before it left Bristol and which now appeared on the deck of the *Molly* for sale. The cargo consisted of firearms and ammunition, textiles, metals and metalwares, alcohol, and other manufactured goods such as caps and beads (arrangoes). The largest part of the cargo were muskets (six hundred), blunderbusses, flints, and gunpowder. Then, in order of decreasing value, an array of cloths, produced in England and India, such as nicanees, romauls, and chelloes; iron bars and copper rods, knives and iron pots; and a few miscellaneous items. Captain Jenkins also had on board "1885 Galls of Brandy in Casks" as well as bottles and numerous smaller casks called "caggs."[44]

The most remarkable thing about the document Jenkins kept was his careful recording of his business dealings with African merchants, beginning with the king of Bonny, to whom he paid trading duties and fees for wood and water. Jenkins recorded the traders each and every one by name. He gave *dashee* to "Lord York," "Black Tom," "Cudjoe," "Parlement Gentleman," "Gallows," and seventy-five others who clustered in two main networks, one associated with the king and another with the big merchant John Mendoss. But of the eighty who got *dashee,* fifty-eight never brought the *Molly* a single slave. One of the largest notations was, "The King of Bonny: Trust," followed by a variety of items to be given in exchange for slaves on a future voyage. Jenkins clearly intended to build and sustain working relationships.[45]

Most of the purchases were small as traders brought 1, 2, or 3 slaves on board at a time, as was typical on almost all areas of the Guinea coast. Only three sellers provided more than 20 altogether; another six brought more than 10, and these only a few at a time. The leading provider was Jemmy Sharp, who visited the ship seven times and sold 28 slaves. Of those who did bring slaves, twenty-four got *dashee,* while twenty-five did not. But the ones who received *dashee* produced 216 slaves, more than three-quarters of the 286 Jenkins would eventually purchase. Among those who sold slaves, all but fifteen came and sold more than once; altogether this group accounted for 267 slaves, 93.3 percent of the total. The *Molly*'s most frequent visitor was a man named Tillebo, who came aboard eleven times to sell slaves. All told, Captain Jenkins conducted 160 transactions to purchase slaves, which allowed him to "slave" his ship more quickly than usual, in only three months. He ended up with a cargo of 125 men, 114 women, 21 boys, and 26 girls. Clearly the contacts were worth the investment, as the captain had transacted his trade successfully. New challenges awaited the captain now that 286 restive African prisoners were aboard his ship.

Brother Captain

Slave-ship captains also established relations with one another, especially over the several months while they were buying slaves on the coast of Africa. Here, at various shipping points, they met repeatedly, taking turns to dine in twos or threes or more on their various ships or with African traders ashore, overcoming their command isolation and sharing useful knowledge and information. William Smith, a surveyor for the Royal African Company, noted that captains and officers of the slave ships in and around the Gambia River in 1726 were "visiting each other daily." The same was true wherever the ships congregated. Even though they were competing with one another—to conduct their trade quickly and advantageously, to get a full cargo of slaves, and to sail expeditiously for the New World—they recognized and acted on their common interests.[46]

John Newton visited and communicated with other captains regularly, exchanging useful information of all kinds, about the state of trade, the availability and price of slaves, the news of danger and disaster. He asked one captain to take his mutinous sailors and rebellious slaves, another to lend his surgeon. He engaged in "raillery" with his peers, much of it apparently sexual banter. The others teased Newton for his slavish devotion to a single woman, his wife, Mary; he countered by saying that "some of them are mere slaves to a hundred," some no doubt women they bought on the coast. Slave-ship captains resorted with familiar ease to the idiom of their industry.

Some of the information the captains exchanged could be a matter of life or death. They talked repeatedly of disasters—slave ships "cut off" by local Africans, bloody insurrections, seamen gone missing, explosions, and shipwrecks. Captain Street suggested the importance of such concourse when he reported from Rio Pongas on the Windward Coast in 1807: he listed thirteen slave ships and when they would be "slaved" and leave the coast; he noted that their captains were having a hard time buying rice, which they needed to feed the slaves during their Middle Passages; he described how two vessels had been damaged by a countertide at a local slave-trading factory. He also noted an attempted murder and mutiny against Captain McBride aboard the *Hind,* the same ship's high mortality, and a mass runaway of sailors from the *Byam.*[47]

Mostly the captains talked about business at their meetings—the availability and prices of slaves perhaps above all else, but also their relationships with black traders (who could be trusted and who could not) and what kinds of goods such traders were eager to buy. They might also share resources, lend skilled labor (a carpenter or a surgeon), supplies (medicines), food, or trade goods as long as such sharing would not damage the interests of the merchants and shipowners for whom they worked. Pride of place in these meetings would belong to the captain who knew the region best. Seaman William Butterworth described a custom in which the "oldest" captain in the gathered group (meaning the most experienced) would lead the vessels up the Calabar River to the canoe house to trade.[48]

Captains also compared notes on their officers, sailors, and slaves. Here the reputation of a rising officer might be enhanced or damaged, as all captains would take note of skilled and dependable men they might wish to hire, or others they would refuse to hire, on future voyages. They also talked, and often complained, about surgeons and their qualifications. They were quick to blame a surgeon who could not prevent mortality, and in a few instances serious conflicts developed

The passage from expropriation and enslavement in Africa to exploitation in America often involved transportation by canoe from shore to ship, as shown by this illustration of watercraft on the Gold Coast in the late seventeenth century.

"Black Bart" Roberts was a mate on a slave ship when captured by pirates in 1719. He joined them and soon became the most notorious captain of the "golden age of piracy." His disruption of the slave trade moved Parliament to increase naval patrols in West Africa, one of which killed Roberts in battle in 1722. Fifty-two members of his multiracial crew were hanged at Cape Coast Castle.

London's leading slave trader in the early eighteenth century, Humphry Morice was one of the most powerful people of his day as governor (highest officer) of the Bank of England and a Member of Parliament. David Le Marchand sculpted his portrait in ivory, likely from Africa.

Henry Laurens was British North America's leading slave trader in the middle of the eighteenth century. He used capital accumulated in the slave trade to rise to the highest levels of South Carolina and early American society and politics. He became president of the Continental Congress in 1777.

Sharks followed slavers across the Atlantic, feeding hungrily on the corpses of sailors and especially slaves who died and were thrown over the side of the ship. Captains of slave ships consciously used the sharks to augment their ruling terror.

Former sailor and artist Nicholas Pocock drew Sydenham Teast's Bristol shipyard in 1760, showing what appear to be three large deep-water vessels, perhaps slavers, all at different stages of construction and surrounded by artisans and workers, a couple of them apparently of African descent.

Liverpool was the greatest British slaving port and indeed by late in the eighteenth century the greatest in the world. The city's merchants employed dozens of large three-masted ships like the one painted by the maritime artist William Jackson, circa 1780.

Common to the slave trade were smaller vessels such as the sloop and schooner, especially popular among North American merchants, and larger two-masted craft such as the brigantine (and the snow, or snauw).

The barricado was a bulwark behind which the crewmen could retreat to escape an uprising and fire their weapons to restore order. This unrealistic depiction of an early-nineteenth-century French slave ship shows a barricado that is too short, too open at the seams, and too fragile, but it does show how men and women were separated and treated differently on the slave ship.

An imam of the Senegambia region, Job Ben Solomon was captured by African traders and sold to a slaver in 1730. Distinguished by his elite carriage and learning, he was eventually freed and repatriated by the Royal African Company, which he in turn assisted in its various business affairs.

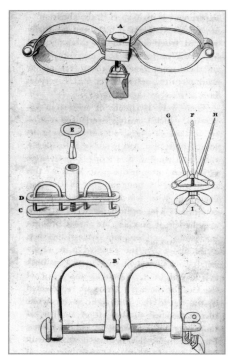

Slave ships routinely carried manacles for the wrists and shackles for the ankles of the captives. Captains used thumbscrews (center left) to torture rebellious captives and the *speculum oris* (center right) to force open throats and pour gruel into those who refused to eat.

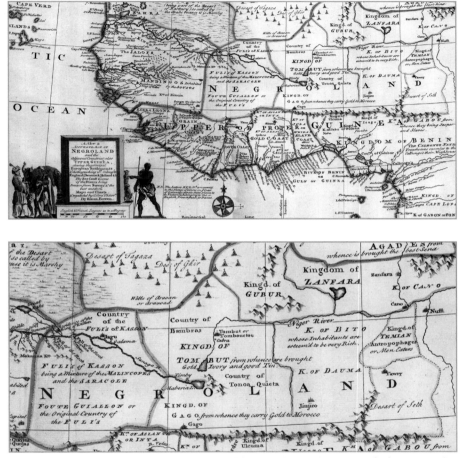

Alongside the customary "Guinea" as a description of the main slave-trading region of Africa, mapmaker Emmanuel Bowen added in 1747 the more racially charged "Negroland," demonstrating how the Atlantic slave system was creating new ways of thinking about the order of humankind.

The history of the trading fort at Anomabu on the Gold Coast reflected fierce imperial rivalry over gold and slaves. It was occupied by the Dutch, the Swedes, the Danes, the Anomabu themselves, and finally the English, who made it one of their six main forts in the late eighteenth century.

Dahomey was a strategically located kingdom on the "Slave Coast," a region whose name owed something to the enslaving power of the army, shown here during a religious procession. Seven European vessels lurk in the background, no doubt waiting for the big business of slaving to resume.

The Vili kingdom of Loango, in the Kongo region, was one of the greatest sources of slaves in all of Africa. A slaving gang in the foreground would carry prisoners to the coast and an endless train of slave ships. An estimated million souls passed through Loango in the eighteenth century alone.

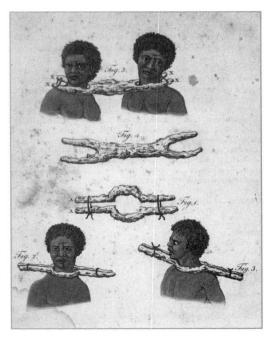

As ever larger numbers of Guineamen appeared on the coast of West Africa in the eighteenth century, the catchment area for slaves expanded more deeply into the interior, resulting in longer marches to the sea. These constraints allowed African merchants to control and move the coffles toward the ships.

Olaudah Equiano, also known as Gustavus Vassa, was the "voice of the voiceless" in the eighteenth-century slave trade, penning the most influential literary work of the abolitionist movement from an African perspective, that of an eleven-year-old boy who experienced the "astonishment and terror" of the slave ship.

James Field Stanfield sailed to Benin in 1774 aboard the slave ship *Eagle*. When the abolitionist movement emerged in the late 1780s, Stanfield wrote an exposé of the slave trade from the perspective of the common sailor, showing the horrors experienced by those who sailed the ships.

John Newton made four voyages, one as mate and three as captain, between 1748 and 1754. Later in life he became an evangelical minister, wrote the famous hymn "Amazing Grace," and finally declared himself a staunch opponent of the human commerce from which he had once made his livelihood.

The slave ship was a floating prison in which the captives outnumbered the guards by an order of ten to one and sometimes more; hence the male prisoners (and rebellious females) were shackled to limit their capacity to resist.

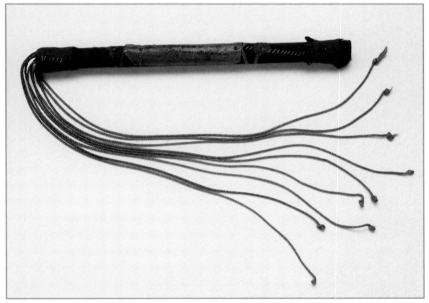

The "cat" was used to move people around the decks, to "stow" them belowdecks, and to punish them for any and all infractions, from refusing to eat to attempted insurrection. The nine knotted tails were designed to lacerate the flesh and maximize the pain of the person being flogged.

Captain Edward Kimber reportedly flogged to death a fifteen-year-old girl who refused to dance naked. He was brought to trial and acquitted, not because it was proven that the alleged killing did not happen but because the two members of his crew who reported it were shown to have a grudge against him.

Captains and doctors alike believed that exercise was essential to the health of the enslaved aboard the ship, so they organized dancing on deck every day, for men and women prisoners, assisted sometimes by music but more commonly by whips, which the mates at the left and right use to make the men move.

The Slave Deck of the Albaroz, *Prize to the* Albatross, *1845* is a rare eyewitness depiction of the lower deck of a slaver. It was painted by Lieutenant Francis Meynell of the British Royal Navy after his vessel, the *Albatross*, captured the Brazilian or Portuguese slaver and liberated the three hundred slaves on board.

The Dying Negro illustrated a poem written in 1773 by John Bicknell and Thomas Day after the authors read a London newspaper article about a suicide at sea. The image shows how the resistance of the enslaved circulated from the slave ship back to the metropolis to influence developing antislavery discourse.

REPRESENTATION of an **INSURRECTION**
on board
A SLAVE-SHIP.

Shewing how the crew fire upon the unhappy Slaves from behind the
BARRICADO, *erected on board all Slave ships, as a security whenever*
such commotions may happen.

In stark contrast to the supine, orderly bodies of African captives pictured in the famous graphic of the slave ship *Brooks*, this representation of a slave insurrection shows the opposite, resistance and disorder. The crewmen have retreated behind the barricado, firing their muskets down on the rebels, some of whom leap overboard.

This depiction of a slave market in early-nineteenth-century Brazil reveals how the enslaved studied the slave ship. A boy at the left with his back turned (detail, right) draws graffiti—a slave ship—on the wall, no doubt the very same vessel on which he and the others in the market just crossed the Atlantic.

Thomas Clarkson traveled to Bristol and Liverpool in 1787 to gather evidence against the slave trade. When slave merchants and captains learned his intentions, they refused to speak to him. He turned to dissident common sailors, many of them victims of the trade, who instructed him in violent detail how a slave ship actually worked.

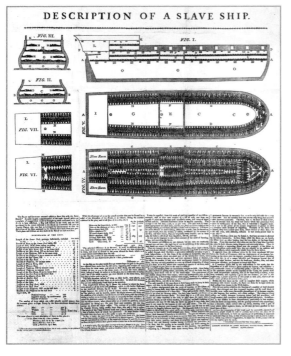

The Society for Effecting the Abolition of the Slave Trade used the measurements of a real slave ship, the *Brooks* of Liverpool; added Clarkson's research about the nightmarish social reality of all slave ships; and published a broadside that would become its most powerful propaganda against the slave trade.

between captains and their usually more educated and occasionally "enlightened" physicians.[49]

Conversations about sailors and slaves tended to concentrate on rebelliousness and health. The blacklisting of working seamen was an order of business in these meetings, and so, too, were decisions to remove mutinous sailors to nearby men-of-war when possible. Captains compared notes on punishments, offering encouragement to one another for torturing innovations. Conversations about African slaves were not dissimilar, although undoubtedly laced with more racist invective, about the various ethnic groups and their responses to being on the ship. There existed an unwritten rule of the fraternity of slave-ship captains on the coast: they would, regardless of nationality, come to one another's assistance in dealing with their crews and especially their slaves, particularly in moments of rebellion.[50]

A collective of slave-ship captains sometimes acted as a sort of government on the coast of Africa. When an issue of concern to all slavers in a given area had to be addressed, someone called a council meeting to be attended by all nearby captains. Like naval officers who met to confer on battle strategy, the slave-ship captains deliberated and gave their collective judgment on the best course of action. They might decide the fate of the ringleader of a failed insurrection, as William Snelgrave asked a group of eight to do in 1721: their verdict was to gather all the ships close together, bring all slaves upon deck, hoist the malefactor into the air, then shoot him while elevated so everyone could see and thereby imbibe the lesson of terror. The slave in question argued with Snelgrave, convinced that he had too much economic value to be executed. He was wrong. Snelgrave and the other captains were determined to send the message that this is what would happen to any African who killed "a white Man." Hugh Crow called a meeting of all the captains at Bonny to ask what should be done with a mate who was often drunk, fomenting mutiny among the crew, and causing the captain to fear for his life. Their verdict was to allow him to keep his cabin (because he was from a "respectable family in Liverpool") but to remove him from duty.[51]

The captains also bragged much among themselves about their fraudulent trading practices—watered spirits, false heads in kegs of gunpowder, big pieces cut from the middle of a bolt of cloth, cheating in "number, weight, and measure, or quality of what they purchase, in every possible way." Newton recalled that "the man who was most expert in committing frauds was reckoned the most handy and clever fellow in the business." This was the art of the trade. The captains, in sum, showed camaraderie, a community of interest, a consciousness of kind. Their meetings represented a sort of propertied white man's mutual-aid society.[52]

Jailer

The long, slow purchase of the enslaved was conducted within a "warlike peace" on the coast of West Africa. Slaves spent six months and more on the ship while the purchase was being completed and six to ten weeks aboard during the Middle Passage. A few captains tried to randomize their "cargo," mixing peoples of different African cultures and languages to minimize their ability to communicate, cooperate, and resist, but this was difficult, costly, and in the end impractical. Given the competitiveness of the slave trade and the nature of its organization on the African side, captains had very little control over which slaves they could buy, so they took what they could get. During this long stretch of time, the captain and indeed every member of the crew assumed that the people brought on board were held against their will and that they would do anything possible to escape captivity. The captain's power depended first and foremost on brute force.

The captain usually made initial contact with an enslaved person at the moment of inspection and purchase, whether in a fortress, in a factory, in a coastal village, or on the ship. At that time the captain and the doctor assessed that individual's age, health, and working capacity, according to the criteria of his employer. He would also "read" that person's "country marks," ritual scars distinctive to each West African cultural group, and he would, based on experience, ascribe likely behaviors rooted in stereotypes—Igbos, the wisdom among captains went, were prone to suicide and must be watched; Coromantees were rebellious and must be chained; Angolas were passive and need not be chained. Related to this was an assessment of attitude—that is, each individual's probability of cooperation with or resistance to the shipboard regime. If the captain decided to purchase a given person, he offered a combination of goods to the traders and haggled until they closed the deal. From that moment forward, the enslaved person, whether man, woman, boy, or girl, would be known to the captain as a number. The first purchased was Number 1, and so on, until the ship was fully "slaved" and ready to sail to the Americas.

Captains varied in their degree of involvement in the daily activities of the ship. After delegating authority, most seem to have remained somewhat aloof and remote, to be seen only at certain, limited times, usually pacing the quarterdeck. Some might go forward among the male slaves, but only occasionally and under heavy guard, and few seem to have gone below among the enslaved on the lower deck under any circumstances. Captain Francis Messervy of the *Ferrers* galley discovered why, the hard way, in 1721. According to fellow captain William Snelgrave, Messervy was guilty of "over-care, and too great Kindness to the Negroes on board his Ship," helping, for example, to prepare and serve their food. Snelgrave wrote, "I could not forbear observing to him, 'How imprudent it was in him to do so: For tho' it was proper for a Commander sometimes to go forward, and observe how things were managed; yet he ought to take a proper time, and have a good many of his white People in Arms when he went; or else they having him so much in their Power, might incourage the Slaves to mutiny.'" Messervy apparently disdained the advice, for soon, while walking among the men slaves at mealtime, they "laid hold on him, and beat out his Brains with the little Tubs, out of which they eat the boiled Rice." They then exploded into a long-planned insurrection, during and after which eighty Africans were killed or died, by gunshot, by drowning (after they jumped overboard), or by hunger strike (refusing to eat after the initial slaughter). The moral of the story for Snelgrave was that captains must be circumspect about their involvement in the daily routines of the slaves, not least because the captives studied the ship's hierarchy and would always strike first, given the opportunity, at the most powerful person aboard: "they always aim at the chief Person in the Ship, whom they soon distinguish by the respect shown him by the rest of the People." It was never hard to figure out who was the big man on a slave ship.[53]

Every time a new group of slaves came on board, captain and crew would watch closely to see who among them might prove to be what they called "guardians" or "confidence slaves."[54] These were Africans the captain and officers felt they could trust and who might therefore be recruited to help maintain order on board the ship. Those who seemed well disposed to their captors, especially if they were people of some influence among their own countrymen and -women on board, might be offered a deal. "Guardians" might be chosen to "domineer over the rest." Anyone who knew English could serve as a translator among his or her own countrypeople and perhaps others. Women might be offered jobs as cooks, maybe even the captain's cook (which would probably imply other responsibilities). One African man found a job in the shipboard division of labor as a tailor. But most important would be those who would help to manage the enslaved, keep them in order. The captain (or the mate) might offer incentives to boys, who had the run of the ship, if they would spy on the men and inform of conspiracies.[55]

William Snelgrave explained how a slave might be used to help manage the ship. An older woman, who was apparently close to the king of Dahomey, perhaps even a wife, fell out of favor and was sentenced to death: she was, on his orders, thrown overboard from a canoe, hands tied, to the sharks. Somehow the woman survived the ordeal and was rescued unharmed by Snelgrave's sailors and brought aboard the ship. Snelgrave feared that the king would take revenge if he learned that he had saved the woman, so he apparently kept her hidden. The "sensible" woman, conscious that her advanced age made her "useless" as a slave, felt grateful to Snelgrave for saving her life and did everything she could to assist him during the voyage. Because of her high social standing, she was well known to many of the other enslaved people on board. She used her influence to convince them that the "white People" were not as bad as they had been told; she consoled the captives, made them "easy in their Minds." She had special influence, wrote Snelgrave, among the "female *Negroes,* who used always to be the most troublesome to us, on account of the noise and clamour they made." They "were kept in such Order and Decorum by this Woman, that I had never the like in any Voyage before." Snelgrave expressed his gratitude in return, finding the woman a "generous and good" master, Charles Dunbar of Antigua. A strategy of co-optation could help to keep order on the ship.[56]

Another kind of co-optation, or deal making, was less voluntary and was in some ways indistinguishable from the rape and sexual abuse of the African women on board. Captains, and less frequently officers, took "favorites" from among the enslaved women, moving them from the lower deck to the captain's cabin, which meant more room, more and better food, greater freedom, and perhaps in some cases less-violent discipline. Such appears to have been the case with a slave woman on board John Fox's slave schooner who was known as Amba to the Africans and as Betsey to the captain and other Europeans. Thomas Boulton complained of an African woman who used her privileged relationship to (mulatto) Captain John Tittle in order to wield power on the ship. He wrote of "Dizia, an *African* Lady":

> Whose sooty charms he [the captain] was so wrapt in,
> He strait ordain'd her second captain;
> So strict was she in ev'ry matter,
> She even lock'd the jar of water;
> And whil'st in that high station plac'd,
> No thirsty soul a drop must taste.

Whenever the captain tired of current favorites, he removed them from that "high station" and found replacements right outside his cabin door, which on many slave ships abutted the women's apartment.[57]

Captains also offered incentives for what they considered good behavior. Hugh Crow trained some enslaved men to work the ship's cannon in 1806, in the event of an attack by a French privateer. In return, he explained, the enslaved "were each provided with a pair of light trowsers, a shirt, and a cap." They "were very proud of this preferment" and thereby came to resemble the crew more than the other slaves. A substantial number of captains rewarded the enslaved for work they did aboard, giving tobacco or brandy, for example, for scrubbing the apartments of the lower deck. Other incentives might be beads, extra food, or the privilege, for a man, of getting out of chains. During an insurrection of 1704, a seventeen-year-old male slave shielded the captain from a rebel's blow with a stave, suffered a fractured arm for it, and was rewarded with his freedom upon arrival in Virginia. These positive inducements were important to the captain's power to keep order aboard the slave ship, but they should not be overemphasized. Relatively few of the enslaved got any special deal, and the vast majority on any given ship were ruled by brute force and abject terror.[58]

The government of the slave ship depended on what was called exemplary punishment and its hoped-for deterrent effect. If, therefore, the captain's instruments of discipline helped to establish and maintain power among the sailors, they were even more decisive among the enslaved. The cat was used in full, flailing force whenever the enslaved were on deck, especially at mealtime. The mates and the boatswain employed it to "encourage" people to obey orders—to move quickly, to line up in orderly fashion, to eat properly. The person who refused food could expect a longer lashing from the cat, and indeed this was the only way many could be made to eat. A substantial number still refused, which often brought into play another functional instrument of terror, the *speculum oris*. The lower deck itself might also be used to discipline the rebellious, as a passenger aboard a slaver noted in 1768: the "Captain would not suffer a soul on deck for several days, designing, as he said, to lower their spirits by a sweating." When he did finally let them come on the main deck, they revolted, prompting him, after regaining control, to say that "not a soul should see the sun till they arrived in Barbados."[59]

A more common approach in the aftermath of failed insurrections was for the captain to whip, torture, and execute the rebels on the main deck, to maximize the terror. Here was a moment when the captain shed his remoteness and demonstrated his power with utmost effort—and effect. During these exemplary public punishments, the captain himself usually wielded the cat or turned the thumbscrews, to torture the rebels and terrorize their compatriots. Another preferred instrument was called "the tormentor." This was a large cook's fork, which was heated white hot and applied to the flesh of rebels. Nothing more certainly called forth the raw power of the captain than the will of the enslaved to resist it.[60]

The Savage Spirit of the Trade

When Captain Richard Jackson muttered, on setting off, that he had a hell of his own aboard the *Brownlow,* he cast himself as the devil. Many on board his ship would come to see him that way, including his chief mate, John Newton, who by the time he recounted his memories of Jackson had reinvented himself as a saint. Yet in talking about his floating hell, Jackson conveyed something of great significance about himself and slave-ship captains in general, including Newton. Their power in some inescapable measure depended on inflicting cruelty and suffering as a means of human control; it depended, in a word, on terror. This is why hell, as a place of deliberately imposed torment, was such a good and useful analogy and in the end why abolitionists found it so easy to demonize the slave-ship captain in their propaganda. Not all masters of Guineamen were devils, but almost each and every one had the devil in him. This was not a flaw of individual personality or character. It was a requirement of the job and the larger economic system it served.[61]

Newton came to understand this toward the end of his life. He had been aboard many slavers, as sailor, mate, captain, and visitor, learning the lore and watching the practices of numerous captains. He insisted that there were "a few honest and humane men" in the trade. He had known "several commanders of African ships who were prudent, respectable men, and who maintained a proper discipline and regularity in their vessels; but there were too many of a different character." Among the "too many," including Jackson, cruelty came to be the defining feature of the captain's power, and this was reflected in the broader culture of slave-ship captains.[62]

Newton saw the cruelty in all its colors—mostly purples, blues, and reds. Captains accused sick seamen of being lazy, then lashed them, after which they died. Captains entertained themselves by tormenting sailors during the monotonous hours of a long voyage: "the chief study and amusement of their leisure seems to be, how to make the sailors, at least such of them as they take a dislike to, as miserable as they can." For the enslaved, of course, the terror was much more pervasive. Captains unleashed sexual terror on women captives. For men the terror was equally great, although different in its methods. Newton saw "unmerciful whippings, continued till the poor creatures have not had power to groan under their misery, and hardly a sign of life has remained." He saw the enslaved agonizing for hours and indeed days in thumbscrews. He knew one captain who "studied, with no small attention, how to make death as excruciating as possible."

Newton could not bring himself to convey the full story of terror on the slave ship to the readers of his pamphlet *Thoughts upon the African Slave Trade* nor to the select committee of the House of Commons before whom he testified. But he did tell all in a private letter to the abolitionist Richard Phillips in July 1788. He made it clear that he was talking about a captain he had sailed with, who would have been Richard Jackson, hell-master aboard the *Brownlow* in 1748–49. Newton "frequently heard the details of his cruelties from his own mouth." (Note the "frequently" and the implied pride.) After a failed insurrection, Jackson sentenced the rebellious slaves to die, then selected their mode of punishment. The first group

he jointed; that is, he cut off, with an axe, first their feet, then their legs below the knee, then their thighs; in like manner their hands, then their arms below the elbow, and then at their shoulders, till their bodies remained only like the trunk of a tree when all the branches are lopped away; and, lastly, their heads. And, as he proceeded in his operation, he threw the reeking members and heads in the midst of the bulk of the trembling slaves, who were chained upon the main-deck.

The terror so far was insufficient, so Captain Jackson then punished the second group:

He tied round the upper parts of the heads of others a small soft platted rope, which the sailors call a point, so loosely as to admit a short lever: by continuing to turn the lever, he drew the point more and more tight, till at length he forced their eyes to stand out of their heads; and when he had satiated himself with their torments, he cut their heads off.

It is not clear whether Newton merely heard about these punishments or whether he saw and perhaps even participated in them. The memory sounds rather more vivid than would have been conveyed through a story. Indeed Newton might have been describing a specific event that took place aboard the *Brownlow,* where the slaves rose up in insurrection only to be suppressed and suffer what must have been savage punishments. Safety trumped humanity. If Newton was involved in these horrific practices—and the ship's chief mate would have been involved, possibly as executioner—it would not have been the only time he conveniently confused what he did with what he claimed merely to know. In *Thoughts upon the African Slave Trade,* he wrote that he had "seen" the use of the thumbscrews, "a dreadful engine, which, if the screw be turned by an unrelenting hand, can give intolerable anguish." This was, in a narrow and technical sense, the truth: Newton had "seen" the thumbscrews in operation *because he himself had used them*—on children, no less. Newton wrote to Mary that he was "absolute in my small dominions (life and death excepted)." But as Newton's story of Captain Jackson made clear, having a hell of one's own meant that matters of life and death were not excepted.

Newton developed a theory about why violence, cruelty, and terror were intrinsic to the slave trade. He explained that most, though not all, captains of Guineamen were brutal or, as he put it in a more Christian parlance, "hard hearted," to a degree that would have been almost incomprehensible to anyone who had no experience of the trade. He wrote, "A savageness of spirit, not easily conceived, infuses itself (though, as I have observed, there are exceptions) into those who exercise power on board an African slave-ship, from the captain downwards. It is the spirit of the trade, which, like a pestilential air, is so generally infectious, that but few escape it." Violence and suffering were so pervasive on the slaver that the "work" itself—meaning the discipline and control of the human "cargo"—tended directly to "efface moral sense, to rob the heart of every gentle and humane disposition, and to harden it, like steel, against all impressions of sensibility." The slave trade thus produced and reproduced, in both officers and crew, a callous, violent moral insensibility.

The most savage and insensible spirit of all belonged to the captain, the sovereign of the wooden world, the man "absolute in his command." For those who were "bred up" to the trade, the gaining of knowledge and the hardening of the heart went together. Newton explained, "Many of the captains are brought up in the business; and pass through the several stages of apprentices, foremastmen, and mates, before they are masters, and gradually acquire a cruel disposition together with their knowledge of the trade." Learning cruelty was intrinsic to learning the trade itself, as Captain Bowen realized when he tried to restrain the ferocious violence of a mate "regularly initiated at Liverpool" in the human commerce. Bowen pronounced the man "incurable," got rid of him, and himself made that the one and only slaving voyage he ever captained. Newton, too, was part of a system of terror that applied to both sailors and slaves, one that not only practiced ruthless violence but glorified it.[63]

Newton's understanding was echoed by numerous others involved in the trade. Of the officers on his own ship, seaman William Butterworth explained, "The Cyclops might have forged their case-hardened hearts." Seaman Silas Told, who was "saved" from the slave trade by a Christian conversion in Boston in 1734, recognized that the captain's cruelty and terror were not an individual matter but a systemic one. He said of himself with startling honesty, "I probably might (by promotion to the rank of captain) have proved as eminent a savage as the most notorious character among them." William Leigh, writing as "Africanus" about the slave trade in 1787–88, made the same point. The "cruel conduct of a few individuals" as captains was not the issue. It was rather "the general cruelty of the system." This was the ultimate meaning of Richard Jackson's hell aboard the *Brownlow*.[64]

CHAPTER 8

The Sailor's Vast Machine

As they walked the streets of the Liverpool waterfront at five o'clock on a still-dark morning, 1775, the two men listened for a fiddle. One was the captain of a slave ship, the other likely its surgeon; they "were upon the look out for hands" to carry the slaver to Cape Mount, Africa, where they would pick up a human cargo and cross the Atlantic for American plantations. They soon heard the telltale sound, located the house it was coming from, and "naturally concluded that none but sailors at such a time & in that house could be awake." They had found what they were looking for.[1]

It was not a good moment to be recruiting for the trade, and they knew it. Tensions were running high in Liverpool, as slave-trade merchants had slashed wages, and soon thousands of angry sailors would pour into the very streets they were walking. Still, they had to raise a crew, so they stepped nervously through the door and toward the scraping fiddle. There they found the landlady of the establishment, asleep, or passed out, or perhaps even knocked out, sitting on a chair "bareheaded, with her eyelids as black as coal, a large lump upon one corner of her forehead, & the remains of a couple of streams of blood from each nostril bedaub'd the underpart of her face." Nearby was a man, her husband, they surmised, lying by an overturned table with empty drinking vessels, a tin quart and a pint bottle, strewn around. He, too, was in bad shape. His wig had been thrown behind the nearby chimney, his coat was off, his hand held a broken pipe, and his stockings were down about his ankles, revealing bruised shins. The ship's officers steered clear of these two and pressed on toward the music, "if musick it might be called." Climbing some stairs, they got to the top, "where a door half open invited us to look in."[2]

They saw a blind fiddler and a single sailor, who was "skipping & capering round the room in his shirt & trousers." The dancing tar did not immediately notice his visitors, but finally, in one of his "revolutions" around the room, he stopped, sized them up, and glowered. In salty language he asked what they wanted. The surgeon explained that "it would have been dangerous to speak out"—that is, to answer that they were recruiting for a slave ship—so they "modestly hinted to him" that they might want someone to work on a ship whose destination was left discreetly unstated.

The sailor replied "with a Volley of Oaths" and upbraided the visitors for their stupidity. They must know very little of sailors, he explained, "to think he would go to sea while he could keep a fiddler & dance all night & sleep as long in the day as he pleas'd." No, he would not go to sea until economic necessity required him to do so, and he still had fifteen shillings in his pocket. He expected to spend that money soon: "that I believe will go today, But no matter for that!" He had dancing yet to do.

The captain and surgeon listened carefully and decided that these were "unanswerable reasons." So they turned to leave. But the sailor called to them, "Hark ye Gentle[me]n." He said, "that B——h below there with the black eyes has a design to shabb me off tomorrow"—by which he meant play a dirty trick to get rid of him, turn him over to the constable, who would slap him in jail for debt. She would then do as all Liverpool landlords and ladies did—sell him to an outward-bound Guineaman and collect his two or three months' advance wages to pay off his debt. If the gentlemen would call again tomorrow, the sailor might, he said, "play the Jade a trick" and leave town before she could do her dirty work. The sailor then declared that he had "forgot to ask where you are bound" but waved it off, saying never mind.

Turning back to the order of the day, he bellowed, "Play up you old blind rascal."

Here was jolly jack-tar in almost stereotypical form—a dancing, carousing, foul-mouthed "rolling stone," unconcerned about tomorrow. But here, too, was a man of independent spirit who cherished the autonomy his full pockets could provide, and someone who had contempt for his so-called betters and would-be employers. Would he go to Africa? Perhaps; he left the possibility open. With a cosmopolitan fatalism, he implied that it did not matter where his shipboard labors might take him. His motivations in seeking a berth would be fundamentally economic. As a proletarian, he depended on the money wage. He would go back to sea when his pockets were empty.

This kind of encounter often took place in a context of war, of two distinct but related kinds. The first was war between nations, which was common in the eighteenth century. Indeed, Britain and her American colonies were at war, usually against France or Spain, over markets, commerce, and empire, for almost half the years between 1700 and 1807. When the slave-ship recruiters conversed with the dancing sailor in Liverpool in 1775, fighting had already begun in what would be the American War for Independence. Britain would undertake a massive mobilization of military labor.

This mobilization would intensify a second, older, and less-formal kind of war between classes, over maritime labor power, between royal officials, magistrates, merchants, captains, and officers on the one side, sailors on the other. The former group struggled to find seamen enough to man their ships of war, trade, and privateering, and not infrequently members of the group battled one another over the right to employ the seaman as they collectively battled the seaman himself. They resorted to violence and special allurements, to the press-gang and the crimp, as well as to higher wages and better working conditions. Within this war over his labor, the seaman fought for his own autonomy and interests.

Did the dancing sailor join the slave ship? The surgeon did not say. But it is clear that many thousands of men like him did. Year after year merchants and captains, one way or another, found workers enough to sail their dozens of ships to the west coast of Africa. In order to ship 3.5 million slaves to the New World, they hired crews that would have totaled 350,000 men. About 30 percent of these would have been officers and skilled workers, who had special inducements and who therefore made more repeat voyages than did common sailors. If each such person made three voyages, the core of skilled seafaring officers would have been roughly 35,000. If each common sailor (including apprentices and landmen) made one or two voyages (one and a half on average), the total involved would have been about 210,000.

How did merchants and captains do it? How did they win the war for maritime labor, or at least win often enough to accomplish their economic objectives in the slave trade? How did they manage to find thousands of workers for a trade in which working conditions were harsh, wages were modest, food was poor, and the dangers of mortality (by accident, overzealous discipline, slave revolt, or disease) were great? This chapter explores the collective work and experience of sailors in the slave trade and thereby places the life and writing of sailor-poet James Field Stanfield in a broader context. It is a tale of war, money, class, violence, race, and death, all linked, for sailors, to a floating workplace, what Stanfield called the "vast machine."[3]

From Port to Ship

Surveying the war over maritime labor, the surgeon's conclusions about manning a slave ship echoed those of Stanfield. The "Toil of shipping People," he thought, was "by far the most disagreeable [part] of a disagreeable voyage." Seamen did not like the Guinea trade; they despised the long confinement and "bad usage" by their officers. Like the dancing man with fifteen shillings, most sailors would never "go to Sea with a Farthing in their pocket and nothing but necessity compels them at the last, especially to Guinea." Only after they had spent their cash and piled up debt with a local landlady, and only after they found themselves in or facing jail would they agree to make a Guinea voyage, and then only "as the price of their liberty." Even under these circumstances, sailors experienced "an exchange of confinement [rather] than a release from it, for they are hurried from the prison on board the ship where they remain without the least prospect of getting [on] shore untill the Ship arrives on the Coast and most frequently not untill the West Indies." The pro-slave-trade surgeon and the anti-slave sailor agreed that service on a Guineaman was a prison stint.[4]

Numerous sailors explained how they ended up on a slave ship. Among those who made a voluntary choice was William Butterworth, who as a boy saw a cousin dressed in a uniform of the Royal Navy and decided his future then and there: he would be a sailor. He ran away to Liverpool in 1786, met a crimp, then met an old salt who warned him against the slave trade. Butterworth could not contradict a word he said, so he asked, with invincible ignorance, if "others had risked their lives and fortune, therefore why might not I?" He signed on.[5] William Richardson, a twenty-two-year-old veteran of twenty voyages in colliers (coal ships) from Shields to London, spied "a fine ship" on the Thames, fell in love with it, and joined up, not caring where it was bound.[6] John Richardson was removed from his midshipman's position in the Royal Navy because he had a habit of getting drunk, causing riots, and getting thrown in prison. He showed up on a slave ship, without a sea chest or clothing, and talked his way aboard.[7]

Other seamen found themselves working on slave ships through no choice of their own. Silas Told was apprenticed to the sea at the age of fourteen. His master took him on three West India voyages and then consigned him to Captain Timothy Tucker of the *Loyal George,* bound for Guinea.[8] Thomas Thompson once signed on to sail to the West Indies, only to be "fraudulently taken to Africa."[9] On another occasion the landlords "got hold of him" by debt and forced him, after imprisonment, to take a Guinea voyage with a violent captain he despised.[10] Henry Ellison, who had made ten slaving voyages, thought some tars went into the slave trade voluntarily but that "by far the greater part of them go from necessity." Some went from want, as they could find no other employ; some went because they fell into debt and wanted to escape jail. Ellison had known many such men and known them to be "fine seamen."[11]

Slave-trade seamen came from numerous social backgrounds, from orphanages and jails to respectable working-class and even middle-class families. But sailors as a whole were widely known as among the poorest occupational groups in Britain and America in the eighteenth century, so there were many more of the former group than the latter. Indeed John Newton described slave-trade seamen as "the refuse and dregs of the Nation," refugees of the "prisons and glass houses." He added that most "have generally been bred to it young" (like Told), but some were also "boys impatient of their parents or masters" (like Butterworth) and men "already ruin'd by some untimely vice" (like Richardson).[12] Hugh Crow largely agreed. The "white slaves" who served aboard his ships were essentially the "very dregs of the community": some were jailbirds, a few were landsmen who learned a few sea phrases and signed on under false pretenses, and an even smaller number were the wasted sons of gentlemen.[13] According to the slave-trade merchant James Penny, some of the landsmen who sailed on Liverpool ships were urban proletarians, "idle people from the manufacturing towns," such as Manchester.[14]

Advocates of the slave trade emphasized the significant number of landsmen who went on board slave ships. Some claimed that they made up half or more of each crew.[15] Landsmen did turn up on the muster rolls of slave ships, but in modest numbers. William Seaton took only two when he sailed in the *Swift* in 1775. During a wartime voyage of 1780–81, when labor demand would have been at its peak and landsmen most desirable, the *Hawk* carried only three among its crew of forty-one.[16] Those who began their work at sea as landsmen moved up the hierarchy voyage by voyage, becoming "half sailors," "3/4 sailors," both at lower pay, and finally full, able seamen.[17]

James Field Stanfield underestimated the number of seamen who joined the slave ship by choice, which often operated in tandem with necessity or coercion. Crimps not only "sold" sailors to Guinea captains, they delivered them by consent, as in the case of William Butterworth.

A landlord got Thomas Thompson thrown into jail, whereupon he "agreed" to go aboard a Guineaman. Choice would also be conditioned by necessity for a poor sailor who found a berth in a slave ship at forty shillings per month in peacetime, or sixty shillings and even seventy shillings per month in wartime, both of which were 20 to 25 percent higher than other trades. The same sailor also got a guaranteed food allowance (although of dubious quality) for the duration of the voyage. Many slave-trade merchants allowed sailors to allocate a portion of their pay to wives or mothers, who could collect it monthly in the home port. And even though it was usually forbidden, men who had a little money and signed on to a slaver had the prospect of private trade—carrying with them a few locally produced items such as knives or laced hats, which could then be traded for more valuable items (a parrot or a small piece of ivory) in Africa.[18]

What the slave trade offered above all else was ready money—an advance of two or three months' wages. This was the key to enticing sailors to join a trade they did not like. A common sailor could get £4 to £6 sterling (in 1760), which by today's standards would have been between $1,000 and $1,500, a considerable sum of money for a poor person, especially if times were hard and he had a family to feed. Sometimes the money fed a wild, rakish binge with his mates. The collector of customs in Liverpool made this point before Parliament in 1788. Because sailors were a "thoughtless Set of Men" who cared for today, not tomorrow, advance pay, "before sailing, would carry the far greater Part of them [on] the most dangerous Voyage that was ever undertaken." His stereotype notwithstanding, the collector expressed a fundamental truth. As proletarians with no other means of subsistence, sailors wanted and needed ready money, even when its price might be high.[19]

The slave trade offered prospects for upward mobility, although these were limited, as historian Emma Christopher has emphasized. As in any trade, able and ambitious men might move up the ladder, especially when the people above were dying and falling off, which was common in the Guinea trade. Silas Told went three voyages as an apprentice and then jumped to gunner. Over ten voyages Henry Ellison moved up the ranks from apprentice, as he testified in 1790: "A gunner was the highest [position] that I ever had—I had not learning to be a mate." He hit the wall that separated the poor from those who had acquired some education, which was essential to learning navigation and keeping books.[20]

Slave-trade sailors were a "motley crew" from "all over the globe." Many, perhaps a majority, were British in the broad sense—from England, Scotland, Wales, Ireland, and from British colonies (or new nations) overseas—but the ships also included significant numbers of other Europeans, Africans, Asians (especially lascars), and others. The *Bruce Grove* had a crew of thirty-one that included four Swedes, a Portuguese, an East Indian (lascar), and the proverbial black cook. The portledge bill of an American vessel, the *Tartar,* lists a smaller crew of fourteen, but one no less motley, from the coastal United States (Massachusetts to South Carolina), Denmark, France, Prussia, Sicily, and Sweden. The cooper was a "freeman" from St. Domingue, the new revolutionary republic of Haiti, and the cook had been born in Rio Pongas on the Windward Coast of Africa, where the vessel was bound.[21]

Like the cook of the *Tartar,* numerous men joined the slavers from along the African littoral, and many, such as the Fante and the Kru, had maritime backgrounds. Some were "grumettoes" who worked for short periods aboard the slave ships on the coast. Others made transatlantic voyages. The wage book of the *Hawk,* sailed by Captain John Smale and crew from Liverpool to the Gold Coast to the Cameroons River, to St. Lucia in 1780–81, listed Ackway, Lancelots Abey, Cudjoe, Quashey, Liverpool, and Joe Dick, all "fantyemen" who earned wages for the voyage. Four of them had been given wage advances in gold while on the African coast. Free sailors of African descent also joined the ships as their voyages began in European and American ports, not least because they had relatively few employment opportunities and seafaring was one of the most open and available. James Field Stanfield might not have understood the motives of such men, nor the lure of money to sailors poorer than himself, which in turn caused him to underestimate the role of choice, constrained though it was by necessity for so many.[22]

The Culture of the Common Sailor

Every sailor who went aboard a slave ship did so within a profound relationship of class. He had signed a contract, even if it meant drawing his best X on it, with a merchant and a captain, promising labor on the voyage for a money wage. For the next ten to fourteen months, he would experience the social life of the ship: he would sail to Africa and America and perform various kinds of labor along the way; he would live, eat, and sleep under a rigid hierarchy and harsh discipline. He would be a part of the miniature, class-riven society of the ship.[23]

Yet each sailor did not come aboard the ship as an autonomous individual. He came, in most cases, as someone who was already a member of a strong and distinctive culture, as Samuel Robinson discovered during his two voyages as a boy aboard slave ships, between 1800 and 1804. Sailors, he learned, had their own way of talking (full of sea phrases and metaphors), their own way of walking (with a wide gait to keep balance on rolling decks), their own way of seeing and acting upon the world. All of it was based on their work, which was cooperative and dangerous. Seamen depended on one another for their lives, and their social attitudes and relations reflected this fundamental fact. Robinson noted that they formed "strong attachments to their mates and vessels." Solidarity was the occupational order of the day, and indeed a favorite saying among sailors was "One and all."

Robinson also noted that sailors had a strong attachment to their work, as sailoring was the only life for a man of spirit. Cultural outsiders could and would be treated roughly. Sailors had little respect for landlubbers and notorious contempt for soldiers, with whom they brawled at the drop of a hat. The implications of this for Africans, especially those who came from inland societies, would be significant. On board the ship, apprentices, boys, and green hands were routinely pranked, cuffed around, sometimes even tormented. But over time these newcomers would be incorporated into the world of the deep-sea sailor, partly by learning the work and partly by ritual initiation and inclusion, as, for example, when newcomers were baptized by King Neptune on "crossing the line," the Tropic of Cancer or the equator, on a first long-distance voyage. Emma Christopher has noted that sailors practiced "fictive kinship" to incorporate workingmen of many different national, cultural, and racial origins. The motley crew found unity in their work. They were "brother tars."

Learning to be a sailor meant learning to face danger without fear and to live with want. Physical and mental toughness were therefore central to the cultural outlook of sailors, as Robinson noted: "It was well known that seamen, as a class, are of a jovial, reckless temperament, disposed to look at everything on the bright side, unwilling to look for breakers a head, desirous to bear up unflinchingly under privations and fatigue which would dishearten and paralyze almost any other class of men, [and] what they consider comfort is only misery in disguise." Shared peril and suffering bonded sailors together and gave rise to an ethic of mutual aid. Robinson found seamen to be "kind, openhearted and generous." This was not merely a moral stand but a survival strategy, based on the assumption that an equal distribution of life's risks helped everyone. Better to share what little one had, in the hope that someone else would share when you had nothing. Anything and everything for your brother tars. The corollary of this belief, Robinson noted, was, "The desire for wealth is deemed a meanness unworthy of any one except the lowest wretch."

Deeply embedded in this culture was an oppositional sensibility, which Robinson captured in a description of mealtime, when meat and bread were divided among the sailors aboard his ship. Rather than "expressing thankfulness," as Robinson thought they should have done, "every one commences cursing his own eyes and limbs in particular, if ever he was on board such a bloody hooker in his life, and expressing a general wish that the ship, captain and owners, all and sundry, may be sent to a certain place which need not be named." This set of attitudes would find expression over the course of the voyage in various forms of resistance: desertion, mutiny, and piracy. Against the concentrated power of the captain, common sailors would assert power of their own, from below. They also wielded power over those below them, who defined the limits of their occupational culture.

Work on the Ship

On the outward passage from a British or American port to West Africa, sailors by and large did what they did on most deep-sea vessels. They were organized into watches, starboard and larboard, the captain taking one, the chief mate the other on the smaller ships, the mates taking charge on the larger ones. Everyone would be on deck working all day, from 8:00 A.M. to 6:00 P.M., then four hours on and four hours off until the next morning. The mate or the boatswain would mark the changing of the watch by clanging the ship's bell or blowing a whistle. The modest amount of time each sailor had off might easily be lost to a change in the weather, when all hands were called up to set sail and adjust the ship's course. William Butterworth complained that he "never enjoyed a sound sleep during the entire voyage."[24]

Within each watch, groups of five or six seamen were organized into messes, to which food would be allocated by the mate on a weekly basis. According to a slave-trade merchant in 1729, "The usual Allowance given to Marriners on board of the Merchant Men on the Coast [of Africa] aforesd is Five Pounds of Bread a Week each Man, a piece of Beef weighing between Four and Five Pounds before it is salted between five men a Day with pease and flower the allowance being generally of Pease half a Pint& flour half a pound each day when allowed the same." This allowance might be supplemented by fish if the sailors were skillful enough to catch them. Grog and sometimes brandy were also important parts of the customary weekly allowance, and they could be matters of sharp contention. Sometimes the captain would put the men to short allowance, reducing the amount of food and drink given to each mess, which inevitably brought curses, especially if the allowance in the captain's cabin continued as before, which it always seemed to do.[25]

The work to be done at this point in the voyage was the usual for a common seaman—to hand, reef, and steer—that is, to manage the sails (often aloft) by extending or reducing them as the situation required and to direct the ship's movements by the helm (usually two hours per stint), all under the direction of the mate of the watch. Many captains swore there would be no idleness aboard their ships, so every working hour was filled, sometimes with scrubbing, or holystoning, the decks. Sailors also wove mats, thick webs of spun yarn or small ropes, used to protect the standing rigging from the friction of other ropes. They made sinnet, a braided cordage. When the vessel neared the African coast, sailors would go below, into the hold and the lower deck, to hoist and maneuver the trade goods for exchange.

Some aspects of work, however, were distinctive to the slaver. On a ship in which armed watch would be a matter of life and death, the gunner urgently checked and cleaned the small arms. He also tended to the blunderbusses and swivel cannon, while the sailors assembled ammunition, cartridges of shot. Sailors also knitted the netting, which would be used to prevent slaves from escaping the ship and unwelcome traders from coming aboard. Captain William Miller of the *Black Prince* noted in his journal in 1764, "The People Emp[loy]'d about netting and other necessarys." Sailors also counted and bagged cowrie shells for trade.[26]

When a slave ship arrived on the coast of Africa, sailors soon became something more than sailors. They continued to do the work of the ship—dropping and raising anchor and setting sails to take the vessel here and there, especially if the captain had in mind a "coasting voyage" in which he would buy slaves at several locations, as was common on the Windward Coast. Seamen also maintained the ship—cleaning, mending sails, repairing rigging, and tending to stores. At the same time, they would, as James Field Stanfield explained, build a thatched or tarpaulin roof over a large portion of the ship's deck, to provide shade against the tropical sun and to constrain the captives whom the captain would purchase. Once the actual buying and selling began, sailors would be redeployed to the yawl and longboat, rowing, sometimes great distances, back and forth from ship to shore and to other ships, hauling trade goods, people, and provisions (yams, corn, rice, water). As soon as the trade goods were people—that is, as soon as the captain began to buy slaves—the seamen's social function changed: they suddenly became prison guards. They would remain so for the coming seven to ten months or more—five to seven months or more on the coast, two to three months in the Middle Passage—until the vessel arrived in its American port of delivery.

As soon as the enslaved came aboard the vessel, "keeping watch" acquired a new meaning. The captain mobilized a guard, to be present and vigilant on the main deck anytime the enslaved were there. Each member would be armed, some with pistols, some with muskets, and all, apparently, with a cutlass, the handle of which featured a lanyard, which the sailor wound around his wrist so that a rebelling slave might not take it away from him.[27] The primary worries at this point in the voyage were escape and insurrection, both of which were encouraged by the proximity of the ship to the shore and the prospect of getting back to one's native society (even though recapture and resale were likely as the runaway tried to make his or her way home over many miles inland). The primary purposes of the sailor's work were now to keep a vigilant watch and to preserve the new human property of his captain and shipowner.

After about ten men slaves had been brought on board, all of them, and every man thereafter, would be manacled and shackled. Under the direction of the captain and mate as well as the armorer or gunner, the sailors would hammer the cuffs into place, linking the men by twos, the left wrist and ankle of one to the right wrist and ankle of the other. Thereafter, whenever the men came upon the main deck, the sailors would reeve a chain through their leg shackles and lock them in groups of ten to a ringbolt. Sailors were to check the men's irons carefully and regularly, at least twice a day, morning and night.[28] Women and child slaves were not normally constrained, unless rebellious. As soon as the house was dismantled, members of the crew manned the barricado and trained their muskets through "Loop

Holes." Two sailors took their stations at elevated four-pound cannon, "loaded with a Cannister of Musket Balls to rake the Main deck, if there should be any Occasion for it."[29]

As the ship filled up, sailors oversaw the routines of the captives on both the lower and main decks. Belowdecks the sailor would assist in "stowing" the slaves—that is, the assignment of a particular space where each person was to lie or sit whenever belowdecks, while on the coast and during the Middle Passage. The chief mate and the boatswain, cat-o'-nine-tails in hand, supervised stowing the men; the second mate and gunner, the women. The sailors helped to pack the enslaved together tightly, "adjusting their arms and legs, and prescribing a fixed place for each." Those who did not "get quickly into their places" were compelled by the cat. George Millar, who served on the *Canterbury* on a voyage to Old Calabar in 1767, recalled, "I was the person that had the care of the men Slaves, and when stowed, there was not room to put down the point of a stick between one and another."[30]

When the enslaved were on the main deck during the daytime hours, a detachment of sailors went below to clean their apartments. Sometimes this work would be done by the enslaved themselves, but more commonly by the sailors, who frankly despised it. This work had several aspects, some daily, others more occasional. One constant task was emptying the necessary tubs of urine and excrement. Alexander Falconbridge wrote, "In each of the apartments are placed three or four large buckets, of a conical form, being near two feet in diameter at the bottom, and only one foot at the top, and in depth about twenty-eight inches; to which, when necessary, the negroes have recourse." The seamen also scrubbed the deck and the beams, using sand and other abrasives to remove dried filth, vomit, and mucus. Once every week or two, the sailors would, after cleaning, fumigate the apartments, which was done in various ways. Captain William Littleton had them put a "a red hot loggerhead into vinegar," confine the smoke, and let it suffuse the woodwork. Seaman Samuel Robinson wrote that on his ships the lower deck was kept "scrupulousley clean, washed and scrubbed with sand twice a week, dried with fire-pans, and fumigated with vinegar and tobacco smoke; while large tubs, with close covers, are placed at proper distances for necessary purposes."[31]

Another detested piece of service among sailors was guard duty belowdecks among the men slaves overnight. Not all captains required this; some were content to lock the slaves below and tend to them again the following morning. But other ships did require the duty, and William Butterworth left a detailed record of what it entailed. In the aftermath of a failed insurrection, Captain Jenkin Evans of the *Hudibras* "deemed it necessary that a person should be stationed in the men's apartment during the night." When he heard the news, Butterworth was mortified. He thought, "Unenviable situation! uncoveted post!" But as the captain's will (fate) would have it, he and another man were chosen for the duty. Wishing suddenly that the enslaved were "all in their native woods" and that he himself was "safe in my own native town," Butterworth hid himself to try to avoid duty. To no avail: he was found out and made to go below for four hours. When he arrived at his post, he found the man he was replacing "on the top of the ladder" that led up from the lower deck, "with his hands [gripping] hold of the gratings, and tears in his eyes." He was terrified, as was Butterworth, who fearfully went below and took a seat as far from the slaves as he could get, "keeping a most respectful distance." Time passed slowly as he listened to the clanking irons of the Coromantee and Igbo ringleaders of the insurrection, who were chained together in groups of ten. To his horror he was soon forced to take a second four-hour watch, during which he used his cat-o'-nine-tails—which he called the "credential of authority below deck"—to drive back to his spot an "old offender," already in strong fetters, who had approached him. Eventually Butterworth grew sleepy but feared that he would be ripped limb from limb if he dozed off. Slowly he began to talk to the enslaved Igbo men near the ladder, hoping to cultivate allies. By his watch the following day, he had decided that the policy was working to guarantee his safety. Little did he know that another uprising was being planned. Two of the men Butterworth was "guarding" were soon found to have large knives in their possession. He was apparently considered too insignificant a target.[32]

Another important task sailors carried out was to conduct a daily search among the captives for hard-edged tools or indeed anything that might be used as a weapon—against the crew in insurrection, against themselves in suicide, or against each other in the frequent quarrels that broke out amid the hot, crowded, miserable circumstances of the lower deck. On some ships this meant clipping the fingernails of potential rebels. On almost all it meant keeping an eye on the more mobile women and child slaves, who sometimes passed tools through the gratings to the men below. Sailors were also dispatched to break up fights that flared up from conflicts over space, sickness, cleanliness, or cultural difference. Vaunting his own humanity (with no apparent sense of irony), the slave trader Robert Norris explained that such attention was necessary so that "the strong do not oppress the weak."[33]

Every morning at around eight, when the weather was good, some sailors took their positions under arms while others brought the enslaved up from the lower deck, the men on the forward side of the barricado, the women and children aft. After chaining the men to the deck, seamen would assist in a morning washup of face and hands, then arrange the bodies as the surgeon made his rounds, listened to complaints, and looked for the telltale signs of illness. Around ten o'clock the sailors began to serve the morning meal, which usually consisted of African food according to the region of origin of the enslaved: rice for those from Senegambia and the Windward Coast, corn for those from the Gold Coast, yams for those from the Bights of Benin and Biafra. The sailors also served a pannikin of water. After the meal, sailors collected eating bowls (called "crews") and spoons and made arrangements for a full wash. At noon the sailors began the activities for the afternoon. Of special importance was something called "dancing."

Physicians and slave traders alike believed that exercise would help to maintain the health of the enslaved. Therefore each afternoon the

Africans would be required to dance (and also to sing, on many ships). This could take many forms, from something more or less freely chosen, accompanied by African instruments (more common among the women), to the dreary, forced clanking of chains (more common among the men). Some refused to take part in the exercise altogether; others did so sullenly. These reactions brought the scourge of the cat, wielded by the mate or boatswain.

The same was frequently true of feeding: some people refused to eat, willfully or because they were sick or depressed. Violence would force them. The preferred instrument was the omnipresent cat, used by the officers. Numerous observers noted that it did not always work: many still refused to eat, which brought out other means of force, including hot coals and finally the *speculum oris*. Sailors would have assisted in these tortures but would not have taken the lead.

At some point in the afternoon, bread and sometimes a pipe of tobacco and a dram of brandy would be offered to the men and women. On some ships the women and girls would be given beads with which to make ornaments. The afternoon meal, served around four o'clock, usually consisted of European victuals—horsebeans and peas, with salt meat or fish. Many a cook made "dab-a-dab," a concoction of rice, a little salt meat, pepper, and palm oil. At the end of the day, somewhere between 4:00 and 6:00 P.M., the men were taken and locked below. Women and children usually got to stay on deck longer, until they, too, were taken to their dark apartments for the next twelve to fourteen hours.[34]

"Dancing" and feeding revealed a larger truth about the slave ship: the officers reserved for themselves the primary means of violence. Only the captain and the surgeon, recalled Isaac Wilson, were allowed to chastise the slaves aboard his ship. Others agreed. Alexander Falconbridge said that only the captain, chief mate, and surgeon (himself) were permitted to use the cat-o'-nine-tails. Common sailors rarely wielded the cat, and then usually only in two situations: when they went below and in the brutal aftermath of a failed insurrection.[35]

The final phase of a sailor's work consisted of preparing the enslaved for sale as the ship neared its port of delivery. This, as Emma Christopher has emphasized, was a kind of production in which the sailor transformed the African captive into a commodity for sale. It entailed taking the constraints off the wrists and ankles of the men about ten days before arrival, in order to let the chafing heal. It also included careful cleaning, shaving the men (beard and sometimes head), and using a lunar caustic to hide sores. Gray hair would be picked out or dyed black. Finally, sailors would rub down the African bodies with palm oil. The whole process was one of value creation and enhancement. Thanks to the sailor's labor, a shipload of expensive commodities would soon be available for sale.[36]

Sailors, Slaves, and Violence

The Liverpool writer "Dicky Sam" described the violent reality of the slave ship this way: "the captain bullies the men, the men torture the slaves, the slaves' hearts are breaking with despair." The statement expresses an important truth. Violence cascaded downward, from captain and officers to sailors to the enslaved. Sailors, often beaten and abused themselves, took out their plight on the even more abject and powerless captives under their supervision and control. How this happened on any given ship would depend to a large extent on the captain, who had enormous latitude to run the ship as he wished. Even though captains and officers were the prime agents of disciplinary violence, sailors occupied the front line of social war on the ship. This must be emphasized, because James Field Stanfield, in his dramatic rendering of the slaving voyage, tended to blur the line between sailors and slaves.[37]

The least documented type of violence on the slave ship was probably the most pervasive—the rough, sometimes cruel treatment of daily life. Dr. Ecroyde Claxton, surgeon on the *Young Hero,* noted that Captain Molineux treated the enslaved well but the sailors did not. On one occasion, when a group of sick slaves were brought on deck and covered with a sail, it was soon smeared "with blood and mucus, which involuntarily issued from them." The sailors, who had to clean the sail, flew into a rage and beat them "inhumanly." This made the sick slaves so fearful that they thereafter "crept to the tub, and there sat straining and straining." This, the physician noted, produced "prolapsus ani, which it was entirely impossible to cure." This was one of thousands of instances of everyday terror.[38]

The greatest explosion of violence from a ship's crew followed a failed slave insurrection. Ringleaders would be gruesomely punished by captains and mates on the main deck, in full view of all the enslaved. When the officers tired themselves by repeated lashing, they passed the cat to sailors, who continued the flaying. On other occasions sailors were known to torment defeated rebels by pricking their skin with the points of the cutlasses. In a few cases, the sailors' work included actual execution, by horrific means. Sailors thus not only maintained captivity, they viciously punished those who tried to escape it.

Another extremity of violence enacted by the crew, showing that "work" sometimes included outright murder, was illustrated aboard the *Zong* in 1781. Captain Luke Collingwood sailed with his crew of seventeen and a "cargo" of 470 tight-packed slaves from West Africa to Jamaica. The ship soon grew sickly: sixty Africans and seven members of the crew perished. Fearful of "a broken voyage," Collingwood called the crew together and told them that "if the slaves died a natural death, it would be the loss of the owners of the ship; *but if they were thrown alive into the sea, it would be the loss of the underwriters*" who had insured the voyage. Some members of the crew, including mate James Kelsal, objected, but Collingwood prevailed, and that evening the crew threw 54 slaves, hands bound, overboard. They threw another 42 over the side two days later, and 26 more soon after. Ten of the enslaved watched the hideous spectacle and jumped overboard of their own volition, committing suicide and bringing the number of deaths to 132. Collingwood later pretended a lack of water was the cause of his action, but neither crew nor captives had been put to short allowance, and indeed the ship still had 420 gallons when it docked. The case was tried in court when the insurer refused to pay the claim and the owners sued in response. The trial publicized the cruelty of the slave trade and proved to be a turning point as abolitionists such as Olaudah Equiano and Granville Sharp built a nascent popular movement. It was perhaps the most spectacular atrocity in the four-hundred-year history of the slave trade. It depended on sailors accepting the orders to throw the living overboard.[39]

One of the most important aspects of violence visited by the crew upon the enslaved was addressed by the Reverend John Newton in his pamphlet *Thoughts upon the African Slave Trade,* published in London, 1788. He painted a chilling picture:

> When the women and girls are taken on board a ship, naked, trembling, terrified, perhaps almost exhausted with cold, fatigue, and hunger, they are often exposed to the wanton rudeness of white savages. The poor creatures cannot understand the language they hear, but the looks and manners of the speakers are sufficiently intelligible. In imagination, the prey is divided, upon the spot, and only reserved until opportunity offers. Where resistance or refusal would be utterly in vain, even the solicitation of consent is seldom thought of.

Then he stopped, declaring, "This is not a subject for declamation," even though the "enormities" of what happened on slave ships were, at the time, "little known *here.*" Perhaps he and other abolitionists considered it too delicate a subject for public discussion, or perhaps they shied away because it conflicted with their desire to make the British sailor a victim of the slave trade and an object of popular sympathy. It would not do to depict him as a "white savage," a sexual predator, a serial rapist. Yet that is what some slave-trade sailors were. It is entirely possible that some men signed on to slaving voyages in the first place precisely because they wanted unrestricted access to the bodies of African women. Thomas Boulton implied as much when he had the recruiting mate in *The Sailor's Farewell, or the Guinea Outfit* speak to a potential sailor of the "soft African wench" who awaited him if he signed on. What would a real sailor think as he joined a Rhode Island slave ship named the *Free Love,* Captain Wanton?[40]

Slave-trade merchants did the best they could to downplay the matter, stressing that "good order" aboard the ship meant no abuse of the female slaves by the crew. A member of the investigating parliamentary committee asked Robert Norris, "Is there any Care taken to prevent any Intercourse between White Men and the Black Women?" Norris responded crisply, in captainlike fashion, "Orders are generally issued for that Purpose by the Commanding Officer." A questioner who was apparently more sympathetic to the slave trade may have considered this too weak a response, so he followed up to make sure everyone knew that sexual abuse would not be tolerated. He wondered, "If a British Sailor should offer Violence to a Negro Woman, would he not be severely punished by the Captain?" Norris answered, "He would be sharply reproved certainly." John Knox added that it was usually a matter of contract that any sailor proved guilty of "vice" while on the voyage would lose one month's pay.[41]

The "good order" described by the merchants was not unknown, but according to Newton (whose knowledge of the slave trade was based in an earlier era), it was relatively uncommon. Speaking of the crew, he wrote, "On shipboard they may be restrained, and in some ships they are; but such restraint is far from being general." It all depended on the captain, who had the power to protect the women slaves if he chose to do so. Newton knew several commanders who maintained what he considered proper discipline, but these were probably a minority: "In some ships, perhaps in the most, the license in this particular was almost unlimited." Anyone who did his work and did it properly "might, in other respects, do what they pleased." The Reverend William Leigh added that Guinea voyages often exhibited "promiscuous intercourse" and wild "scenes of debauchery." Questions of morality, both ministers lamented, were never posed.[42]

Questions of class aboard the ship were posed. Most observers of slave-shipboard life agreed that officers had unlimited access to slave women but that common sailors did not. Alexander Falconbridge wrote that "on board some ships, the common sailors are allowed to have intercourse with such of the black women whose consent they can procure." The officers, on the other hand, "are permitted to indulge their passions among them at pleasure, and sometimes are guilty of such brutal excesses as disgrace human nature." Reverend Leigh agreed: "the Captain and Officers still indulge their desires unrestrained, and the common sailors are allowed to take for the voyage any female Negro whose consent they can obtain." Neither writer paused to consider what "consent" could have meant in a situation where women had no protection, no rights, and were, in Newton's words, "abandoned, without restraint, to the lawless will of the first comer."

And yet sketchy evidence suggests that some African women formed relationships with sailors that involved some degree of consent. This may have been a woman's way to make the best of a bad situation, that is, to make a strategic alliance with one man as a protection against other predators. The higher up the ship's hierarchy the protector, the better and more reliable the protection would be. When a sailor did pair off with a woman, he apparently gave her access to his provisions, which saved the merchant and captain money. Leigh suggested that some of these unions resulted in tragic scenes when the ship arrived in the American port and the time came for the sale of the enslaved. He said that "Negroe women, when being separated by sale from the sailors who cohabited with them," sometimes tried "destroying themselves, and sometimes jumping overboard, on the attempt to force them from the ship."[43]

There is no reason to think that the process described by John Newton—the hardening of the captain's heart—would apply less to sailors, and indeed it may have applied more, because sailors were in intimate daily contact with the enslaved, sharing close quarters for anywhere between two and ten months on a voyage. Several ship captains spoke of the need to restrain their sailors, to intervene against a socialization process over which they themselves presided. William Snelgrave was sure that the desperate insurrections of the enslaved were caused by "the Sailors ill usage of these poor People, when on board the Ships wherein they are transported to our Plantations." Captain John Samuel Smith of the Royal Navy testified in 1791 that he had trouble impressing slave-trade sailors for the king's service because they were so sick and ulcerated as to pose a risk of infection to the other men aboard his vessel. But the two he was able to press "turned out to be such cruel inhuman fellows, that we were under the necessity of dismissing them from the ship, although good seamen."[44]

The Dead List

Along the coast of West Africa, common sailors encountered a barrier reef of an unusual kind. It was pathogenic, made of microbes, and it made the area a "White Man's Grave." Half of all Europeans who journeyed to West Africa in the eighteenth century, most of them seamen, died within a year. The primary causes of the high mortality were "fevers," malaria and yellow fever, both mosquito-borne, and both reproducible within the slave ship itself, as the insects bred in the stagnant bilgewater that collected in the hull. Other causes of death were dysentery, smallpox, accidents, murder, and occasionally scurvy. The prevalence of disease (and the absence of immunity), coupled with difficult working and living conditions (fatiguing work, poor food, and harsh discipline), meant that the crew aboard the slave ships often died in even greater proportions than did the enslaved, although of different causes, within a different chronological pattern during the voyage (more while on the coast and early in the voyage), and with variations according to African region: the Gold Coast was comparatively healthy, the Bights of Benin and Biafra deadly. In surveying crew mortality for 350 Bristol and Liverpool slavers between 1784 and 1790, a House of Commons committee found that 21.6 percent of the sailors died, a figure that was in keeping with Thomas Clarkson's estimates at the time and is consistent with modern research. Roughly twenty thousand British slave-trade seamen died between 1780 and 1807. For sailors as for African captives, living for several months aboard a slave ship was in itself a struggle for life.[45]

The history of the slave trade is full of horror stories of crew mortality, of ships so disabled by disease and death that voyages ended in failure if not outright catastrophe. One captain in 1721 referred to his sick sailors as "walking ghosts." Later in the century, another noted in his journal the "squal'd immassiated appearance" of his sailors, who reminded him of the "resurrection of the Dead." In many instances there was only death and no resurrection. Captain David Harrison brought news to Providence, Rhode Island, in 1770 from the river Gambia, where the "whole crew" of the brig *Elizabeth* had died, leaving a ghost ship at anchor. In 1796, Captain Cooke of Baltimore "lost all his hands, except a negro man and boy." Sometimes entire seafaring families were devastated. When Josiah Bowen of Barrington, Rhode Island, died on the coast of Africa in 1801, the newspaper noted that his father had lost five sons at sea over the past five years.[46] Observers were not referring to the enslaved alone when they called slave ships "floating" or "marine lazar-houses," places filled with people suffering from all kinds of mortal diseases.[47]

A macabre portrait of the wounded and the dead emerges from petitions by sailors or their families to the Society of Merchant Venturers in Bristol on behalf of men who had worked on company ships for five years or more. John Fielding got a "high scurvy," which caused him to lose the toes on his left foot. Benjamin Williams contracted ulcers in his legs; the right one was amputated. William Victor had both of his legs broken when a tent frame (which he was erecting for the sale of slaves in Virginia) collapsed on him. John Smith and Cornelius Calahan "were seized with a Distemper in their Eyes then raging amongst the Slaves which has deprived them of their sight." The maimed were the lucky ones. John Grenville died after falling from the main deck into the hold. Richard Ruth "was lost by the oversett of a canoe on the coast of Africa"; William Davis and six others apparently drowned when their longboat capsized. James Harding was poisoned by African traders, while George Hancock was killed by "a Rising of the Slaves."[48]

Conditions on the ships were so bad that sailors occasionally committed suicide, especially when they had been bullied by a captain or a mate. Captain Thomas Tucker abused cook John Bundy so badly, whipping and at one point stabbing him in the face, that the poor man's life, wrote Silas Told, became "grievously burthensome to him." When he hinted that he would throw himself overboard, his ship-mates tried to dissuade him, but one morning at eight o'clock he "plunged himself into the sea." Thomas Jillett, a fifteen-year-old boy aboard the *Bruce Grove,* declared after mistreatment by the ship's mate that he "was weary of his life" and soon disappeared over the side. An Irish boy named Paddy did likewise aboard the *Briton* in 1762: threatened by the mate with a severe flogging for not boiling the teakettle in time, he jumped overboard and drowned.[49]

The physical decline of the crew, which began on the coast of Africa and increased throughout the Middle Passage, created a literally fatal contradiction: crews sickened, weakened, and died just as ever-larger numbers of the enslaved were coming on board, leaving too few workers to sail the ship and guard against a slave insurrection. An observer aboard a slave ship wrote, "[We conceal] ye death of ye Sailours from ye Negros by throwing them overboard in ye night, lest it might give them a temptation to rise upon us, seeing us so much weaken'd by ye death of 8, & most of ye rest sick but my self, we being now but 12 in all, that were left." Moreover, one of the advantages of the barricado was that the men slaves could not see over it and thereby count how many sailors were still alive, working on the other side.[50]

When a sailor died, a simple burial ceremony might be held, as seamen were "plain dealers" who did not care for elaborate rituals. If on the coast of Africa, the captain usually made efforts to bury the body ashore (the slave-trading port of Bonny, for example, had a burial ground for sailors on the river). If at sea, the corpse was sewn up in a hammock or an old canvas sail and weighted down with a cannonball to sink it. But even this modest interment faced challenge, mostly from sharks, which were known to rip the dead body to pieces before it could sink. Many a sailor ended up not only in an unmarked grave but as "food for the fishes of the deep." It was an ignominious end to life.[51]

Such men left few traces. Common sailor George Glover's life came to an end, cause unknown, aboard the *Essex,* commanded by Captain Peter Potter, on November 13, 1783. Potter arranged to take an inventory of his few worldly goods. According to sailors' custom, these were sold "at the mast" to his shipmates, the proceeds to go to a widow or family member. Glover's most valuable possession was his jacket, sold for thirteen shillings, sixpence. He had two pairs of trousers, one of which was "good for nothing." Other items included two shirts (one check, one flannel), shoes, stockings, a pair of drawers, a pair of buckles, a bag, and a worthless hat. One of the shirts, the shoes, and the hat he had bought from the captain during the voyage at high prices. In the end, everything Glover owned aboard the ship was worth less than a pound and a half, and even this value is largely inflated because seamen always paid, to help the surviving family, considerably more than any given item was worth. Other common seamen who died left a little more than Glover, some a little less. One man left "1 parrot the Cooper has in his care."[52] When ships like the *Essex* returned to Liverpool, a "melancholy ceremony" was enacted. The family and friends of the original crew assembled on the dock where the vessel arrived to hear someone on board read out the "dead list."[53]

Mutiny and Desertion

Off the Gold Coast in 1749, Captain Thomas Sanderson of the *Antelope* commanded his sailors to turn out on deck. A group of them refused. Those who still accepted his authority apparently answered a second command to secure the five men who remained below. They clapped Edward Suttle, Michael Simpson, John Turner, William Perkins, and Nicholas Barnes in irons. Sanderson wanted to get them off the ship, so he transferred them to another merchant vessel anchored nearby. Meanwhile three other members of the crew seized the longboat and deserted.[54]

Captain Sanderson had a problem, and not only with mutiny. He had a significant number of captive slaves belowdecks, and he had now lost a third of his crew. He therefore brought the five mutinous ones back aboard, but again they refused to work, and this time they armed themselves with cutlasses to make sure he got the point. When

Sanderson persisted, giving an order to weigh anchor, John Turner "threatned to knock down the first Man that should put a Handspike into the Windlass to heave up the Anchor." At this point Sanderson appealed for help to another slave trader, Captain Holmes, who came aboard and reprimanded the crew. The mutineers threatened to heave him overboard. Sanderson now apparently felt that he could no longer count on the obedience of his own crew, so he appealed to a Dutch captain, who dispatched a group of his own sailors. They quelled the disturbance and put the mutineers once again in irons.

Still short of hands, Sanderson released the men again, probably after securing a promise of obedience, which soon evaporated into the coastal mist. This time the sailors took up handspikes and demanded that Sanderson "surrender himself prisoner." They captured the ship and turned the world upside down, locking Sanderson, the surgeon, and a few others in chains but assuring them that they would not be harmed. Later they put the captain and his supporters in a boat, with food, and sent them ashore. The vanquished were taken aboard the slave ship *Speedwell* by Captain Joseph Bellamy, who came to the aid of a fellow captain in distress. He immediately went in pursuit of the *Antelope*. Eventually the mutineers were retaken and found themselves fastened in irons a third time.

After the recapture of his ship, Captain Sanderson went aboard and discovered many empty bottles and, more disturbingly, gunpowder at the ready (whether to defend or destroy the vessel, he did not say). He also found that containers of his valuable cargo, "India goods" (cotton fabrics), had been broken open by the crew and distributed "to the Women Slaves on board." When someone asked the men in chains what they had planned to do with the ship, one of them, perhaps "Captain Turner," as he was called, said that "some of the Crew were for carrying her to Brazil & Others for carrying the same to Eustatia & there to dispose of them." He referred to the slaves belowdecks. The mutiny was only a limited liberation.

The courtroom testimony of surgeon's mate William Steele made clear the causes of the mutiny. First, several seamen thought Sanderson had violated custom, the main one being the sailors' iron right to grog. Complaining that Sanderson made no "Allowance of strong Liquors which it was usual for Masters of other Ships on the Coast to do," two seamen decided to take the matter into their own hands. They broke into a storage room, found the spirits to refresh their spirits, got drunk, and quarreled with Captain Sanderson. A second cause was "the uneasy & unsettled Life they lived on board the Ship by the Captain's Behaviour to them," which apparently included violence. When Sanderson announced that they would be sailing farther east down the Guinea coast, there was much "grumbling upon Deck." The sailors "said the Captain had used them so ill in the former Part of the Voyage they thought it was very hard for them to be obliged to go windward for that they expected that if they did he would use them worse when he got [away] from among the Rest of the Ships," meaning those trading in the area. His tyranny would increase in isolation. A third, more specific cause (or perhaps an illustration of the second) was a beating the captain gave the boatswain. When this happened, several members of the crew dared to object, saying he "should not beat the old Man (meaning ye Boatswain who was a very old Man)." A shouting match ensued, in which the crew gave the captain "ill language." The confrontation, which apparently took place the night before the first work stoppage, may have been the breaking point.[55]

In comparative terms Captain Sanderson was lucky to escape unharmed or even with his life.[56] Mutineers aboard the *Endeavour* in 1721 flogged Captain John Wroe, while others gruesomely killed captains, usually over the same causes that existed on the *Antelope*.[57] A mutineer aboard the *Abington* in 1719 commented on the conditions of working life by saying, "Damn it, it was better to be hanged than live so."[58] The sailors aboard the *Buxton* in 1734 decapitated Captain James Beard with an ax. After it was over, common seaman Thomas Williams sighed with relief, "Damn the Dog I have done it at last. I wish it had been don long enough agoe." More than two years later, grumbling sailors aboard the *Pearl Galley* engaged in a war of nerves, asking Captain Eustace Hardwicke and others if anyone remembered the fate of Captain Beard, implying, with menace, that the same thing could happen again, soon.[59] Aboard the *Tewkesbury* in 1737, the "young Lads" among the sailors axed their captain in the face and threw him overboard. Mutineer John Kennelly was heard to say that now "they should have Rum enough," while John Rearden boasted that now the captain would not *kill half a dozen of us.*" Captured and taken to Cape Coast Castle, where they were tried and convicted, two of the rebels were made seven-year indentured servants to the traders and five others were hanged at the waterside gates of the fort.[60]

Some mutineers set up as pirates, especially in the 1710s and 1720s, when slave-trade sailors like "Black Bart" Roberts roamed the seas, captured prizes, and created a crisis in the Atlantic trading system. That generation of pirates was crushed by a bloody campaign of grisly executions and more rigorous naval patrolling, but nonetheless mutineers on the coast of Africa occasionally set up as pirates. An official from the slave-trading port of Anomabu notified merchants in 1766 that "the Coast is very much infested with Pirates, and that one, in particular, is a Schooner, copper sheathed, commanded by one Hide, has on board thirty four Men, and is extremely well fitted with Swivels, and Small Arms." The pirate had taken twelve to fourteen small vessels and "had on board 1200. Sterling in Goods, and 50 ounces of Gold Dust." After a mutiny aboard the *Black Prince* in 1769, sailors "hoisted the black flag" and changed the name of the ship to the *Liberty.*[61]

Sailors engaged in other forms of resistance in addition to mutiny and piracy, most commonly desertion. Emma Christopher has shown that running away on the coast of Africa was frequent. Yet for sailors as for slaves who escaped the ships, freedom was hard to find, since African slave traders and their allies almost always (for a fee) captured and returned runaways to the captain. The sharks that slowly circled the ships in West African waters also deterred many a seaman who had a desire to desert, although a few were willing to face one monster to escape another. Another limitation on desertion was the attitude of the sailors themselves, one of whom explained in court that he and his mates "intended to have made their escape" from their captain in Bonny but did not because it was "a wild place inhabited by Cannibals."[62]

End of the Voyage

For a sailor on a slave ship, the voyage always ended in one of four ways: in death; in resistance (desertion or mutiny, which could have several outcomes, from escape to hanging); in legal or illegal discharge at the delivering port after the Middle Passage; or in discharge at the home port after the homeward passage.

At the end of the Middle Passage, many captains faced a problem. A two-hundred-ton ship that required a crew of thirty-five to handle 350 enslaved people now would carry a cargo of sugar (or even ballast) back to the home port, requiring only sixteen, perhaps even fewer, if the captain wanted to economize, as he often did. What would happen to the suddenly superfluous crew members? Some had died and some had had their fill of captain and ship and deserted with glee, even at the cost of forfeiting substantial wages. But many seamen wanted to keep their hard-earned money and return to their home port, not least to return to family and community. Slave captains devised a strategy to deal with this surplus of labor.[63]

Toward the end of the Middle Passage, just as the treatment of the enslaved began to improve (to ready them for market), the captain started driving the crew, or at least a portion of the crew, very hard, in the hope that some of them would desert when they reached port. This was bullying full bore. Not all captains did it, but enough did so that the practice was widely known. No less a person than Lord Rodney, naval war hero, savior of the British Empire, "Knight of the Most Honourable Order of the Bath, Admiral of the White, and Vice Admiral of England," testified in Parliament of slavers in 1790, "I believe there have been many instances of harsh treatment in captains of those ships to get rid of their men" in the West Indies.[64]

This was by design, and indeed merchants sometimes gave explicit instructions to get rid of extra crew before completing the voyage. Miles Barber wrote to Captain James Penny in 1784, "I wish you to ship a few foreign seamen if practicable at St. Kitts or St. Thomas's, discharging such part of your crew as are disorderly." He knew that this was illegal, so he advised Penny to tell the mates "not to mention it." Even if merchants did not mention getting rid of seamen, captains did it routinely. Captain Francis Pope wrote to a Rhode Island merchant named Abraham Redwood in 1740, "I think to keep as few men as Possable for tis to your advantage." The profits of the voyage expanded by saving on labor expenditure, as even the proslavery Lord Sheffield was forced to admit. But there were other considerations, too. Given the hard usage and explosive tensions of the slave ship, captains might want to get rid of the rebellious or "disorderly." Another part of the calculation was that a substantial number of sailors, in some cases a majority of the crew, were in such bad health by the time the slaving voyage ended that they could no longer work. They suffered from malaria, ophthalmia (an eye disease), "Guinea worms" (parasites that grew to enormous size, usually in the legs), and ulcers of various kinds, especially the "yaws," a contagious African skin disease.[65]

These sailors arrived in the West Indies in a sorry state. In Barbados, seaman Henry Ellison saw "several Guinea seamen in great distress, and in want of the common necessaries of life, with their legs in an ulcerated state, eaten up by the chicres [chiggers], and their toes rotting off, without any person to give them any assistance, or to take them in." The human landscape along the docks was similar in Jamaica, where seamen were "lying on the wharfs and other places in an ulcerated and helpless state." They were cankerous from "the knee pan to the ankle, and in such a state, that no ship whatever would receive them." Some of these men he knew personally. They had been "used in a barbarous manner," then bilked of their wages. Ellison took them food from his own ship. They were variously known as "wharfingers," "scow-bankers," or, when there were no docks, "beach horners." They sometimes crawled into empty sugar casks on the docks to die.[66]

These sailors were the equivalent of the "refuse slaves" who were too sick to be sold at full value, but with a difference: "white men," of course, could not be sold, but, on the other hand, these broken-down sailors had no value to anyone and negative value to the people for whom they had worked for the past many months. They could not be sold but they could be dumped, forced off the ship. Poor, sick sailors would become beggars on the docks of almost every slave-delivery port in the Americas.

This grew into a big enough problem that various colonial and port city governments took action, and several created special hospitals for sailors. At Bridgetown, Barbados, the poorhouse was crowded with slave-ship sailors. They likewise turned up on the beaches and in the harbors of Dominica and Grenada. A report out of Charleston in 1784 noted that "no less than sixty seamen belonging to African ships have been thrown on this city, the greater part of which died, and were buried at the expence of the city." Jamaica passed legislation as early as 1759—and renewed it long thereafter—dealing with "maimed" and disabled seamen, and it was noted in 1791 that a "very great proportion of those who are in Kingston Hospital are Guineamen." The abandonment of "lame, ulcerated, and sick seamen" was such "a very great nuisance and expence to the community at Kingston" that the Jamaican legislature passed a law requiring shipmasters to give a security against leaving the disabled ashore.[67]

Two sailors who were themselves wharfingers described their plight. William Butterworth, who had lacerated his leg in a fall down the hatchway, was discharged by his captain in Kingston. He felt he had been "turned adrift, in a strange country, weak, lame, and possessing but little money!" James Towne found himself in a similar situation: "I was myself left on shore at Charles Town, South Carolina, with two others, without either money or friends. The two died."[68]

Insurrection: Liverpool, 1775

The sailors had just finished rigging the *Derby* in preparation for its voyage to Angola and Jamaica. Captain Luke Mann had engaged them a month earlier at the rate of thirty shillings per month but informed them now, on August 25, he would pay only twenty shillings, because "there were plenty of hands to be had," owing to a glut of out-of-work sailors in the harbor. The decision came directly from the owners of the ship, especially, it seems, a local merchant, Thomas Yates. The crewmen of the *Derby* were incensed. They promptly cut down the rigging and left it in a tangled heap on the main deck.[69]

Someone summoned the constables, who arrested nine sailors, carried them before the magistrates, and threw them into jail. Meanwhile word of the original direct action and the imprisonment swept the waterfront, and soon two or three thousand sailors (the accounts varied) took up handspikes and clubs, the traditional weapons of sailors in mobs, and marched to Old Tower on Water Street to free their brother tars. The sailors broke windows and got into the prison office, where they destroyed documents and records. The jailers capitulated, released eight of the sailors, and desperately hoped the ordeal was over. As the cheering mob carried away the liberated, they realized that they had left one of their comrades behind, so back they went. They found the man and freed him, and likewise a woman who had been jailed for assisting the rioters. The sailors then paraded around the docks until midnight, terrifying some of the local inhabitants as they exulted loudly in their victory. They soon set about unrigging as many ships in the harbor as they could.[70]

The incident aboard the *Derby* grew from a direct action on the job into a strike and finally an urban insurrection. Saturday and Sunday, August 26 and 27, were quiet, but each night the sailors, prompted by the continuing efforts of merchants to slash wages, crept around the docks cutting rigging, striking sails, and immobilizing the vessels of the dynamic port city. Early Monday morning, sailors went from ship to ship to encourage people to join the work stoppage. Those who refused were forcibly removed, as seaman Thomas Cocket explained: the seamen were "boarding all the vessels and taking out all the People." The strike had spread, and the normally bustling waterfront went quiet. Meeting later in the day at their headquarters, North Lady's Walk overlooking the city, the sailors decided to take their wage grievance to the merchants at the Mercantile Exchange, where they would demand redress. They were angry, but they went peacefully, unarmed. They met with no success. As they left the exchange, some of them apparently threatened to return the following day to pull the building down. The merchants took these menacing words to heart. In fear of a second, more violent confrontation, they shuttered and barricaded the exchange. They also recruited and armed military volunteers, some of whom were gentlemen of "superior quality," and paid another 120 workers to defend the building.[71]

At noon on Tuesday, August 29, the sailors returned, in larger numbers and a militant mood, "shouting and huzzaing." They were still willing to negotiate, but again their grievances were not answered. The increasingly nervous local authorities read the Riot Act and demanded that they disperse. The sailors refused and eventually formed themselves into a menacing ring around the exchange. A few protesters began to throw staves and bricks at the windows. Seaman John Fisher smashed the glass of the imposing building with a rake. As the tensions escalated, someone from within the exchange, perhaps merchant Thomas Radcliffe or a member of the dock watch named Thomas Ellis, fired a gun at the protesters. Then followed a roar of shot, after which several seamen fell dead. The "cries and groans of the wounded," recalled an observer, "were dismal." The chaos of the scene made it difficult for anyone to know the precise extent of the casualties. As few as two and as many as seven seamen were killed; a minimum of fifteen and as many as forty were wounded. Everyone knew, after the shootings, that the sailors would strike back, so houses were shuttered and plans for self-defense made. The wealthy hid their valuables and sent their children away from home. Slave-trade merchant Thomas Staniforth concealed his silver in a hayloft.[72]

Wednesday morning a thousand seamen took to the streets sporting red ribbons on their hats. They broke into gunsmith shops and warehouses, taking three hundred muskets from one, gunpowder from another, blunderbusses and pistols from a third. But even these weapons were too little to serve their design, so they commandeered horses, led them to the dockside, and used them to drag ship's cannon on a cart up the hill to the exchange.[73] Soon the "clattering of swords and cannon" filled the city's cobblestone streets. Sailors marched en masse behind George Oliver, who carried the "bloody flag," signifying to one and all that the sailors would neither take nor give quarter. This would be a fight to the death. By noon they had set up their cannon in strategic locations on Dale Street and Castle Street so they could attack the exchange from north and south. They then spent "the greatest part of the day" bombarding the building with cannonballs and gunshot. "Aim at the goose!" was the cry. The enraged sailors trained their cannon and muskets on the carved stone "liver bird," symbol of the all-powerful Corporation of Liverpool and indeed the city itself. They pulverized it. The concussion of their fire was such that there was "scarce a whole pane of glass in the neighbourhood." The steady bombardment resulted in something of a siege and eventually, according to one reporter, the deaths of four more people.[74]

As shot rained down on the center of business, privilege, and power, terror gripped the city. Merchants stood on the street corners observing the battle "with fear painted in their faces." One man wrote with surprising candor, "I am a coward its true, but I think this would have alarmed any one." The city's rulers recognized their own inability to defend the city against the rage of the sailors, so they called for help. Two gentlemen hurried to Manchester to explain that unless a military force arrived quickly, "Liverpool would be laid in ashes and every inhabitant murdered." This was an exaggeration, of course, meant to get Lord Pembroke's Royal Regiment of Dragoons moving. As the rulers gathered their defenses, the sailors expanded their struggles in new directions. During the late afternoon, some went door-to-door, terrifying propertied inhabitants as they "requested" money, sometimes at gunpoint, to be used to bury those who had been murdered at the exchange. Others organized companies to march, in formation, with drums rolling and flags flying, to the homes of specially targeted slave-trade merchants. An eyewitness said that they "marched there under a Ships ensign or fflag and a great Number of Sailors carried with them such Arms as Blunderbusses, muskets & other Arms & Weapons."[75]

The first merchant they went after was Thomas Radcliffe, who was believed to have fired the first shot at them the day before. He lived in Frog Lane, Whitechapel, northeast of the exchange. When the sailors arrived, a group of them went inside and began throwing Radcliffe's property out into the streets. According to an eyewitness, they brought out expensive furniture and splintered it. They removed cabinets with drawers full of fine-fabric clothes, which they "tore in pieces." They destroyed fine china and parchment documents. They threw out "feather-beds, pillows, &c, ripped them open and scattered the feathers in the air." They discovered, to their surprise, that the gentleman had filled the beds of the servants not with feathers but the chaff of wheat, an insult the lower orders of Liverpool would not soon forget. Not everything was destroyed, however, for women in the mob, called the "whores" of the sailors, carried some items away.[76]

Next they went to Rainford Gardens and the home of William James, one of the most powerful African merchants who at one point had twenty-nine ships in the slave trade. James somehow got advance notice of the crowd's intentions and was able to remove valuables to a country home and even to fortify the house against the assault, but to no avail. A sailor broke the shutters, smashed a window, and yelled to the crowd, "Here goes. Let's break the house down." Joseph Black and other members of the mob trained guns on the building in case anyone was home and cared to offer resistance. Into the house went the seamen, and out came furniture (beds, chairs, desks), bedding, clothes, pewter goods, china, and silver spoons. Once again the prerogatives of money were dishonored and thrown about in the streets. Damages ran to £1,000 ($177,000 in 2007 dollars) or more. The rioters also made two discoveries—a cellar stocked with wine and rum, which they most emphatically did not destroy, and, inside a grandfather clock, a "little negro boy," who had gone there to hide. He was apparently unharmed.[77]

Two other merchants' homes were also attacked, although less destructively: Thomas Yates, owner of the *Derby* (where the whole dispute began), who lived on Cleveland Square, and John Simmons, who lived on St. Paul's Square. In none of the four targeted places were the merchants at home when the sailors arrived. According to the merchant Thomas Middleton, they all would have been murdered if they had been. Ominously, the sailors gave out the news that "they mean to go to all of the Guinea merchants in town." They had a mind to continue the "daring outrages."[78]

It was a time to settle scores, and not only with the merchants. Slave-ship captain Henry Billinge testified that seaman Thomas Pearson, "on hearing a Woman say that this Inform't was a Guinea Captain," pounded him with his club. Captain Thomas Blundell of the *Benin* saw the sailors' mob and "went off towards Hanover Street to avoid them." Captain Anthony Taylor of the *Ferret* went into hiding, "being afraid to appear publickly as the rioters had threatened his Life." A terrified observer was forced to admit, "they behaved very well to every one, excepting those to whom they owed a grudge."[79]

On Thursday morning the merchants waved an olive branch, sending a delegation to North Lady's Walk to negotiate, offering the sailors work if they would cease their protest. At the moment most of the sailors were busy burying their dead, and hence they could not consider the proposal. The delegates did, however, manage to speak briefly to George Hill, a London sailor and a leader of the insurrection. Hill was apparently a ship's gunner; he spoke affectionately of his cannon, which he called "his old wife." He did not care for the proposal, telling the visitors that "he was a Sailor and could not use a Spade." Moreover, he felt that he and his mates had unfinished business. He "swore he would not be content till the Exchange was brought down and nothing else would satisfy him." As soon as his comrades were properly buried, they would bring even bigger cannon to bear on the exchange: "they were determined not to have one stone upon another." With these words the merchants' representatives took their leave.[80]

Meanwhile Lord Pembroke's regiment had marched all night through the rain from Manchester. According to a gentleman who accompanied the troops, when they arrived in Liverpool around 4:00 P.M. on Thursday, they found the "respectable" people of Liverpool peering out from behind their shuttered windows and soon cheering their arrival. They also found the sailors gathered for a showdown, but they were quickly dislodged from their positions by cavalry and forced to retreat in confusion. The troops rounded up around fifty protesters and threw them into Lancaster jail. By Friday morning the insurrection was over. The Dragoons were later lauded for "saving the Town and Shipping from impending destruction." Sailors had not, however, attacked all shipping, captains, or merchants, rather only those connected to the slave trade.[81]

The Return of the Dancing Sailor

Did the dancing sailor join the Liverpool insurrection? As the "disturbances" began, he was already cursing his betters and vaunting his own independence. It is not hard to imagine him joining with his brother tars to express raw class hatred—through slashed rigging, cannon fire on the exchange, and the trashed finery of the hated slave-trade merchants, lying in the streets. He would have helped to create the modern practice called the "strike," which was named at this particular historical moment for the militant action of sailors who "struck"—took down—the sails of their vessels. He also would have helped to make one of the biggest municipal uprisings of the late-eighteenth-century Atlantic, and one of the only ones in which the crowd used cannon against state and business authority.

Or did the sailor, alternatively, meet the captain and the surgeon the day after his dancing by fiddle and sign on to the slave ship, the "vast machine"? He would have found on the ship two overlapping and conflicting communities, one vertical, the other horizontal. The first was a corporate community linking the entire crew from the top of the laboring hierarchy to the bottom; it was summed up in the phrase "We're all in this ship together." The second was a class community, in which he would have been arrayed alongside other common sailors against the captain and officers (with the junior mates and lesser skilled workers in between, usually leaning to one side or the other). On the outward-bound voyage to Africa, as the captain asserted his distended powers of discipline, the relationship between officers and sailors would be the main line of tension, the primary contradiction in shipboard society.

When the ship arrived on the African coast and large numbers of enslaved people came on board, everything changed. Now the sailor would oversee the forced dancing of African captives. He worked as a prison guard, holding hundreds of Africans on the ship, against their wills, by violence. Suddenly it mattered little how he had first come aboard or how much he may have hated the captain. Conflicts that had arisen back in port or during the outward voyage began to be eclipsed. A new social cement called fear bonded the entire crew, from captain to cabin boy, whose lives now depended on their unity of vigilance and action, their cooperation against a more numerous and potentially powerful group of captives in their midst. As the sailor and the captain moved closer together, the corporate community grew stronger and the class community weakened, although it did not disappear. Now a deeper antagonism ruled the ship, and with it came a new discipline. It would be called "race."

It also mattered little what had been the cultural or ethnic background of the sailor, for he would, on the ship and coast of Africa, become "white," at least for a time, as the "vast machine" helped to produce racial categories and identities. It was the common practice for everyone involved in the slave trade, whether African or European, to refer to the ship's crew as the "white men" or the "white people," even when the crew was motley, a portion of it "colored" and distinctly not white. The sailor's status as a "white man" guaranteed that he would not be sold in the slave-labor market, and it marked him as someone who could dispense violence and discipline to the enslaved on behalf of the merchant and his capital. One of the lessons of the slave ship, as William Snelgrave pointed out, was that the enslaved must never "make a Disturbance, or offer to strike a white Man"; otherwise, they would be "severely punished," perhaps executed for it. But such status did not guarantee that the sailor himself would not be the target of violence and discipline from the captain and officers, nor did it guarantee other standards of treatment aboard the ship.[82]

The original and primary contradiction on the ship, between captain and crew, became, on the coast of Africa and through the Middle Passage, secondary. And even though sailors began to get the "wages of whiteness," they nonetheless had their complaints about the new situation. They complained bitterly—and, it must be stressed, self-servingly and dishonestly—that the enslaved were treated better on board the ship than they were. They complained about shelter: when the African captives came aboard, they had nowhere to sleep. They complained about health care: a sailor from the slave ship *Albion* came aboard HMS *Adventure* on the Windward Coast in 1788–89 and announced that the Guineaman's "surgeon neglected the sick seamen, alledging that he was only paid for attending the Slaves." They complained loudest about food: the slaves ate better than they did. Their provisions were fresher and more plentiful, but, according to Samuel Robinson, should the sailor "be found snatching a handful of the slaves mess when dealing it out, he would be severely punished." One seaman complained that sailors were sometimes "obliged to beg victuals of the slaves." The so-called free workers were treated worse than the slaves, in whom both the merchant and captain had a much greater vested interest as valuable property. Sailors also discovered that "white skin privilege," such as it was, could be reversed, even on the Middle Passage, when toward the end of the voyage they became expendable, surplus labor. Sailors were abused, dumped, left to fend for themselves, often in a sickly state. Class came back with a vengeance.[83]

The sailor was a third party between two much bigger, heavier dancers: the merchant, his capital, and his class on the one hand and the African captive, her labor power, and her class-in-the-making on the other. In fighting to maintain a middle position and to limit his own exploitation in a dangerous line of work, the sailor resisted wage cuts, as in Liverpool in 1775, but he did not strike *against* the slave trade. He struck for a better wage deal within it. Such was the hard limit of his radicalism, his practice of solidarity.[84] His contradictory position was expressed in a drunken, perhaps insane, and utterly tragic manner aboard a slave ship that arrived from the coast of Guinea, at North America, in 1763. A sailor, "being in Liquor, stript off his Cloaths, and divided them among the Slaves; then taking up a Negro Boy in his Arms, said, *He would have a Servant of his own;* and leaping with him into the River, they were both drowned."[85]

CHAPTER 9

From Captives to Shipmates

The man refused to eat. He had been sick, reduced to a "mere skele-ton." He had apparently made a decision to die. Captain Timothy Tucker was outraged, and probably fearful that his example might spread to the other two hundred–plus captives aboard his ship, the *Loyal George,* as it made its way across the Atlantic to Barbados in the year 1727. The captain turned to his black cabin boy, Robin, and com-manded him to fetch his whip. This was no cat-o'-nine-tails but rather something much bigger, a horsewhip. He tied up the man and lashed him: "from his neck to his ancles, there was nothing to be seen but bloody wounds," said Silas Told, an apprentice seaman and crew mem-ber who recounted the story years later. All the while the man made no resistance and said nothing, which incensed the captain, who now threatened him in his own language: "he would *tickeravoo* him," that is, kill him, to which the man answered, *"Adomma,"* so be it.[1]

The captain then left the man "in shocking agonies" to take his din-ner on the quarterdeck, eating "like a hog," thought Told. After he had finished his meal, Captain Tucker was ready to resume the punish-ment. This time he called another ship's boy, John Lad, to bring him two loaded pistols from his cabin. Captain Tucker and John Lad then walked forward on the main deck, approaching the nameless hunger striker, who was sitting with his back against the larboard gunnel of the ship. With a "malicious and virulent grin," Tucker pointed a pistol at the man and repeated that he would kill him if he did not eat. The man answered simply, as before, *"Adomma."* The captain put the barrel of the pistol to the man's forehead and pulled the trigger. The man "instantly clapped his hands to his head, the one behind, the other before," and stared the captain directly in the face. Blood gushed from the wound, like the "tapping [of] a cask," but he did not fall. The captain, infuriated, cursed, turned to the cabin boy, and screamed, "This will not kill him," so he clapped the other pistol to the man's ear and fired again. To the utter amazement of Told and surely everyone else who looked on, "nor did he drop, even then!" Finally the captain ordered John Lad to shoot the man through the heart, whereupon "he then dropt down dead."

In consequence of this "uncommon murder," the rest of the male captives rose in vengeful wrath "upon the ship's company with full purpose to slay us all." The crew scrambled to retreat behind the barricado. Once there they took up their positions at the swivel guns, raking the main deck with shot and sending the rebels flying in all directions. Some of the men dove belowdecks seeking cover, while others jumped overboard. As soon as the crew had regained control of the main deck, they took to the boats to save the men in the water but were able to rescue only one or two from the "violence of the sea" and the men's own concerted efforts to drown themselves. A large but unknown number perished. Thus did an individual act of resistance spark a collective revolt and one form of resistance give rise to another. The refusal to eat had led to a kind of martyrdom, to an insurrection, and, once that failed, to mass suicide.[2]

Scenes like this played out on one slave ship after another. They epitomized a deep dialectic of discipline and resistance—on the one hand, extreme violence enacted by the captain against an enslaved individual, with an expectation that the resulting terror would help him to rule the others, and, in response from the enslaved, extreme opposition to that violence and terror, individually and in the end collectively. Beneath the response, however, is a question: how did a multiethnic mass of several hundred Africans, thrown together in a slave ship, learn to act collectively? From the time they were first brought aboard the ship, they were socialized into a new order, one designed to objectify, discipline, and individualize the laboring body through violence, medical inspection, numbering, chaining, "stowing" belowdecks, and various social routines, from eating and "dancing" to working. Meanwhile the captives communicated among themselves and fought back, individually and collectively, which meant that each ship contained within it a process of culture stripping from above and an oppositional process of culture creation from below. In the shadow of death, the millions who made the great Atlantic passage in a slave ship forged new forms of life—new language, new means of expression, new resistance, and a new sense of community. Herein lay the maritime origins of cultures that were at once African-American and Pan-African, creative and hence indestructible.[3]

Boarding the Ship

Depending on the ship's location in Africa and how the trade was organized locally, some of the enslaved who came aboard would have been inspected by the physician and captain (or mate) on shore, while others would be examined as they stood for the first time on the main deck of the vessel. The physical condition of the captives varied widely, according to how they had been enslaved, how far they had traveled, and under what conditions. Some were sick, some were wounded, some were emaciated, some were still in shock or had begun to slip into "melancholy." Still, they had to be in reasonable, or at least recuperable, condition, or the slave traders would not buy them.

The process of stripping began, under threat of violence from both the black traders and the white, with clothes. It soon extended to name, identity, and to some extent culture, or so the new captors hoped. Various merchants and captains gave the official reason for removing clothes: to "preserve their health"—that is, to reduce the likelihood of vermin and disease. Some of the women, when stripped, immediately squatted to hide their genitals. (Some unknown number of ship captains gave women a small square of fabric to wear around their waists.) Perhaps just as important—although this reason for removing clothes was rarely mentioned—captains did not want the enslaved to have any place on their person where they might hide a weapon of any kind.[4]

The mental state of the captives varied considerably. A twenty-seven-year-old woman who had apparently traveled hundreds of miles to get to the coast eyed the members of the ship's crew with the "greatest astonishment." She had never seen white people before and was brimming over with curiosity. Slave trader John Matthews described a man of even "bolder constitution" who looked at "the white man with amazement, but without fear." He carefully examined the white man's skin, then his own, the white man's hair, then his own, "and frequently burst into laughter at the contrast, and, to him no doubt, [the] uncouth appearance of the white man." On the other hand, Matthews also noted that a much greater number came aboard in abject terror, in "a state of torpid insensibility" in which they remained for some time. These people thought that "the white man buys him either to offer him as a sacrifice to his God, or to devour him as food."[5]

Cannibalism was one of the idioms through which the war called the slave trade was waged. Europeans had long justified the trade, and slavery more broadly, by saying that Africans were savage man-eaters, who must be civilized by exposure to the more "advanced" life and thought of Christian Europe. Many Africans were equally sure that the strange pale men in the houses with wings were the cannibals, eager to eat their flesh and drink their blood. This belief was apparently strengthened as some African elites used the slave trade to discipline their own slaves: "the Masters or Priests hold out as a general Doctrine to their Slaves, that the Europeans will kill and eat them, if they behave so ill as they do to their respective Masters, by which Means the Slaves are kept in better Order, and in great Fear of being sold to the Europeans." In any case a huge number of people, like Equiano, arrived at the ship in morbid fear of being eaten alive. The belief was more common in some regions of Africa than others: people from the interior were more likely to believe it than were people from the coast; the Igbo more likely than the Akan. The fear of being eaten would prove to be a powerful motive to resistance of all kinds, from hunger strike to suicide to insurrection.[6]

Perhaps the most infamous symbols of control aboard the slave ship were the manacles, shackles, neck rings, and chains that made up the hardware of bondage. Many of the enslaved were already constrained when they came aboard the ship, especially the so-called stout men (physically strong adults), but moving from African cordage or vine to the iron technology of the Europeans evoked a special horror. Manacles took several forms, from handcuffs to rounded clamps. Leg shackles, also known as bilboes, consisted of a straight iron rod, on which were slid two U-shaped metal loops. The rod had a finished end, large and flattened, and a slotted end with a lock or, more commonly, a hammered ring, through which a chain might be reeved when two captives came on deck. The most punishing constraint was reserved for the most rebellious slaves, whose necks were locked into large iron collars, which made it even more difficult to move, lie down, or rest. The point was to limit movement and control potential resistance.

The general rule was, all men manacled and shackled at the wrist and leg, women and children left unconstrained. But captains did vary in their uses of fetters. Some apparently always chained certain groups of Africans (Fante, Ibibio) but not others (Chamba, Angola), who were considered unlikely to rise up. The Asante might be chained, depending on how and why they ended up on the ship. Several captains swore that they let even the men out of chains once they had left the African coast, although equally experienced captains did not believe it. Some captains used only manacles or shackles, not both. One captain said he let men out of chains once they seemed to be "reconciled" to their fate on board the ship. Women who proved rebellious were also fettered, and quickly.[7]

The iron constraints excoriated the flesh. Even minimal movement could be painful. Trying to get oneself and a partner through a mass of bodies on the lower deck to the necessary tubs could be excruciating, and the forced "dancing" on the main deck for exercise could be torture.

In the late 1780s, the youthful John Riland befriended (in England) an old African named Caesar, who still bore the scars of the fetters he wore on the slave ship. The skin on his ankles was "seamed and rugged," not least because he had been chained to a man whose language he did not understand, which made it difficult for them to coordinate their movements. When his partner sickened and convulsed with starts and twitches, the movements against the metal lacerated both men. The experience of wearing these fetters, Caesar explained to Riland, would never be forgotten: "the iron entered into our souls!"[8]

Early in the history of the slave trade, Europeans took control of slave bodies by branding them, burning symbols of European ownership into the flesh, usually on the shoulder, upper chest, or thigh. Branding was most common when the purchasing trader was the representative of a large chartered company such as the Royal African Company or the South Sea Company. Some merchants also required captains to brand their privilege slaves to hold them accountable for the loss in case of mortality. But the practice of branding seems to have diminished over time. By the early 1800s, it was rarely mentioned.[9]

Other, more "rational" means arose in order to transform human beings into property. Gaining strength throughout the eighteenth century was an accounting system that operated aboard each ship to reduce all captives to the deadened anonymity of numbers. Each person who was purchased was assigned a number, and sometimes a new name. But a numbering system was more pervasive and functional, for both captains and surgeons, who routinely referred in their logs and journals to the death of man "No. 33," a boy "No. 27," a woman "No. 11," or a girl "No. 92." According to the official records of the voyage, each slave was a nameless entry in a bookkeeping system. Captains numbered the living as they came aboard; surgeons numbered the dead as they flung them overboard.[10]

Working

A significant number of the enslaved worked aboard the vessel, at a wide variety of tasks central to the shipboard economy. Probably the most common work was "domestic" in the broad sense, part of the necessary daily reproductive labors of the ship. A substantial number of women seem to have been involved in food preparation. They performed what were likely familiar duties: they cleaned rice, pounded yams, and ground corn. Women also worked as cooks, in place of or in some instances alongside the ship's cook, to prepare food for the hundreds on board. Occasionally an enslaved woman (considered trustworthy) might cook the higher-quality food to be served to the captain's table. Other Africans, men and women, washed and cleaned the decks and scraped and sanitized the slave apartments. Some found a niche in the shipboard economy washing and mending the clothes of the crew. They often got "pay" for these tasks—a dram of brandy, tobacco, or extra food.[11]

Other labors were more commonly the result of crisis. In the event of a storm or damage to the vessel, African men might be mobilized to work at the pumps. Captain John Rawlinson of the *Mary* "let the Negroes out of Irons to assist in pumping the Ship" in 1737, as did Captain Charles Harris of the *Charles-Town* in 1797. In the latter, reported explorer Mungo Park, "It was found necessary, therefore, to take some of the ablest of the Negro men out of irons, and employ them in this labour; in which they were often worked beyond their strength." Their strength might have been the difference between capsizing and making it to port.[12]

In wartime some captains elected to train a portion of the men in the use of knives, swords, pikes, small arms, or cannon in case of an attack by an enemy privateer. Captain Edwards of the snow *Seaflower* faced a Spanish privateer in 1741 with only six sailors and a boy, but 159 slaves. Rather than surrender, he opened a chest of small arms and "put Firelocks, Pistols, and Cutlasses into the Hands of some of the Negroes," who "fought so desperately in their Way, shooting, slashing, and throwing Fire into the Privateer, when they attempted twice to board him, that by their Bravery they sav'd the Ship and Cargo," that "cargo" being themselves! The privateer was obliged to "sheer off" with no booty and having done little damage. Captain Peter Whitfield

Branker testified before the House of Lords that on a voyage of 1779 he trained a large number of slaves every night during the Middle Passage: "I had at least a Hundred and fifty Slaves to work the Guns, Sails, and Small Arms; I had Twenty-two Marines; there were ten Slaves in each Top, that lived there continually, that were exercised to hand the Sails as Top Men in His Majesty's Ships."[13]

The last comment points toward the most common work of all for boys and men: helping to sail the ship. This, too, was often a matter of necessity. When ten sailors deserted the *Mercury* in 1803–4, their "places were filled by negro slaves." More commonly, however, it was not desertion but sickness and death that set the enslaved to work as sailors. When nineteen of the twenty-two crew members of the *Thetis* fell ill in 1760, they "set sail with the assistance of our own slaves, there being no possibility of working the ship without them," wrote the ship's carpenter, who was himself slowly going blind from a "distemper" in his eyes. Many captains declared that they could never have brought their ships to port without the labors of the enslaved.[14]

African boys on board the ship worked with the sailors and indeed some were being trained to become sailors. A few were the captain's privilege slaves, trained to enhance market value. One captain claimed that the boys were "allowed to go aloft, work with the Sailors, and are reckoned upon as a Part of the Ship's Company." This was an exaggeration, but it contained a truth confirmed by others. When the slave ship *Benson* came near his own vessel, the *Neptune,* in the early 1770s, mate John Ashley Hall "could only see two White men upon her yards handing the sails, the rest were Black boys, Slaves." Aboard the *Eliza* in 1805, three "working boys" named Tom, Peter, and Jack not only helped sail the ship, they talked with the other captives and reported what they learned to the crew.[15]

Fighting

Violence lay at the very heart of the slave ship. The gunned ship itself was an instrument of war making and empire building, and of course violence of one kind or another had brought most everyone aboard.

Moreover, almost everything that happened on the slave ship had the threat or actuality of violence behind it. It comes as no surprise, therefore, that the Africans brought together on the slave ship sometimes fought among themselves, especially given the fear, rage, and frustration they all must have felt. The reasons for conflict among Africans were first and foremost circumstantial, related to the brutal conditions of enslavement and incarceration, especially on the hot, crowded, stinking lower deck. But cultural causes can also be discerned in shipboard ruckus.

The noisome conditions of the lower deck caused an endless number of fights, especially at night when the prisoners were locked below without guards. Most fights were occasioned by the efforts of the captives to get through the mass of bodies to the necessary tubs to relieve themselves. The fighting was worst in the men's apartment, not only because men were more apt to fight but because they were manacled and shackled, which made getting to the tubs more difficult. In 1790 a member of the House of Commons committee investigating the slave trade asked Dr. Alexander Falconbridge, "Have you known instances of quarrels between Slaves who have been shackled together?" He answered, "It is frequently the case, I believe, in all Slave ships." And so it was. Among the men belowdecks, there were "continual quarrels."[16]

Any man who had to answer the call of nature had to coordinate the trip with his partner, who might not wish to be disturbed, and this in itself could cause a fight. If the partner proved willing, two people then tried to make their way through the multitude of bodies, all the while negotiating the rolling motions of the ship. Inevitably one person stepped or fell on another, who, "disturbed by the shock, took umbrage at it" and hit the "accidental offender." Then someone else struck back to defend the person who had been hit. The escalation of the clash in such crowded circumstances was rapid, and soon the incident had grown into what seaman William Butterworth called a "battle."[17]

These difficulties pale, however, when compared to what happened when sickness—especially dysentery or any other malady that produced diarrhea—swept through the lower deck. Suddenly the afflicted could not always get to the tubs in time, or in some instances they were simply too weak to make the effort, especially if the tubs were at a distance. When the sick "ease[d] themselves" where they lay, furious disturbances broke out. This, and indeed the entire filthy condition of the lower deck, was a special torment to West Africans, who were known to pride themselves on personal cleanliness. Fighting was therefore chronic.[18]

Another aspect of fighting was cultural, and here each ship captain faced a dilemma. Captain James Bowen observed that when "Men of different Nations" were shackled together, they would frequently "quarrel and fight." Rather than coordinate movement, one man "would drag the other after him," causing a row. Some captains said they would not link men who could not understand each other's language. But this was dangerous. Should a captain chain men together who were from the same nation and thereby risk cooperation and hence conspiracy, or should he shackle men of different nations and risk fighting, disorder, and injury? Bowen opted to reduce the fighting, or so he claimed, but other captains may have chosen differently.[19]

The Fante and the Chamba, both from the Gold Coast, were a case in point in the late eighteenth century. The coastal Fante had long been major slave-trading partners of the British, but even so, some of their people ended up as slaves aboard the ships when convicted of a crime. The Chamba (sometimes mistakenly called the Dunco), a more rural people from the interior, were convinced that they ended up on the ships because of the machinations of the man-stealing Fante: "they consider these people as the authors of their misfortunes," wrote a slave-ship captain, "and the chief instruments used in removing them from their country." When these two groups were on the same ship, they fought bitterly. Indeed when the Fante rose up in rebellion, as they often did, the Chamba, "as if to be revenged on them, always assisted the crews in suppressing these mutinies, and keeping them in subjection." The Fante, in other words, were bigger enemies than the European crew; if they wanted something, the Chamba wanted the opposite.[20]

Sometimes the fighting among the enslaved resulted in serious injury, disability, even death. At mealtime aboard the *Florida* in 1714, the enslaved "were much given to fighting, & biting one another, & some of their bites prov'd mortal." Something similar must have happened on the *Sandown*, as Captain Samuel Gamble noted in his log for April 4, 1794: "At 6 PM the Doctor Amputated a Mans finger that was begun to mortify, having been bit by another Slave. at 5 PM he Departed this Life, No 10." A captain trading at New Calabar wrote of the "cruel and bloody" temper of the slaves he had purchased there. They were "always quarrelling, biting, and fighting, and sometimes choking and murdering one another, without any mercy, as happened to several aboard our ship." Some captains seemed to think they had on board a chaotic and gruesome war of each against all.[21]

Most of the fighting went on belowdecks, but it did occasionally break out on the main deck, when, for example, because of a prolonged Middle Passage or an inability to purchase adequate provisions in Africa, everyone on board had been put to short allowance of victuals. In this situation hungry people fought over food, thereby permitting slave captains to brag that they humanely protected the weak captives from the strong. Enslaved women were also known to fight over the beads they had been given in order to make ornaments during their daytime hours on the main deck. Younger captives sometimes taunted the older ones: "it is not unusual for the Boy Slaves, who are brought on Board, to insult the Men, who, being in Irons, cannot easily pursue and punish them for it."[22]

Dying

Sickness and death were central to the African experience aboard the slave ship. Despite the efforts of merchants, captains, and surgeons, all of whom had a direct material interest in the health and survival of their captives, illness and mortality plagued slave ships even as the percentage of deaths declined over the course of the eighteenth century. Some captives arrived at the ships in a poor state of health, because of inadequate nutrition and the harsh, harmful conditions of their enslavement and march to the coast. Those from the Gold Coast seemed to be healthiest and therefore suffered lower mortality aboard the ships, while those from the Bights of Benin and Biafra died in significantly greater numbers. Yet even comparatively healthy voyages, in which only 5 to 7 percent of the enslaved died, were in many ways traumatic, for death on a ship, a small, crowded, intimate place, was always highly visible and poignant. Uncontrollable, catastrophic epidemics erupted from time to time, which is why the slave ship was called a "marine lazar house" and a "floating bier." The famous rendition of the slave ship *Brooks,* it has been remarked, resembled a huge coffin with hundreds of bodies arranged neatly inside. The thin, ghostly cries wafted from belowdecks endlessly: *"Yarra! Yarra!"* (We are sick) or *"Kickeraboo! Kickeraboo!"* (We are dying).[23]

A "sickly ship," everyone agreed, was a horror beyond imagination. The ill lay on bare planks, without bedding, as friction caused by the rolling motion of the ship rubbed away the skin from their hips, elbows, and shoulders. A man belowdecks sometimes awoke in the morning and found himself shackled to a corpse. Most ships did not have room for a "hospital," and even if one did, the demand for it might quickly exceed its capacity. Louis Asa-Asa noted that many sick people on his ship got no medical attention. Some would not have wanted it in any case. Captain James Fraser wrote that Africans were "naturally averse to taking medicines," by which he meant Western medicines. Probably the most famous image of a sickly ship was provided by Dr. Alexander Falconbridge, who wrote about his visits to a lower deck ravaged by fluxes and fevers: "the deck was covered with blood and mucous, and approached nearer to the resemblance of a slaughter-house than any thing I can compare it to, [and] the stench and foul air were likewise intolerable."[24]

Surgeons' journals kept between 1788 and 1797 (and submitted to the House of Lords) revealed the main causes of death, which were, as described, variously precise, fuzzy, and revealing. The greatest killer was dysentery (bacillary and amebic), which was called at the time the "flux" or "bloody flux." The second leading cause of death was a generic listing, "fever," noted by doctors in several types: "nervous" or "hectic," "pleuratic," "intermittent," "inflammatory," "putrid," and "malignant." These fevers included malaria (the deadly *Plasmodium falciparum,* as well as the debilitating *P. vivax* and *P. ovale*) and yellow fever, even though many West Africans had partial immunities to these diseases. Other, less frequent causes of death were measles, smallpox, and influenza, although any of them could devastate a ship at any time.[25] Scurvy was better understood as a vitamin C deficiency as the eighteenth century progressed, but it did strike with deadly force now and again against those ships whose captains did not or could not stock up on fresh provisions and citrus fruits. Yet another cause of mortality was dehydration, always a deadly danger in the tropics, on the infernal lower deck of a ship with a limited water supply. More occasional causes of death included depression ("fixed melancholy"), infection ("mortification"), stroke ("apoplexy"), heart attack ("decay of the muscular functions of the Hart"), and, to a lesser extent, parasites ("worms") and skin disease (yaws). Less precise causes appeared in the journals as "inflammation," "convulsions," and "delirium." Finally, social (as opposed to medical) causes of death included "the sulks," "jump'd overboard," "choked himself," and "insurrection." Most ships experienced several of these maladies, and a few combined the deadliest kinds. The *Comte du Nord* in 1784 suffered a lethal combination of dysentery, measles, and scurvy, which for a while killed 6 to 7 captives per day, 136 deaths altogether. The last word on cause of death belongs not to a doctor but rather the abolitionist J. Philmore. Some people, he suggested, died of a "broken heart."[26]

One can only guess at the meanings Africans attached to this endlessly repeated catastrophic death and the cavalier dumping of bodies over the rail of the ship, often to sharks waiting below. But we can perhaps understand something of its cultural magnitude by realizing that many peoples from West African societies believed that sickness and death were caused by malevolent spirits. An observer who knew the Windward Coast well noted that death was always thought to be the handiwork of "some malicious enemy." Nicholas Owen, who had lived for years in Sierra Leone, believed that Africans in that region "never think that any sickness comes but by a witch or devil." It is not hard to imagine who the malicious enemy aboard the slave ship would be, but the conclusions to be drawn from the identification remain elusive. Added to this would have been the violation of almost all West African cultural precepts about how death was to be handled in ritual fashion—how a person was to be buried, with what kinds of accoutrements, and how the spirit was to be sent to the next world. Not that the multiethnic Africans would have necessarily agreed about these things; the point is that their enslavement and incarceration precluded customary grieving and closure. Even though the ship's physician did what he could to keep the enslaved alive, there can be no doubt but that sickness and death were central to the experience of terror aboard the slave ship.[27]

Building Babel

West Africa is one of the world's richest linguistic zones, and it has long been known that the peoples who came aboard the slave ships brought scores of languages with them. European and American slave traders were conscious of this, and indeed they saw in it an advantage. Richard Simson expressed this clearly in his late-seventeenth-century ship's log: "The means used by those who trade to Guinea, to keep the Negros quiet, is to choose them from severall parts of ye Country, of different Languages; so that they find they cannot act joyntly, when they are not in a Capacity of Consulting with one an other, and this they can not doe, in soe farr as they understand not one an other." Royal African Company surveyor William Smith expressed the same idea. The languages of the Senegambia region were "so many and so different," he wrote, "that the Natives, on either Side of the River, cannot understand each other." By taking some "of every Sort on board [the slave ship], there will be no more Likelihood of their succeeding in a Plot, than of finishing the Tower of *Babel*." This, he noted, "is no small Happiness to the Europeans." Conversely, traders worried about cooperation and rebellion when they had too many people on a slaver who were "of one Town and Language."[28]

It is true that any given slave ship had several African cultures and languages aboard and that intelligibility could be an issue among the enslaved. Captain William Snelgrave was convinced that captives from the Windward Coast on board the *Elizabeth* had not been involved in an insurrection because they "did not understand a word" of the language of its Gold Coast organizers. The extreme case of unintelligibility came with the appearance of someone on board with whom no one else could converse. This happened rarely, but when it did, the consequences could be tragic, as explained by Dr. Ecroyde Claxton: "there was one man who spoke a language that was unknown to any one of them, which made his condition truly lamentable, and made him always look very much dejected—this I believe produced a state of insanity."[29]

Recent scholarship, however, has begun to emphasize the multilingualism and mutual intelligibility of West Africans to one another, at least within certain large cultural regions, and to suggest that linguistic divisions aboard the slave ships were less extreme than once thought. It now appears that means of communication had been worked out over time and broad distances through the process of trade, especially along West Africa's coastline and on its many large rivers and hydrographic systems that extended deeply into the interior of the continent. Especially important in inter-African communication was what one observer called "maritime tongues."[30]

Some of the maritime tongues were pidgins, formed to permit trade between speakers of different languages. In West Africa, English- and Portuguese-based pidgins were most commonly used. Others were African languages, such as Manding, Fante, and Igbo, which served the same purpose. According to Captain James Rigby, all coastal peoples who lived and labored from Cape Mount to Cape Palmas on the Windward Coast, a distance of about 250 miles, understood one another. Thomas Thompson, a missionary who lived on the Gold Coast, noted the small, "parish-sized" linguistic zones but also noted the existence of seafaring languages that connected people over broad distances, for example, the 300 miles from Cape Apollonia to the river Volta. Sierra Leoneans in the 1790s spoke a lingua franca, but they also spoke "English, French, Dutch, or Portuguese with tolerable fluency." Captain William McIntosh discovered in the 1770s that the enslaved he purchased at Galam, who had originated in the interior of Senegal, "perfectly understood the language of those slaves I purchased on the Gold Coast." Both groups had apparently come from so far inland as to have mutually intelligible languages.[31]

Africans also communicated with one another by learning English on board the ship, most of them by speaking with sailors. This involved normal conversation as well as the technical language of seafaring work. The latter would have been essential for the boys who labored alongside the seamen. But learning English could be a matter of urgency for most anyone. When a captive named Cape Mount Jack, from the Windward Coast, was forced aboard the *Emilia* in 1784, "he spoke very little English," but over time "he learnt more" and used it to tell the story of his kidnapping. Here was another maritime tongue and one that would grow increasingly important to those people who were bound to English-speaking colonies.[32]

The variety of formal languages spoken on the ship did not exhaust the possibilities for communication; far from it. Sailors William Butterworth and Samuel Robinson recalled speaking with captives by "sign and gesture," and of course Africans spoke to one another the same way. And then, on every ship, there were various and important forms of expressive culture: singing and dancing (of the self-chosen, not forced, variety), drumming (the entire ship, being wooden, was one vast percussive instrument), and storytelling. Observers noted the "wonderful" and "surprising" memories of Africans, which was of course a reference to the oral tradition, and the telling of stories, by women, "upon the plan of Aesop's fables," Aesop himself having been an African. Another form of expressive culture was drama, which could be performed, with expansive and perhaps therapeutic social meanings, on the main deck of the slave ship as if it were a stage. Dr. Thomas

Trotter noted that "some boys in my ship," the infamous *Brooks* on a voyage of 1783–84, "played a sort of game, which they called Slave-taking, or Bush fighting." In this they acted out the trauma of how marauders had captured them and their families. Trotter continued, "I have seen them perform all the manœuvres, such as leaping, sallying, and retreating, and all other gestures made use of in bush fighting." When Trotter made inquiries about this play among the enslaved women of the ship, "I was only answered by violent bursts of sorrow." The drama of dispossession and enslavement was thus reenacted, discussed, lamented, and committed to memory aboard the ship.[33]

Communicating Belowdecks

The best description of how communication worked among the enslaved belowdecks was written by seaman William Butterworth, in an account of his voyage aboard the *Hudibras,* from Liverpool to Old Calabar to Barbados and Grenada in 1786–87. Captain Jenkin Evans initially purchased 150 people, among whom, noted Butterworth, were "fourteen different tribes or nations." It is not clear how many cultural groups were among the final number, the 360 with whom they commenced the Middle Passage, but it is clear that the dominant group on board were the Igbo, as was almost always the case on ships trading on the Bight of Biafra at this time.[34]

Butterworth demonstrated how communication took place among people who were separated from one another by apartments belowdecks. In the aftermath of a failed insurrection, in which the men slaves on the vessel had risen up "to massacre the ship's company, and take possession of the vessel," but had not been supported by the women, angry recriminations were shouted around the ship. Locked below in the forward part of the ship with armed guards pacing above their heads on the main-deck gratings, the men shouted to the women that they were cowards and traitors "in not assisting them to regain their liberty." The women hollered back that "they thought the plot was discovered, and their plan frustrated." Earlier, when confronted by the captain, the women had denied knowing anything about the plot, but the midnight conversation now suggested otherwise. The crew on deck heard the entire heated exchange. Some of them would have understood what they heard, likely including Captain Evans, who had made at least two previous voyages to the Bight of Biafra. Any deficiencies of understanding would be overcome by an African boy named Bristol, who understood all languages of the region and acted as the ship's interpreter.

Undeterred by what the captain and crew might or might not know, some of the men began to organize a second insurrection, again with the women, who seemed determined to give a better account of themselves this time. Correspondence was now carried on "through the medium of the boys; which prevented the necessity of shouting from the two extremities of the ship." The boys would run back and forth between bulkheads at each end of their apartment, carrying whispered messages from the men to the women and back again. Occasionally someone would break the rule of secrecy and speak aloud, most notably in this instance a powerful woman called "Boatswain Bess," who was, in Butterworth's eyes, "an Amazon, in every sense of the word." She had been appointed "superintendent of her country women" and given sailor's slops by Captain Evans. The rebel plan now was to break down the bulkheads and force their way up onto the main deck, whereupon Bess and the other women would arm themselves with the cook's utensils—forks, knives, an ax—and lead the uprising. The plot was extinguished before it could be put into action, with the help of Bristol. The male ringleaders were flogged, while Boatswain Bess and four other women were wrapped up in a wet canvas sail and dropped on deck to "cool off."

Butterworth also noted other important means of communication, especially among the female slaves with whom he was stationed and whom he observed closely. He noted how one nameless woman was "universally esteemed" among the bondwomen and especially among her own "countrywomen." She was "an oracle of literature"—an "orator" and a "songstress." One of her main purposes was to "render more easy the hours of her sisters in exile." Her cultural background is unknown, although it would appear that she was not Igbo, as Butterworth could not understand her. She was, however, more than successful in addressing a multiethnic audience, as her premature death caused a long and loud outpouring of grief among her fellow female captives.

When this woman spoke or sang, the female slaves of the *Hudibras* arranged themselves on the quarterdeck in circles, "the youngest constituting the innermost circle, and so on, several deep, the most aged always being found outermost." The singer stood, or rather knelt, at the center of the inner circle, singing "slow airs, of a pathetic nature," no doubt capturing the sorrows of dispossession and enslavement. Judging from the tone, mood, and emotions on display, Butterworth surmised that "they might be speaking of friends far distant, and of homes now no more." She also gave orations, some of which, Butterworth believed, were recitations from memory, perhaps epic poetry. These pieces "moved the passions; exciting joy or grief, pleasure or pain, as fancy or inclination led," depending on the tale and the circumstances. The surrounding women and girls were closely involved in the event through the traditional African pattern of call-and-response. They joined in as "a kind of chorus, at the close of particular sentences." It was a deeply communal occasion, and an "air of solemnity ran through the whole." The effect, even on the young Englishman who could not understand the words, was moving: he found, to his surprise, that he "shed tears of involuntary sympathy." He considered the gatherings of the women to be "melancholy" and thought-provoking.

Butterworth also showed how information could make its way from one part of the lower deck throughout the entire ship, quickly and explosively. As it happened, Dr. Dickinson, the ship's surgeon, mentioned (perhaps in jest) to an enslaved woman that after stopping in Barbados they still had a long voyage of two months or more ahead of them—and this after a grueling eight-week Atlantic crossing. The woman was furious that their agonies at sea should be prolonged, and she conveyed both the news and her anger to the other women with whom she was confined belowdecks. Suddenly, wrote Butterworth, "like a train of gunpowder, ignited at one end, it ran through the apartment of the boys, to that of the men, the great magazine of suppressed discontent." Butterworth heard the "loud murmurs which now ascended from below" and feared a "dreadful explosion." So did Captain Evans, who promptly summoned Dr. Dickinson as well as male and female captives from belowdecks to a highly visible public meeting. The captain explained to the assembled (and indeed to the whole ship) that what the doctor had said was false, as they would arrive soon in Grenada. He reprimanded the surgeon and forced him to make a public apology, all to keep the social order in the aftermath of the angry murmurs.

Singing

As Butterworth made clear, one of the recurrent sounds of a slave ship was song. The sailors sometimes played instruments and sang, but more commonly, day and night, the Africans sang. Some of their singing was forced, but some of it was "of their own accord." Everyone, it seems, took part. "Men sing their Country Songs," from and about their native cultures, explained a former slave-ship captain, "and the Boys dance to amuse them." The leading part in singing aboard the slave ship was by all accounts, including Butterworth's, played by women.[35]

Song was an essential means of communication among people who were not meant to communicate. The barricado across the main deck might separate men and women, even prevent them from seeing one another, but it could not block sound or keep them from hearing or conversing with one another. A mate named Janverin, who made four voyages to Africa in the late 1760s and early 1770s, explained in an interview, "They frequently sing, the men and women answering one another, but what is the subject of their songs [I] cannot say."[36]

And of course that was the point: singing in African languages permitted among the captives a kind of communication that many of the European captains and crew members could not understand. Singing was also a way of finding one's kin, fellow villagers, and countrymen and -women, and identifying which cultural groups were on board the ship. It was a way of communicating important information about conditions, treatment, resistance, and events, about where the ship was going. Singing was a means of creating a common base of knowledge and forging a collective identity.

Some members of the crew, however, knew the languages in which people sang, or they got someone to translate either the general or specific meaning of the lyrics. Cases in point were two sea surgeons who made voyages in the late 1780s—one to Gabon, the other to Bonny. They described forced singing, which could vary considerably in tone and message. With African drums beating and the cat-o'-nine-tails cracking around their bodies, the enslaved were required to sing specific lyrics: *"Messe, Messe, Mackaride"*—that is, "Good Living or Messing well among White men." The enslaved, explained one of the physicians with sarcasm, were thus required to "praise us for suffering them to live so well." On the other vessel, the enslaved sang songs not of praise but of protest: *"Madda! Madda! Yiera! Yiera! Bemini! Bemini! Madda! Aufera!"* These lyrics meant that "they were all sick, and by and by they should be no more." This surgeon added that "they also sung songs expressive of their fears of being beat, of their want of victuals, particularly the want of their native food, and of their never returning to their own country."[37]

Not all songs were protests, however, as singing could serve several different purposes. The enslaved aboard the *Anne,* anchored off Old Calabar in 1713, sang a song of praise to Captain William Snelgrave after he had saved the child of a woman on board from sacrifice by a local African king. Those aboard the *Hudibras* sang "songs of joy" after their restive "murmuring" had forced an apology and clarification from the captain about the length and destination of their voyage. The singing apparently continued into the night, expressing their hopes for life in "Makarahrah country." Vice Admiral Richard Edwards of the Royal Navy noted something similar: on slave ships arriving in West Indian ports, "the Negroes usually appeared chearful and singing—That you are apprized of the Arrival of a Guineaman by the Dancing and Singing of the Negroes on Board." What they had to be cheerful about, the vice admiral did not say.[38]

Happy songs seem to have been exceptions. More commonly, be-lowdecks at night, whenever captives, especially women, were on their own, they sang songs of "lamentation," or so they were called by one observer after another. These were sad, mournful songs about loss—about dispossession, enslavement, alienation—often accompanied by collective tears. "Some of the women used to sing very sweetly, and in a plaintive tone, when left to themselves," recalled John Riland. They sang of having been taken away from their family, friends, country-men; their songs were "melancholy lamentations of their exile from their native country." Thomas Clarkson noted the singing of women who slowly went insane while chained to a mast on the main deck of a Guineaman: "In their songs they call upon their lost Relations and Friends, they bid adieu to their Country, they recount the Luxuriance of their native soil, and the happy Days they have spent there. At other Times they neither sing nor speak, but are melancholy and low, and pour forth their Grief in repeated Torrents of Tears. At other Times they dance, shriek, become furious. Such are the dreadful scenes, which one is obliged to behold in the dreary Caverns of a Slave-Vessel."[39]

One aspect of these songs was the active recalling of history, in the style of the griot. Seaman David Henderson heard songs about "the History of their Sufferings, and the Wretchedness of their Situation." Dr. James Arnold also heard the women singing "the History of their Lives, and their separation from their Friends and Country." He went on to note that these songs of resistance were well understood by Cap-tain Joseph Williams, who found them "very disagreeable." He had the women flogged in "a terrible Manner" for daring to remember through song; often their wounds took two to three weeks to heal. The struggle for memory by these women was an effort to retain historical identity in a situation of utter social upheaval. It was a central element of an ac-tive and growing culture of opposition aboard the ship.[40]

Resistance: Refusing to Eat

If the common experiences of expropriation and enslavement, includ-ing the violent, densely communal regimentation of the slave ship, created the potential for community among African prisoners, and if social practices—working, communicating, and singing—helped to realize it, nothing was more important to the collective project of creating group identity than resistance. This was in itself a new language, a language of action employed every time people refused food, jumped over the side of the ship, or rose up in insurrection. It was a universal language, which everyone understood regardless of cultural background, even if they chose not to speak it actively themselves. Every act of resistance, small or large, rejected enslavement and social death as it embraced creativity and a different future. Each refusal bound people together, in ever-deeper ways, in a common struggle.[41]

The Atlantic slave trade was, in many senses, a four-hundred-year hunger strike. From the beginning of the waterborne human commerce in the early fifteenth century to its end in the late nineteenth century, enslaved Africans routinely refused to eat the food given to them. When some of the enslaved came on board the ship, they fell into a "fixed melancholy," a depression in which they responded to nothing their captors said or demanded, including instructions to eat. Others got sick and were unable to eat even if they had wanted to. And yet even among some of the depressed and the sick, and among a much larger group who was neither, the refusal to eat was a conscious choice, which served several important purposes among the enslaved. Because the captain's main charge from the merchant was to deliver as many live, healthy African bodies as possible to a New World port, anyone who refused sustenance, for any reason whatsoever, endangered profits and subverted authority. Refusing to eat was therefore first and foremost an act of resistance, which in turn inspired other acts of resistance. Second, it proved to be a tactic of negotiation. Mistreatment could trigger a hunger strike. Third, it helped to create a shipboard culture of resistance, a "we" against a "they." Among the messages of the hunger strike were these: we will not be property; we will not be labor power; we will not let you eat us alive.

On John Riland's ship the *Liberty* in 1801, several of the enslaved rejected their food. The officer on watch first swore he would throw them overboard if they did not eat; then he threatened them with the cat, which seemed to work, or so he thought: "The slaves then made a show of eating, by putting a little rice into their mouths; but whenever the officer's back was turned they threw it into the sea." Seaman James Morley also saw slaves pretend to eat, holding food in their mouths "till they have been almost strangled." The officers would damn them "for being sulky Black b———." They would try to force them to eat, using the cat, the thumbscrews, a "bolus knife" or a stick (to open the mouth), or a *speculum oris* or a "horn" to force food down obstinate throats.[42]

Anyone who resisted food posed a direct challenge to the captain's powers, as the example might spread, with disastrous results. This was made chillingly clear by seaman Isaac Parker when he testified before the House of Commons committee investigating the slave trade in 1791. Aboard the *Black Joke* in 1765, a small child, whose mother was also on board, "took sulk, and would not eat," refusing both the breast and standard fare of rice mixed with palm oil. Captain Thomas Marshall flogged the child with the cat as enslaved men looked on through the crevices of the barricado: they made "a great murmuring" in protest. Still the child refused to eat, and day after day the captain wielded the cat but also tied a mango log, eighteen to twenty inches long and twelve to thirteen pounds in weight, around its neck by a string. "The last time he took the child up and flogged it," explained Parker, he "let it drop out of his hands" to the deck, saying, "Damn you. . . . I will make you eat, or I will be the death of you." In less than an hour, the child died. In a final act of cruelty, the captain commanded the child's mother to throw the small corpse overboard. When she refused, he beat her. Eventually she complied, and afterward, "She seemed very sorry, and cried for several hours." Even the smallest rebel, a nine-month-old child who refused to eat, could not be tolerated aboard the *Black Joke*.[43]

What captains like Marshall feared, the contagion of resistance, was illustrated in a case that came before the High Court of Admiralty in 1730. James Kettle, captain of the *City of London* (owned by the South Sea Company), charged that seaman Edward Fentiman was too violent in his carriage toward the enslaved. He had beaten an unnamed slave woman, after which all the others—and there were 377 on board—refused to take sustenance. This in turn earned Fentiman a beating from Kettle, who explained to the court that what had happened here was one instance of a larger problem: it is "the nature & disposition of Negroes & so frequently happens on board of Merchant Ships that when any one of them have been beat or abused for the whole Company of them on Board to resent it & grow Sullen and refuse to eat and many of them thereby to pine away and die."[44]

Dr. T. Aubrey reinforced Captain Kettle's point and raised it to a higher level of generalization. In his vade mecum for slave-trade surgeons, he explained that the violent mistreatment of the enslaved often resulted in their refusal to eat. Once they stop, "then they lose their Appetites, and perhaps fall sick, partly thro' fasting, and partly with Grief to see themselves so treated." More tellingly still, once they had taken their resistance to heart, "all the Surgeon's Art will never keep them alive; they will never eat any thing by fair Means, or foul, because they choose rather to dye, than be ill treated." He referred, of course, to the various violent means used to make people eat. These would be resisted, in his view, and would in the end be useless against the will to refuse all sustenance. Like Kettle, Aubrey made it clear that the hunger strike was a tactic employed in the struggle that raged aboard every slave ship.[45]

The hunger strike aboard the *Loyal George,* as recalled by Silas Told, led directly to an insurrection and, once that failed, to mass suicide. The process of resistance also worked the other way, as hunger strikes often followed failed insurrections. After the captives rose aboard the *Ferrers Galley* in 1721, "near eighty" were killed or drowned. Most of those who survived, wrote Captain William Snelgrave, "grew so sullen, that several of them were starved to death, obstinately refusing to take any Sustenance." After an uprising on an unnamed vessel in the Bonny River in 1781, three of the wounded leaders "came to the resolution of starving themselves to death." They were threatened, then beaten, but "no terrors were effectual, for they never tasted any sustenance after their resolution, and they died in consequence of it." Likewise aboard the *Wasp* in 1783, when two insurrections took place. Following the first, in which the women captives seized the captain and tried to throw him overboard, twelve died of wounds and the refusal to eat. Following the second, even bigger explosion, fifty-five Africans died of "bruises, swallowing salt water, chagrins at disappointment, and abstinence."[46]

Jumping Overboard

Perhaps an even more dramatic form of resistance than self-starvation was jumping overboard. Some jumped in the hope of escape when docked in an African port, while others chose drowning over starvation as a means to terminate the life of a body meant to slave away on New World plantations. This kind of resistance was widely practiced and just as widely feared by the organizers of the trade. Merchants warned captains about it in their instructions, formal and informal. Captains in turn made sure their ships had nettings all around. They also had the male captives chained to a ringbolt whenever they were on the main deck, and at the same time they made sure that vigilant watches were always kept. When the enslaved did manage to get overboard, captains urgently dispatched emergency rescue parties, in boats, to catch and bring them back aboard.

African women had greater freedom of movement on the ship than men did, so they played a prominent role in this kind of resistance. In 1714 four women, one of them "big with child," jumped overboard as the *Florida* departed Old Calabar. As a man on board noted, they "shew'd us how well they could swim, & gave us ye slip." The crew immediately went after them but caught only the pregnant one, because she "could not shift so well as the rest." In Anomabu on the Gold Coast in 1732, Captain James Hogg discovered in the middle of the night that six women had jumped overboard and afterward was sure that only a brisk effort from the crew prevented the rest from following. Such escapes were dangerous, even for expert swimmers, as many of the enslaved from coastal regions happened to be. Anyone retaken in the water—and most who jumped overboard were—could expect severe punishment, in some cases death (as a deterrent to others), once back aboard the ship. Even if the fugitives got to shore, chances were that their African captors would catch them and return them to the slaver. Finally, many of the waterways near shore where people jumped overboard were shark-infested. Captain Hugh Crow recalled two Igbo women who went over the side of one of his vessels, only to be torn apart immediately by sharks.[47]

Some captives went overboard spontaneously, in response to a specific event, rather than in a calculated bid for freedom. In 1786 a gang of six, "enraged or terrified" at seeing the corpse of their deceased countryman cut open by a ship's doctor for anatomical analysis, "plunged into the sea, and were instantly drowned." A couple of years before, another forty or fifty jumped into the sea during a scramble, a deliberately terrifying manner of selling slaves on the ship's deck in Jamaica. One hundred men jumped off the *Prince of Orange* after they had been released from chains upon the docking of the vessel at St. Kitts in 1737. Thirty-three refused assistance from the sailors and drowned. They were "resolv'd to die, and sunk directly down." The cause of the mass action, according to Captain Japhet Bird, was that one of the countrymen of the enslaved came aboard and "jokingly" told them they would be blinded and eaten by the white men.[48]

One of the most illuminating aspects of these suicidal escapes was the joy expressed by people once they had gotten into the water. Seaman Isaac Wilson recalled a captive who jumped into the sea and "went down as if exulting that he got away." Another African man, who knew that the nettings had been loosened to empty the lower deck's necessary tubs, got free of a group of sailors and "darted himself through the hole overboard." When the sailors went after him, and almost caught him, the man dived down and popped up again some distance away, eluding his would-be captors. All the while, recalled the ship's surgeon, he "made signs which it is impossible for me to describe in words, expressive of the happiness he had in escaping from us." Finally he went down again, "and we saw him no more." After a bloody insurrection had been suppressed aboard the *Nassau* in 1742, the captain ordered all injured slaves on deck: everyone whose wounds made recovery doubtful was "to jump into the sea," which many of them did, going to their deaths with "seeming chearfulness," according to the person who had been the cabin boy on the voyage. The same thing happened aboard the infamous *Zong*. As Captain Luke Collingwood ordered 122 sick captives thrown overboard, another 10 jumped of their own accord.[49]

Hunger strikes and jumping overboard were not the only means of self-destruction. Some sick people refused medicine because "they want to die." Two women found ways to strangle themselves to death aboard the *Elizabeth* in 1788–89. Others cut their own throats, with hard-edged tools, sharp objects, or their own fingernails. A sailor named Thompson noted that he "has known all the slaves [locked belowdecks] unanimously [to] rush to leeward in a gale of wind, on purpose to upset the ship, choosing to drown themselves, than to continue in their situation, or go into foreign slavery."[50]

The least common but most spectacular mass suicides involved blowing up the entire ship. In January 1773 the enslaved men belowdecks aboard the *New Britannia,* using tools slipped to them by the more mobile boys, cut through the bulkheads and got into the gun room, where they found weapons and used them to battle the crew for more than an hour, with significant loss of life on both sides. When they saw that defeat at the hands of the crew was inevitable, "they set fire to the magazine, and blowed the vessel up," killing almost everyone on board, as many as three hundred altogether. When Captain James Charles learned in October 1785 that Gambian captives had successfully captured a Dutch slaver (and killed the captain and crew), he resolved to go after the vessel, not least because the insurgents, if defeated, might become his property. Following a chase of three hours and an indecisive engagement, a party of his own crew volunteered to board the freedpeople's craft under fire. Ten men and an officer went aboard and, after a smart contest on deck, "drove the mutinous slaves into the hold." As the battle continued, someone apparently blew the vessel up "with a dreadful explosion, and every soul on board perished." Part of the wreckage fell upon the deck of Captain Charles's vessel, the *Africa*.[51]

Even though suicides run like a bloodred thread through the documentation of the slave trade, it is difficult to be sure how common they were. One measure, for a limited time period, may be found in the journals that slave-ship surgeons were required to keep in the aftermath of the Dolben Act, or Slave Carrying Bill, of 1788. For the period from 1788 to 1797, physicians for eighty-six vessels recorded in their journals the cause of death for all the Africans under their charge, and in these suicide looms rather large. Twenty-five surgeons recorded what appeared to be one or another kind of self-destruction: eight ships had one or more person jump overboard; three others listed captives "missing" (no doubt overboard) after an insurrection; three others experienced nonspecific forms of suicide; and another twelve gave causes such as "lost," "drowned," "sulkiness," and "abortion." Almost one-third of the vessels in the sample witnessed a suicide, and even this is likely a serious understatement, as surgeons had vested interests not to report suicides in this era of charged debate about the inhumanity of slave ships.[52] Another reason to reduce or conceal the number of suicides was the ruling of an English court, Judge Mansfield presiding, in Trinity Term 1785: insurance companies would be required to pay for insured slaves who died in an insurrection but would not be required to pay for those who died of chagrin, abstinence, or despair. More specifically, "all who died by leaping into the sea were not to be paid for."[53]

Rising Up

Hundreds of bodies packed together belowdecks were a potent source of energy, as could be seen in material emanation anytime a slave ship sailed through cool, rainy weather. On these occasions steam billowed up from the mass of hot bodies on the lower deck, through the gratings, and onto the main deck where the crew worked. Aboard the slave ship *Nightingale* in the late 1760s, seaman Henry Ellison saw "steam coming through the gratings like a furnace." Not infrequently the human furnace down below exploded—into full insurrection. The peculiar war that was the slave trade would now be waged openly on the ship.[54]

Yet insurrection aboard a slave ship did not happen as a spontaneous natural process. It was, rather, the result of calculated human effort—careful communication, detailed planning, precise execution. Every insurrection, regardless of its success, was a remarkable achievement, as the slave ship itself was organized in almost all respects to prevent it. Merchants, captains, officers, and crew thought about it, worried about it, took practical action against it. Each and all assumed that the enslaved would rise up in a fury and destroy them if given half a chance. For those who ran the slave ship, an insurrection was without a doubt their greatest nightmare. It could extinguish profits and lives in an explosive flash.

Collective action began in communication among people who identified common problems and searched together for common solutions. They began to converse in small groups, probably twos and threes, literally conspiring (breathing together) in the dank, fetid air belowdecks, probably at night, away from the ears of captain and crew. The lower deck was usually crowded, but mobility among the enslaved was often possible, even among the shackled and manacled men, so potential rebels could move around, find one another, and talk. Once they had formulated a plan, the core conspirators might take a "sangaree," an "Oath to stick by each other, and made by sucking a few Drops of one another's Blood." They would then organize others, mindful of a dangerous contradiction: the greater the number of people involved in the plot, the greater the chance of success, but at the same time, the greater the chance that someone would snitch. Many would therefore opt for a smaller number of more committed militants, wagering that once the insurrection was under way, others would join them. Most conspirators would proceed carefully and wait for their moment to strike.[55]

Everyone involved in running the slave trade assumed, correctly, that the most likely insurrectionists were African men, who were therefore fettered and chained at almost all times, whether on the lower or the main deck. But women and children had important roles to play as well, not least because of their greater mobility around the ship. Indeed women sometimes played leading parts in uprisings, as, for example, when they seized Captain Richard Bowen aboard the *Wasp* in 1785 and tried to throw him overboard. The captives on board the *Unity* (1769–71), like those aboard the *Thomas* (1797), rose up "by the means of the women." On other occasions women used their proximity to power and freedom of movement to plan assassinations of captains and officers or to pass tools to the men below. The boys on board the *New Britannia,* anchored in Gambia, passed to the men down below "some of the carpenter's tools where-with they ripped up the lower decks, and got possession of the guns, beads, and powder."[56]

Crucial to any uprising was the previous experience of those involved. Some of the men (like the Gola) and perhaps a few of the women (from Dahomey) had been warriors and hence had spent their lives mastering the courage, discipline, and skills of warfare. They would have been trained to fight at close quarters, to act in coordinated ways, and to hold position, not retreat. Others had valuable knowledge of Europeans, their ways, even their ships. Seaman William Butterworth described several captives "who, by living at Calabar and the neighbouring towns, had learned the English tongue so as to speak it very well; men who, for the commission of some misdemeanour, had forfeited their freedom, and who, desirous of regaining their liberty at any risk, had for some time been sowing the seeds of discontent in the minds of the less guilty, but equally unfortunate slaves, of both sexes." Such savvy men and women from the port cities could "read" their captors in ways others could not, and some could even read their ships. A special port-city denizen was the African seafarer, skilled in the ways of deep-sea sailing ships and probably the most valuable person to an insurrectionary attempt. The Kru of the Windward Coast and the Fante of the Gold Coast were known to be especially knowledgeable about

European ships and sailing, although lots of other coastal and riverine peoples were as well. For these reasons captives known to have come from the waterside were considered by slave-ship captains to be special security risks.[57]

Knowledge of European arms was evident aboard the *Thomas,* which lay in the Gambia River in March 1753. All eighty-seven of the enslaved "privately got off their Irons," came up on deck, and threw the chief mate overboard. Alarmed, the seamen fired their small arms and drove the rebels back below. But some of the captives noticed that the seamen's firearms were not working properly, whereupon they picked up "Billets of Wood, and Pieces of Board" and came back up on deck, battling the crew, who numbered only eight at the moment, driving them to the longboat, in which they escaped, leaving "the Sloop in Possession of the Slaves"—who suddenly were slaves no longer. When two slave-ship captains tried to recapture the sloop, they got a blistering engagement, "the Slaves making use of the Swivel guns, and trading Small Arms, seemingly in an experienced Manner against them." Such use of firearms was not uncommon, provided the enslaved could get to them.[58]

Certain cultural groups were widely known for their rebelliousness. Several observers noted that captives from the Senegambia region had a special hatred for slavery, which made them dangerous on board the ships. According to an RAC employee named William Smith, "the Gambians, who are naturally very idle and lazy, abhor Slavery, and will attempt any Thing, tho' never so desperate, to obtain Freedom." The Fante of the Gold Coast were ready to "undertake any hazardous enterprise," including insurrection, noted Dr. Thomas Trotter based on his experience of the 1780s. Alexander Falconbridge agreed: those from the Gold Coast were "very bold and resolute, and insurrections happen more frequently among them, when on ship-board, than amongst the negroes of any other part of the coast." The Ibibio of the Bight of Biafra, also known as "Quaws" and, in America, the "Moco," were, according to Captain Hugh Crow, "a most desperate race of men," always "foremost in any mischief or insurrection amongst the slaves" in the late eighteenth century. They killed many crew members and were known to blow up ships. "The females of this tribe," added Crow, "are fully as ferocious and vindictive as the men." Indeed the Ibibio were considered so dangerous that captains were careful "to have as few of them as possible amongst their cargoes." When captains did take them aboard, they "were always obliged to provide separate rooms for these men between decks." The Ibibio were the only group known to warrant special quarters for their rebelliousness, which the captains sought to contain by isolation.[59]

Each of the major lines of recruitment, among women, boys, and cultural groups, contained within them potential divisions. Numerous were the times when either the men or the women rose up in insurrection, unsupported by the other, which of course made it much easier for the crew to put down the uprising. The men, for example, did not act when the women attacked Captain Bowen of the *Wasp* in 1785, while the women did not rise up with the men on the *Hudibras* in 1786. Boys were known to pass not only hard-edged tools to the enslaved men but also information to the crew about designs afoot belowdecks. And if certain African groups were inclined to rebellion, it did not necessarily follow that their militant ways were agreeable to others on the ship. The Ibibio and Igbo were called "mortal enemies," the Chamba despised the Fante, and, during the middle of an insurrection in late 1752, Igbo and Coromantee insurgents began to fight each other. It is not always clear in any given case whether the divisions arose from previous history, inadequate communication and preparation, or the desirability of insurrection as a goal.[60]

Uprisings required familiarity with the ship; hence one of the things that people whispered about was what they knew of the hold, the lower deck, the main deck, the captain's cabin, the gun room, and how they should therefore proceed based on this knowledge. They found that they needed three specific kinds of knowledge about Europeans and their technologies, and that these were related to three distinct phases of an uprising: how to get out of the chains, how to find and use weapons against the crew, and how to sail the ship if they were successful. Insurrections tended to break down and suffer defeat at one of these moments in the process.

The iron technology of manacles, shackles, and chains was largely effective for its purpose, as its continued use, for centuries, on the enslaved and on all kinds of other prisoners, makes perfectly clear. But it is also clear that male captives on the lower deck regularly found ways to get out of these fetters. Sometimes the irons fit too loosely, and the enslaved could, with lubrication and effort, simply squirm out of them. In other cases they used nails, picks, slivers of wood, and other instruments to pick the locks, or a hard-edged tool of some kind (saw, adze, knife, hammer, chisel, hatchet, or ax, likely passed below by one of the women or boys) to cut or break through the iron. An additional challenge was to use the tools quietly so as not to be discovered in the process of breaking free. Once the chains were off, the rebels had to get through the fortified gratings, which were always locked overnight. Surprise at the morning opening frequently represented the best opportunity, unless someone could trick a member of the crew to open the gratings at night.[61]

The next step was to unleash the explosive energy from belowdecks, the sounds of which were, to a terrified crew member, "an uncommon uproar" and "several dreadful shrieks," perhaps "from a sailor being killed." African war cries would pierce the morning quiet. Striking with speed, surprise, force, and fury was important, because it could shock the crew into running for the longboat in an effort to escape the insurrection. Meanwhile hand-to-hand combat engulfed the forward part of the ship, and if a substantial number of the enslaved managed to get out of their irons, they would have had a decided numerical advantage over the sailors assigned to guard them. The sailors, however, had cutlasses, and the insurgents had no weapons other than what they could pick up from the deck, such as belaying pins, staves, perhaps an oar or two. If the women had risen in coordination with the men, fighting would have broken out in the aft part of the ship, behind the barricado, where they would have had access to better implements, such as fishgigs and the cook's hatchet. Most insurrectionists found themselves in the situation of one group who had burst onto a moonlit deck at midnight: "They had no fire arms, and no weapons, except the loose articles which they could pick up on the deck."[62]

As all hands rushed on deck to quell the uprising, they picked up pistols and muskets and took their positions at the barricado, firing through the peepholes at the men. They also manned the swivel guns at the top of the barricado, which allowed them to sweep the deck with shot. This was a decisive moment. If the enslaved had any hope of victory, they had to breach the barricado, not least to get into the gun room, which was located as far from the men's section as possible, in the stern of the vessel, near the captain's cabin, where crew members would be around to guard it. Many insurrectionists therefore tried to crash through the small door of the barricado or scale its wall, which ranged from eight to twelve feet high, with spikes at the top. If they managed to get through or over, if they could fight their way to the gun room and break it open, and if they knew how to use European firearms (as many African men with military experience did), they might have an outcome like the enslaved aboard the ship *Ann* in 1750: "the Negroes got to the Powder and Arms, and about 3 o'Clock in the Morning, rose upon the Whites; and after wounding all of them very much, except two who hid themselves: they run the Vessel ashore a little to the Southward of Cape Lopez, and made their Escape."[63]

As the fighting raged on, the rebels would act on previous planning. What would they do about the crew? For the most part, they had a straightforward answer: they would kill them. Such would appear to have been the choice on an unnamed vessel out of Bristol when, in 1732, the enslaved "rose and destroyed the whole Crew, cutting off the Captain's Head, Legs and Arms." This issue was complicated, however, by another one—that is, whether the Africans had any among them who knew how to sail the ship. The absence of such knowledge was always considered by Europeans to be one of their greatest bulwarks against insurrection once the ship was out at sea, as John Atkins remarked in 1735: "it is commonly imagined, the *Negroes* Ignorance of Navigation will always be a Safeguard." Some insurrectionaries therefore made it a point to keep several crew members alive, to assist with navigation and sailing the ship back to Africa.[64]

Insurrections aboard slave ships usually had one of three outcomes. The first of these was exemplified in 1729 aboard the *Clare* galley. Only ten leagues out to sea off the Gold Coast, the enslaved "rose and making themselves Masters of the Gunpowder and Fire Arms" drove the captain and crew into the longboat to escape their wrath and then took control of the ship. It is not clear whether the successful rebels sailed the vessel or simply let it drift toward the shore, but in any case they made landfall and their escape to freedom not far from Cape Coast Castle. An even more dramatic uprising occurred off the Windward Coast in 1749. The enslaved picked the locks of their shackles, grabbed large billets of wood off the deck, fought the crew, and after two hours overpowered them, forcing them to retreat to the captain's cabin and lock themselves inside. The following day, as the captives ripped open the quarterdeck, five members of the crew jumped overboard in an attempt to escape but discovered the hard way that some of the Africans knew how to use firearms; they were shot and killed in the water. The successful insurrectionists then ordered the rest of the crew to surrender, threatening to blow up the powder room if they refused. The vessel soon ran aground, and, before leaving, the victors plundered it. Some of them went ashore, not in the nakedness required on the ship but now clad in the clothes of the crew.[65]

Sometimes an insurrection resulted in the mutual destruction of the contending sides. Such would appear to have been the case aboard a "ghost ship," discovered adrift in the Atlantic in 1785 by another vessel. The unnamed slave schooner had sailed about a year earlier with a Newport, Rhode Island, crew to the coast of Africa. Now it had no sails and no crew, only fifteen Africans on board, and they were in "very emaciated and wretched condition." It was supposed by those who found them that they had "been long at sea." It was also supposed that the enslaved had waged an insurrection on board, "had rose and murdered the Captain and crew," and that during or after the uprising "many of the Blacks must have died." Perhaps no one knew how to sail the vessel and they slowly starved to death.[66]

By far the most common outcome of shipboard rebellion was defeat, which always featured torture, torment, and terror in its aftermath. Those who had played a leading role in the insurrection would be made examples to the rest. They would be variously flogged, pricked, cut, razored, stretched, broken, unlimbed, and beheaded, all according to the overheated imagination of the slave-ship captain. The war would continue through these savage punishments, the insurgents refusing to cry out when they were whipped or going to their deaths calmly, as the Coromantee notoriously did, despising "punishment, even death it self." Sometimes the body parts of the defeated would be distributed among the remaining captives, throughout the ship, as a reminder of what happened to those who dared to rise up. It was proven again and again that the slave ship was a well-organized fortress for the control of human beings. It was, by design, extremely difficult for its prisoners to take it over and sail to freedom.[67]

The main cause of slave revolts was slavery. And indeed Africans themselves offered their own explanations aboard the ship that proved the observation true. Seaman James Towne, who knew the primary trading language of the Windward Coast "nearly as well as English," conversed with the enslaved and learned their grievances. Asked by an MP in 1791 whether he had ever known them to attempt an insurrection on board a slave ship, he said that he had. He was then asked, "Did you ever inquire into the causes of such insurrections?" He replied, "I have. The reasons that were given me were, 'What business had we to make Slaves of them, and carry them away from their own country? That they had wives and children, and wanted to be with them.'" Other considerations that made insurrection more likely on any given ship were, for some, proximity to shore (worries about navigation once the vessel was out to sea) and poor health or lax vigilance among the crew. The captives' previous experience in Africa of warfare in the expansion of slaving operations would add to the likelihood of insurrection.[68]

The historian David Richardson has shown that insurrections aboard slave ships materially affected the conduct of the trade. They caused losses, raised shipping costs, and created disincentives for investors, as a writer in the *Boston News-Letter* recognized in 1731: "What with the Negroes rising, and other Disappointment, in the late Voyages thither [Gold Coast], have occasioned a great Reduction in our Merchants Gains." Richardson estimates that as many as one in ten vessels experienced an insurrection, that the average number of deaths per insurrection was roughly twenty-five, and that, all told, one hundred thousand valuable captives died as a result. Insurrections also generated other economic effects (higher costs, lower demand) that "significantly reduced the shipments of slaves" to America—by a million over the full history of the slave trade, by six hundred thousand in the period from 1698 to 1807.[69]

Insurrections also affected the reading public, as newspapers on both sides of the Atlantic endlessly chronicled the bloody uprisings of the enslaved. Alongside and sometimes within this coverage, opponents of the slave trade also gave voice to the struggles from the lower deck, noting the "desperate resolution, and astonishing heroism" displayed by the enslaved. They often insisted that the prisoners were trying to recapture their "lost liberty," their natural right. Moreover, when public debate about the slave trade exploded in Britain and the United States after 1787, abolitionists repeatedly used the resistance of the enslaved to disprove everything the slave-trading interest said about the decency of conditions and treatment aboard the ships. If slave ships were what merchants and captains said they were, why would anyone starve him- or herself to death, throw him- or herself over the side of the vessel, or rise up against long odds and suffer likely death in insurrection?[70]

Thomas Clarkson wrote of the "Scenes of the brightest Heroism [that] happen repeatedly in the Holds or on the Decks of the Slave-Vessels." So great and noble were these acts that the "Authors of them often eclipse by the Splendour of their Actions the celebrated Character both of Greece and Rome." He continued:

But how different is the Fate of the one and of the other. The Actions of the former are considered as so many Acts of Baseness, and are punished with Torture or with Death, while those of the latter have been honoured with publick Rewards. The Actions of the former again are industriously consigned to oblivion, that not a trace, if possible, may be found, while those of the latter have been industriously recorded as Examples for future Times.[71]

Clarkson was right about the heroism, the torture, the death, and about the endless glorification of the history of Greece and Rome, but he was wrong about the legacy of the rebels. The effect of insurrection was probably greatest upon the enslaved aboard the ship, and this despite their various degrees of participation in the project. Those who refused to accept slavery initiated a struggle that would go on for hundreds of years. As martyrs they would enter the folklore and long memory of those on the lower deck, the waterfront, and the slave plantation. The rebels would be remembered, and the struggle would continue.[72]

Going Home to Guinea

The experience of death, and the impulse to all forms of resistance, was linked to a broadly held West African spiritual belief. From the beginning of the eighteenth century to the time of abolition, most captives seem to have believed that in death they returned to their native land. This allowed them to "meet their fate with a fortitude and indifference truely their own." The belief seems to have been especially prominent among peoples from the Bight of Biafra, but it was also present among those of Senegambia, the Windward Coast, and the Gold Coast. It persisted long after the Middle Passage. Among people of African descent in North America and the West Indies, funerals often featured rejoicing, even rapture, because the deceased was "going home to Guinea."[73]

Early in the eighteenth century, an unnamed observer noted of those dying aboard his ship, "Their opinion is that when they dye, they go to their own country, which made some of them refuse to eat their victuals. Striving to pine themselves, as [the most ex]peditious way to return home." A woman of Old Calabar who starved herself to death aboard a slaver in the 1760s said to other women captives the night before she died that "she was going to her friends." Late in the century, Joseph Hawkins wrote that after death the Ibau "must return to their own country, and remain forever free of care or pain." Abolitionists knew of the belief in the transmigration of souls, as explained by Thomas Clarkson: "It is an opinion, which the Africans universally entertain, that, as soon as death shall release them from the hands of their oppressors, they shall immediately be wafted back to their native plains, there to exist again, to enjoy the sight of their beloved countrymen, and to spend the whole of their new existence in scenes of tranquility and delight: and so powerfully does this notion operate upon them, as to drive them frequently to the horrid extremity of putting a period to their lives." When someone died, the other Africans said that *"he has gone to his happy country."*[74]

A European observer who talked to various captives aboard his ship noted that among the majority this belief was "so gross as to allow them to inhabit the same country with the same bodies." Some even thought they would go back to life just as it was before, even to inhabit their "old dwellings." Others (denominated the "more intelligent" Africans) thought they would return to "a portion of this vast continent which alive they can never know." In an "African paradise," they would enjoy the joys and luxuries of life with none of its fears. The Islamic slaves on board the slave ship referred to the "law . . . which is to be the inheritance of all true Musselmen!" But they seemed to have a difference of opinion about who would accompany them into the afterlife, whether they would "carry their old wives along with them" or "blew eyed virgins." According to the man who collected the lore, the anthropological foray led nowhere: "Their opinion of this matter however must be acknowledged to be so dark and unintelligible as scarce to deserve our attention."[75]

Slave-trade merchants and ship captains begged to differ. They gave the belief a great deal of attention, in contemplation and action. They not only hooked up the nettings to prevent suicides and readied the implements of forced feeding, they also resorted to studied terror. Since many Africans believed that they would return to their native land in their own bodies, captains terrorized the dead body, and all who would look upon it, as a "preventative." One captain brought all the enslaved onto the main deck to witness as the carpenter cut off the head of the first slave who died, throwing the body overboard and "intimating to them, that if they were determined to go back to their own country, they should go back without their heads." He repeated the grisly ritual with each subsequent death. Captain William Snelgrave had the same idea. After decapitating a man who had been executed for leading an insurrection, he explained, "This last part was done to let our Negroes see that all who offended thus, should be served in the same manner, For many of the Blacks believe, that if they are put to death and not dismembred, they shall return again to their own Country, after they are thrown overboard." Hugh Crow knew that the belief often led to "the utter annihilation of the culprit." To the many roles played by the slave-ship captain in the burgeoning capitalist economy of the Atlantic must be added another: terrorist.[76]

The determination to "go home to Guinea" also suggests that the goal of an insurrection was not always the capture of the ship. The objective on many occasions was collective suicide, as Thomas Clarkson explained: the captives often "determine to rise upon the crew, hoping by those means to find that death which they have wished for, and indulging a Hope at the same time, that they shall find it at the Expence of some of the Lives of their Oppressors." Given this objective, a much larger number of insurrections must be counted as successful from the point of view of those who made them. In death and spiritual return, insurgents reversed their expropriation, enslavement, and exile.[77]

Bonding

The violence of expropriation and enslavement shattered the structures of kinship that had ordered the lives of almost all who had been forced aboard the slave ship. As deep, disruptive, and disorienting as this was, the enslaved did not suffer it passively. They did everything they could to preserve whatever may have survived of these kin relations, and, just as important, they set about building new ones, on the ship if not earlier, in the coffles, "slave-holes," factories, and fortresses along their way to the ship. Olaudah Equiano developed new connections to his "countrymen," a word that could refer to his fellow Igbo or to all the African people with whom he found himself sharing the ship. What anthropologists have called "fictive kinship" was actually an endlessly reproduced series of miniature mutual-aid societies that were formed on the lower deck of the slave ship. The kindred would call themselves "shipmates."

The first point to be emphasized about kinship is that it was real and commonplace aboard the slave ship. Husbands and wives, parents and children, siblings, members of families both extended and nuclear found themselves on the same ships, as one observer after another pointed out. One of the primary means of enslavement in Africa made this likely. The "grand pillage" of entire villages, set afire in the middle of the night, meant that families, indeed clans and sometimes communities, were swept up by marauding enemy forces, carried to the coast, and often sold together as "prisoners of war." As John Thornton has written, "An entire slave ship might be filled, not just with people possessing the same culture, but people who grew up together."[78]

Kinfolk met regularly aboard the Guineamen. An Igbo man, an *embrenché* "styled of the higher class" (like Equiano's father), encountered on the main deck of his vessel a woman of similar "countenance and color," his sister. The two then "stood with silence and amazement," looked at each other with the greatest affection, and "rushed into each other's arms." An "extremely clever and intelligent" fifteen-year-old girl was brought aboard another slaver only to find, three months later, that a "girl with similar features," her eight-year-old sister, had been forced to join her. "They very soon embraced each other, and went below." It happened repeatedly on slave ships that "relations are brought on board, such as Brothers and Sisters, Wives and Husbands, and these at Separate Times." Brothers ate together, as did sisters. But because men and women were separated, it was not easy for all kin to maintain contact. Communication between husbands and wives, for example, "was carried betwixt them by the boys which ran about the decks."[79]

Slowly, in ways surviving documents do not allow us to see in detail, the idiom of kinship broadened, from immediate family to messes, to workmates, to friends, to countrymen and -women, to the whole of the lower deck. Central to the process was the additive nature of many West African cultures, as explained by John Matthews: the people of Sierra Leone had an extraordinary "facility with which they form new connexions." Captain James Bowen described the bonding process among the enslaved. On his ship there were among the Africans "many relations." These were not, he made clear, traditional kin relations but something of more recent formation. These were people "who had discovered such an attachment to each other, as to have been inseparable, and to have partaken of the same food, and to have slept on the same plank during the voyage." They had, in short, shared violence, terror, and difficult conditions, as well as resistance, community, and finally survival on the lower deck of the slave ship. They built "new connexions": they were shipmates.[80]

Dr. Thomas Winterbottom explained the significance of the term. He worked as a physician in the Sierra Leone colony in the early 1790s and observed the connection between kinship in Africa, aboard the ship, and in the New World. He noted that at a certain age "the title of pa, or father, is prefixed to the names of the men, as a token of respect," and the "title of ma, or mother, is also added to the names of the women." This, he noted, was "also practised among the slaves in the West Indies." Then he showed how the ship provided a link: "it is worthy of remark, that those unfortunate people who have gone to the West Indies in the same vessel, ever after retain for each other a strong and tender affection: with them the term *ship-mate* is almost equivalent to that of brother or sister, as it is rarely that matrimonial connection takes place between them." This phenomenon prevailed throughout the Atlantic colonies: in the Dutch colonies, those who came over on the same ship called one another *sibbi* or *sippi*. In Portuguese Brazil, the word for seafaring kinship was *malungo*. In French Caribbean Creole, it was *bâtiment*. And from Virginia to Barbados to Jamaica and beyond, it was "shipmate." Such kinship would be extended when those who sailed together on a ship would later instruct their children to call their shipmates "uncle" or "aunt." Speaking of the changed social relationships aboard his own ship during the Middle Passage, seaman William Butterworth noted how "much were things altered in a few weeks sailing."[81]

Evidence of such bonds appeared in the extreme anxiety and pain of shipmates as they were sold and separated at the end of the voyage. Part of their agitation was of course the fear of the unknown that lay ahead on the plantation, but part of it was losing what had been built, in anguish and desperate hope, aboard the ship. In the House of Commons hearings on the slave trade between 1788 and 1792, surgeon Alexander Falconbridge and seaman Henry Ellison were asked the same question by an MP: "Have you ever known the Slaves on board your ship to appear exceedingly distressed when they were sold in the West Indies?" They agreed that yes, "they seemed sorry to be parted from one another." Falconbridge had witnessed four such sales, while the long-experienced Ellison had seen ten. Between them they had seen more than four thousand Africans sold off the ships. They spoke not just of formal kin, who would have been in a small minority in any case; rather they generalized about the enslaved of each ship as a whole who were "sorry to be parted from one another."[82]

Others added depth to the observation. Dr. Thomas Trotter wrote that the people from his ship "were crying out for their friends with all the language of affliction at being parted." He added that "on this occasion some husbands and wives were parted," but also noted that there were "many other relations of different degrees of kindred"—in other words, from closest family to extended kin, to fellow villagers, to countrymen, to new shipmates. Captain Bowen tried to keep together for group sale (in a scramble) those "connected by consanguinity or attachments," but he failed in his design. With "shrieking and dismay," even fainting, the attached were parted, probably, the captain thought, never to meet again. A final sale and separation involved three young girls "of the same country" whose vessel docked in Charleston, South Carolina, in 1804. This produced "the most piercing anguish" among one of the three, who was "overloaded with horror and dismay at the separation from her two friends." They in turn "looked wistfully at her, and she at them. At last they threw themselves into each others arms, and burst into the most piteous exclamations.—They hung together and sobbed and screamed and bathed each other with their tears." At last they were torn apart, whereupon one of the girls took "a string of beads with an amulet from her neck, kissed it, and hung it on her friend's."[83]

Another instance of a shipboard community in formation appeared in the comments of Captain Thomas King, veteran of nine Guinea voyages between 1766 and 1780. Captain King had witnessed instances in which "religious Priests" of certain groups had been brought aboard among the captives and had proceeded to encourage insurrection. These spiritual leaders induced others "to make those attempts, with the expectation that they should get the ship to some shore, where they would form a little community of their own." Here, on the ship, was a new community in formation. It began when the African Adam and Eve came aboard, and it would continue in plantation communities, maroon communities, church communities, and urban communities. Here was the alchemy of chains mutating, under the hard pressure of resistance, into bonds of community. The mysterious slave ship had become a place of creative resistance for those who now discovered themselves to be "black folks." In a dialectic of stunning power, the community of mortal suffering aboard the slave ship gave birth to defiant, resilient, life-affirming African-American and Pan-African cultures.[84]

CHAPTER 10

The Long Voyage of the Slave Ship *Brooks*

By the late 1780s, slave ships had crossed the Atlantic in the thousands, delivering millions of captives to New World plantations and helping to create a powerful new Atlantic capitalist economy. Suddenly, in 1788–89, they were all called home, in a manner of speaking, by abolitionists, who realized that what happened on these ships was morally indefensible and that their violence needed to be known in the home ports of London, Liverpool, and Bristol in England, in Boston, New York, and Philadelphia in the United States. The opponents of the slave trade thus began an intensive campaign to make the slave ship real to a metropolitan reading public, to bring the vessels that had long operated beyond the bounds of civil society into the glare of public scrutiny and, they hoped, under new political control.[1]

Making the slave ship real was accomplished in a variety of ways—in pamphlets, speeches, lectures, and poetry, for example—but probably the most powerful means was visual. Abolitionists produced images of the slave ship that would prove to be among the most effective propaganda any social movement has ever created. The best known of these, in its own day and since, was the slave ship *Brooks,* first drawn and published by William Elford and the Plymouth chapter of the Society for Effecting the Abolition of the Slave Trade in November 1788. The *Brooks* would be redrawn and republished many times around the Atlantic in the years that followed, and indeed it would come to epitomize the cruelties of the Atlantic slave trade in the eighteenth and nineteenth centuries, as well as the many-sided struggles against it. Thomas Clarkson explained in his history of the abolitionist movement that the image made "an instantaneous impression of horror upon all who saw it." It gave viewers "a much better idea than they could otherwise have had of the horrors of [the Africans'] transportation, and contributed greatly . . . to impress the public in favour of our cause."[2]

The creation of the image of the *Brooks* was part of a larger strategy to educate, agitate, and activate people in Britain and America, and indeed anywhere the slave trade went on. Manchester radical Thomas Cooper explained the approach in 1787: "Every man condemns the trade in general; but it requires the exhibition of particular instances of the enormity of this Commerce, to induce those to become active in the matter, who wish well to the cause upon the whole." Knowledge of the slave trade must be concrete, material, and human in order to build a movement. It must not be exaggerated, indeed must be a "narration of miseries which cannot be exaggerated; which extend to millions of our fellow creatures," miseries that were "increased and authorised, not alleviated, by laws, which avarice and oppression have enacted and enforced." It is, he concluded, "*particular* distress, with its attendant circumstances, which is calculated to excite compassion" and motivate people to act. Cooper thus articulated the principles that would guide much successful abolitionist work.[3]

The *Brooks* represented the miseries and enormity of the slave trade more fully and graphically than anything else the abolitionists would find. The result of their campaign was the broad dissemination of an image of the slave ship as a place of violence, cruelty, inhuman conditions, and horrific death. They showed in gruesome, concrete detail that the slaver was itself a place of barbarity, indeed a huge, complex, technologically sophisticated instrument of torture. In making the public case against it, they demonstrated that the vessel that had carried millions of Africans into slavery also carried something else: the seeds of its own destruction.[4]

Why the Brooks?

The voyage of the *Brooks* toward infamy began with a simple notation. It was written by a Captain Parrey of the Royal Navy, who had been dispatched to Liverpool to measure the tonnage and internal dimensions of several slave ships. He noted: "Ship Brooks—burthen 297 Tons contains in her different apartments for the Negroes 4178 square feet, which allows for one half the number she carried (609). 5 feet 6 Inches Length & 18 Inches breadth, & the other half 5 feet length & 13 Inches breadth, or 6 feet 10 Inches to each person on board." Parrey had inspected twenty-six vessels and taken the measurements of nine, three of which were larger than the *Brooks*, five smaller. When the square footage of each vessel was divided by the number of slaves carried on the last voyage, the *Brooks* had the second-smallest allocation of space per slave. In all other respects it seemed more or less typical.[5]

The *Brooks* came to be featured in abolitionist propaganda after the Plymouth and London abolition committees gained access to Parrey's list of measurements, likely through Prime Minister William Pitt, who had sent Parrey to Liverpool in the first place. In the original broadside text, Elford provided part of the rationale by introducing the *Brooks* as "a capital ship." The London committee, which apparently approved the Plymouth broadside, thought it necessary, in Clarkson's words, "to select some one ship, which had been engaged in the Slave-trade, with her real dimensions, if they meant to make a fair representation of the manner of the transportation." The *Brooks* therefore offered three advantages: it was, by chance, the first that appeared on Captain Parrey's list, so it was randomly chosen. It would also admit of "no complaint of exaggeration" by the opponents of abolition. It was, finally, "a ship well known in the trade."[6]

The *Brooks* had been built in 1781 and named for Liverpool slave-trading merchant Joseph Brooks Jr., who commissioned it and was its first owner. It was a big ship by the standards of the day, even for a Guineaman, at 297 tons (average was about 200). It was built "for the [slave] Trade," as Captain Parrey noted in his report. Evidence lay in the fourteen scuttles or air ports cut in the sides of the ship to ventilate the lower deck where the enslaved would be stowed. (Other "cargoes"—except perhaps cattle and convicts—did not require such ventilation.) The *Brooks* had a long life as a slaver, making ten successful voyages over almost a quarter of a century. Its captains purchased an estimated total of 5,163 Africans, 4,559 of whom they delivered alive, giving the ship a mortality rate of 11.7 percent, close to the average for ships over the four centuries of the slave trade (12.1 percent), but high for its own day (average for British ships between 1775 and 1800 was 7.95 percent). Before the Dolben Act, the *Brooks* carried considerably more slaves than would be shown in the various diagrams: 666 slaves in 1781–83; 638 in 1783–84; a staggering 740 in 1785–86; and 609 in 1786–87, the last voyage before Captain Parrey's inspection.[7]

The First Image: Plymouth

At the top of the large broadside created by Elford and the Plymouth Committee was the image of the *Brooks* with 294 Africans tightly packed and arranged in orderly fashion in four apartments, labeled from left (the stern of the vessel) "Girls Room," "Womens Room," "Boys Room," and "Mens Room." Each person was distinctly and individually drawn and wore only a loincloth. The men were chained at the ankles. On a broadside that measured twenty by thirty inches, the ship took up less than a quarter of the space. Immediately below the image was the heading "Plan of an AFRICAN SHIP'S Lower Deck with NEGROES in the proportion of only One to a Ton." In the middle of the heading was another image, an oval featuring a supplicant slave in chains, hands raised and asking, "Am I not a Man and a Brother?" At the left of the oval were manacles and at the right a whip, a cat-o'-nine-tails. This was an early use of what would become the primary emblem of the abolition society.[8]

Beneath the image and heading were two columns (eight paragraphs) of explanatory text, which took up the other three-fourths of the broadside. It began: "The above Plate represents the lower deck of an African ship of 297 tons burden, with the Slaves stowed in it, in the

The *Brooks*, original Plymouth edition, reproduced in Bristol proportion of not quite one to a ton." The next paragraph describes spatial allocation: men got six feet by sixteen inches; boys, five feet by fourteen inches; women, five feet ten inches by sixteen inches; girls, four feet by fourteen inches. The height between decks was five feet eight inches. Then followed a brief description of social conditions aboard the ship—how the men were fettered, how the enslaved were brought upon deck to be fed. The recently passed Dolben Act, which limited the number of slaves to be carried according to the tonnage of the vessel, is mentioned before the text returns to the question of stowage and then to the "thousand other miseries" suffered by the enslaved— being torn from their kin and native land, the "unremitting labours of slavery, without recompense, and without hope," and ultimately premature death.

Then came an explanation that the current abolition campaign concerned the slave trade only, not the emancipation of the slaves, as some had falsely alleged, which would injure "private property." On the contrary, the ending of the slave trade would result in better treatment for the slaves already in possession: "Thus then the value of private property will not only suffer no diminution, but will be very comfortably inhanced by the abolition of the Trade."

A penultimate short paragraph rebuts an argument put forward by supporters of the trade "that the suppression of it will destroy a great nursery for seamen, and annihilate a very considerable source of commercial profit." Thomas Clarkson's research had recently demonstrated that the slave trade was not a "nursery" for seamen but rather a graveyard. Moreover, the precarious and uncertain nature of the trade made it a dangerous, sometimes ruinous, investment for merchants.

The text concluded with a call to activism. It noted the current parliamentary investigation of the slave trade and called on citizens "to stand forward" and provide relevant information to "throw the necessary lights on the subject," presumably into the dark lower deck of the *Brooks* and other slave ships. It closed by noting the power and agency of an incipient social movement: "people would do well to consider, that it does not often fall to the lot of individuals, to have an opportunity of performing so important a moral and religious duty, as that of endeavouring to put an end to a practice, which may, without exaggeration, be stiled one of the greatest evils at this day existing upon the earth." The Plymouth committee resolved that "1500 plates, representing the mode of stowing slaves on board the African traders, with remarks on it, be struck off and distributed gratis."[9]

Transit: Philadelphia and New York

The earliest versions of the *Brooks* produced in Philadelphia and New York followed the Plymouth model in image and text. The first of these was published by Mathew Carey in *American Museum* in May 1789 and subsequently in a print run of twenty-five hundred copies as a broadside. Carey repositioned both image and text, putting the *Brooks* at the top of an oblong page, placing the original headline above the image and "Remarks on the Slave Trade" below it. He shrank the size of the whole to roughly thirteen by sixteen inches (thirty-three by forty centimeters), probably because it was published in a magazine. The New York printer Samuel Wood combined the Philadelphia text and the Plymouth layout. His version was larger than Carey's at roughly nineteen by twenty-four inches (forty-eight by sixty centimeters), though smaller than the original from Plymouth.[10]

The American printers made three major changes to the text, two by subtraction, one by addition, which distinguished—and radicalized— their variants of the broadside. First, Carey removed the kneeling slave and cut in its entirety the paragraph explaining how the campaign against the slave trade did not imply the emancipation of the slaves and how it would not damage but rather enhance private property. He then added a new paragraph at the beginning of the text to make clear that this was the work of the "Pennsylvania society for promoting the ABOLITION of slavery." The broadside would now be used to attack slavery itself.

The new paragraph also sought to strengthen the viewer's identification with the "unhappy Africans" aboard the *Brooks:* "Here is presented to our view, one of the most horrid spectacles—a number of

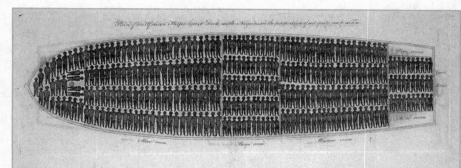

The *Brooks,* Philadelphia edition

human creatures, packed, side by side, almost like herrings in a barrel, and reduced nearly to the state of being buried alive, with just air enough to preserve a degree of life sufficient to make them sensible of all the horrors of their situation." Transoceanic travel was rough enough, as Carey himself would have known from his forced migration from Ireland to Philadelphia in 1784, but these "forlorn wretches" in the picture suffered something vastly worse, cramped, as they were, in close quarters, unable to sit up or turn over, and suffering from seasickness and disease. Of the image of the ship, Carey wrote, "we do not recollect to have met with a more striking illustration of the barbarity of the slave trade."[11]

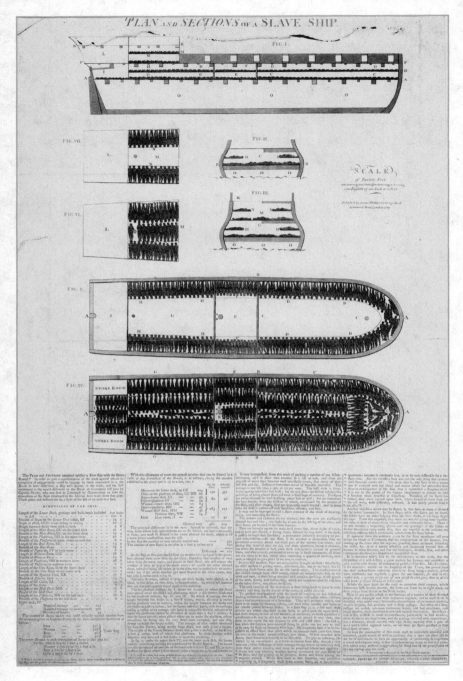

The *Brooks*, London edition

An "Improved" Image: London

In *The History of the Rise, Progress, and Accomplishment of the Abolition of the African Slave-Trade by the British Parliament* (1808), Thomas Clarkson wrote of the image of the *Brooks*, "The committee at Plymouth had been the first to suggest the idea; but that in London had now improved it." The improvement took the form of dramatic change and expansion—of both image and text—in a broadside now entitled, more concisely, "Plan and Sections of a Slave Ship," which would eventually evolve into the more famous "Description of a Slave Ship." All alterations made in London reflected a deeper and more practical understanding of how slave ships looked and worked, which is to say that they reflected the knowledge of Clarkson himself, who likely oversaw the drawings and certainly wrote the new text. He demonstrated a more empirical and scientific approach to the *Brooks* in all respects. The declared goal was to be objective—that is, to present "facts" about a slave ship that could not be disputed "by those concerned in it."[12]

The single view of the lower deck of the *Brooks* in the Plymouth illustration was now replaced by seven views—a side sectional (or "longitudinal") view of the entire vessel; two top-down views of the lower deck, one showing the arrangement of bodies on the deck planks and another on the platforms two and a half feet higher; two similar views of the half deck toward the stern of the vessel; and two transverse views showing the vertical configuration of decks and platforms. The amount of text below the images doubled, from two columns of twelve hundred words to four columns of twenty-four hundred words. The broadside as a whole remained large—roughly twenty by thirty inches (fifty by seventy-one centimeters)—and the views of the ship took up more space, about two-thirds of the whole. The *Brooks* now contained 482 men, women, boys, and girls, as allowed by the Dolben Act. Each one was carefully stowed in the appropriate apartment.[13]

The new images of the *Brooks* were shaped by a specific moment and process of transformation. During the late eighteenth and early nineteenth centuries, shipbuilding in England was moving from craft to modern industry. The shipwright's art and mystery were being interrogated and "improved" by those who followed the new laws of science. The London committee's plan and sections of the *Brooks* were, as the cultural critic Marcus Wood has pointed out, rendered in the "enlightened" style. They were drawn in a way associated, for example, with the Society for the Improvement of Naval Architecture, which was formed around the same time to organize international cooperation, for the public good, on the new science of shipbuilding.[14]

The empirical and scientific approach was also evident in the expanded text, the first half of which concerned the practical question of stowing human bodies aboard the *Brooks*. Captain Parrey's report on the ship was conveyed in precise detail: the text included his twenty-five measurements of length, breadth, and height on the seven sectional views; tonnage (297 nominal, 320 measured); number of seamen recently employed (45); number of slaves recently carried (609), broken down by category: men (351), women (127), boys (90), girls (41). The amount of space for an individual of each category is specified, followed by a calculation of how many people can be stowed in each specific part of the vessel, comparing hypothetical to actual numbers. Then follows a detailed discussion of deck height and "headroom," in which it is shown that beams (carlings) and the platforms themselves reduced vertical space to two feet six inches, too little to allow an adult to sit up. It is emphasized that the diagram presents a bare minimum of crowding, as it features only 482 slaves rather than the 609 the *Brooks* actually carried, and it does not allow space in each apartment for the "poopoo tubs" or the "stanchions to support the platforms and decks." It also allowed more space per slave than had been allowed in practice, according to the observations of both Parrey and various Liverpool delegates who testified before the House of Commons. It was therefore a graphic understatement.[15]

The second half of the London text moves from the social organization of shipboard space (and away from an explicit discussion of the *Brooks*) to the experience of the enslaved aboard the ship, encouraging direct identification with the sufferings of "our fellow-creatures," whose bodies were bruised and skins rubbed raw by the friction of chains and bare boards with the rolling of the ship. Brief description is given to the routines of daily life aboard the ship (feeding, "airing," and "dancing") and to sickness and death. Mortality is discussed using both statistics and the eyewitness testimony of Dr. Alexander Falconbridge, who vividly describes the horrors of life belowdecks, especially during outbreaks of sickness that made ships' decks look like a "slaughterhouse." "It is not in the power of the human imagination," explained Falconbridge, "to picture to itself a situation more dreadful or disgusting."[16]

The final column turned to conditions for the sailors. They had no room for their bedding on the overcrowded slavers; they suffered from the effluvia wafting up from belowdecks; and they grew sick and died in great numbers, thereby making the slave trade not a nursery but "constantly and regularly a grave for our seamen." The London text, like those reproduced in Philadelphia and New York, cut out the paragraph about the protection of "private property," but it retained the final sentence urging viewers of the broadside to take action to abolish the evil slave trade.[17]

"First-Rate Nautical Knowledge"

In June 1787, less than a month after the London abolition committee had been formed, Clarkson and his fellow members found themselves in a bind. They had resolved to abolish the slave trade, but they did not know much about it. Clarkson had written an M.A. thesis on slavery at Cambridge, but its sources were limited and it was not enough to educate either the public or members of Parliament, whose already-rumored hearings "could not proceed without evidence." The committee resolved on June 12 that Clarkson should go to Bristol, Liverpool, and elsewhere to "collect Information on the Subject of the Slave Trade."[18]

Clarkson devised a strategy for gathering evidence. He would act the part of historian, a social historian at that. He would go to the merchants' halls and the customs houses of Bristol and Liverpool, where he would immerse himself in historical records such as ship muster rolls, from which he would compute mortality rates. He would gather the names of twenty thousand sailors to see what became of them. He would collect documents such as articles of agreement, wage contracts both printed and unprinted, through which to explore the conditions of seafaring employment. Most important, he would search the waterfront for people to interview. He took an approach based on oral history, which would, unexpectedly, become a history from below.

Clarkson began his tour of the ports on June 25, 1787; he journeyed first to Bristol. He suffered a moment of despair on entering the city, when he suddenly realized what he was up against. He feared the power of the wealthy, self-interested people he knew he would have to challenge. He anticipated persecution as he attempted to gather evidence. He even dared to wonder "whether I should ever get out of it alive." Some of his fellow activists in London must have wondered the same thing, for over the next few weeks they wrote their friends in Bristol to ask whether Clarkson was still among the living.[19]

Clarkson initially sought out Quakers and other allies, who would sustain him through the visit. But the people he really wanted to talk to were credible, "respectable" witnesses, merchants and ship captains who knew the slave trade firsthand. But when these people learned his intentions, they shunned him. Passing him on the street, they crossed to the other side, as if, Clarkson recalled, "I had been a wolf, or tiger, or some other dangerous beast of prey." Shipowners and merchants also forbade anyone in their employ to speak to him. Clarkson was soon "obliged to give up all hope of getting any evidence from this quarter." He would be forced to turn to the only others who had concrete experience and knowledge: common sailors.[20]

Clarkson recorded in a personal journal his first encounters with slave-trade sailors. As he crossed the Avon River on July 3, he "saw a Boat painted Africa on her stern." Clarkson hailed the sailors and asked whether they belonged to the Guineaman *Africa,* to which they answered yes, they did. He then asked if they were not afraid to go to Africa because of the high death rate for sailors. The response revealed a mentality of cosmopolitan fatalism. One man explained, "If it is my Lot to die in Africa, why I must, and if is not, why then I shall not die though I go there. And if it is my Lot to live, why I may as well live there as anywhere else." The conversation then turned to a slaver called the *Brothers,* lying at Kingroad and ready to sail. It was delayed because Captain Hewlett, "a cruel Rascal," was having trouble getting a crew. A large group had signed on, gauged the temper of their new commander, and deserted immediately. Clarkson noted this information. He might have also noted that his own education had entered a new phase.[21]

Clarkson later reflected on the significance of this meeting:

I cannot describe my feeling in seeing those poor Fellows belonging to the Africa. They were seven in Number—all of them young, about 22 or 23, and very robust—they were all *Seamen;* and I think the finest fellows I ever beheld—I am sure no one can describe my feelings when I considered that some of them were devoted [doomed], and whatever might be their spirits now, would never see their native Home more. I considered also how much the glory of the British Flag was diminishing by the destruction of such Noble Fellows, who appeared so strong, robust, and hardy, and at the same so spirited, as to enable us to bid defiance to the Marine of our enemies the French.

With a touch of homoeroticism and his nationalist feeling stirred by these "pillars of the state," Clarkson would henceforth make sailors and their experience central to the abolition movement. He would increasingly come to rely on them for evidence and information, for the light they could carry into the lower deck of the slave ship.

Clarkson soon met his first informant, John Dean, a black sailor whose mutilated back was gruesome evidence of his torture while working aboard a slaver. He met an Irish publican named Thompson who between midnight and 3:00 A.M. led him up and down Marsh Street and into the sailors' dives, which were full of "music, dancing, rioting, drunkenness, and profane swearing." He met seamen who were lame, blind, ulcerated, and fevered. He learned of the murder of William Lines by the chief mate of the *Thomas*. He tracked down crew members and gathered enough evidence to have the mate arrested and charged at the Mayor's Court, where he got nothing but "savage looks" from the "slave-merchants" in attendance. Such open hostility scared Bristol's middle-class opponents of slavery, who were "fearful of coming forward in an open manner." Sailors, however, flocked to the abolitionist to describe their "different scenes of barbarity." Clarkson had finally found those "who had been personally acquainted with the horrors of the slave trade."[22]

Clarkson heard that the slave ship *Alfred* had just returned to port with a man named Thomas, who had suffered severe injury at the hands of Captain Edward Robe. After a long search, he found Thomas in a boardinghouse, in bad shape. His legs and body were wrapped in flannel as a comfort to his wounds. Delirious, Thomas could not figure out who Clarkson was. He grew frightened and agitated by the stranger's presence. Was he a lawyer? He repeatedly asked, Clarkson wrote, "if I was come with an Intent to take Captain Robe's Part." Was he come to kill him? Clarkson "answered no, [and said] that I was come to take his [part] & punish Captain Robe." Thomas could not understand—perhaps because he was in such a disordered state, perhaps because he could not imagine a gentleman taking his side. Unable to interview the man, Clarkson pieced together what he could from his shipmates. Robe had beaten Thomas so often that he tried to commit suicide by leaping overboard into shark-infested waters. Saved by his mates, he was then chained by the captain to the deck, where the beatings continued. Thomas died a short time after the visit, but the image of the abused, deranged surgeon's mate haunted Clarkson "day and night." Such encounters created "a fire of indignation within me."[23]

Liverpool—the home of Joseph Brooks Jr. and the *Brooks*—would prove even rougher, as one might expect of a port that had four times as many slave ships as Bristol. When word got out that a man who sought to abolish the slave trade—and hence destroy the "glory" of the city— was in town and could moreover be found dining in public each night at the King's Arms, curious people turned up to see and converse with him. These were mostly slave merchants and captains. They engaged Clarkson in spirited debate, which rapidly degenerated into insults and threats. Clarkson was happy to have at his side the abolitionist Dr. Alexander Falconbridge, "an athletic and resolute-looking man" who had made four slaving voyages and could add muscle to the argument in more ways than one. Whenever Clarkson went out at night, Falconbridge went with him, always "well armed." Anonymous letters threatened death if Clarkson did not leave town immediately. Not only did he refuse to leave, he refused to change lodgings, as this would betray "an unmanly fear of my visitors" and reflect badly on the cause.[24]

Most of Liverpool's slave-trading merchants and captains now began to shun Clarkson, and the ones who did not shun him tried to kill him. One stormy afternoon a gang of eight or nine men (two or three of whom he had seen at the King's Arms) tried to throw him off a pier-head. He was undeterred, or rather more determined than ever. Clarkson soon gathered what he thought was enough evidence to prosecute the merchant, the captain, and the mate responsible for the murder of a seaman named Peter Green, but his friends in Liverpool panicked at the prospect, swearing that he would be "torn to pieces, and the house where I lodged burnt down." The abolitionist Dr. James Currie criticized Clarkson for preferring the testimony of the "lowest class of seamen" over that of virtuous citizens. The problem was, "respectable" people who opposed slavery, like Currie, lived in terror of the powerful slave merchants and would not speak out. The same had been true in Bristol.[25]

Meanwhile, word of Clarkson's presence and purposes spread along the waterfront, and sailors began to show up in twos and threes at the King's Arms to tell their tales of brutal mistreatment. Clarkson wrote, "though no one else would come near me, to give me any information about the trade, these [seamen] were always forward to speak to me, and to tell me their grievances, if it were only with the hope of being able to get redress." In the end Clarkson helped the sailors bring prosecutions in nine cases in Bristol and Liverpool. None of them came to court, but Clarkson managed in each and every instance to win monetary settlements for the abused seamen or their families. He made these small victories possible by keeping nineteen witnesses, all sailors, at his own expense in order to make sure the evidence for conviction would be at hand, rather than on a ship in the middle of the Atlantic. Based on the violence done to sailors, he concluded that the slave trade was "but one barbarous system from the beginning to the end."[26]

Writing about himself in the third person, Clarkson summed up his experience with the sailors in Bristol and Liverpool: "A certain person, totally unconnected with the law, had no less than sixty-three applications made to him in three months, to obtain redress for such seamen, as had experienced the fury of the officers of their respective ships." All but two had labored on slave ships. Clarkson was affected not only by the tales but by the physical condition of the tellers. Explaining in the preface of the pamphlet the evidence he had gathered among John Dean and the other sailors, he wrote, "I have also had *ocular demonstration,* as far as a sight of their mangled bodies will be admitted as a proof."[27]

Almost everything Clarkson would do in the abolitionist movement in the coming years was shaped by his dealings with these sailors. The knowledge he gained from and about them loomed large in *An Essay on the Impolicy of the African Slave Trade,* published in July 1788, and *An Essay on the Comparative Efficiency of Regulation or Abolition as applied to the Slave Trade,* which appeared in April 1789. But perhaps most important in this regard was a collection of twenty-two interviews with seafaring people, entitled *The Substance of the Evidence of Sundry Persons on the Slave-Trade Collected in the Course of a Tour Made in the Autumn of the Year 1788,* published in April 1789, the very moment when the London committee was also preparing the "Plan and Sections of the Slave Ship," both of which were then distributed to all MPs in advance of the vote on the slave trade scheduled to take place on May 11. Sixteen of the people interviewed had worked in the slave trade, and the other six had observed it at close range, most of them on African tours of duty in the Royal Navy. Half of those who had worked on slavers did so at the lowest level of the ship's hierarchy, as "foremastmen" (common seamen) or "boys" (apprentices). Two had been captains in the trade, and six had been mates or skilled workers (although three of these had risen from the lower ranks).[28]

It is instructive to view the image and text of the *Brooks* alongside the sailors' interviews, for here, in grim detail, was the information for which Clarkson had been dispatched by the London committee in June 1787. Sailor after sailor had explained to him the arrangement of decks on a slave ship—the hold, the lower deck, the main deck; how male slaves were chained together; how the enslaved were stowed belowdecks; how they were fed, guarded, and forced to "dance" for exercise; how sickness, disease, and high mortality were the lot of both slave and sailor. Sailors told Clarkson that the slave trade was not a "nursery" for sailors, as its advocates insisted, but rather a cemetery. It is of first importance that almost every single fact to be found in the text accompanying the image of the *Brooks* can be found in the interviews Clarkson conducted with sailors in the period immediately before the broadside was conceived, published, and circulated.[29]

There was cruel irony in the emergence of the sailor as an object of sympathy within the growing abolitionist movement. Sailors perpetrated many of the horrors of the trade. To be sure, Clarkson and the members of the London committee also stressed the plight of the "injur'd Africans," but they were not gathering *their* stories of the slave ship and the Middle Passage, as they might easily have done in London, Liverpool, and Bristol at this time. The slaves' experience was, after all, the most profound history from below (literally, from belowdecks), and indeed it would seem that Olaudah Equiano understood very well both the exclusion and the consequent need for an African voice when he published his influential autobiography, *The Interesting Narrative of the Life of Olaudah Equiano, or Gustavus Vassa, the African* (1789). By emphasizing the dismal lot of sailors, Clarkson and his fellow abolitionists were wagering that the British government and public would respond to an appeal based on race and nation. Still, it was a risky bet, for the use of lowly sailors as sources did not pass without vicious class ridicule. When seaman Isaac Parker was introduced during the House of Commons hearings in March 1790, an observer wrote that the "whole Committee was in a laugh." The pro-slavery members then taunted William Wilberforce, abolition's leader in Parliament, "will you bring your ship-keepers, ship-sweepers, and deck cleaners in competition with our admirals and men of honor? It is now high time to close your evidence, indeed!" Undaunted and speaking in short, simple sentences, Parker described, among other things, the flogging, torture, and death by Captain Thomas Marshall of the enslaved child who would not eat aboard the *Black Joke* in 1764. Like dozens of other seamen, Parker spoke truth to power; his detailed testimony damned the trade in ways that abstract moral denunciation could never have done.[30]

Thomas Clarkson, a young and somewhat naive middle-class, Cambridge-educated minister, came face-to-face with the class struggle that raged on the ships and along the waterfront in the slave-trading ports. He joined it, fearlessly, on the side of the sailors. By doing so he gained credibility among seamen and knowledge that would be invaluable to the abolitionist movement. He found the deserters, the cripples, the rebels, the dropouts, the guilty of conscience—in short, the dissidents who knew the slave trade from the inside and had chilling stories to tell about it. He would use these stories to make the trade, which to most people was an abstract and distant proposition, into something concrete, human, and immediate. The *Brooks* was thus one triumph among many for Clarkson's radical investigative journalism along the waterfront. With great and far-reaching agitational effect, he had brought into the movement what he called "first-rate nautical knowledge." It was a foundational achievement.[31]

The Brooks *in the Debate*

Opponents and supporters of the slave trade waged a furious debate between the years 1788 and 1792, in which slave ships in general and the *Brooks* in particular played central parts. Clarkson's work among the sailors made possible a new circulation of proletarian experience, a conversion of one kind of experience and knowledge into others. He linked the slave-trade seamen to members of Parliament who were conducting an investigation of the human commerce, and then to a metropolitan reading public hungry for information about dreadful things that for the most part happened beyond the shores of their own experience. By publicizing seamen's stories, Clarkson allowed them to appear in new oral and printed forms, in speeches (William Wilberforce), lectures (Samuel Taylor Coleridge), poems (Robert Southey, Hannah More), sermons (Joseph Priestley), illustrations (Isaac Cruikshank), testimony, statistical tables, articles, pamphlets, and books, around the Atlantic. The image and reality of the slave ship, like almost all aspects of Clarkson's research, were disseminated far and wide. The *Brooks* was reproduced and circulated in thousands of copies to Paris, Edinburgh, and Glasgow, and across the Atlantic to Philadelphia, New York, and Charleston, and to Newport and Providence, Rhode Island, where newspapers reported the availability for purchase of a "Number of elegant and afflicting Copperplate Representations of the Sufferings of our Fellow-Men in a Slave-Ship." The *Brooks* became a central image of the age, hanging in public places during petition drives and in homes and taverns around the Atlantic.[32]

William Wilberforce coined a memorable phrase when he observed of the slave ship, "So much misery condensed in so little room is more than the human imagination had ever before conceived." These words signaled a strategic choice of topic and the task at hand. Abolitionist after abolitionist hammered away at the horrors of the slave ship—the beatings, the casual cruelty, the tyranny of the captain, the sickness and mortality, in short, all of the themes identified by Clarkson during his time among the sailors. If the slave trade had long survived because it was carried on far beyond the metropolis, its opponents now determined to bring home its stinking, brutal reality in ways that could not be avoided.[33]

Those trying to fend off the attack, for example the official delegates from the city of Liverpool who testified in the parliamentary hearings, bravely presented the slave ship as a safe, modern, hygienic technology. Robert Norris, formerly captain and now merchant in the trade, explained to the Privy Council and the parliamentary committee that the enslaved had clean quarters (treated with frankincense and lime); good food; much music, singing, and dancing; and even luxuries: tobacco, brandy, and, for the women, beads. The captives slept on "clean boards," which were more wholesome than on "Beds or Hammacks." Captain Norris had even given up his mattress for the bare board himself! Close stowing was not a problem, because the enslaved "lay there as close to each other, by Choice." They actually preferred to "crowd together." Above their heads were "spacious Gratings," and "a Row of Air Ports [were] all round the Sides of the Ship, to admit a free Circulation of fresh Air." Norris thus did the best job he could defending the slave ship, but his descriptions, placed against the gruesome evidence produced by abolitionist witnesses, sounded absurd, inviting Wilberforce to offer ridicule of his own in his famous speech of May 12, 1789: what with the perfumed chambers, fine food, and onboard amusements, Norris spoke as if "the whole were really a scene of pleasure and dissipation." Were these Africans really "rejoicing at their captivity"?[34]

The proponents of the trade were losing the debate about the slave ship, and they knew it. This was indicated in two basic ways—first, by how quickly they adopted some of the language of their antagonists, speaking in the idiom of "humanity." The purchase of slaves was actually a humanitarian act because the unbought would routinely be slaughtered by their savage African captors. English slavers were saving lives! An even more telling sign was strategic retreat. Facing damning, endlessly reiterated evidence of the horrors of the slave ship, pro-slave-trade representatives agreed that there were "abuses" and embraced the cause of regulation in an effort to fend off total abolition. They then quickly fell back on their long-preferred economic argument: human commerce might have its regrettable aspects, but the slave trade and indeed the entire complex of slavery in the anglophone Atlantic strongly supported the national and imperial economic interests of Great Britain. The Africa trade was essential to commerce, industry, and employment, explained merchants, manufacturers, and workers from Liverpool, Bristol, London, and Manchester in their petitions. To dismantle the trade—or, more worrying to many, to turn it over to archrival France—was unthinkable. Throughout the debate the most effective way for supporters of the slave trade to deal with the abolitionist attack on the slave ship was to change the subject.[35]

The image of the slave ship in general and the *Brooks* in particular figured significantly in parliamentary debate. Sir William Dolben, a moderate MP who represented Oxford University, went aboard a slave ship at anchor in the Thames, and it changed his life. Suddenly able to imagine the fate of the "poor unhappy wretches" who were crammed together, he led a campaign to reduce the crowding of slave ships. When the normally eloquent Charles James Fox addressed the House of Commons in April 1791, he grew speechless in the face of the Middle Passage, so he referred his fellow MPs "to the printed section of the slave-ship; where the eye might see what the tongue must fall short in describing." Not long afterward Lord Windham likewise struggled to express the sufferings caused by the trade: "The section of the slave-ship, however, made up the deficiency of language, and did away [with] all necessity of argument, on this subject."[36]

The *Brooks* also made an impact in revolutionary Paris, where Clarkson spent six months in 1789 organizing on behalf of the cause, disseminating the image at every opportunity. He reported that after seeing the slave ship, the bishop of Chartres declared that now "there was nothing so barbarous which might not readily be believed" about the slave trade. When the archbishop of Aix first saw it, he "was so struck with horror, that he could scarcely speak." Count Mirabeau, the great orator of the French Revolution, was captivated by the image and immediately summoned a woodworking artisan to make a model, with "little wooden men and women, which were painted black to represent the slaves stowed in their proper places." He kept the three-foot miniature in his dining room and planned to use it in a speech against the slave trade in the National Assembly. When King Louis XVI asked the director-general and minister of state Jacques Necker

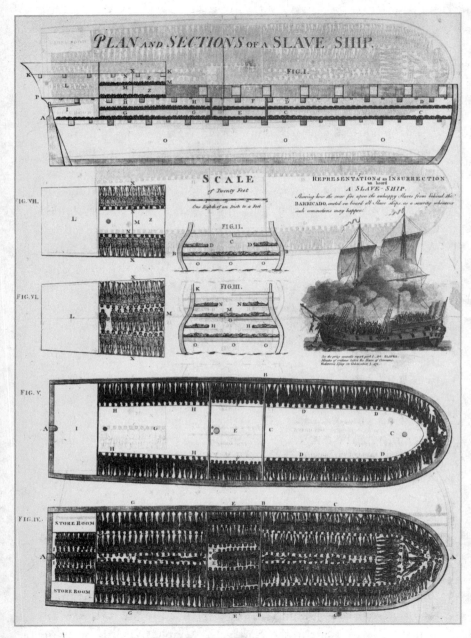

The *Brooks*, with insurrection

to bring him materials so that he might learn about the suddenly controversial commerce in human flesh, the adviser brought Clarkson's essay *The Impolicy of the Slave Trade* and "specimens of the manufactures of the Africans" but decided against taking the plan of the slave ship. He "thought it would affect His Majesty too much, as he was then indisposed."[37]

During the broader public debate, radical abolitionists were not content merely to expose the sufferings of enslaved Africans; they detailed individual and collective acts of rebellion against the conditions they encountered on the slave ships. They defended the right of slaves to rise up in insurrection and recover their stolen "liberty." Clarkson went so far as to defend the Haitian Revolution, claiming that the self-emancipated slaves there were "endeavouring to vindicate for themselves the unalterable Rights of Man." The prospect and reality of insurrection also appeared in the text that accompanied the image of the *Brooks:* the Plymouth, Philadelphia, and New York broadsides each mentioned it once, the London version twice. Abolitionists transformed their visual propaganda to include an image of slave insurrection at sea. An illustration entitled "Representation of an Insurrection on board a Slave-Ship," which appeared in Carl Bernard Wadstrom's *An Essay on Colonization, particularly applied to the Western coast of Africa . . . in Two Parts* (London, 1794) and showed a crew firing from behind a barricado on rebellious slaves, was subsequently added to the sectional view of the *Brooks.*[38]

A New Debate

The role of the *Brooks* in the debate expanded when a new drama involving the ship took national center stage at Westminster in 1790. Parliamentary hearings featured Dr. Thomas Trotter and Captain Clement Noble, who had sailed together on the *Brooks* in 1783–84. The doctor was a young man who had been a surgeon in the Royal Navy, was demobilized after the American War, and signed aboard the slaver. He was horrified by the experience and now opposed the trade.[39] The captain had made nine voyages to Africa, two as mate, seven as captain, four of the latter on the *Brooks* before the plan and sections of his ship was published. He had prospered and become a shipowner and merchant. He was a staunch defender of the trade.[40]

As if to provide verbal embellishment of the print of the *Brooks,* Trotter explained to the committee that conditions belowdecks were abysmal. The enslaved were packed by the chief mate every morning and "locked spoonways, according to the technical phrase." Anyone out of place would be driven to his or her designated spot by the violence of the cat. The result was a mass of humanity packed so tightly that Trotter, who went below daily, could not "walk amongst them without treading upon them." Moreover, the claustrophobic confinement caused the enslaved to gasp for breath and live in "dread of suffocation." Some, he believed, died of asphyxiation. Trotter also noted the "dancing" that took place on the *Brooks.* Those confined in irons "were ordered to stand up, and make what motion they could." Those who resisted "were compelled to it by the lash of the cat," but many continued to resist and "refused to do it, even with this mode of punishment in a severe degree."[41]

The line of questioning continued with Captain Noble. When asked how much space each slave had, no doubt by someone who had seen the diagram of the *Brooks,* Noble answered, "I do not know the space; I never measured it, or made any calculation of what room they had; they had always plenty of room to lay down in, and had they three times as much room they would all lay jammed up close together; they always do that before the room is half full." Conditions on the lower deck were good, he testified, and of course he would know, because he, unlike some captains, went down there frequently. He admitted that some of the slaves were dejected when they first came aboard, "but they in general soon mend of that, and are in general in very good spirits during the time they are on board the ships." In contrast to Trotter, he added that the men slaves were "very fond of dancing." A few proved sulky, and they might have to be "persuaded to dance" by the mate. If persuasion failed, "they let them do as they please."[42]

On the matter of authority, Trotter stated that the sailors were, like the African captives, oppressed by a tyrant "whose character was perfectly congenial to the trade." Trotter once heard Captain Noble bragging to a group of captains about a punishment he devised for a sailor on a previous voyage. The captain was transporting on his own account (as private trade) a dozen small, exotic African birds to be sold in the West Indies. They died, and he suspected a mutinous black seaman from Philadelphia of having killed them. He ordered the man to be lashed and then chained for twelve days to one of the masts, during which time all he was given to eat each day was one of the tiny dead birds (which were, in size, between a sparrow and a thrush). Noble told this parable of power with "a degree of triumph and satisfaction that would have disgraced an Indian scalper." When he finished, his fellow captains cheered—they "applauded his invention for the novelty of the punishment." Trotter was appalled by this "wanton piece of barbarity." He added that several sailors on his own voyage were "unmercifully flogged" and that Noble's ill usage almost provoked a mutiny.[43]

Captain Noble responded by presenting himself as a reasonable and humane man, someone who ran a happy ship. He treated his sailors and slaves well and consequently suffered minimal mortality. On the voyage with Trotter, he lost only three sailors—one to smallpox, one to drowning, one to a "natural death." He lost fifty-eight slaves, suggesting as a possible cause only that Dr. Trotter was "very inattentive to his duty" and "spent a great deal too much time in dress." (Was Trotter a dandy?) Noble claimed that no slave of his had ever died because of "correction." He recalled disciplining a seaman "for abusing the Slaves, and being very insolent to myself—I believe it was the only time that any of the seamen were flogged that voyage." Indeed he was such a good and kind master that his seamen always wanted to sail with him again after they had completed a voyage. "I hardly ever knew an instance to the contrary," he stated confidently.[44]

Unfortunately for Captain Noble, the muster rolls of the *Brooks* support Trotter's account of captain-crew relations, for during his three voyages as captain only 13 of 162 men signed on again for another voyage, and most of these were mates (who had special inducements), family members, or apprentices, who had no choice. It would be generous to say that the captain's memory failed him before the parliamentary committee, but it would be more accurate to say that he lied.[45]

Trotter went beyond the diagram of the *Brooks* by bringing some of the faceless, supine captives to life through his testimony. He followed Clarkson, bringing oral history to the parliamentary committee. He had talked to the men, women, and children who were taken on board—some in English, some in sign language ("gesture and motion" he called it), and some through interpreters. He explained, "Few Slaves came on board of whom I did not enquire, why they were made Slaves?" Trotter noted two main ethnic groups on board the *Brooks,* who as it happened had a long history of antagonism between them in Africa: coastal Fantes and those he called "Duncos," who were, in fact, inland Chambas ("Dunco" being a Fante word for "stupid fellow"). Unlike Captain Noble, who urged the black traders "to get him Slaves by any means," never doubted their authority to sell them, and never inquired how people became slaves, Trotter asked how they came to be on the ship and discovered that most had been kidnapped. They would be described, falsely, as "prisoners of war." He also learned that separation from family and home led to despair. At night Trotter often heard the slaves make "a howling melancholy kind of noise, something expressive of extreme anguish." He asked a woman who served as an interpreter to discover its cause. She reported that the visceral cry came when people awoke from dreams of being back at home with loved ones, only to discover themselves belowdecks aboard the ghastly ship.[46]

The surgeon's account of the *Brooks* paralleled the abolitionist text that accompanied the image of the ship published a year and a half earlier. The major themes were the treatment of the sailors and, more important, the slaves; how the latter were fettered and stowed in a small space; how they were organized; how they did or did not survive. The parallel is no accident. By the time Trotter took the stand before the House of Commons Select Committee in May 1790, the abolitionist movement had already shaped public discourse about the slave trade by drawing attention to these themes. By a curious twist of fate, the image of the *Brooks* helped to shape the public testimony about what had actually happened on the *Brooks*. Thomas Clarkson and his fellow abolitionists had already distributed the "Plans and Sections of a Slave Ship" throughout Parliament and moreover had worked with William Wilberforce and other MPs to develop a set of questions, based on previous knowledge, to ask Trotter, Noble, and many other witnesses—about stowage and spatial allocation, social routine, and the treatment of both sailors and slaves.

Impact

Clarkson always insisted that the power of the image of the *Brooks* lay primarily in its ability to make the viewer identify and sympathize with the "injured Africans" on the lower deck of the ship. The broadside was "designed to give the spectator an idea of the sufferings of the Africans in the Middle Passage, and this so familiarly, that he might instantly pronounce upon the miseries experienced there." The image would thus agitate and move the viewer to join the debate about the slave trade, as Thomas Cooper hoped, and to do so with a new, more human understanding of what was at stake. In conveying the horrors of transportation, the picture would appeal to the emotions of the observer and seal the issue in his or her memory: "It brought forth the tear of sympathy in behalf of the sufferers, and it fixed their sufferings in his heart." In so doing, the image became "a language, which was at once intelligible and irresistible." Clarkson thus anticipated what modern scholars have said about the "iconographic vocabulary" and "visual identity" of the abolitionist movement.[47]

Clarkson was undoubtedly right in these judgments of effect. After all, he himself passed the broadside from hand to hand, and he talked to a lot of people about it. Because he used the image as an instrument of organization, he needed to know how it moved people and how he could build on the feelings and understandings it engendered. He therefore deserves pride of place as an interpreter of the meaning of the *Brooks*. And yet, all that said and properly acknowledged, Clarkson did not fully explain the power of the image. It had another dimension that Clarkson understood but rarely discussed.

The original title of the Plymouth print was "Plan of an AFRICAN SHIP'S Lower Deck with NEGROES in the proportion of only One to a Ton." The reference to proportion, to the number of people per ton of the ship's carrying capacity, referred specifically to the debate surrounding the Dolben Act, or the Slave Carrying Bill, which received royal assent in July 1788, four months before the image of the *Brooks* was created. The debate concerned the profitability of the slave trade. The *Brooks* image and text must be read not only alongside the interviews collected and published in *Substance of the Evidence* but also *An Essay on the Comparative Efficiency of Regulation or Abolition as applied to the Slave Trade,* the pamphlet Clarkson was writing when the image of the slave ship was first published.

Clarkson began the pamphlet with statements made by the representatives of the Liverpool slave-trading interest before the House of Commons in 1788. Mr. Piggot, "Counsel for the Merchants of Liverpool," testified that "one man to one ton . . . will operate as a virtual abolition of the trade." The other delegates formed a chorus singing the same refrain. Robert Norris added that at one to one "there would be no profit." Alexander Dalziel argued that the slave trade was already in decline and that any restriction on the numbers of slaves to be carried would "help it on." James Penny suggested that anything less than two slaves to a ton would make it impossible for the "trade to be carried on with advantage"; one and a half to one or one to one would equal abolition. John Tarleton explained that he was *"authorized by the Merchants of Liverpool* to say that *less than two slaves per ton* (and it perfectly coincides with my opinion) would totally abolish the *African slave trade."* John Matthews provided a more detailed calculus, estimating profits and losses on a one-hundred-ton ship, at two and a half to one (plus £761.5.6); at two to one (plus £180.3.6); at one and a half to one (minus £206.19.9); and at one to one (minus £590.1.0). The Liverpool delegates had thus opposed regulation, and they had suffered a partial defeat with the passage of the Dolben Act, which set the ratio of slaves to tons at five to three on the first two hundred tons, one to one thereafter. But soon they decided to swim with the tide they could not stem and embraced limited reform and regulation as a way of fending off total abolition.

The *Brooks* image was not simply a critique of the slave trade but equally a critique of the supposedly more humane regulated slave trade. The diagram showed not the 609 slaves the ship had most recently carried from Africa to America but the smaller, more civilized number of 482. Like Clarkson's pamphlet, it showed that even regulation was horrific. Many, Clarkson noted, looked at the plate and "considered the regulation itself as perfect barbarism."[48]

The concept of "barbarism" is a key to understanding the hidden meaning of the *Brooks*. Matthew Carey called the image "a striking illustration of the barbarity of the slave trade." The bishop of Chartres thought the *Brooks* made all tales about the barbarism of the slave trade believable. Many of these tales had come from sailors who described their own treatment as barbaric. After hearing them Clarkson concluded that the commerce in human flesh was barbarous from beginning to end. Abolition alone could "destroy forever the sources of barbarity" in the slave trade. Who were the agents of this violent, cruel barbarism? Or, to put the same question another way, who imagined this horrific ship? Who designed it? Who thought of stowing people this way aboard it? The *Brooks* brought forth not only "the tear of sympathy" but the shock of moral astonishment.[49]

The power of these questions increased as the image of the *Brooks* evolved. As the symbol of the supplicant slave of the Society for Effecting the Abolition of the Slave Trade disappeared from the Plymouth broadside, as the reference to "fellow creatures" dropped from the accompanying text, as the text itself and even the headings were reduced and eventually removed, many people who viewed the *Brooks* would not have known that they were looking at abolitionist propaganda. They would have assumed that it was the work of a naval architect in the pay of a slave-trade merchant. The ambiguity was most useful to the abolitionist movement, for it allowed them to demonize their enemies. Who was the barbarian after all? It certainly was not the Africans, nor was it the sailors, who despite their technical know-how appeared as secondary victims of the slave trade.

The practical agent of violence, cruelty, torture, and terror was the slave-ship captain, as sailors repeatedly told Clarkson. In *An Essay on Comparative Efficiency,* he called the slave captain "the most despicable character on earth." Captain Clement Noble might claim that he did not "know the space" of his own ship, that he "never measured it, or made any calculation of what room [the slaves] had," but he certainly knew how to stow hundreds of bodies in a tight space, as the diagram of the *Brooks* made clear. He did it in a less orderly way, perhaps using experience rather than scientific knowledge, but he did it, with violence and profit. He was, according to Thomas Trotter, a practitioner of "barbarity."[50]

There was a bigger, more violent barbarian above the captain's head; this was his employer, the merchant, with whom Clarkson was engaged in mortal combat. He addressed *An Essay on the Comparative Efficiency* to all sections of the public except the "slave merchants," who had, after all, tried to kill him. Here was the hidden agent behind the *Brooks,* the creator of the instrument of torture. He was the one who imagined and built the ship, he was the ultimate architect of the social order, he was the organizer of the commerce and the one who profited by the barbarism.[51]

The merchant's violence was twofold, practical and conceptual. Both were essential to how the slave ship worked as a machine to produce the commodity "slave" for a global labor market. A violence of enslavement and a violence of abstraction developed together and reinforced each other. As more and more bodies were captured, enslaved, transported, and exploited, merchants learned to calculate short- and long-term labor needs and to gauge and regulate the transnational flow of labor power in and through slave ships, plantations, markets, and an entire system of Atlantic capitalism.[52]

The genius of the image of the *Brooks* was to illustrate—and critique—both kinds of violence, imbuing both with a sinister industrial quality. The image had what a Scottish abolitionist described as a "rigorous oeconomy" in which "no place capable of holding a single person, from one end of the vessel to the other, is left unoccupied." It suggests the carefully designed mass production of bodies and a deliberate, systematic annihilation of individual identity. It depicted the violence and terror of the ship and at the same time it captured the brutal logic and cold, rational mentality of the merchant's business—the process by which human beings were reduced to property, by which labor was made into a thing, a commodity, shorn of all ethical considerations. In a troubled era of transition from a moral to a political conception of economy, the *Brooks* represented a nightmarish outcome of the process. Here was the new, modern economic system in all its horrifying nakedness, capitalism without a loincloth, as Walter Rodney noted. Not for nothing was the *Brooks* called "a capital ship." It was itself a concentration of capital, and it was the bearer of capitalist assumptions and practices about the world and the way it ought to be.[53]

The violent reduction of human beings to property entailed not only social death but physical death, which was also manufactured on the slave ship—even though merchants and captains tried to preserve the lives of their slaves in order to sell them in the Americas and the lives of their sailors for the sake of labor and security. Even so, merchants built death into the social planning of each and every voyage. Slaves and sailors would die, but these were simply neutral empirical facts of business life. Latter-day military thinkers would call these deaths "collateral damage"; to merchants and captains they were "wastage" of cargo and labor. It was not accidental, scholars have noted, that the *Brooks* was shaped like a coffin.[54]

The most radical abolitionists construed these deaths as murder. Throwing 122 living people off the main deck of the *Zong* was clearly murder, and abolitionists such as Olaudah Equiano and Granville Sharp denounced it as such. But what about the people who were whipped to death after a failed bid for freedom? What about the ones who died simply because they found themselves in deadly circumstances? Perhaps this was "social murder." Numerous critics of the slave trade, from Ottobah Cugoano to J. Philmore, had no doubts: this slave trade was calculated murder. On every voyage, merchants and captains like Joseph Brooks Jr. and Captain Clement Noble confronted these issues concretely and made "diabolical calculations," about violence, terror, and death. Their murderous logic and practice of killing by "calculated inches" were exposed to public view by the "plans and sections of a slave ship," the *Brooks*.[55]

Final Port

By using the *Brooks* and every other means of agitation and persuasion at their disposal, abolitionists in both Britain and America eventually forced national reckonings on the slave trade. These unfolded in different ways on each side of the Atlantic during roughly the same years, 1787–1808. They involved significant transatlantic collaboration and cooperation among activists on means and ends, and they resulted in both cases in formal abolition. Ships like the *Brooks* would no longer be legally allowed to sail from British or American ports to gather slaves in Africa and carry them to the plantation societies of the Americas.

An intense agitation of less than five years came to a climax on April 2, 1792, in an all-night parliamentary debate that featured some of the highest oratory that chamber had ever heard. The result was a compromise, offered by the savvy Scot Henry Dundas, to abolish the slave trade "gradually." Soon after, the international context of abolition changed as revolutions in France and St. Domingue exploded into new phases and domestic radicalism emerged in England to send ruling elites into a terror of their own. The gradual abolition bill that passed in the House of Commons met sustained resistance in the House of Lords. When war with France broke out in February 1793, the questions of national and imperial interest trumped everything else, forcing abolitionists and their cause into the background for years. Clarkson, on the edge of collapse, retired from public life in 1794. Small victories nonetheless continued to accumulate to the cause—for example, the Slave Carrying Bill of 1799, which expanded restrictions first established under the Dolben Act of 1788. In 1806 abolitionist activity began to revive, and in that year Parliament passed the Foreign Slave Trade Bill, banning British trade to Spanish and Dutch New World colonies. This prepared the way for formal abolition, which was declared on May 1, 1807.[56]

Abolition happened differently in the United States, where the primary issue was not shipment by merchants but rather importation and purchase by planters. Quakers like Anthony Benezet waged a struggle against the slave trade during the 1770s as the American movement for independence from Britain fashioned an ideology of liberty. The Continental Congress declared itself in 1774 to be against British imports, including slaves. Abolitionists discovered unlikely allies in Chesapeake slave owners such as Thomas Jefferson and James Madison, whose slaves reproduced themselves and made regional importation by slave ship not only unnecessary but frankly uneconomic. Jefferson soon excoriated King George III for his conduct of the slave trade in an early draft of the Declaration of Independence, but the passage offended patriots from South Carolina and Georgia, who craved slave labor. A compromise would be reached in the constitutional debates of 1787: Article I, Section 9 would allow the slave trade to go on until 1808. But abolitionists continued to work at the state level, and in 1788–89 they managed to pass laws limiting the trade in New York, Massachusetts, Rhode Island, Pennsylvania, Connecticut, and Delaware. They simultaneously expanded cooperation with activists in England and began to petition Congress in 1790. In 1791 revolution exploded in St. Domingue, causing fearful American masters to close their ports to slave ships. After long political infighting, an abolition act was passed on March 2, 1807, to take final effect on January 1, 1808. The act was almost toothless, which meant that illegal trading would continue for decades, but a victory had been won.[57]

Through it all—acrimonious debates, world-shaking revolutions in France and Haiti, and domestic upheaval and reaction in Britain, America, and around the Atlantic—the *Brooks* kept sailing. The vessel made seven more terror-filled voyages to Africa, beginning in 1791, 1792, 1796, 1797, 1799, 1800, and finally in May 1804, all from its life-long home port, Liverpool. On the last of these, Captain William Murdock sailed to the Kongo-Angola coast with a crew of 54 to gather 322 captives. After a Middle Passage into the South Atlantic, in which only 2 Africans and 2 sailors died, the *Brooks* sailed to Montevideo on the Rio de la Plata, where it disgorged 320 souls. The ship had sailed its last. Already old for a slaver and no doubt decayed in the hull after having spent so much time in tropical waters over twenty-three years, the storied ship was condemned and presumably destroyed late in the year. The entire trade would be dismantled only three years later. The vessel that had played such a role in the slave trade and in the struggle against it came to a quiet, rotten end far from the eyes of both merchants and abolitionists. Yet its image sailed on, around the Atlantic, for decades to come, epitomizing the horrors of the trade and helping to advance a worldwide struggle against slavery.[58]

Endless Passage

Captain James D'Wolf, a member of New England's most powerful slave-trading family, had just returned to Newport, Rhode Island, after a voyage to the Gold Coast in the *Polly,* a smallish two-masted slaver. He had gathered 142 Coromantee captives and delivered 121 of them alive to Havana, Cuba. One of his sailors, John Cranston, appeared before a federal grand jury on June 15, 1791, to testify about "a Negro Woman . . . thrown over Board the said Vessel, while living." Had Captain D'Wolf committed murder?[1]

The woman, Cranston stated, was

taken Sick, which we took to be the small Pox. The Captain orderd her to be put in the Main top for fear she should give it to the others. She was there two Days. The night after being (then 2 Days) the Watch was called at 4 O'Clock then Capt Wolf called us all aft—& says he—if we keep the Slave here—she will give it to the rest—and [I] shall lose the biggest part of my Slaves. Then he asked if we were willing to heave her overboard. We made answer no. We were not willing to do any such thing. Upon that he himself run up the Shrowds, saying she must go overboard & shall go overboard—ordering one Thos. Gorton to go up with him—who went—then he lashed her in a Chair & ty'd a Mask round her Eyes & Mouth & there was a tackle hooked upon the Slings round

343

the Chair when we lowered her down on the larboard side of the Vessel.

Captain D'Wolf was not only afraid of losing his human property, he was apparently afraid to touch the sick woman, which is why he used a chair to hoist and lower her to the deck. At this point another sailor, Henry Clannen, joined in to help lift her overboard and drop her into the water. As the captain engineered the woman's death, Cranston and other sailors "went right forward & left them."[2]

Cranston had seen the woman alive in the maintop (high up the mainmast) about two minutes before she was hoisted down to the main deck.

> Q: Did you not hear her speak or make any Noises when she was thrown over—or see her struggle?
>
> A: No—a Mask was ty'd round her mouth & Eyes that she could not, & it was done to prevent her making any Noise that the other Slaves might not hear, least they should rise.
>
> Q: Do you recollect to hear the Capt. say any thing after the scene was ended?
>
> A: All he said was he was sorry he had lost so good a Chair.
>
> . . .
>
> Q: Did any person endeavour to prevent him throwing her [over]board?
>
> A: No. No further than telling him that they would not have any thing to do with it.

Cranston concluded by saying that neither he nor the rest of the crew was afraid of the smallpox and that they actually wished for exposure to it, to develop immunity.[3]

The port and region buzzed about the scandal. No fewer than five newspapers reported the incident, and a public clamor arose. This was expressed most forcefully in early July when the grand jury indicted Captain James D'Wolf for murder.[4]

Yet the wily Captain D'Wolf was a step ahead of his sailors, the abolitionists, and the authorities. He had seen the charges coming and quickly left Newport on another voyage to the Gold Coast. He wanted to let the agitation subside. In October 1794—more than three years after the event in question—he arranged for two other members of the crew of the *Polly,* Isaac Stockman and Henry Clannen, to give depositions, not in Rhode Island but in St. Eustatius, a slave-trading port in the West Indies.[5]

Stockman and Clannen confirmed most of what Cranston had said about the event but emphasized that they had no choice except to do what they did. The woman posed a danger because, had a number of the crew sickened and died, they would have been unable to control their large and unruly cargo of Coromantee captives, as they were "a Nation famed for Insurrection." These potentially deadly circumstances "compelled them to adopt this disagreeable alternative, being the only one from which, in this Situation, they could obtain the necessary relief."[6]

In any case the "Situation" of the crew of the *Polly* was one largely of D'Wolf's making. As shipowner and captain, it had been his decision to maximize profits by taking a small crew and no surgeon. It had been his decision to buy members of "a Nation famed for Insurrection." He was the one who had signed an insurance policy that would reimburse him only for the death of more than 20 percent of the enslaved, thereby creating a material incentive to kill one, save many, and profit.[7]

Other aspects of the situation were decidedly *not* of D'Wolf's making, and these suggest the imminent demise of the slave ship as an organizing institution of Atlantic capitalism. A first line of force emanated from the Gold Coast. The captain and crew of the *Polly* feared the Coromantee captives because these very people had a long history of leading revolts—on slave ships and in the slave societies of the New World. (A generation earlier they had led Tacky's Revolt in Jamaica, one of the Atlantic's bloodiest slave uprisings.) Another line stretched from abolitionist circles in Britain and America to the ship. In the aftermath of the *Zong* incident, when Captain Luke Collingwood in

1781 commanded his sailors to throw 122 captives overboard, opponents of the slave trade raised the cry of murder and insisted that slave-ship captains did not have the right to kill African captives with impunity. John Cranston's brave appearance before the grand jury—during the peak years of abolitionist agitation, 1788–92—suggests that the ideas of the abolitionist movement were now gaining currency among sailors, the people on whom the slave trade depended. Here, on the *Polly,* and in the Rhode Island courtroom in 1790–91, was the embryonic alliance that would in time destroy the slave trade: rebellious Africans and dissident sailors, in league with middle-class metropolitan antislavery activists. They combined to change the Atlantic field of force and to limit the power of the slave-ship captain.[8]

They were not yet strong enough: Captain D'Wolf beat the murder charges. The testimony of Stockman and Clannen helped, as did a ruling by a judge in St. Thomas in April 1795 that D'Wolf was innocent of the murder charges—this at a hearing in which there was no one present to testify against him. Just as important was the immense power of his family, several members of which would have been working behind the scenes. For years after the grand jury returned its murder charge, the marshal of Bristol, Rhode Island, population 1,406, seemed to have a lot of trouble finding James D'Wolf—a prominent member of an eminent and highly visible family—in order to arrest him. Surely he did not try very hard, and after five years he stopped trying altogether. The American charges were never formally dropped, but the issue itself was. The powerful D'Wolf clan had triumphed.[9]

The fates of the three principal actors in the drama underline the divergent experiences of the slave trade. John Cranston disappeared into the waterfront. The enslaved woman, whose name is forever lost, drowned, no doubt struggling against the lashings that bound her to the chair of which Captain D'Wolf was so fond. Her Coromantee shipmates were delivered in Havana, Cuba, in early 1791. They likely spent their numbered days cultivating sugar, which, the abolitionist movement was busy explaining, was made with blood. Some of them may have ended up on one of the three plantations Captain D'Wolf eventually bought on the island. They would have carried on their tradition of resistance.[10]

Captain James D'Wolf prospered in the heart of darkness, gathering immense riches in the slave trade. He financed and profited from another twenty-five voyages as sole or primary merchant and shipowner, and he also invested in numerous other voyages, usually in partnership with his brother John. He became not only the wealthiest member of the elite D'Wolf family but the wealthiest man in the state, if not the entire region. From his riches—denounced by an abolitionist as "the gains of oppression"—he built Mount Hope, one of the most sumptuous mansions in all of New England. He eventually became a United States senator.[11]

The "Most Magnificent Drama" Revisited

By the time Great Britain and the United States abolished the slave trade in 1807–8, what had the slave ship wrought? It had already carried 9 million people out of Africa to the New World. (Another 3 million were yet to come.) British and American slave ships alone had carried 3 million during the long eighteenth century. The human costs of the traffic were staggering: around 5 million died in Africa, on the ships, and in the first year of labor in the New World. For the period 1700–1808, some 500,000 perished on the way to the ships, another 400,000 on board, and yet another quarter million or so not long after the ships docked. By the time of abolition, roughly 3.3 million slaves were working in the Atlantic "plantation complex," for American, British, Danish, Dutch, French, Portuguese, and Spanish masters. Approximately 1.2 million of these labored in the United States, another 700,000 in the British Caribbean colonies. Their production was staggering. In 1807 alone, Britain imported for domestic consumption 297.9 million pounds of sugar and 3.77 million gallons of rum, all of it slave-produced, as well as 16.4 million pounds of tobacco and 72.74 million pounds of cotton, almost all of it slave-produced. In 1810 the enslaved population of the United States produced 93 million pounds

of cotton and most of 84 million pounds of tobacco; they were themselves, as property, worth $316 million. Robin Blackburn has estimated
that by 1800 the slave-based production of the New World "had cost
the slaves 2,500,000,000 hours of toil" and sold for "a gross sum that
could not have been much less than £35,000,000," or 3.3 billion 2007
dollars.[12]

As W. E. B. DuBois noted, the slave trade was the "most magnificent drama in the last thousand years of human history"—"the transportation of ten million human beings out of the dark beauty of their
mother continent into the new-found Eldorado of the West. They descended into Hell," a place of torment and suffering. It was certainly so
for the murdered, masked woman and for her Coromantee shipmates,
who, with the millions, were torn from their native land, transported
across the Atlantic, and forced to work, to produce wealth, in "Eldorado," for others. DuBois referred, of course, to the entire experience
of slavery, but he knew that the slave ship was a special circle of the
inferno. So did captains like James D'Wolf and Richard Jackson, who
turned their ships into floating hells and used terror to control everyone aboard, sailors and slaves, or "white slaves" and "black slaves," as
one captain called them: there was not, in his view, "a shade of difference between them, save in their respective complexions." The instruments in the task were masks, chairs, and tackle, the cat-o'-nine-tails,
thumbscrews, the *speculum oris,* cutlasses, pistols, swivel guns, and
sharks. The ship itself was in many respects a diabolical machine, one
big tool of torture.[13]

The drama, however, was larger than what happened on the ship, as
DuBois—and D'Wolf—knew well. The slave ship was a linchpin of a
rapidly growing Atlantic system of capital and labor. It linked workers
free, unfree, and everywhere in between, in capitalist and noncapitalist
societies on several continents. The voyage of the slaver originated in
the ports of Britain and America, where merchants pooled their money,
built or bought a vessel, and set a transnational train of people and
events in motion. These included, in their home ports, investors, bankers, clerks, and insurance underwriters. Government officials, from

customs officers to the Board of Trade to legislatures, played regulating roles small and large. In assembling the ship's various and expensive cargo to be traded on the coast of Africa, merchant-capitalists mobilized the energies of manufacturers and workers in Britain, America, Europe, the Caribbean, and India to produce textiles, metalwares, guns, rum, and other items. In building the ship, the merchant-capitalist called upon the shipwright and a small army of artisans, from woodworkers to sailmakers. Strong-backed dockworkers helped to load the cargo into the hold of the vessel, and of course a captain and crew would sail it around the Atlantic.

On the coast of Africa, the captain worked as the representative of merchant capital, conducting business with other merchants, some of them European, who ran the forts and factories, more of them African, who controlled the trade and mobilized their own officials, fee takers, and regulators, local and state, according to region. Like their British and American counterparts, African merchants coordinated workers of various kinds in their own spheres of influence: direct producers of "nonslave" commodities; captors of "slaves"—armies, raiders, and kidnappers (distinguished by the scale of their slave-capturing operations); and finally canoe-men and other workers on the waterfront, who cooperated directly with the slave-ship captains and sailors in getting the merchandise, human and otherwise, aboard the ship. A significant number of Africans would become sailors on the slavers, for shorter or longer periods of time.

After the slave ship completed the Middle Passage and arrived in an American port, the original British and American merchant-capitalists now used a new set of contacts to make the sale, and realize the profits, of the human cargo. Receiving merchants, under the oversight of colonial officials, took charge of transactions, connecting the slave-ship captain and crew, through local dockworkers black and white, to the labor-hungry planters who bought the captives. After the sale, slave-produced commodities from local plantations would often (ideally) be purchased by the captain and loaded onto the ship as a cargo for the homeward passage. Through these far-flung connections, merchants used the slave ship to create and coordinate a primary circuit of Atlantic capitalism, which was as lucrative for some as it was terror-filled and deadly for others.

The slave ship had not only delivered millions of people to slavery, it had prepared them for it. Literal preparations included readying the bodies for sale by the crew: shaving and cutting the hair of the men, using caustics to hide sores, dying gray hair black, and rubbing down torsos with palm oil. Preparations also included subjection to the discipline of enslavement. Captives experienced the "white master" and his unchecked power and terror, as well as that of his "overseers," the mate, boatswain, or sailor. They experienced the use of violence to hold together a social order in which they outnumbered their captors by ten to one or more. They ate communally and lived in extreme barracklike circumstances. They did not yet work in the backbreaking, soul-killing ways of the plantation, but labor many of them did, from domestic toil to forced sex work, from pumping the ship to setting the sails. It must also be noted that in preparing the captives for slavery, the experience of the slave ship also helped to prepare them to resist slavery. They developed new methods of survival and mutual aid—novel means of communication and solidarities among a multiethnic mass. They gathered new knowledge, of the ship, of the "white men," of one another as shipmates. Perhaps most important, the ship witnessed the beginnings of a culture of resistance, the subversive practices of negotiation and insurrection.

Reconciliation from Below

As John Cranston testified before the Rhode Island grand jury, many of his "brother tars," the very people who had helped to build the fortunes of Captain D'Wolf and his class, found themselves in a different situation after slaving voyages. Those called "wharfingers," "scowbankers," and "beach horners"—sick, broken-down seamen all, forced by captains off the slave ships—haunted the docks and harbors of almost all American ports, from the Chesapeake to Charleston, to Kingston, Jamaica, and Bridgetown, Barbados. They had no work, because no one would hire them for fear of infection. They had no money, because they had been bilked of their wages. They had no food and shelter, because they had no money. They drifted around the waterfront, sleeping under the balconies of houses, under the cranes used to hoist cargo in and out of the ships, in the odd unlocked shed, inside empty sugar casks—anywhere they could find to protect themselves from the elements.

They were nightmarish in appearance. Some had the bruises, blotches, and bloody gums of scurvy. Some had burning ulcers caused by Guinea worms, which grew up to four feet long and festered beneath the skin of the lower legs and feet. Some had the shakes and sweats of malaria. Some had grotesquely swollen limbs and rotting toes. Some were blind, victims of a parasite (*Onchocerca volvulus*) spread by blackflies in fast-flowing West African rivers. Some had a starved and beaten appearance, courtesy of their captain. They had "cadaverous looks," and indeed many were near death. The more able ones "begg[ed] a mouthful of victuals from other seamen." One well-traveled sea captain called them "the most miserable objects I ever met with in any country in my life." These "refuse" sailors of the slave trade depended on charity. Healthier "brother sailors" brought them food and tried to care for them, but their own means were limited.[14]

There was another source, perhaps unexpected, of assistance. An officer in the Royal Navy, a Mr. Thompson, noted that some of these pathetic sailors died, but "upon others the negroes have taken compassion, and carried them into their huts, where he has often seen them so ill, as to be almost at the point of death." Other observers in other places noticed the same pattern. "Some of them," explained Mr. James, "are taken in by the negroe women, out of compassion, and are healed in time." Seaman Henry Ellison noted that the wharfingers had trouble finding a place to stay dry, "except that a negro was now and then kind enough to take them into his hut." The people who took them in would have known exactly who they were, recognizing the specifically West African maladies from which they suffered, and perhaps how to treat them. Some likely knew the sailors personally.[15]

The compassion did not end with the giving of food, shelter, and nursing. It extended into the afterlife. When the sailors died—"in the greatest misery, of hunger and disease"—they were "buried out of charity, by the same people," said Mr. James. In Kingston, Ellison had seen "negroes carrying their dead bodies to Spring Path to be interred." Another naval officer, Ninian Jeffreys, who was "attending a negro holiday at Spring Path, which is the cemetery of the negroes, has often seen the bodies of these wharfingers brought there, and interred in an adjoining spot."[16]

What was the meaning of this compassion and charity? Is it possible that those who had survived the slave ship as prisoners knew precisely how horrible the experience had been for everyone aboard and that, moved by such knowledge, they could show sympathy and pity to those who had been their prison guards? Might the term "shipmate" have been generous and bighearted enough to allow the oppressed to show humanity to the very people who had presided over their enslavement aboard the slave ship?[17]

Dead Reckoning

To conclude, again, on a personal note. I chose to end this book with the account of Captain James D'Wolf, seaman John Cranston, and the masked African woman, name unknown, for three reasons. First, the story features the three central actors in the "most magnificent drama." It is, moreover, appropriate that the book should end where it began, with the travails of an African woman whose name is unknown to us. Second, it sums up the reality of terror aboard the slave ship and at the same time suggests the gathering forces that would bring it to an end. Third, it calls attention to a fact that requires emphasis: the dramas that played out on the decks of a slave ship were made possible, one might even say structured, by the capital and power of people far from the ship. The dramas involving captains, sailors, and African captives aboard the slave ship were part of a much larger drama, the rise and movement of capitalism around the world.

James D'Wolf is unusual in that he got his hands dirty—perhaps bloody would be a better way to put it—in the trade itself. The hands that threw the masked woman overboard would count profits at the merchant's table and in the end help to craft legislation in the United States Senate. D'Wolf was certainly unusual, though not unique, in this regard, as the people who benefited most from the slave ship were usually distant from its torment, suffering, stench, and death, both physically and psychologically. Merchants, government officials, and ruling classes more broadly reaped the enormous benefits of the slave ship and the system it served. D'Wolf would soon join them, apparently making only one more slaving voyage (to evade the authorities after the murder), then moving up the economic ladder from captain to the more genteel status of slave-trade merchant. Most merchants, like Humphry Morice and Henry Laurens, insulated themselves from the human consequences of their investments, thinking of the slave ship in abstract and useful ways, reducing all to columns of numbers in ledger books and statements of profit and loss.

Like growing numbers of people around the world, I am convinced that the time has come for a different accounting. What do the descendants of D'Wolf, Morice, and Laurens—their families, their class, their government, and the societies they helped to construct—owe to the descendants of the enslaved people they delivered into bondage? It is a complex question, but justice demands that it be posed—and answered, if the legacy of slavery is ever to be overcome. There can be no reconciliation without justice.

It is not a new question. Slave-trade Captain Hugh Crow noted in his memoir, published in the aftermath of abolition, that opportunities existed "to make some reparation to Africa for the wrongs which England may have inflicted upon her." He had in mind philanthropy and what would be called "legitimate trade" to Africa—that is, trade in "commodities" other than human beings. He did not include the people whom he and other captains had transported to the Americas. But even the slave-ship captain admitted that something had to be done to redress a monstrous historical injustice. This applies of course not only to the slave trade but to the entire experience of slavery.[18]

Britain and the United States have made significant progress over the past generation in acknowledging that the slave trade and slavery were important parts of their history. This has come about primarily because various peoples' movements for racial and class justice arose on both sides of the Atlantic in the 1960s and 1970s, demanding new histories and new debates about their meaning. Scholars, teachers, journalists, museum professionals, and others took inspiration from these movements and recovered large parts of the African and African-American past, creating new knowledge and public awareness. Still, I would suggest that neither country has yet come to grips with the darker and more violent side of this history, which is perhaps one reason the darkness and violence continue in the present. Violence and terror were central to the very formation of the Atlantic economy and its multiple labor systems in the seventeenth and eighteenth centuries. Even the best histories of the slave trade and slavery have tended to minimize, one might even say sanitize, the violence and terror that lay at the heart of their subjects.[19]

Most histories of the Middle Passage and the slave trade more broadly have concentrated on one aspect of their subject. Following the lead of eighteenth-century abolitionists, but distrusting their propaganda and sensationalism, many historians have focused on the mortality of the Middle Passage, which has come to stand for the horrors of the slave trade. Hence precisely how many people were transported and how many of them died along the way have been key issues to be studied and debated—rightly so, in my view, but the approach is limited. One of the main purposes of this book has been to broaden the conspectus by treating death as one aspect of terror and to insist that the latter, as a profoundly human drama enacted on one vessel after another, was the defining feature of the slave ship's hell. How many people died can be answered through abstract, indeed bloodless, statistics; how a few created terror and how the many experienced terror—and how they in turn resisted it—cannot.

An emphasis on terror does not make the question of redress easier to answer. Nor is it the place of a historian to answer the question in any case. The price of exploitation, of unpaid labor, might be computed, and should be, as all people, past and present, deserve the full and just value of their labor. Reparations are, in my view, in order, but justice cannot be reduced to a calculus of money, lest proposed solutions play by the rules of the game that spawned the slave trade in the first place. What in any case would be the price of terror? What the price of mass premature death? These are constituent elements of racism, especially when wedded to class oppression, and they are with us still.[20]

In the end I conclude that answers to these questions must be decided by a social movement for justice, led by the descendants of those who have suffered most from the legacy of the slave trade, slavery, and the racism they spawned, joined by allies in a broader struggle to end the violence and terror that have always been central to the rise and continuing operation of capitalism. It is for this reason that I chose to end with the sailors' testimony about enslaved people caring for diseased and dying seamen in Caribbean ports. Theirs was the most generous and inclusive conception of humanity I discovered in the course of my research for this book. These good deeds, taken by people who themselves had little enough food, shelter, health, and space for ritual and burial, seemed to suggest the possibility of a different future. With their inspiration and our hard work, it may still be possible. The long, violent passage of the slave ship might finally come to an end, and the "most magnificent drama" might become magnificent in an entirely new way.

ACKNOWLEDGMENTS

I could never have written this book without family, friends, colleagues, and no small number of helpful strangers. I thank the staffs at the National Maritime Museum, Greenwich; Bristol Record Office (especially Pat Denney, archivist of the Society of Merchant Venturers); Bristol University Library; Bristol City Museum; Merseyside Maritime Museum (Tony Tibbles and Dawn Littler in particular); Liverpool Record Office; St. John's College Library and Cambridge University Library; National Archives; House of Lords Record Office; Royal College of Surgeons; Friends House Library; Bristol (RI) Historical Society; Newport (RI) Historical Society; John Carter Brown Library; Providence Public Library; Baker Library, Harvard Business School; New-York Historical Society; Seeley G. Mudd Manuscript Library, Princeton University; Robert W. Woodruff Library, Atlanta University Center; Charleston County Public Library; Avery Research Center and Special Collections, Addlestone Library, College of Charleston; South Caroliniana Library; South Carolina Historical Society. I am also grateful to the wonderful staff at my home library, Hillman, at the University of Pittsburgh, especially Phil Wilkin, who helped me to get essential research materials.

Thanks to the National Endowment of the Humanities and the American Council of Learned Societies for fellowship support. My research has also been facilitated in various and generous ways at the University of Pittsburgh, by support from the Center for Latin American Studies, the Center for West European Studies, the University Center for International Studies, the Central Research Development Fund, George Klinzing and Provost's Office of Research, and Dean N. John Cooper and the Faculty of Arts and Sciences.

It was my good fortune to speak about this project before many engaged and responsive audiences. Thanks to the facilitators of the events and those who came and spoke their minds: Eric Cheyfitz, Cornell University; Karen Kupperman, Sinclair Thomson, and Michael Gomez, New York University; Madge Dresser, University of the West of England; Peter Way, Bowling Green State University; Andrew Wells and Ben Maddison, University of Wollongong; Cassandra Pybus, Centre for the Study of Colonialism and Its Aftermath, University of Tasmania; Rick Halpern, University of Toronto; Pearl Robinson, Tufts University; William Keach, Brown University; Simon Lewis, College of Charleston; Modhumita Roy, Marxist Literary Group; Phyllis Hunter, University of North Carolina-Greensboro; Kirk Savage, Department of History of Art and Architecture, and Alejandro de la Fuente, Department of History, University of Pittsburgh. I also benefited from the thoughts and suggestions of colleagues who gathered in Fremantle, Australia, in July 2005 at the conference "Middle Passages: The Oceanic Voyage as Social Process," organized by Cassandra Pybus, Emma Christopher, and Terri-Ann White.

As I worked in maritime archives over the last thirty years, it took a long time to see that it might be possible to write a history of the slave ship and longer still to accept its challenge. The idea first came to me in the late 1990s as I visited prisoners on death row in Pennsylvania and worked to abolish capital punishment, a modern system of terror. Thanks to the many people I have met through this long and continuing struggle: our common work is reflected in countless ways, subtle and deep, in these pages. A critical moment in deciding to write the book was a meeting in 2003 with a host of talented scholars in the Sawyer Seminar on "Redress in Social Thought, Law, and Literature," at the University of California-Irvine. Especially valuable then and since have been communications with Saidiya Hartman, author of the powerful new book *Lose Your Mother: A Journey Along the Atlantic Slave Route.*

Many of my colleagues and students at the University of Pittsburgh have helped me in countless ways. Joseph Adjaye has long been a vital source of knowledge and wisdom about African history. Stefan

Wheelock encouraged me to think about the technology of enslavement, while Jerome Branche helped me to understand the concept "shipmate." Seymour Drescher and Rebecca Shumway read chapters and gave me the benefit of their expertise. Patrick Manning has been a paragon of scholarly and comradely generosity, encouraging me at the beginning of the project, guiding me through the middle, and helping me in numerous and practical ways at the end. Rob Ruck has shared the ups and downs of this book and much else, not least many a Pitt basketball season. These people and others—Alejandro de la Fuente, Lara Putnam, Bill Chase, Reid Andrews, and the members of the Working-Class History Seminar—have helped to make the history department and the University of Pittsburgh my happy home for many years.

I have had excellent research assistance along the way. Three of my former undergraduate students, Heather Looney, Ian Hartman, and Matt Maeder, did truly outstanding work, not only gathering primary sources but asking sharp, probing questions about what they found. My graduate students past and present have been a continual source of enthusiasm, assistance, and inspiration: thanks to Isaac Curtis, John Donoghue, Niklas Frykman, Gabriele Gottlieb, Forrest Hylton, Maurice Jackson, Eric Kimball, Christopher Magra, Michael McCoy, Craig Marin, Scott Smith, Karsten Voss, and Cornell Womack. Special thanks to Niklas, Gabriele, Chris, and Forrest, who helped me with research, as did my son, Zeke Rediker, who lent a hand in his own area of interest, African history.

I owe a special debt to Peter Linebaugh, whose friendship and collaboration over many years were central to the formulation of this project. Michael West, a distinguished scholar-activist of Africa and the Black Atlantic, has given warm encouragement to the project from beginning to end. The splendid maritime artist and writer William Gilkerson lent a sailor's hand with chapter two. George Burgess, coordinator of Museum Operations, and director, Florida Program for Shark Research, Florida Museum of Natural History, and Department of Ichthyology, University of Florida, helped me to understand the history and behavior of sharks, while Pieter van der Merwe of the National Maritime Museum gave generous assistance on James Field Stanfield (chapter five). David Eltis kindly provided recent figures from the updated *Trans-Atlantic Slave Trade: A Database on CD-ROM*. Roderick Ebanks shared his knowledge of historical archaeology in Jamaica. My gratitude to all.

Five superb historians read the entire manuscript and applied their enormous learning. Especially warm thanks to Cassandra Pybus, a gifted writer and historian who helped me to see new possibilities; Emma Christopher, whose pathbreaking study of slave-trade sailors helped to make my own book possible; and Robin Blackburn, whose synthetic, comparative, and comprehensive studies of Atlantic slavery have been exemplary. Ira Berlin, who has brilliantly reconceptualized the slave experience in the New World, made characteristically tough-minded suggestions. Kenneth Morgan, whose own forthcoming study of the British slave trade will reset the scholarly standard, helped me in many ways, sharing his extraordinary knowledge of sources and many careful, detailed comments. I thank all for what they suggested, including the comments I was too hard-headed to accept.

My agent, Sandy Dijkstra, helped me to think my way into the project and to find the right publishers on both sides of the Atlantic. Maureen Sugden provided expert copyediting. Thanks to Eleanor Birne at John Murray, and to my excellent editors at Viking Penguin USA, Wendy Wolf and Ellen Garrison, who accompanied, challenged, and helped me along the way, especially as things got difficult at the end.

Final thanks are reserved for my family. My wife, Wendy Goldman, has read, discussed, argued, and helped endlessly, more than anyone else. The book is dedicated to her and to my children, Zeke and Eva Rediker.

NOTES

ABBREVIATIONS

An Account of the Life	Silas Told, *An Account of the Life, and Dealings of God with Silas Told, Late Preacher of the Gospel wherein is set forth The wonderful Display of Divine Providence towards him when at Sea; His various Sufferings abroad; Together with Many Instances of the Sovereign Grace of GOD, in the Conversion of several Malefactors under Sentence of Death, who were greatly blessed by his Ministry* (London: Gilbert and Plummer, 1785).
BL	British Library, London.
BCL	Bristol Central Library, Bristol, England.
BRO	Bristol Record Office, Bristol, England.
Clarkson, *History*	Thomas Clarkson, *The History of the Rise, Progress, and Accomplishment of the Abolition of the African Slave-Trade by the British Parliament* (London, 1808), vols. 1–2.
Donnan II	Elizabeth Donnan, ed., *Documents Illustrative of the History of the Slave Trade to America* (Washington, D.C.: Carnegie Institution of Washington, 1931), vol. II: *The Eighteenth Century.*
Donnan III	Elizabeth Donnan, ed., *Documents Illustrative of the History of the Slave Trade to America* (Washington, D.C.: Carnegie Institution of Washington, 1932), vol. III: *New England and the Middle Colonies.*
Donnan IV	Elizabeth Donnan, ed., *Documents Illustrative of the History of the Slave Trade to America* (Washington, D.C.: Carnegie Institution of Washington, 1935), vol. IV: *The Border Colonies and Southern Colonies.*
HCA	High Court of Admiralty.
HCSP	Sheila Lambert, ed., *House of Commons Sessional Papers of the Eighteenth Century* (Wilmington, Del.: Scholarly Resources, 1975), vols. 67–73, 82.
HLRO	House of Lords Record Office, Westminster.
HLSP	F. William Torrington, ed., *House of Lords Sessional Papers* (Dobbs Ferry, N.Y.: Oceana Publications, 1974), Session 1798–1799, vols. 2–3.
LRO	Liverpool Record Office, Liverpool.

Memoirs of Crow   *Memoirs of the Late Captain Hugh Crow of Liverpool. Comprising a Narrative of his Life together with Descriptive Sketches of the Western Coast of Africa, particularly in Bonny, the Manners and Customs of the Inhabitants, the Production of the Soil, and the Trade of the Country, to which are added Anecdotes and Observations illustrative of the Negro Character, chiefly compiled from his own Manuscripts: with Authentic Additions from Recent Voyages and Approved Authors* (London: Longman, Rees, Orme, Brown, and Green, 1830; rpt. London: Frank Cass & Co., 1970).

MMM   Merseyside Maritime Museum, Liverpool.

NA   National Archives of the United Kingdom, Kew Gardens, London.

NMM   National Maritime Museum, Greenwich.

Substance   [Thomas Clarkson, ed.], *The Substance of the Evidence of Sundry Persons on the Slave-Trade Collected in the Course of a Tour Made in the Autumn of the Year 1788* (London, 1789).

PL   Records of the County Palantine of Lancaster.

Three Years Adventures   William Butterworth [Henry Schroder], *Three Years Adventures of a Minor, in England, Africa, and the West Indies, South Carolina and Georgia* (Leeds: Edward Barnes, 1822).

TSTD   David Eltis, Stephen D. Behrendt, David Richardson, and Herbert S. Klein, *The Trans-Atlantic Slave Trade: A Database on CD-ROM* (Cambridge: Cambridge University Press, 1999).

Introduction

1. This reconstruction of a woman's experience is based loosely on an account by sailor William Butterworth of one who came aboard his vessel, the *Hudibras,* in 1786 in Old Calabar in the Bight of Biafra. Other details are culled from numerous primary source descriptions of captives transported by canoe to the slave ships. Igbo words are taken from a vocabulary list collected by Captain Hugh Crow during his voyages to Bonny, a different port in the same region. See *Three Years Adventures,* 81–82, and *Memoirs of Crow,* 229–30. See also Robert Smith, "The Canoe in West African History," *Journal of African History* 11 (1970), 515–33. A "moon" was a common West African way of reckoning time, equal roughly to a month.

2. W. E. B. DuBois, *Black Reconstruction in America: An Essay toward a History of the Part Which Black Folk Played in the Attempt to Reconstruct Democracy in America, 1860–1880* (New York: Harcourt, Brace and Company, 1935), 727. The significance of this quotation by DuBois was emphasized in Peter Linebaugh, "All the Atlantic Mountains Shook," *Labour/Le Travailleur* 19 (1982), 63–121. I am indebted to this article, and to our joint work, for many of the fundamental ideas of this book. See also Peter Linebaugh and Marcus Rediker, *The Many-Headed Hydra: Sailors, Slaves, Commoners, and the Hidden History of the Revolutionary Atlantic* (Boston: Beacon Press, 2000).

3. These numbers and others throughout the book are based on the updated but not yet final and published new edition of the *TSTD,* as kindly provided by David Eltis. On the origins and growth of the Atlantic slave system, see David Eltis, *The Rise of African Slavery in the Americas* (Cambridge: Cambridge University Press, 2000), and Robin Blackburn, *The Making of New World Slavery: From the Baroque to the Modern, 1492–1800* (London: Verso, 1997). Jerome S. Handler has emphasized how little first-person African testimony has survived. See his "Survivors of the Middle Passage: Life Histories of Enslaved Africans in British America," *Slavery and Abolition* 23 (2002), 25–56.

4. Estimates of death before boarding range widely. For Angola, Joseph Miller has suggested that 25 percent of the enslaved died on the way to the coast and another 15 percent while in captivity once there. See his *Way of Death: Merchant Capitalism and the Angolan Slave Trade, 1730–1830* (Madison: University of Wisconsin Press, 1988), 384–85. Patrick Manning settles on a lower range, 5 to 25 percent (Patrick Manning, *The African Diaspora: A History Through Culture* [New York: Columbia University Press, forthcoming, 2008]). Paul Lovejoy suggests a narrower range of 9 to 15 percent; see his *Transformations in Slavery: A History of Slavery in Africa* (Cambridge: Cambridge University Press, 2000), 2nd edition, 63–64. Herbert S. Klein likewise suggests that mortality on the coast was likely as low or lower than on the Middle Passage (that is, about 12 percent or less). See his *The Atlantic Slave Trade* (Cambridge: Cambridge University Press, 1999), 155.

5. Ottobah Cugoano, *Thoughts and Sentiments on the Evil of Slavery* (orig. publ. London, 1787; rpt. London: Penguin, 1999), 46, 85.

6. East Africa (including Madagascar) became a source of a few thousand captives in the 1790s but did not qualify as an important trading zone for the period as a whole.

7. Dalby Thomas to the Royal African Company, February 15, 1707, quoted in Jay Coughtry, *The Notorious Triangle: Rhode Island and the African Slave Trade, 1700–1807* (Philadelphia: Temple University Press, 1981), 43.

8. Richard H. Steckel and Richard A. Jensen, "New Evidence on the Causes of Slave and Crew Mortality in the Atlantic Slave Trade," *Journal of Economic History* 46 (1986), 57–77; Stephen D. Behrendt, "Crew Mortality in the Transatlantic Slave Trade in the

Eighteenth Century," *Slavery and Abolition* 18 (1997), 49–71. The ditty about Benin is quoted in Marcus Rediker, *Between the Devil and the Deep Blue Sea: Merchant Seamen, Pirates, and the Anglo-American Maritime World, 1700–1750* (Cambridge: Cambridge University Press), 47. The *TSTD* shows that the mortality rate for British vessels between 1700 and 1725 was 12.1 percent and that it had dropped to 7.95 percent for the period 1775–1800.

9. Sidney W. Mintz and Richard Price, *The Birth of African-American Culture: An Anthropological Perspective* (orig. publ. 1976; Boston: Beacon Press, 1992). A small sample of the creative and rapidly expanding work on cultural connections between Africa and the Americas would include John Thornton, *Africa and Africans in the Making of the Atlantic World, 1400–1800* (Cambridge: Cambridge University Press, 1992; 2nd edition, 1998); Judith A. Carney, *Black Rice: The African Origins of Rice Cultivation in the Americas* (Cambridge, Mass.: Harvard University Press, 2001); Linda M. Heywood, ed., *Central Africans and Cultural Transformations in the American Diaspora* (Cambridge: Cambridge University Press, 2002); James H. Sweet, *Recreating Africa: Cultu re, Kinship, and Religion in the African-Portuguese World, 1441–1770* (Chapel Hill : University of North Carolina Press, 2003); Toyin Falola and Matt D. Childs, eds., *The Yoruba Diaspora in the Atlantic World* (Bloomington: Indiana University Press, 2004); José C. Curto and Paul E. Lovejoy, eds., *Enslaving Connections: Changing Cultures of Africa and Brazil During the Era of Slavery* (Trenton, N.J.: Africa World Press, 2005); James Lorand Matory, *Black Atlantic Religion: Tradition, Transnationalism, and Matriarchy in the Afro-Brazilian Candomblé* (Princeton, N.J.: Princeton University Press, 2005).

10. *TSTD,* #15123, #20211.

11. Ralph Davis, *The Rise of the English Shipping Industry in the Seventeenth and Eighteenth Centuries* (London: Macmillan, 1962), 71, 73; D. P. Lamb, "Volume and Tonnage of the Liverpool Slave Trade, 1772–1807," in Roger Anstey and P. E. H. Hair, eds., *Liverpool, the African Slave Trade, and Abolition* (Chippenham, England: Antony Rowe for the Historical Society of Lancashire and Cheshire, 1976, rpt. 1989), 98–99. The continuities in the operation of the slave ship make it possible to explore its history in topical and thematic ways in the pages that follow.

12. For exceptions to this neglect, see George Francis Dow, *Slave Ships and Slaving* (Salem, Mass.: Marine Research Society, 1927), a combination of narrative and primary sources; Patrick Villiers, *Traite des noirs et navires negriers au XVIII siècle* (Grenoble: Éditions des 4 Seigneurs, 1982), a useful although limited exploration; and Jean Boudriot, *Traite et Navire Negrier* (self-published, 1984), a study of a single ship, *L'Aurore*. A recent addition is Gail Swanson, *Slave Ship* Guerrero (West Conshohocken, P.A.: Infinity Publishing, 2005).

13. Philip D. Curtin, *The African Slave Trade: A Census* (Madison: University of Wisconsin Press, 1969); Miller, *Way of Death;* Hugh Thomas, *The Slave Trade: The Story of the African Slave Trade, 1440–1870* (New York: Simon and Schuster, 1999); Robert Harms, *The Diligent: A Voyage Through the Worlds of the Slave Trade* (New York: Basic Books, 2002); Eltis, et al., *TSTD*. Other important works are W. E. B. DuBois, *The Suppression of the African Slave-Trade in the United States of America, 1638–1870* (orig. publ. 1896; Mineola, N.Y.: Dover Publications, Inc., 1970); Basil Davidson, *The African Slave Trade* (Boston: Little, Brown, 1961); Daniel P. Mannix and Malcolm Cowley, *Black Cargoes: A History of the Atlantic Slave Trade, 1518–1865* (London: Longmans, 1963); James A. Rawley, *The Transatlantic Slave Trade: A History* (New York: W. W. Norton, 1981); and more recently Anne C. Bailey, *African Voices of the Atlantic Slave Trade: Beyond the Silence and the Shame* (Boston: Beacon Press, 2005).

14. Toni Morrison, *Beloved* (New York: Alfred A. Knopf, 1987); Charles Johnson, *Middle Passage* (New York: Plume, 1991); Barry Unsworth, *Sacred Hunger* (New York: W. W. Norton, 1993); Fred D'Aguiar, *Feeding the Ghosts* (London: Chatto & Windus, 1997); Caryl Phillips, *The Atlantic Sound* (New York: Alfred A. Knopf, 2000); Manu Herbstein, *Ama: A Novel of the Atlantic Slave Trade* (Capetown: Picador Africa, 2005).

15. Much of what is new is coming from younger scholars, to whose work I am much indebted: Emma Christopher, *Slave Ship Sailors and their Captive Cargoes, 1730–1807* (New York: Cambridge University Press, 2005); Stephanie E. Smallwood, *Saltwater Slavery: A Middle Passage from Africa to American Diaspora* (Cambridge, Mass: Harvard University Press, 2006); Eric Robert Taylor, *If We Must Die: Shipboard Insurrections in the Era of the Atlantic Slave Trade* (Baton Rouge: Louisiana State University Press, 2006); Vincent Brown, *The Reaper's Garden: Death and Power in the World of Atlantic Slavery* (Cambridge, Mass.: Harvard University Press, forthcoming); Alexander Xavier Byrd, "Captives and Voyagers: Black Migrants Across the Eighteenth-Century World of Olaudah Equiano," Ph.D. dissertation, Duke University, 2001; Maurice Jackson, " 'Ethiopia shall soon stretch her hands unto God': Anthony Benezet and the Atlantic Antislavery Revolution," Ph.D. dissertation, Georgetown University, 2001.

16. Seymour Drescher, "Whose Abolition? Popular Pressure and the Ending of the British Slave Trade," *Past & Present* 143 (1994), 136–66.

17. Unsworth, *Sacred Hunger,* 353. I am indebted to Gesa Mackenthun, "Body Counts: Violence and Its Occlusion in Writing the Atlantic Slave Trade," paper presented to the Francis Barker Memorial Conference, 2001.

18. Derek Sayer, *The Violence of Abstraction: The Analytic Foundations of Historical Materialism* (Oxford: Basil Blackwell, 1987).

Chapter 1: Life, Death, and Terror in the Slave Trade

1. John Atkins, *A Voyage to Guinea, Brasil, and the West Indies; In His Majesty's Ships, the Swallow and Weymouth* (London, 1735; rpt. London: Frank Cass, 1970), 41–42, 72–73.

2. *TSTD,* #16303.

3. Testimony of Henry Ellison, 1790, *HCSP,* 73:376. See *TSTD,* #17707.

4. Testimony of Thomas Trotter, 1790, *HCSP,* 73:83, 88, 92; Testimony of Clement Noble, 1790, in ibid., 111, 114–15. Trotter noted in his study *Observations on the Scurvy, with a Review of the Theories lately advanced on that Disease; and the Theories of Dr. Milman refuted from Practice* (London, 1785; Philadelphia, 1793) 23, that Fante and "Dunco" (i.e., Chamba) were the main two groups on the ship. The Fante were coastal and more likely to speak English than were the Chamba.

5. *Three Years Adventures,* 80–81, 108–9, 111–12.

6. *TSTD,* #81890.

7. Samuel Robinson, *A Sailor Boy's Experience Aboard a Slave Ship in the Beginning of the Present Century* (orig. publ. Hamilton, Scotland: William Naismith, 1867; rpt. Wigtown, Scotland: G.C. Book Publishers Ltd., 1996); *TSTD,* #88216 (*Lady Neilson* or *Nelson*), #80928 (*Crescent*).

8. Captain Charles Johnson, *A General History of the Pyrates,* ed. Manuel Schonhorn (London, 1724, 1728; rpt. Columbia: University of South Carolina Press, 1972), 194–287; *TSTD,* #76602; Robert Norris, *Memoirs of the Reign of Bossa Ahádee, King of Dahomy,*

an Inland Country of Guiney, to which are added the Author's Journey to Abomey, the Capital, and a Short Account of the African Slave Trade (orig. publ. London, 1789; rpt. London: Frank Cass and Company Limited, 1968), 67–68. For background on Roberts's generation of pirates, see Marcus Rediker, *Villains of All Nations: Atlantic Pirates in the Golden Age* (Boston: Beacon Press, 2004).

9. Nicholas Owen, *Journal of a Slave-Dealer: A View of Some Remarkable Axedents in the Life of Nics. Owen on the Coast of Africa and America from the Year 1746 to the Year 1757,* ed. Eveline Martin (Boston: Houghton Mifflin, 1930). One of Owen's voyages was on the *Prince Shurborough,* Captain William Brown, *TSTD,* #36152.

10. Captain William Snelgrave, *A New Account of Some Parts of Guinea and the Slave Trade* (London, 1734; rpt. London: Frank Cass & Co., Ltd., 1971), introduction; *TSTD,* #25657.

11. Interview of Henry Ellison, *Substance,* 224–25; *TSTD,* #17686.

12. Testimony of James Fraser, 1790, *HCSP,* 71:5–58; Testimony of Alexander Falconbridge, 1790, *HCSP,* 72:293–344. The quote by Burges is in Clarkson, *History,* vol. I, 318.

13. In Fraser's early voyages, he did not retain crew members in significant numbers from one voyage to the next, but by the late 1780s as many as two-thirds of his men, an extraordinary number, signed on again after a previous voyage. See "A Muster Roll for the Ship Alexander, James Fraser Master from Bristol to Africa and America," 1777–78; "A Muster Roll for the Ship Valiant, James Fraser Master from Africa and Jamaica," 1777–78; "A Muster Roll for the Ship Tartar, James Fraser Master from Bristol to Africa and America," 1780–81; "A Muster Roll for the Ship Emilia, James Fraser Master from Dominica," 1783–84; "A Muster Roll for the Ship Emilia, James Fraser Master from Jamaica," 1784–85; "A Muster Roll for the Ship Emilia, James Fraser Master from Jamaica," 1785–86; "A Muster Roll for the Ship Emilia, James Fraser Master from Africa," 1786–87; "A Muster Roll for the Ship Emilia, James Fraser Master from Africa," 1787–88; Muster Rolls, 1754–94, vols. 8 and 9, Society of Merchant Venturers Archives, Bristol Record Office; *TSTD,* #17888, #17895, #17902, #17920, #17933, #17952, #17967, #17990.

14. Anonymous, *A Short Account of the African Slave Trade, Collected from Local Knowledge* (Liverpool, 1788); Norris, *Memoirs of the Reign of Bossa Ahádee,* v; Testimony of Robert Norris, 1788, *HCSP,* 68:3–19; Testimony of Robert Norris, 1790, *HCSP,* 69:118–20, 202–3; "The Log of the *Unity,* 1769–1771," Earle Family Papers, D/EARLE/1/4, MMM; *TSTD,* #91567.

15. "List of the Slaves that Dyed on Board the Katharine Galley, John Dagge Commander," 1728, "Trading Accounts and Personal Papers of Humphry Morice," vol. 5; Humphry Morice to William Clinch, September 13, 1722, M7/7; Humphry Morice to Captain William Boyle, May 11, 1724, M7/10. Humphry Morice Papers, Bank of England Archives, London ; *TSTD,* #76558. Throughout his section I am indebted to James A. Rawley, "Humphry Morice: Foremost London Slave Merchant of his Time," in his *London: Metropolis of the Slave Trade* (Columbia and London: University of Missouri Press, 2003), 40–56. See also "Humphry Morice," *Dictionary of National Biography,* ed. Sidney Lee (London: Oxford University Press, 1921–22), 13: 941.

16. Basnett, Miller, and Mill to Humphry Morice, Kingston, November 9, 1722, f. 29–30, Correspondence of Humphry Morice, Miscellaneous Letters and Papers, Add. Ms. 48590B, BL.

17. Henry Laurens to Hinson Todd, April 14, 1769, in George C. Rogers, David R. Chesnutt, and Peggy J. Clark, eds., *The Papers of Henry Laurens* (Columbia: Uni-

versity of South Carolina Press, 1978), vol. 6, 438 (first quotation); see also vol. 1, 259 (second quotation). This section draws upon James A. Rawley, "Henry Laurens and the Atlantic Slave Trade," in his *London: Metropolis of the Slave Trade*, 82–97, and C. James Taylor, ed., "Laurens, Henry," *American National Biography Online,* February 2000, http://www.anb.org/articles/01/01-00495.html. See also Daniel C. Littlefield, *Rice and Slaves: Ethnicity and the Slave Trade in Colonial South Carolina* (Champaign-Urbana, Ill.: University of Illinois Press, 1981); James A. McMillan, *The Final Victims: Foreign Slave Trade to North America, 1783–1810* (Columbia: University of South Carolina Press, 2004).

18. Of 1,382 slaving voyages that brought 264,536 slaves to the American colonies/United States between 1701 and 1810, 761 delivered 151,647 to ports in the Carolinas, the overwhelming majority of these in Charleston. These figures represent 55 percent of voyages and 57 percent of slaves disembarked. Computations based on *TSTD.*

19. On sharks in the river Gambia, see Mungo Park, *Travels into the Interior of Africa, Performed Under the Direction and Patronage of the African Association, in the Years 1795, 1796, and 1797,* ed. Kate Ferguson Marsters (orig. publ. 1799; rpt. Durham, N.C., and London: Duke University Press, 2000), 28; in Sierra Leone, see John Matthews, *A Voyage to the River Sierra Leone, on the Coast of Africa, containing an Account of the Trade and Productions of the Country, and of the Civil and Religious Customs and Manners of the People; in a Series of Letters to a Friend in England* (London: B. White and Son, 1788), 50; in the Bonny River, see Alexander Falconbridge, *An Account of the Slave Trade on the Coast of Africa* (London, 1788), 51–52, 67; in the Kongo River, see "A Battle Between a Tiger and an Alligator; Or, wonderful instance of Providential Preservation, described in a letter from the Captain of the Davenport Guineaman," *Connecticut Herald,* June 28, 1808. For a survey of African sharks, see Henry W. Fowler, "The Marine Fishes of West Africa, Based on the Collection of the American Museum Congo Expedition, 1909–1915," *Bulletin of the American Museum of Natural History* (New York: American Museum of Natural History, 1936), 70, 1:23–92. See also J. Cadenat and J. Blache, *Requins de Méditerranée et d'Atlantique (plus Particulièrement de la Côte Occidentale d'Afrique)* (Paris: Éditions de l'Office de la Recherche Scientifique et Technique Outre-Mer, 1981). For the origins of the English word "shark" in the slaving voyages of Captain John Hawkins during the 1560s, see *Oxford English Dictionary,* s.v. "Shark," citing *Ballads & Broadsides* (1867) 147, BL. See also José I. Castro, "On the Origins of the Spanish Word Tiburón and the English Word 'Shark,'" *Environmental Biology of Fishes* 65 (2002), 249–53.

20. "Natural History of the Shark, from Dr. Goldsmith and other eminent Writers," *Universal Magazine* 43 (1778), 231; Robinson, *A Sailor Boy's Experience,* 29–32; *Memoirs of Crow,* 264; William Smith, *A New Voyage to Guinea: Describing the Customs, Manners, Soil, Climate, Habits, Buildings, Education, Manual Arts, Agriculture, Trade, Employments, Languages, Ranks of Distinction, Habitations, Diversions, Marriages, and whatever else is memorable among the Inhabitants* (London, 1744; rpt. London: Frank Cass & Co. Ltd., 1967), 239. See also Testimony of Fraser, *HCSP,* 71:24.

21. *An Account of the Life,* 40; Atkins, *A Voyage to Guinea,* 46. Told did not say whether the man was a slave or a sailor. It appears that it was the latter, because he told the story in the context of dangerous work performed by the crew. See also Falconbridge, *Account of the Slave Trade,* 67, who noted that Africans buried their dead at a "distance from the sea that the sharks cannot smell them."

22. Falconbridge, *Account of the Slave Trade,* 67; Smith, *New Voyage,* 239. See also "Voyage to Guinea, Antego, Bay of Campeachy, Cuba, Barbadoes, &c." (1714–23), Add.

Ms. 39946, BL; [John Wells], "Journal of a Voyage to the Coast of Guinea, 1802," Add. Ms. 3,871, Cambridge University Library; Ship's Log, Vessel Unknown, 1777–78, Royal African Company, T70/1218, NA.

23. Willem Bosman, *A New and Accurate Description of the Coast of Guinea* (London, 1705), 282. West Africans had their own extensive local knowledge of sharks and their own relationships with them. The people of New Calabar were said to consider the shark sacred, but not so the nearby people of Bonny nor the Fante, who called it *samya* and ate it with zeal, as, apparently, did many other seaside peoples. Supporters of the slave trade often emphasized that Africans used sharks in their own systems of social discipline: those convicted of crimes were in some areas thrown into shark-infested waters. Those who survived "trial by shark," and some did, were deemed innocent of the criminal charges. See Captain John Adams, *Sketches taken during Ten Voyages to Africa, Between the Years 1786 and 1800; including Observations on the Country between Cape Palmas and the River Congo; and Cursory Remarks on the Physical and Moral Character of the Inhabitants* (London, 1823; rpt. New York: Johnson Reprint Corporation, 1970), 67; Thomas Winterbottom, *An Account of the Native Africans in the Neighbourhood of Sierra Leone, to which is added An Account of the Present State of Medicine among them* (London, 1803; rpt. London: Frank Cass & Co., 1969), 256; "From a speech given by Mr. Shirley to legislature of Jamaica," *City Gazette and Daily Advertiser,* December 19, 1788; Testimony of Fraser, 1790, *HCSP,* 71:18; *Memoirs of Crow,* 36, 44, 84.

24. *Norwich Packet or, the Country Journal,* April 14, 1785; *Memoirs of Crow,* 266. There are roughly 350 species of sharks in the world today, and about a quarter of these can be found in West African waters. The two most common sharks around the slave ships would have been the bull shark and the tiger shark. Both are common from Senegal to Angola, and both frequent brackish and freshwater bays, lagoons, estuaries, and rivers, moving into waters clear or muddy and shallow, a mere three feet deep, and around jetties and wharves in the harbors, close to human populations. Both have indiscriminate appetites. John Atkins wrote in 1735 of the sharks he encountered in the Sierra Leone River, "In short, their Voracity refuses nothing; Canvas, Ropeyarns, Bones, Blanketing, &c." (Atkins, *A Voyage to Guinea,* 46.) Once trained (in some cases over several months) to regard the ship as a source of food, bull and tiger sharks could have made transatlantic migrations. But a slave ship, as a big floating object, a "moving reef" of sorts in deep oceanic waters, also attracted deep-water species, the blue shark, silky shark, shortfin mako, and oceanic whitefin, which are thinner, faster, and also known to eat human beings. The number of predators would have increased in American coastal waters, as the bull and tiger sharks of the western Atlantic joined the red wake. Sharks thus followed the ships both continuously and in a relay. See Leonard J. V. Compagno, comp., *Sharks of the World: An Annotated and Illustrated Catalogue of Sharks Known to Date* (Rome: United Nations Development Programme, 1984), part 2, 478–81, 503–6.

25. *Connecticut Gazette,* January 30, 1789; *Memoirs of Crow,* 266. For an account of a shark attack in the West Indies in 1704 as recounted by a man who was at the time a sailor deserting a naval vessel, see *A narrative of the wonderful deliverance of Samuel Jennings, Esq.* (no place of publication, 1765).

26. "Natural History of the Shark," 222–23, 231–33; Thomas Pennant, *British Zoology* (Chester: Eliza. Adams, 1768–70), vol. III, 82–83.

NOTES FOR PAGES 41-44

Chapter 2: The Evolution of the Slave Ship

1. Thomas Gordon, *Principles of Naval Architecture, with Proposals for Improving the Form of Ships, to which are added, some Observations on the Structure and Carriages for the Purposes of Inland Commerce, Agriculture, &c.* (London, 1784), 23. See also Robin Blackburn, *The Making of New World Slavery: From the Baroque to the Modern, 1492-1800* (London: Verso, 1997), 376. On the transition to capitalism, see Maurice Dobb, *Studies in the Development of Capitalism* (New York: International Publishers, 1964); Immanuel Wallerstein, *The Modern World-System: Capitalist Agriculture and the Origins of the European World-Economy in the Sixteenth Century* (New York: Academic Press, 1974); Rodney Hilton, ed., *The Transition from Feudalism to Capitalism* (London: New Left Books, 1976); Eric Wolf, *Europe and the People Without History* (Berkeley: University of California Press, 1982).

2. Romola and R. C. Anderson, *The Sailing-Ship: Six Thousand Years of History* (orig. publ. 1926; New York: W. W. Norton, 1963), 129; Basil Greenhill, *The Evolution of the Wooden Ship* (New York: Facts on File, 1988), 67-76. Fascinating work has been done recently by nautical archaeologists, who have excavated and analyzed the material culture of slave ships. See Madeleine Burnside and Rosemarie Robotham, *Spirits of the Passage: The Transatlantic Slave Trade in the Seventeenth Century* (New York: Simon & Schuster, 1997), about the *Henrietta Marie;* Leif Svalesen, *The Slave Ship Fredensborg* (Bloomington: Indiana University Press, 2000). For an overview by an author who has her own important book on the subject forthcoming, see Jane Webster, "Looking for the Material Culture of the Middle Passage," *Journal of Maritime Research* (2005), available online at http://www.jmr.nmm.ac.uk/server/show/ConJmrArticle.209.

3. Carlo Cipolla, *Guns, Sails, and Empires: Technological Innovation and the Early Phases of European Expansion, 1400-1700* (New York: Pantheon Books, 1965).

4. *Memoirs of Crow,* 137. King Holiday made these remarks in 1807, angry that the slave trade was coming to an end. England's king, because he had the big ship, could send "bad people" far away, to Botany Bay, Australia, for example, but now King Holiday could not.

5. Philip Curtin, *The Rise and Fall of the Plantation Complex: Essays in Atlantic History* (Cambridge: Cambridge University Press, 1990), ch. 2.

6. C. L. R. James, *The Black Jacobins: Touissant L'Ouverture and the San Domingo Revolution* (orig. publ. 1938; New York: Vintage, 1989), 85-86; Blackburn, *Making of New World Slavery,* 350.

7. Samuel Martin, *An Essay on Plantership* (London, 1773).

8. Blackburn, *Making of New World Slavery,* 515. The contribution of slavery to the rise of capitalism remains fiercely debated. Highlights and opposing perspectives include Eric Williams, *Capitalism and Slavery* (Chapel Hill: University of North Carolina Press, 1944); Seymour Drescher, *Econocide: British Slavery in the Era of Abolition* (Pittsburgh: University of Pittsburgh Press, 1977); David Eltis and Stanley L. Engerman, "The Importance of Slavery and the Slave Trade to Industrializing Britain," *Journal of Economic History* 60 (2000), 123-44; Kenneth Morgan, *Slavery, Atlantic Trade and the British Economy, 1660-1800* (Cambridge: Cambridge University Press, 2001); Joseph Inikori, *Africans and the Industrial Revolution in England: A Study in International Trade and Economic Development* (Cambridge: Cambridge University Press, 2002).

9. For background on the "floating factory," see Conrad Gill, *Merchants and Mariners in the 18th Century* (London: Edward Arnold, 1961), 91-97.

10. James Field Stanfield, *Observations on a Guinea Voyage, in a Series of Letters Addressed to the Rev. Thomas Clarkson* (London: James Phillips, 1788), 5. For two elaborate listings of outward-bound cargoes, see "Estimate of a Cargo for the *Hungerford* to New Calabar for 400 Negroes, May 1769" and "Estimate of a Cargo for 500 Negroes to Bynin, 1769," both D.M.15, Bristol University Library.

11. Marcus Rediker, *Between the Devil and the Deep Blue Sea: Merchant Seamen, Pirates, and the Anglo-American Maritime World, 1700–1750* (Cambridge: Cambridge University Press, 1987), ch. 2; Emma Christopher, *Slave Ship Sailors and Their Captive Cargoes, 1730–1807* (Cambridge: Cambridge University Press, 2006), ch. 5.

12. James Field Stanfield, *The Guinea Voyage, A Poem in Three Books* (London: James Phillips, 1789), 26; *An Apology for Slavery; or, Six Cogent Arguments against the Immediate Abolition of the Slave Trade* (London, 1792), 45.

13. Malachy Postlethwayt, *The African Trade, the Great Pillar and Support of the British Plantation Trade in America* (London, 1745) and the same author's *The National and Private Advantages of the African Trade Considered: Being an Enquiry, How Far It concerns the Trading Interests of Great Britain, Effectually to Support and Maintain the Forts and Settlements of Africa* (London, 1746).

14. For a discussion of how Postlethwayt's views shifted in the 1750s and 1760s, emphasizing what would come to be called "legitimate commerce" over and against the slave trade and thereby providing an argument for abolitionists such as Thomas Clarkson, see Christopher Leslie Brown, *Moral Capital: Foundations of British Abolitionism* (Chapel Hill: University of North Carolina Press, 2006), 272–74.

15. K. G. Davies, *The Royal African Company* (New York: Atheneum, 1970). For surveys of the slave-trade forts and factories later in the eighteenth century, see "Transcripts of Official Reports and Letters Relating to the State of British Settlements on the Western Coast of Africa in 1765," King's MS #200, BL, and "Sundry Books and Papers Relative to the Commerce to and from Africa delivered to the Secretary of State of the African and American Department by John Roberts, Governor of Cape Coast Castle, 13th December 1779," Egerton 1162A-B, BL. See also Eveline C. Martin, *The British West African Settlements, 1750–1821* (London: Longmans, 1927).

16. John Lord Sheffield, *Observations on the Project for Abolishing the Slave Trade, and on the Reasonableness of attempting some Practicable Mode of Relieving the Negroes* (orig. publ. London, 1790; 2nd edition London, 1791), 21; Roger Anstey, *The Atlantic Slave Trade and Abolition, 1760–1810* (London, 1975) ch. 2, esp. 48, 57; David Richardson, "Profits in the Liverpool Slave Trade: The Accounts of William Davenport, 1757–1784," in Roger Anstey and P. E. H. Hair, eds., *Liverpool, the African Slave Trade, and Abolition* (Chippenham, England: Antony Rowe for the Historical Society of Lancashire and Cheshire, 1976, rpt. 1989), 60–90; Herbert S. Klein, *The Atlantic Slave Trade* (Cambridge: Cambridge University Press, 1999), 98–100; Kenneth Morgan, "James Rogers and the Bristol Slave Trade," *Historical Research* 76 (2003), 189–216.

17. Joseph Manesty to John Bannister, August 2, 1745, John Bannister Letter-Book, no. 66, f. 2, Newport Historical Society, Newport, Rhode Island. The letter is reproduced in Donnan III, 137. On the *Chance*, see *TSTD*, #90018.

18. We have an accounting of one of Manesty's slave-trading voyages. The *Adlington*, John Perkins master, sailed from Liverpool to several locations on the African coast in 1754–55. Perkins delivered 136 slaves (50 men, 25 women, 38 boys, and 23 girls, a few of them "maugre and disordered") to the merchant firm of Case & Southworth in Kingston, Jamaica. After paying the captain's commission, the surgeon's "head money," and the

agent's fee, Manesty received a remittance of £5,047.15.6 (about $1 million in 2007), out of which he would have paid the cost of original trading cargo and the wages for the crew (both unknown). See "Sales of 136 Negroes being the Ship Adlington's Cargoe John Perkins Master, from Africa on acct of Joseph Manesty & Co. Merchts in Liverpool," Case & Southworth Papers, 1755, 380 MD 35, LRO.

19. Manesty to Bannister, June 14, 1747, Bannister Letter-Book, no. 66. Manesty was the primary owner of the ships *Adlington, African, Anson, Bee, Chance, Duke of Argyle, June, Perfect,* and *Spencer.* He owned smaller portions of other vessels, such as the *Swan* and the *Fortune.* Between 1745 and 1758, he would invest in nineteen voyages. See *TSTD,* #90018, #90136–41, #90174, #90350, #90418–9, #90493–5, #90558, #90563, #90569, #90653, #90693. According to Elizabeth Donnan, John Bannister was descended of Boston merchants and came to Newport after 1733. He was himself a merchant and an investor in privateering. It seems likely that he was a middleman who offered connections to shipbuilders rather than a shipbuilder himself. Bannister would soon order his own vessel for the slave trade. He was sole owner of the *Hardman,* Joseph Yowart, master, a snow that made three voyages from Liverpool to Africa and the West Indies between 1749 and 1754 (*TSTD,* #90150–90152).

20. Joseph Manesty to Joseph Harrison, from Liverpool, September 10, 1745, in Donnan III, 138.

21. For two other orders for likely slavers, placed by members of the leading slave-trading family of New England, the D'Wolfs of Bristol, Rhode Island, see "Agreement between William and James D'Wolf and John, Joseph and Joseph Junr Kelly of Warren," January 8, 1797, Folder B-10, Ship's Accounts; and "Memorandum of an Agreement between John and James D'Wolf and builder William Barton," March 13, 1805, Folder B-3, *Orozimbo,* Captain Oliver Wilson; both in the James D'Wolf Papers, Bristol Historical Society, Bristol, Rhode Island.

22. M. K. Stammers, "'Guineamen': Some Technical Aspects of Slave Ships," *Transatlantic Slavery: Against Human Dignity,* ed. Anthony Tibbles (London: HMSO, 1994), 40. It should be noted that slavers got smaller, faster, and cheaper after abolition, to avoid detection and escape capture by naval patrols and to lessen expense if taken. Regarding the pitch and roll of a vessel, see the complaint by merchant John Guerard that many slaves "by fatigue and Tumbling about have suffered insomuch that they are now very much the worse for it." See John Guerard to William Jolliffe, August 25, 1753, John Guerard letter book, 164–67, South Carolina Historical Society, Charleston.

23. Here and throughout the book, ship tonnage refers not to weight but to carrying capacity, and this none too precisely. The "tun" in medieval times referred to a cask (roughly forty cubic feet in capacity) for the shipment of wine between France and England. A vessel that could carry a hundred "tuns" was a one-hundred-ton vessel. But over time tonnage took on other meanings and was computed in a variety of ways, from nation to nation and within nations. A transition from "registered ton" to "measured ton" was mandated in Britain by an act of Parliament in 1786. I have made no effort to standardize tonnage figures and have consistently given them as originally reported in primary sources. For a survey of the subject, see Frederick C. Lane, "Tonnages, Medieval and Modern," *Economic History Review* 17 (1964), 213–33.

24. One of these vessels might have become the *Anson,* built in Newburyport, Massachusetts, and named for the admiral who circumnavigated the globe and captured a vessel in Spain's treasure fleet in 1744–45, or the *Swan,* which was built in Swansea, Massachusetts. See *TSTD,* #90174, #90160–90162. For prices of other slave ships, see

Ralph Inman to Peleg Clarke, Boston, May 11, 1772, in Donnan III, 257; Roderick Terry, ed., "Some Old Papers Relating to the Newport Slave Trade," *Bulletin of the Newport Historical Society* 62 (1927), 12–13; *Wilson v. Sandys,* Accounts for the Slave Ships *Barbados Packet, Meredith, Snow Juno, Saville,* and *Cavendish:* Liverpool, St. Christophers, Grenada, 1771, Chancery (C) 109/401, NA.

25. Manesty to Harrison, in Donnan III, 138.

26. J. H. Parry, *Trade and Dominion: The European Oversea Empires in the Eighteenth Century* (London: Weidenfeld and Nicolson, 1971), 12; Anderson and Anderson, *The Sailing-Ship,* 178; Joseph A. Goldenberg, *Shipbuilding in Colonial America* (Charlottesville: University of Virginia Press, 1976), 32–33; Stephen D. Behrendt, "Markets, Transaction Cycles, and Profits: Merchant Decision Making in the British Slave Trade," *William and Mary Quarterly* 3rd ser. 58 (2001), 171–204.

27. Ronald Stewart-Brown, *Liverpool Ships in the Eighteenth Century, including the King's Ships built there with Notes on the Principal Shipwrights* (Liverpool: University of Liverpool Press, 1932), 75.

28. David M. Williams, "The Shipping of the British Slave Trade in its Final Years, 1798–1807," *International Journal of Maritime History* 12 (2000), 1–25.

29. This paragraph draws heavily on Goldenberg, *Shipbuilding in Colonial America,* 55–56, 89. On the hearth and furnace, see John Fletcher to Captain Peleg Clarke, London, October 16, 1771, Peleg Clarke Letter-Book, Newport Historical Society, no. 75 A.

30. See William Sutherland, *The Shipbuilder's Assistant* (1711); idem, *Britain's Glory; or, Ship-Building Unvail'd, being a General Director for Building and Compleating the said Machines* (1729); John Hardingham, *The Accomplish'd Shipwright* (1706); Mungo Murray, *Elements of Naval Architecture* (1764); Fredrik Henrik af Chapman, *Architecturia Mercatoria Navalis* (1768); Marmaduke Stalkartt, *Naval Architecture* (1787); William Hutchinson, *Treatise on Naval Architecture* (1794); David Steel, *The Elements and Practice of Rigging and Seamanship* (London, 1794); idem, *The Ship-Master's Assistant and Owner's Manual* (London, 1803); idem, *The Elements and Practice of Naval Architecture* (1805); Thomas Gordon, *Principles of Naval Architecture.* No books on shipbuilding were published in British North America in the eighteenth century, so shipwrights used these books and followed European design. See Howard I. Chapelle, *The Search for Speed Under Sail, 1700–1855* (New York: W. W. Norton, 1967), 6–8.

31. Chapelle, *Search for Speed,* 412–14.

32. William Falconer, *Universal Dictionary of the Marine* (London: T. Cadell, 1769; revised edition, 1784), s.v., "architecture (naval)"; *Rules and Orders of the Society for the Improvement of Naval Architecture* (London, 1791); *An Address to the Public, from the Society for the Improvement of Naval Architecture* (London, 1791); *Catalogue of Books on Naval Architecture* (London, 1791); *An Address to the Public, from the Society for the Improvement of Naval Architecture* (London, 1792); *Report of the Committee for Conducting the Experiments of the Society for the Improvement of Naval Architecture* (London, 1799), 1 (quotation).

33. "An Account of Men Belonging to the Snow Peggy the 13th of August 1748," Anthony Fox, Master, 1748–1749, Muster Rolls, vol. I (1748–1751), Society of Merchant Venturers Archives, BRO. See *TSTD,* #77579. For background see Ralph Davis, *The Rise of the English Shipping Industry in the Seventeenth and Eighteenth Centuries* (London: Macmillan, 1962), chs. 6–7; Rediker, *Between the Devil and the Deep Blue Sea,* ch.2; Peter Earle, *Sailors: English Merchant Seamen, 1650–1775* (London: Methuen, 1998).

34. Barnaby Slush, *The Navy Royal: or a Sea-Cook Turn'd Projector* (London, 1709), viii. For a typical wage scheme for all members of a ship's crew, see "A List of the Seamen

on board Ship Christopher Ent'd 19 June 1791," in "Ship Christopher's Book, 4th Voyage," Rare Book, Manuscript and Special Collections Library, Duke University.

35. W.S. (William Snelgrave), "Instructions for a First Mate When in the Road at Whydah," n.d., Humphrey Morice Papers, Bank of England Archive, London.

36. Rhode Island mate Thomas Eldred testified that it was "the common Practice, in Ships trading from America to Africa, to have no Surgeon on board." Rather, they administered medicine "by a Book of Directions which they had on Board." See Testimony of Thomas Eldred, 1789, *HCSP*, 69:166.

37. The quotations in this and the following paragraph come from Clarkson, *History,* 1:327–30. One of the small vessels may have been the *Fly*, a twenty-seven-ton vessel commanded by Captain James Walker, which departed Bristol on August 7, 1787, for Sierra Leone, where it would pick up thirty-five captives and take them to Tortola. See *TSTD*, #17783. For information on the larger London vessel with the same name, see *TSTD*, #81477.

38. On how much space captives had belowdecks, see Charles Garland and Herbert S. Klein, "The Allotment of Space for Slaves Aboard Eighteenth-Century British Slave Ships," *William and Mary Quarterly* 3rd ser. 42 (1985), 238–48.

39. *TSTD*, #90950, #3777, #4405, #36299, #36406.

40. Stewart-Brown, *Liverpool Ships in the Eighteenth Century,* 29, 127–29. See *TSTD,* #83006. For examples of other major disasters, see *TSTD,* #90157 (*Marton,* with 420 captives, reported in the *Georgia Gazette,* December 3, 1766); #78101 (*New Britannia,* with 330 captives, reported in *Connecticut Journal,* August 20, 1773); #82704 (*Mercury,* with 245 captives, reported in *Enquirer,* September 26, 1804); #25648 (*Independence,* with 200 captives, reported in the *American Mercury,* August 20, 1807).

41. Hayley and Hopkins to Aaron Lopez, London, July 20, 1774, in Donnan III, 291; Walter Minchinton, "Characteristics of British Slaving Vessels, 1698–1775," *Journal of Interdisciplinary History* 20 (1989), 53–81. According to data in the *TSTD*, Dutch slave ships tended to be the eighteenth century's largest, at an average of 300 tons, followed by French slavers at 247 tons. The average vessel sailing out of North America was about 100 tons. Stephen D. Behrendt makes an important point: "In general, merchants sent small Guineamen to politically decentralized coastal markets with intermittent slave supplies and larger Guineamen to ports or lagoon sites with the political centralization and commercial infrastructures to maintain large-scale slave shipments." See his "Markets, Transaction Cycles, and Profits," 188.

42. *Newport Mercury,* January 7, 1765.

43. *Pennsylvania Gazette,* June 21, 1753. Falconer, *Universal Dictionary of the Marine,* s.v., "sloop."

44. *City Gazette and Daily Advertiser,* November 28, 1796; Falconer, *Universal Dictionary of the Marine,* s.v., "ship."

45. *South-Carolina State Gazette and Timothy's Daily Adviser,* May 7, 1800; Sir Jeremiah Fitzpatrick, M.D., *Suggestions on the Slave Trade, for the Consideration of the Legislature of Great Britain* (London: John Stockdale, 1797), 6, 17, 62. A bark was another three-masted ship, square-rigged on the fore and mainmasts but fore-and-aft-rigged on the mizzen, without a mizzen topsail. It was much less common than the ship.

46. Reverend John Riland, *Memoirs of a West-India Planter, Published from an Original MS. With a Preface and Additional Details* (London: Hamilton, Adams & Co., 1827). Riland was born in Jamaica in 1778 and sent as a youth to England for schooling. Adam Hochschild has pointed out that the editors of this posthumously published volume in-

cluded plagiarized passages from an account of a slaving voyage by the abolitionist Zachary Macaulay, which had been published in the *Christian Observer* in 1804. It was republished in Viscountess Knutsford, ed., *Life and Letters of Zachary Macaulay* (London: Edward Arnold, 1900), 86–89. See Adam Hochschild, *Bury the Chains: Prophets and Rebels in the Fight to Free an Empire's Slaves* (Boston: Houghton Mifflin, 2005), 253–55, 398. Readers should keep in mind that the evidence presented in this section comes from not one but two distinct voyages and sources.

47. I have discovered two vessels named *Liberty,* although neither comports with Riland's time line. The first sailed in 1795–1796, probably from London to an unidentified port in Africa and from there to Barbados. The second sailed from Liverpool to Angola to St. Kitts in 1806–1807. Macaulay sailed on the *Ann Phillipa* from Liverpool to Sierra Leone to Kingston in 1794–1795. For more information about each, see *TSTD,* #82252, #82254, #80291.

48. When Riland sailed on the slaver he was a person of mixed allegiances. He had sympathy for the antislavery cause, but he also had a strong vested interest in the slave system as he himself readily acknowledged. Once aboard the ship, he began to feel that his "fortunes [were] identified with the commercial prosperity of the colonies," which included the slave trade. He was also conscious that his voyage "was a very favorable specimen of such adventures."

49. I have inferred the tonnage of Riland's vessel from the number of slaves brought on board, using a ratio created by the Dolben Act of 1788—roughly 1.8 slaves per one ton carrying capacity. Macaulay's vessel (144 tons) loaded 244 enslaved Africans and delivered 225 alive in Kingston.

50. According to William Falconer's *Universal Dictionary of the Marine,* gratings were "a sort of open covers for the hatches, formed by several small laths or battens of wood, which cross each other at right angles, leaving a square interval between. They are formed to admit the air and light from above into the lower apartments of the ship, particularly when the turbulence of the sea or weather renders it necessary to shut the ports between decks."

51. Falconer, *Universal Dictionary of the Marine,* s.v., "boat," "long-boat," "yawl"; Stammers, "Guineamen," 40.

52. Thomas Clarkson noted that "the Stern Part of the Vessel is the place, first, where the Arm Chest stands, and secondly, where the Vessel is principally worked. Hence the weakest [captives, often little girls] are put into Stern Division." See Clarkson to Comte de Mirabeau, November 17, 1789, ff. 3–4, Papers of Thomas Clarkson, Huntington Library, San Marino, California. For a public auction of "Four large IRON BOILERS, suitable for a guineaman or vessel of war," see *South-Carolina State Gazette and Timothy's Daily Adviser,* June 14, 1799. On "Guinea casks," see William B. Weeden, *Economic and Social History of New England, 1620–1789* (New York: Hillary House Publishers, Ltd., 1963), vol. II, 458.

53. On sheathing methods see the *Providence Gazette; and Country Journal,* July 7, 1770, and April 9, 1774.

54. *Newport Mercury,* March 25, 1809. The earliest reference I have found to copper sheathing appeared in the records of the Royal African Company in the 1720s. See Ship's Book (unidentified), 1722–24, Treasury (T) 70/1227, NA.

55. According to a letter from Liverpool of August 15, 1791, "This day a new ship for the African trade, called the Carnatic, was launched from a slip near the king's dock, for the same respectable merchant; she is sheathed upon a new principle of coppering—the

sheets being all wrought cold, instead of the usual mode by fire, from which great advantages are expected." See *City Gazette and Daily Advertiser,* October 26, 1791 and *TSTD,* #80733.

56. Falconer, *Universal Dictionary of the Marine,* s.v. "windsail."

57. *Connecticut Centinel,* August 2, 1804.

58. *Providence Gazette; and Country Journal,* August, 5, 1790.

59. *Providence Gazette,* July 19, 1800.

Chapter 3: African Paths to the Middle Passage

1. This and the next three paragraphs are based on Joseph Hawkins, *A History of a Voyage to the Coast of Africa, and Travels into the Interior of that Country; containing Particular Descriptions of the Climate and Inhabitants, particulars concerning the Slave Trade* (Troy, N.Y.: Luther Pratt, 2nd edition, 1797), 18–149. Hawkins was a young man of no property but some education, who worked as supercargo aboard the slave ship *Charleston* on a voyage of 1794–95. For a survey of the Rio Pongas region in this period, see Bruce L. Mouser, "Trade, Coasters, and Conflict in the Rio Pongo from 1790 to 1808," *Journal of African History,* 14 (1973), 45–64.

2. Hawkins called the adversaries in this war "Galla" and "Ebo." Location inland from the Windward Coast suggests that the former were the Gola but that the latter were not the Igbo, who lived several hundred miles to the east in present-day Nigeria. I have tentatively identified the "Ebo" as Ibau based on information in George Peter Murdock, *Africa: Its People and Their Culture History* (New York: MacGraw-Hill Book Company, 1959), 91.

3. J. D. Fage questioned (but did not finally reject) the authenticity of Hawkins's account in "Hawkins' Hoax? A Sequel to 'Drake's Fake,'" *History in Africa* 18 (1991), 83–91. Additional evidence has now come to light to support its credibility. First, Fage did not know about the Ibau and therefore wrongly assumed that Hawkins had misplaced the Igbo on the Windward Coast. Second, the clearance of the *Charleston* was noted in the *City Gazette and Daily Advertiser* on January 5, 1795, and its return in July 1795 in the same newspaper (July 24, 1795, August 5, 7, and 15, 1795) and in the *Columbian Herald or the Southern Star* (August 14, 1795), where a sale of a "cargo of Prime Slaves" was advertised. These dates square with Hawkins's account. Third, Hawkins advertised his book in Charleston's *City Gazette and Daily Advertiser* (March 14 and 15, 1797, August 16, 1797), which he would not likely have done had it been fraudulent.

4. The idea of the Middle Passage as concept, linking expropriation in one location to exploitation in another, was suggested in Peter Linebaugh and Marcus Rediker, *The Many-Headed Hydra: Sailors, Slaves, Commoners, and the Hidden History of the Revolutionary Atlantic* (Boston: Beacon Press, 2000). The idea was developed in various ways in essays that appeared in Marcus Rediker, Cassandra Pybus, and Emma Christopher, eds., *Many Middle Passages: Forced Migration and the Making of the Modern World* (Berkeley: University of California Press, 2007).

5. In this section and the six that follow (on the basic regions of trade), I have drawn on the following major interpretive works: Walter Rodney, "The Guinea Coast," in J. D. Fage and Roland Olivier, eds., *The Cambridge History of Africa* (Cambridge: Cambridge University Press, 1975), vol. 4, *From c. 1600 to c. 1790;* J. D. Fage, *A History of West Africa* (London: Cambridge University Press, 1969), 4th edition; J. F. Ajayi and Michael Crowder, *History of West Africa* (London: Longman, 1971, 1974), 2 vols.; Elizabeth Allo Isichei, *A*

History of African Societies to 1870 (Cambridge: Cambridge University Press, 1997); John Thornton, *Africa and Africans in the Making of the Atlantic World, 1400–1800* (Cambridge: Cambridge University Press, 1992; 2nd edition, 1998); Michael A. Gomez, *Exchanging Our Country Marks: The Transformation of African Identities in the Colonial and Antebellum South* (Chapel Hill: University of North Carolina Press, 1998); Paul E. Lovejoy, *Transformations in Slavery: A History of Slavery in Africa* (Cambridge: Cambridge University Press, 2000), 2nd edition; Christopher Ehret, *The Civilizations of Africa: A History to 1800* (Charlottesville: University of Virginia Press, 2002); Michael A. Gomez, *Reversing Sail: A History of the African Diaspora* (Cambridge: Cambridge University Press, 2005); and Patrick Manning, *The African Diaspora: A History Through Culture* (New York: Columbia University Press, forthcoming, 2008). Also valuable have been Herbert S. Klein, *The Middle Passage: Comparative Studies in the Atlantic Slave Trade* (Princeton: Princeton University Press, 1978); idem, *The Atlantic Slave Trade* (Cambridge: Cambridge University Press, 1999); Johannes Postma, *The Atlantic Slave Trade* (Westport, Conn.: Greenwood Press, 2003). Specialized studies for each region are listed in following sections.

6. Manning, *African Diaspora*; Eric Wolf, *Europe and the People Without History* (Berkeley: University of California Press, 1982), 206.

7. Walter Rodney, *A History of the Upper Guinea Coast, 1545–1800* (Oxford: Clarendon Press, 1970), 114.

8. *South Carolina Gazette,* August 3, 1784.

9. A more modern transcription would be Ayub ibn Suleiman, ibn Ibrahim, or Ayuba Suleyman Diallo.

10. Thomas Bluett, *Some Memoirs of the Life of Job, the Son of Solomon, the High Priest of Boonda in Africa, Who was a Slave about two years in Maryland; and afterwards being brought to England, was set free, and sent to his native Land in the year 1734* (London, 1734), 12–17, 44–48; Job ben Solomon to Mr. Smith, January 27, 1735–36, in Donnan II, 455; Francis Moore, *Travels into the Inland Parts of Africa* (London, 1738), 69, 204–9, 223–24. See also Arthur Pierce Middleton, "The Strange Story of Job Ben Solomon," *William and Mary Quarterly* 3rd series, 5 (1948), 342–50; Douglas Grant, *The Fortunate Slave: An Illustration of African Slavery in the Early Eighteenth Century* (London: Oxford University Press, 1968).

11. Richard Roberts, *Warriors, Merchants, and Slaves: The State and the Economy in the Middle Niger Valley, 1700–1914* (Stanford, Calif.: Stanford University Press, 1987), ch. 3.

12. Sylviane A. Diouf, *Servants of Allah: African Muslims Enslaved in the Americas* (New York: New York University Press, 1998), 164–66; Michael A. Gomez, *Black Crescent: The Experience and Legacy of African Muslims in the Americas* (Cambridge: Cambridge University Press, 2005), 68–70; James F. Searing, *West African Slavery and Atlantic Commerce: The Senegal River Valley, 1700–1860* (New York: Cambridge University Press, 1993); Boubacar Barry, *Senegambia and the Atlantic Slave Trade* (Cambridge: Cambridge University Press, 1998); Donald R. Wright, *The World and a Very Small Place in Africa* (London: ME Sharpe Inc., 2004).

13. Nicholas Owen, *Journal of a Slave-Dealer: A View of Some Remarkable Axedents in the Life of Nics. Owen on the Coast of Africa and America from the Year 1746 to the Year 1757,* ed. Eveline Martin (Boston: Houghton Mifflin, 1930), 76; John Newton, *Journal of a Slave Trader, 1750–1754,* ed. Bernard Martin and Mark Spurrell (London: Epworth Press, 1962), 43.

14. Walter Hawthorne, *Planting Rice and Harvesting Slaves: Transformations Along the Guinea-Bissau Coast, 1400–1900* ((Portsmouth, N.H.: Heinemann, 2003), ch. 3; George E. Brooks, *Eurafricans in Western Africa: Commerce, Social Status, Gender, and*

Religious Observance from the Sixteenth to the Eighteenth Century (Athens: Ohio University Press, 2003), 178, 246–47; Rosalind Shaw, *Memories of the Slave Trade: Ritual and the Historical Imagination in Sierra Leone* (Chicago: University of Chicago Press, 2002); L. Day, "Afro-British Integration on the Sherbro Coast, 1665–1795," *Africana Research Bulletin* 12 (1983), 82–107; Rodney, "The Rise of the Mulatto Traders" in *History of the Upper Guinea Coast.*

15. Accounts of Fort Commenda, October 23, 1714; "Diary and Accounts, Commenda Fort, In Charge of William Brainie, 1714–1718," in Donnan II, 186; David Henige, "John Kabes of Kommenda: An Early African Entrepreneur and State Builder," *Journal of African History* 13 (1977), 1–19. Henige writes, "Kabes was an employee of the Royal African Company in the sense that he was on its payroll and unquestionably performed useful services in its behalf. But he was not—and did not consider himself to be—its 'servant' " (10).

16. Yaw M. Boateng, *The Return: A Novel of the Slave Trade in Africa* (New York: Pantheon Books, 1977), vii.

17. Ray A. Kea, *Settlements, Trade, and Polities in the Seventeenth-Century Gold Coast* (Baltimore: Johns Hopkins University Press, 1982); Kwame Yeboa Daaku, *Trade and Politics on the Gold Coast: 1600–1720: A Study of the African Reaction to European Trade* (New York: Oxford University Press, 1970); Rebecca Shumway, "Between the Castle and the Golden Stool: Transformations in Fante Society, 1700–1807," Ph.D. dissertation, Emory University, 2004; William St. Clair, *The Grand Slave Emporium: Cape Coast Castle and the British Slave Trade* (London: Profile Books, 2006). See also two articles by Peter C. W. Gutkind, "Trade and Labor in Early Precolonial African History: The Canoemen of Southern Ghana," in Catherine Coquery-Vidrovitch and Paul E. Lovejoy, eds., *The Workers of the African Trade* (Beverly Hills: Sage, 1985), 25–50; "The Boatmen of Ghana: The Possibilities of a Pre-Colonial African Labor History," in Michael Hanagan and Charles Stephenson, eds., *Confrontation, Class Consciousness and the Labor Process* (New York: Greenwood Press, 1986), 123–66.

18. James Field Stanfield, *Observations on a Guinea Voyage, in a Series of Letters Addressed to the Rev. Thomas Clarkson* (London: James Phillips, 1788), 20; Interview of Henry Ellison, in *Substance,* 218–19; Testimony of Henry Ellison, 1790, in *HCSP,* 368–69, 383.

19. C. W. Newbury, *The Western Slave Coast and Its Rulers* (Oxford: Clarendon Press, 1961); Patrick Manning, *Slavery, Colonialism and Economic Growth in Dahomey, 1640–1960* (Cambridge: Cambridge University Press, 1982); Robin Law, *The Slave Coast of West Africa 1550–1750: The Impact of the Atlantic Slave Trade on an African Society* (Oxford: Clarendon Press, 1991); Robin Law, *The Oyo Empire, c.1600–c.1836: A West African Imperialism in the Era of the Atlantic Slave Trade* (Oxford: Clarendon Press, 1977); Robin Law and Kristin Mann, "West Africa in the Atlantic Community: The Case of the Slave Coast," *William and Mary Quarterly* 3rd series, 54 (1999), 307–34.

20. Antera Duke's diary appears in two forms, an original text in pidgin English and a "modern English version," in C. Daryl Forde, ed., *Efik Traders of Old Calabar . . . ; The Diary of Antera Duke, an Efik Slave-Trading Chief of the Eighteenth Century* (London, 1956), 27–115. See the entries for the following days: June 5, 1787; August 29, 1785; January 27, 1788; April 8, 1785; September 26, 1785; December 25, 1787 (a Christmas Day party); October 9, 1786; October 5, 1786; May 26, 1785; October 23, 1785; Mar. 21, 1785; January 30, 1785; August 9, 1786 June 27, 1785. Early in his career, in late 1769 and early 1770, Duke was one of thirty Old Calabar traders who sold slaves to Captain John Potter of the *Dobson.* Duke himself sold thirty-seven, along with a thousand yams, for which

he earned 4,400 coppers, the equivalent of 1,100 iron bars or 550 kegs of gunpowder. See P. E. H. Hair, "Antera Duke of Old Calabar—A Little More About an African Entrepreneur," *History in Africa* 17 (1990), 359–65.

21. Twenty vessels (which made twenty-five voyages) mentioned by Duke can be found in the slave-trade database. The actual and (in eight cases) imputed number of slaves shipped on these voyages was 10,285 (although not all from Old Calabar), an average of 411 per ship. See *TSTD*, #81258, #82312, #81407, #81841, #82233, #82326, #83268, #83708, #81353, #81559, #81560, #81583, #82362, #82543, #83063, #81913, #82327, #83168, #83169, #83178, #84050, #83365, #83709, #84018, #84019.

22. For an excellent study of an important event in the history of the region, see Randy J. Sparks, *The Two Princes of Calabar: An Eighteenth-Century Atlantic Odyssey* (Cambridge, Mass.: Harvard University Press, 2004).

23. Robin Horton, "From Fishing Village to City-State: A Social History of New Calabar," in Mary Douglas and Phyllis M. Kaberry, eds., *Man in Africa* (London: 1969), 37–61; A. J. H. Latham, *Old Calabar, 1600–1891: The Impact of the International Economy upon a Traditional Society* (Oxford: Clarendon Press, 1973); David Northrup, *Trade Without Rulers: Pre-Colonial Economic Development in South-Eastern Nigeria* (Oxford: Clarendon, 1978); Elizabeth Allo Isichei, *A History of the Igbo People* (New York: St. Martin's Press, 1976); Douglas B. Chambers, " 'My own nation': Igbo Exiles in the Diaspora," *Slavery and Abolition* 18 (1997), 72–97; David Northrup, "Igbo: Culture and Ethnicity in the Atlantic World," *Slavery and Abolition* 71 (2000); Douglas B. Chambers, "Ethnicity in the Diaspora: The Slave Trade and the Creation of African 'Nations' in the Americas," *Slavery and Abolition* 22 (2001), 25–39; Douglas B. Chambers, "The Significance of Igbo in the Night of Biafra Slave-Trade: A Rejoinder to Northrup's 'Myth Igbo,' " *Slavery and Abolition* 23 (2002), 101–20; Douglas B. Chambers, *Murder at Montpelier: Igbo African in Virginia* (Jackson: University of Mississippi Press, 2005).

24. Robert Harms, *River of Wealth, River of Sorrow: The Central Zaire Basin in the Era of the Slave and Ivory Trade, 1500–1891* (New Haven: Yale University Press, 1981), 7, 8, 27, 33, 35, 92.

25. David Birmingham, *Trade and Conflict in Angola: The Mbundu and Their Neighbors Under the Influence of the Portuguese, 1483–1790* (Oxford: Oxford University Press, 1966); John K. Thornton, *The Kingdom of Kongo: Civil War and Transition, 1641–1718* (Madison: University of Wisconsin Press, 1983); Harms, *River of Wealth, River of Sorrow*; Joseph Miller, *Way of Death: Merchant Capitalism and the Angolan Slave Trade, 1730–1830* (1988); Herbert S. Klein, "The Portuguese Slave Trade from Angola in the Eighteenth Century," *Journal of Economic History* 32 (1972), 894–918.

26. Testimony of Robert Norris, 1789, in *HCSP* 69:38–39. See also John Thornton, *Africa and Africans*, 99–105.

27. "Anonymous Account of the Society and Trade of the Canary Islands and West Africa, with Observations on the Slave Trade" (n.d., but c. 1784), Add. Ms. 59777B, f. 42v, BL; John Matthews, *A Voyage to the River Sierra Leone, on the Coast of Africa, containing an Account of the Trade and Productions of the Country, and of the Civil and Religious Customs and Manners of the People; in a Series of Letters to a Friend in England* (London: B. White and Son, 1788), 85–86; John Atkins, *A Voyage to Guinea, Brasil, and the West Indies; In His Majesty's Ships, the Swallow and Weymouth* (London, 1735; rpt. London: Frank Cass, 1970), 176; Testimony of Thomas Trotter, 1790, in *HCSP*, 73:83–84; Thomas Clarkson, *An Essay on the Slavery and Commerce of the Human Species, particularly the African, translated from a Latin Dissertation, which was honoured with the First Prize in the*

University of Cambridge for the Year 1785, with Additions (London, 1786; rpt. Miami, Fla.: Mnemosyne Publishing Co., 1969), 45; Testimony of Henry Ellison, 1790, *HCSP,* 73:381. See also John Thornton, *Warfare in Atlantic Africa: 1500–1800* (London: Routledge, 1999), 128. On the import of guns into West Africa, especially for the period 1750–1807, see J. E. Inikori, "The Import of Firearms into West Africa 1750–1807: A Quantitative Analysis," *Journal of African History* 18 (1977), 339–68 and W. A. Richards. "The Import of Firearms into West Africa in the Eighteenth Century," *Journal of African History* 21 (1980), 43–59.

28. Moore, *Travels into the Inland Parts of Africa,* 30; Rodney, *History of the Upper Guinea Coast,* 114.

29. Barry, *Senegambia and the Atlantic Slave Trade,* 6–7.

30. Atkins, *A Voyage to Guinea,* 180; Bruce Mouser, ed., *A Slaving Voyage to Africa and Jamaica: The Log of the* Sandown, *1793–1794* (Bloomington: Indiana University Press, 2002), 81–82; Thomas Clarkson, *Letters on the Slave-Trade and the State of the Natives in those Parts of Africa which are Contiguous to Fort St. Louis and Goree* (London, 1791).

31. Robert Norris wrote that the "Mahees" resisted enslavement by the king of Dahomey in the 1750s and 1760s by escaping to rugged, inaccessible mountain terrain, where they defended themselves. See his *Memoirs of the Reign of Bossa Ahádee, King of Dahomy, an Inland Country of Guiney, to which are added the Author's Journey to Abomey, the Capital, and a Sort Account of the African Slave Trade* (orig. publ. London, 1789; rpt. London: Frank Cass and Company Limited, 1968), 21–22. See also Ismail Rashid, "'A Devotion to the Idea of Liberty at Any Price': Rebellion and Antislavery in the Upper Guinea Coast in the Eighteenth and Nineteenth Centuries," in Sylviane A. Diouf, ed., *Fighting the Slave Trade: West African Strategies* (Athens: Ohio University Press, 2003), 137, 142.

32. Alexander Falconbridge, *An Account of the Slave Trade on the Coast of Africa* (London, 1788), 20. On children, see Audra A. Diptee, "African Children in the British Slave Trade During the Late Eighteenth Century," *Slavery and Abolition* 27 (2006), 183–96, and Paul E. Lovejoy, "The Children of Slavery—the Transatlantic Phase," ibid., 197–217.

33. Captain William Snelgrave, *A New Account of Some Parts of Guinea and the Slave Trade* (London, 1734; rpt. London: Frank Cass & Co., 1971), 49; *Memoirs of Crow,* 199–200; Patrick Manning, "Primitive Art and Modern Times," *Radical History Review* 33 (1985), 165–81.

34. The grand pillage is described in Clarkson, *Letters on the Slave-Trade,* based on his conversations with Geoffrey de Villeneuve, aide-de-camp to the French governor of the slave-trading port Goree in Senegambia. See Letter II.

35. Louis Asa-Asa was apparently born soon after the movements to abolish the slave trade had succeeded in Britain and the United States, then transported out of West Afria on a French ship, and on both scores his life falls outside the formal boundaries of our exploration. Yet what he conveyed fits well with surviving evidence of the British and American trades in the earlier period, and in any case African narratives of the slave trade are so rare as to make his brief but vivid account extremely valuable. See "Narrative of Louis Asa-Asa, a Captured African," in *The History of Mary Prince, a West Indian Slave, Related by Herself,* ed. Moira Ferguson (orig. publ. London and Edinburgh, 1831; rpt. Ann Arbor: University of Michigan Press, 1993), 121–24.

36. I have not been able to identify the Adinyé warriors.

37. The chronology of Louis Asa-Asa's life is confused, and indeed he may have worked on a New World plantation, even though the account assembled by Thomas

Prince implies that Asa-Asa came from Sierra Leone directly to England. When he said that "friends and relations" in Egie were captured by the Adinyé and carried away as slaves, he added, "I know this because I afterwards saw them as slaves on the other side of the sea."

38. *Narrative of the Most Remarkable Particulars in the Life of James Albert Ukawsaw Gronniosaw, African Prince, As related by Himself* (Bath, 1770).

39. Mungo Park, *Travels into the Interior of Africa, Performed under the Direction and Patronage of the African Association, in the Years 1795, 1796, and 1797,* ed. Kate Ferguson Marsters (orig. publ. 1799; rpt. Durham, N.C., and London: Duke University Press, 2000), 303.

40. John Newton, *Thoughts upon the African Slave Trade* (London, 1788), 23–24.

41. Testimony of Ellison, in *HCSP,* 73:381.

42. For explorations of the experience see Maria Diedrich, Henry Louis Gates, Jr., and Carl Pedersen, eds., *Black Imagination and the Middle Passage* (New York: Oxford University Press, 1999).

Chapter 4: Olaudah Equiano: Astonishment and Terror

1. Olaudah Equiano, *The Interesting Narrative of the Life of Olaudah Equiano, or Gustavus Vassa, the African. Written by Himself* (London, 1789), reprinted in *The Interesting Narrative and Other Writings* (New York: Penguin, 1995), ed. Vincent Carretta, 55–56 (hereafter cited, Equiano, *Interesting Narrative*). For biographies of Equiano, see James Walvin, *An African's Life: The Life and Times of Olaudah Equiano, 1745–1797* (London: Cassell, 1998) and Vincent Carretta, *Equiano the African: Biography of a Self-Made Man* (Athens and London: University of Georgia Press, 2005); see also the essay by the distinguished Nigerian historian Adiele Afigbo, "Through a Glass Darkly: Eighteenth-Century Igbo Society through Equiano's Narrative," in his *Ropes of Sand: Studies in Igbo History and Culture* (Ibadan: University Press Ltd., 1981), 145–86.

2. I agree with scholars such as Paul Lovejoy and Alexander X. Byrd who have argued that Equiano's deep knowledge of Igbo culture, language included, supports his claim that he was indeed born where he said he was. See Carretta, *Equiano the African,* xi–xix; Alexander X. Byrd, "Eboe, Country, Nation, and Gustavus Vassa's *Interesting Narrative,*" *William and Mary* Quarterly 3rd ser. 63(2006), 123–48; Paul Lovejoy, "Autobiography and Memory: Gustavus Vassa, alias Olaudah Equiano, the African," *Slavery and Abolition* 27 (2006), 317–47. Byrd notes that if Equiano was born in South Carolina, he could only have learned what he did through "prodigious listening" (143). A useful exploration of Equiano's use of African philosophy is Paul Edwards and Rosalind Shaw, "The Invisible *Chi* in Equiano's *Interesting Narrative,*" *Journal of Religion in Africa* 19 (1989) 146–56.

3. Most would agree with Carretta's claim that in writing about enslavement and the Middle Passage Equiano "has spoken for millions of his fellow diasporan Africans." See Carretta, *Equiano the African,* xix; Afigbo, "Through a Glass Darkly," 147. For a useful discussion of the few first-person African accounts of the Middle Passage and the slave trade, see Jerome S. Handler, "Survivors of the Middle Passage: Life Histories of Enslaved Africans in British America," *Slavery and Abolition* 23 (2002), 25–56. I follow Carretta in treating Equiano's depiction of his early life as if true and request that the reader keep in mind that his account might embody a collective lore.

4. Three locations have been suggested as Equiano's birthplace. G. I. Jones put forward Northern Ika Igbo province; Adiele Afigbo advanced Nsukke in northern Igbo

land; and Catherine Obianju Acholonu (along with others) has suggested Isseke. See G. I. Jones, "Olaudah Equiano of the Niger Ibo," in Philip D. Curtin, ed., *Africa Remembered: Narratives by West Africans from the Era of the Slave Trade* (Madison: University of Wisconsin Press, 1967), 61; Afigbo, "Through a Glass Darkly," 156; and Catherine Obianju Acholonu, "The Home of Olaudah Equiano—A Linguistic and Anthropological Survey," *Journal of Commonwealth Literature*, 22 (1987), 5–16.

5. Quotations in this section appear in Equiano, *Interesting Narrative*, 32–33, 35, 37, 38, 46. See also Daryll Forde and G. I. Jones, *The Ibo and Ibibio-Speaking Peoples of South-Eastern Nigeria* (London: Oxford University Press, 1950), 37; G. I. Jones, *The Trading States of the Oil Rivers* (London: Oxford University Press, 1962); G. I. Jones, "Olaudah Equiano of the Niger Ibo," 64. Equiano's familiarity with guns raises questions about whether he was as ignorant of Europeans and the sea as he claimed.

6. On the Aro see Kenneth Onwuka Dike and Felicia Ekejiuba, *The Aro of Southeastern Nigeria, 1650–1980* (Ibadan: University Press Ltd., 1990). This paragraph and indeed this entire section is much indebted to the work of Douglas B. Chambers, " 'My own nation': Igbo Exiles in the Diaspora," *Slavery and Abolition* 18 (1997), 72–97; "Ethnicity in the Diaspora: The Slave Trade and the Creation of African 'Nations' in the Americas," *Slavery and Abolition* 22 (2001), 25–39; "The Significance of Igbo in the Bight of Biafra Slave-Trade: A Rejoinder to Northrup's 'Myth Igbo,' " *Slavery and Abolition* 23 (2002), 101–20; and *Murder at Montpelier: Igbo Africans in Virginia* (Jackson: University of Mississippi Press, 2005), especially ch. 2 and 3.

7. Afigbo, "Economic Foundations of Pre-Colonial Igbo Society," in *Ropes of Sand*, 123–44; John N. Oriji, *Traditions of Igbo Origin: A Study of Pre-Colonial Population Movements in Africa* (New York: Peter Lang, 1990), 4; Chambers, *Murder at Montpelier*, 39–40.

8. David Northrup, *Trade Without Rulers: Pre-Colonial Economic Development in South-Eastern Nigeria* (Oxford: Clarendon, 1978), 15; Chambers, *Murder at Montpelier*, 191; Afigbo, "Through a Glass Darkly," 179.

9. Chambers, "My own nation," 82; Chambers, *Murder at Montpelier*, 59–62.

10. Northrup, *Trade Without Rulers*, 65–76.

11. Quotations in this section appear in Equiano, *Interesting Narrative*, 46–54.

12. Both Carretta (*Equiano the African*, 34) and Lovejoy ("Autobiography and Memory") suggest that the *Ogden* was likely the vessel on which Equiano sailed, and I am inclined to agree. For details on the voyage, see *TSTD*, #90473.

13. Quotations in this section appear in Equiano, *Interesting Narrative*, 55–57. Equiano's reaction to the ship was remarkably similar to that of an English boy, Jack Cremer, who went aboard a naval vessel in 1708 at about eight years of age: "I was not taken notice of for a day or two, nor could I think what world I was in, weather among Spirits or Devills. All seemed strange; different languidge and strange exprefhions of tonge, that I thought myself always a sleep or in a dream, and never properly awake. Every morning a dreadful Noise for Waking Ship, and evenings in boats, that I was always dreading what was the matter." See John Cremer, *Ramblin' Jack: The Journal of Captain John Cremer, 1700–1774*, ed. R. Reynall Bellamy (London: Jonathan Cape, 1936), 43. William Butterworth also pronounced himself "amazed" by the "stupendous pieces of naval architecture" when as a teenager he first saw the Liverpool docks. See *Three Years Adventures*, 4.

14. Femi J. Kolapo, "The Igbo and Their Neighbours During the Era of the Atlantic Slave-Trade," *Slavery and Abolition* 25 (2004), 114–33; Chambers, "Ethnicity in the Diaspora," 26–27; Chambers, "Significance of Igbo," 108–9; David Northrup, "Igbo: Culture and Ethnicity in the Atlantic World," *Slavery and Abolition* 21 (2000), 12. A major

recent finding of scholarship on the slave trade is that there was less randomness, and hence less cultural mixing, in the gathering of slaves than previously believed. On the contrary, the clustering of cultural groups at African slave-trading ports facilitated communication aboard the ship. For more on this issue, see chapter 9. On the cultural flows from Africa to America, important work includes Michael A. Gomez, *Exchanging Our Country Marks: The Transformation of African Identities in the Colonial and Antebellum South* (Chapel Hill: University of North Carlina Press, 1998); Philip D. Morgan, "The Cultural Implications of the Atlantic Slave Trade: African Regional Origins, American Destinations and New World Developments," *Slavery and Abolition* 18 (1997), 122–45; Gwendolyn Midlo Hall, *Slavery and African Ethnicities in the Americas: Restoring the Links* (Chapel Hill: University of North Carolina Press, 2005).

15. Chinua Achebe, "Handicaps of Writing in a Second Language," *Spear Magazine* (1964), cited in Lovejoy, "Autobiography and Memory." See also Byrd, "Eboe, Country, Nation," 127, 132, 134, 137. For a more expansive exploration of the meaning of "Igbo," which includes "the people" and "forest-dweller," see Oriji, *Traditions of Igbo Origins,* 2–4. On Igbo ethnogenesis, see Chambers, "My own nation," 91, and "Ethnicity on the Diaspora," 25–39.

16. It is not known how many people died while the vessel was anchored on the coast and making its Atlantic crossing, only that the captain of the *Ogden* apparently planned to gather a "cargo" of 400 people and actually delivered 243. See *TSTD,* #90473.

17. Quotations in this section appear in Equiano, *Interesting Narrative,* 58–59.

18. Forde and Jones, *Ibo and Ibibio-Speaking Peoples,* 27; Afigbo, "Through a Glass Darkly," 181. Suicide on the slave ship might have been more common among the Igbo than other Africans. Michael Gomez has argued that the stereotype among planters that the Igbo were predisposed to suicide may have had a basis in social reality. See his "A Quality of Anguish: The Igbo Response to Enslavement in the Americas," in Paul E. Lovejoy and David V. Trotman, eds., *Trans-Atlantic Dimensions of the African Diaspora* (London: Continuum, 2003), 82–95.

19. I follow the birth date (1742) and early chronology for Equiano proposed by Lovejoy in "Autobiography and Memory."

20. Quotations in this section appear in Equiano, *Interesting Narrative,* 60–61.

21. On the tendency of the Igbo to see masters as sorcerers, see Chambers, "My own nation," 86.

22. That Equiano had never seen horses supports the argument for his origins in central Igbo land, which because of the tsetse fly did not have horses, rather than the north, which did have them. See Forde and Jones, *Ibo and Ibibio-Speaking Peoples,* 14, and Afigbo, "Through a Glass Darkly," 150.

23. As noted above, the *Ogden* spent eight months on the coast gathering its human cargo.

24. Quotations in this section appear in Equiano, *Interesting Narrative,* 62–67. On the *Nancy,* see Carretta, *Equiano the African,* 37.

25. Equiano, *Interesting Narrative,* 52. The world of the Atlantic slave trade was in some ways a small one. Equiano appeared on the coast for transshipment to America at a time when John Newton (had he ventured farther eastward) might have been the one to carry him to the New World. Moreover, by the time Equiano wrote his memoir in 1789, he had already read James Field Stanfield's *Observations on a Guinea Voyage* and indeed cited him on the character of the people in Benin. It is quite likely that Newton and Stanfield read Equiano's spiritual autobiography, as both were following the debate

on the slave trade closely. For accounts of Stanfield and Newton, see chapters 5 and 6. Quotations in this section appear in Equiano, *Interesting Narrative,* 51, 55, 56, 63, 64.

26. Afigbo, "Through a Glass Darkly," 152.

27. Sidney W. Mintz and Richard Price, *The Birth of African-American Culture: An Anthropological Perspective* (1976, 1992). Chambers is critical of Mintz and Price but writes of the importance of Igbo shipmates in mid-eighteenth-century Virginia. See *Murder at Montpelier,* 94.

28. Byrd, "Eboe, Country, Nation," 145–46; Afigbo, "Economic Foundations," 129.

Chapter 5: James Field Stanfield and the Floating Dungeon

1. James Field Stanfield, *Observations on a Guinea Voyage, in a Series of Letters Addressed to the Rev. Thomas Clarkson* (London: James Phillips, 1788). I would like to thank Pieter van der Merwe of the National Maritime Museum in Greenwich for sharing his own excellent research on the Stanfield family and for his thoughtful advice on many subjects. I am much indebted in what follows to three of his works: "Stanfield, James Field (1749/50–1824)," *Oxford Dictionary of National Biography* (Oxford: Oxford University Press, 2004); "The Life and Theatrical Career of Clarkson Stanfield," Ph.D. dissertation, University of Bristol, 1979; and "James Field Stanfield (1749/1750–1824): An Essay on Biography," paper delivered to the conference on Provincial Culture, Sheffield City Polytechnic, 1981 (copy kindly provided by the author). This expands information also covered in van der Merwe and R. Took, *The Spectacular Career of Clarkson Stanfield, 1793–1867; Seaman, Scene-painter, Royal Academician* (Sunderland Art Gallery exhibition catalog; Tyne and Wear Museums, Newcastle on Tyne, 1979).

2. Clarkson and the London committee paid Stanfield £39.8.9 for the right to publish *Observations on a Guinea Voyage.* It was a considerable sum of money, indeed almost exactly the same amount he would have made in his voyage—twenty months at roughly 40 shillings per month. It is not clear how Stanfield made contact with the abolitionists, nor is it clear whether they encouraged him to write the account or coached him as he did so. The poem, also published by the committee, followed a year later. See Clarkson, *History,* vol. 1, 498.

3. *Providence Gazette; and Country Journal,* September 13–November 8, 1788.

4. James Field Stanfield, *The Guinea Voyage, A Poem in Three Books* (London: James Phillips, 1789). Abolitionist groups in Rhode Island and perhaps elsewhere sold copies of the poem. See *Newport Mercury,* February 22, 1790, and *Providence Gazette; and Country Journal,* March 6, 1790.

5. J. F. Stanfield, "Written on the Coast of Africa in the year 1776," *Freemason's Magazine, or General Complete Library* 4 (1795), 273–74. This was apparently the only commentary Stanfield wrote on the slave trade while he was actually involved in it. *Observations* and *The Guinea Voyage* were written about eleven and twelve years later, respectively, under different circumstances, after the abolitionist movement had emerged and made it possible to talk about the slave trade in new ways. It does not appear that Stanfield kept a diary or journal of his voyage and was hence writing entirely from memory, although, it must be noted, his was a memory that was considered "prodigious" by those who knew him in the theater, where he was known for his "astonishing abilities as to quickness of study"—that is, the speed at which he could memorize his parts. See *Observations,* 36; Tate Wilkinson, *The Wandering Patentee; or, A History of the Yorkshire Theaters* (York, 1795), vol. III, 22.

6. *Guinea Voyage,* iii. Historian J. R. Oldfield has written that Stanfield "clearly set out to shock his readers: some of the scenes he describes were extremely graphic even by the standards of the eighteenth century." He adds that *Observations* is not merely sensationalist, however, but sheds important light on the nature of the slave trade. See his introduction to *Observations,* which is republished in John Oldfield, ed., *The British Transatlantic Slave Trade* (London: Pickering & Chatto, 2003), vol. III: *The Abolitionist Struggle: Opponents of the Slave Trade,* 97–136.

7. *Gentleman's Magazine,* vol. 59 (1789), 933. Years later, when Stanfield's *An Essay on the Study and Composition of Biography* (London, 1813) was published, the subscribers' list included antislavery luminaries such as Thomas Clarkson, James Currie, William Roscoe, and Granville Sharp. See 345–57.

8. *Observations,* 2, 3, 4; *Guinea Voyage,* 2. Of the many who wrote poems about the slave trade, only Stanfield, Thomas Boulton, Thomas Branagan, and Captain John Marjoribanks had actually made a slaving voyage. I am grateful to James G. Basker for discussion of this issue. See his magnificent compilation, *Amazing Grace: An Anthology of Poems about Slavery, 1660–1810* (New Haven: Yale University Press, 2002), 402. Edward Rushton of Liverpool also made a slaving voyage (on which he caught contagious ophthalmia and lost his eyesight). He wrote antislavery poetry, but never specifically about the slave trade. See his *West-Indian Eclogues* (London, 1797).

9. "Written on the Coast of Africa," 273; van der Merwe, "James Field Stanfield (1749/1750–1824): An Essay on Biography," 2. Stanfield's grandson, Field Stanfield (1844–1905), wrote in an unpublished family memoir, "A change at that stage came over his views and he brought his Educational career to an abrupt close. The reaction was indeed so great as to induce him for a time to throw aside all studies notwithstanding the fact that he had progressed to a high degree of attainment both in Classical and Mathematical pursuits. He left these and betook himself to sea and became engaged as a mariner in the slave trade on the Coast of Guinea." See Field Stanfield's unfinished MS memoir of his father Clarkson Stanfield, f.1. I am grateful to Pieter van der Merwe for sharing this document with me and to Liam Chambers for his thoughts on Irishmen who studied in France in this period.

10. "Written on the Coast of Africa," 273; Wilkinson, *The Wandering Patentee,* vol. III, 22. For additional biographical information, not all of it accurate, from contemporaries, see "Notes, James Field Stanfield," *Notes and Queries,* 8th series 60 (1897), 301–2; Transcript of notes by John William Bell (1783–1864) on the facing title of the Sunderland Library copy of *The Guinea Voyage, A Poem in Three Books . . . to which are added Observations on a Voyage to the Coast of Africa, in a series of letters to Thomas Clarkson A.M. by James Field Stanfield, formerly a mariner in the African trade* (Edinburgh: J. Robertson, 1807). It was claimed by two who knew Stanfield that he testified before the House of Commons about the slave trade, but neither Pieter van der Merwe nor I have been able to substantiate this. Sunderland historian Neil Sinclair has recently discovered evidence of Stanfield's involvement in the hearings, not as one who testified but as one who helped to publicize evidence given against the slave trade. See the handbill entitled "Slave Trade" and signed "J.E.S." See DV1/60/8/29, Durham County Record Office, Durham, England.

11. David Roberts, Manuscript Record Book, 1796–1864, f. 197, Yale Center for British Art, New Haven, copy in the Guildhall Library, as cited in van der Merwe, "James Field Stanfield (1749/1750–1824): An Essay on Biography," 1. For a song by Stanfield, see "Patrick O'Neal, An Irish Song," *Weekly Visitant; Moral, Poetical, Humourous, &c* (1806), 383–84.

12. *Observations*, 21, 35, 11. The crew mortality Stanfield witnessed was exceptional, although not unprecedented.

13. *Observations*, 36.

14. The *Eagle* was built in Galway, Ireland, almost thirty years earlier, in 1745, and was therefore more than suitable for retirement as a "floating factory."

15. Captain John Adams described "Gatto" as a main trading town of fifteen thousand inhabitants, located about forty miles inland. See his *Sketches taken during Ten Voyages to Africa, Between the Years 1786 and 1800; including Observations on the Country between Cape Palmas and the River Congo; and Cursory Remarks on the Physical and Moral Character of the Inhabitants* (London, 1823; rpt. New York: Johnson Reprint Corporation, 1970), 29.

16. Captain Wilson filed the muster list with the customs house on May 11, 1776. See Board of Trade (BT) 98/36, Liverpool muster rolls, 1776, NA. Stanfield mistakenly recalled that only three members of the original crew made it back to Liverpool. I am grateful to Christopher Magra for research assistance on this matter. See *Observations*, 5, 19, 26. For more information on the voyage of the *True Blue*, see *TSTD*, #91985.

17. The quotations in this section appear in *Observations*, 7, 6, 8, 9, 7; *Guinea Voyage*, 3–4, 5, 8, 6, 4, 5, 6, 7.

18. "Written on the Coast of Africa," 273.

19. The quotations in this section appear in *Observations*, 10, 13, 14, 11, 12, 15; *Guinea Voyage*, 10.

20. These same insults and indignities during the passage to Africa were reiterated in verse. See *Guinea Voyage*, 23–24.

21. The quotations in this section appear in *Observations*, 15–16, 17–18, 23; *Guinea Voyage*, 19. For another description of seamen working up to their armpits in water, see the Testimony of James Arnold, 1789, in *HCSP*, 69:128.

22. The quotations in this section appear in *Observations*, 21, 19, 20, 25; *Guinea Voyage*, 15, 13, 33, 14, 17, 30, 31, 17, 18, 26, iv, 3, 23, 19. One can see the likely influence of the Quaker Anthony Benezet here. For an excellent account of Benezet's life and thought, see Maurice Jackson, " 'Ethiopia shall soon stretch her hands unto God': Anthony Benezet and the Atlantic Antislavery Revolution," Ph.D. dissertation, Georgetown University, 2001.

23. The story of Abyeda appears in *Guinea Voyage*, 29–31. Stanfield associates Abyeda with a specific place, the Formosa River, when he writes, "Ne'er did such nymph before her brightness lave / Within Formosa's deep, translucent wave" (29). It should also be noted that Quam'no is a variant of the Akan/Gold Coast name Quamino. Thomas Clarkson included an account of an African woman he called "Abeyda" in a letter to Comte de Mirabeau, November 13, 1789, Papers of Thomas Clarkson, Huntington Library, San Marino, California, f. 11. He makes reference in the same letter to the slave ship as a "floating dungeon," a phrase used by Stanfield.

24. van der Merwe, "James Field Stanfield (1749/1750–1824): An Essay on Biography," 3.

25. The quotations in this section appear in *Observations*, 26, 27, 28–29, 30, 31, 32–33, 29; *Guinea Voyage*, iv, 19, 26, 21, 27, 28, 34, 16, 24, 32, 22.

26. The quotations in this section appear in *Guinea Voyage*, 34, 35, vi.

27. *Monthly Review; or, Literary Journal*, vol. 81 (1789), 277–79.

28. *Observations*, 30. Stanfield refers here to parliamentary debates about the slave trade and, it would appear, to Reverend William Robertson, a Scottish Presbyterian theologian and historian who opposed the trade.

Chapter 6: John Newton and the Peaceful Kingdom

1. John Newton, *Letters to a Wife, Written during Three Voyages to Africa, from 1750 to 1754* (orig. publ. London, 1793; rpt. New York, 1794), 61–62.

2. "Amazing Grace," in *The Works of the Reverend John Newton, Late Rector of the United Parishes of St. Mary Woolnoth and St. Mary Woolchurch-Haw, Lombard Street, London* (Edinburgh: Peter Brown and Thomas Nelson, 1828), 538–39; John Newton, *Thoughts upon the African Slave Trade* (London, 1788); Testimony of John Newton, 1789, in *HCSP*, 69: 12, 36, 60, 118; 73: 139–51. For an account of Newton's life as a minister, see D. Bruce Hindmarsh, *John Newton and the English Evangelical Tradition: Between the Conversions of Wesley and Wilberforce* (Oxford: Clarendon Press, 1996). For a history of his most famous hymn, see Steve Turner, *Amazing Grace: The Story of America's Most Beloved Song* (New York: Ecco Press, 2002).

3. John Newton, *Journal of Slave Trader, 1750–1754,* ed. Bernard Martin and Mark Spurrell (London: Epworth Press, 1962); Newton, *Letters to a Wife;* John Newton Letterbook ("A Series of Letters from Mr.—— to Dr. J—— [Dr. David Jennings]," 1750–1760, 920 MD 409, Liverpool Record Office; John Newton, Diaries, December 22, 1751–June 5, 1756, General Manuscripts Co199, Seeley G. Mudd Manuscript Library, Princeton University; Thomas Haweis, *An Authentic Narrative of Some Remarkable and Interesting Particulars in the Life of Mr. Newton, Communicated, in a Series of Letters to the Rev. Mr. Haweis, Rector of Aldwinkle, Northamptonshire* (orig. publ. London, 1764; rpt. Philadelphia, 1783).

4. The quotations in this section appear in *An Authentic Narrative,* 14, 22, 29, 33, 36–37, 41, 44, 43, 47, 56, 57, 58, 74, 76, and other sources as indicated by paragraph.

5. John Newton to David Jennings, October 29, 1755; Newton Letter-book, f. 70.

6. Newton, *Thoughts upon the African Slave Trade,* 98.

7. Newton, *Letters to a Wife,* 21–22.

8. Newton, *Thoughts upon the African Slave Trade,* 101. In the insurrection one crew member and three or four Africans were killed. See Testimony of Newton, *HCSP,* 73:144. For more information on this voyage, see *TSTD,* #90350.

9. Newton to Jennings, August 29, 1752, Newton Letter-book, ff. 28–30. The quotations in this section appear in Newton, *Journal of Slave Trader,* 2, 9–10, 12–15, 17–22, 24–25, 28–34, 37–38, 40, 42–43, 48–50, 52, 54–56, 59, and other sources as indicated by paragraph.

10. *TSTD,* #90350.

11. For another instance of readying the swivel guns at mealtime, see "Voyage to Guinea, Antego, Bay of Campeachy, Cuba, Barbadoes, &c." (1714–23), Add. Ms. 39946, f. 10, BL.

12. Newton, *Thoughts upon the African Slave Trade,* 106, 107.

13. Newton, *Letters to a Wife,* 29.

14. Newton, *Thoughts upon the African Slave Trade,* 110–11; Testimony of John Newton, *HCSP,* 69:118, 73:144, 145.

15. On provisioning on the West African coast, see Stephen D. Behrendt, "Markets, Transaction Cycles, and Profits: Merchant Decision Making in the British Slave Trade," *William and Mary Quarterly* 3rd ser. 58 (2001), 171–204.

16. Newton, *Thoughts upon the African Slave Trade,* 110.

17. Newton, *Letters to a Wife,* 86; Entry for December 22, 1751, Newton Diaries, ff. 2, 5. The quotations in this section appear in Newton, *Journal of Slave Trader,* 65, 69–72, 75–77, 80–81, and in other sources as indicated by paragraph.

18. *TSTD*, #90418. The labors of the crew on this voyage were essentially the same as on the previous one: the carpenter worked on the bulkheads and apartments, the platforms, and the barricado; the gunner on the small arms and the swivel guns; the boatswain on the nettings; everyone else doing the fundamental work of sailing the ship.

19. Newton, *Letters to a Wife*, 77, 71–72; Entry for August 13, 1752, Newton Diaries, f. 37; *An Authentic Narrative*, 85–86.

20. Entry for July 23, 1752, Newton Diaries, f. 23. Around this time Newton wrote to the Anglican divine David Jennings to propose that someone (himself, actually) write a manual of religious instruction especially for sailors, one that would feature a short, simple combination of biblical verse, prayer, and sermon, all geared to the "particular temptations and infirmities incident to foreign voyages." See Newton to Jennings, August 29, 1752, Newton Letter-book, f. 37.

21. On the round-robin, see Marcus Rediker, *Between the Devil and the Deep Blue Sea: Merchant Seamen, Pirates, and the Anglo-American Maritime World, 1700–1750* (Cambridge: Cambridge University Press, 1987), 234–35.

22. Entry for November 19, 1752, Newton Diaries, ff. 49–50.

23. Ibid. For more on the *Earl of Halifax*, see *TSTD*, #77617.

24. Ibid.

25. Entry for December 11, 1752, Newton Diaries, ff. 61, 64.

26. *TSTD*, #90419. The quotations in this section appear in Newton, *Letters to a Wife*, 118–20, 126, 129–30, 143, 149, 188, and in other sources as indicated by paragraph.

27. Newton, *Journal of Slave Trader*, 88, 92–93.

28. Ibid., 88.

29. Ibid., 92–93.

30. Entry for August 29, 1753, Newton Diaries, f. 88.

31. Newton, *Letters to a Wife*, 83–84; *An Authentic Narrative*, 95; Newton to Jennings, August 29, 1852, Newton Letter-book, f. 26; "Amazing Grace," in *The Works of the Reverend John Newton*, 538–39; Testimony of Newton, *HCSP*, 73:151.

32. Entry for December 8, 1752, Newton Diaries, f. 53.

33. Newton, *Letters to a Wife*, 137. See also Testimony of Newton, *HCSP*, 73:151.

Chapter 7: The Captain's Own Hell

1. John Newton to Richard Phillips, July 5, 1788, published in Mary Phillips, *Memoir of the Life of Richard Phillips* (London: Seeley and Burnside, 1841), 29–31.

2. The phrase "subordination and regularity" was used by Lord Kenyon in *Smith v. Goodrich*, in which a mate sued the captain of a slave ship for a violent assault. See the *Times*, June 22, 1792. For similar legal reasoning, see *Lowden v. Goodrich*, summarized in *Dunlap's American Daily Advertiser*, May 24, 1791. For a broader account of the captain's powers in the merchant shipping industry, see Marcus Rediker, *Between the Devil and the Deep Blue Sea: Merchant Seamen, Pirates, and the Anglo-American Maritime World, 1700–1750* (Cambridge: Cambridge University Press, 1987), ch. 5.

3. Letter of Instructions from Henry Wafford to Captain Alexander Speers of the Brig *Nelly*, 28 September 1772, David Tuohy papers, 380 TUO, 4/6, LRO; Captain Peter Potter to William Davenport & Co., November 22, 1776, "Ship New Badger's Inward Accots, 1777," William Davenport Archives, Maritime Archives & Library, MMM, D/DAV/10/1/2. See *TSTD*, #92536.

4. *Memoirs of Crow*, quotations at 67, 13, 2, 29.

5. *TSTD*, #83183. What Crow recalled as his first ship does not appear in the *TSTD*.

6. Stephen Behrendt, "The Captains in the British Slave Trade from 1785 to 1807," *Transactions of the Historical Society of Lancashire and Cheshire* 140 (1990), 79–140; Jay Coughtry, *The Notorious Triangle: Rhode Island and the African Slave Trade, 1700–1807* (Philadelphia: Temple University Press, 1981), 50–53; Africanus, *Remarks on the Slave Trade, and the Slavery of Negroes, in a Series of Letters* (London: J. Phillips, and Norwich: Chase and Co., 1788), 50. See also Emma Christopher, *Slave Trade Sailors and Their Captive Cargoes, 1730–1807* (Cambridge: Cambridge University Press, 2006), 35–39. Behrendt writes that the British captains who survived several voyages "often acquired great wealth in the slave trade," especially if they were among the 10 percent who were also part owners of their vessels. Herbert Klein notes that a captain could accumulate a "respectable fortune" in two or three voyages. See his *The Atlantic Slave Trade* (Cambridge: Cambridge University Press, 1999), 83. For examples of captains who got in trouble with employing merchants, see Amelia C. Ford, ed., "An Eighteenth Century Letter from a Sea Captain to his Owner," *New England Quarterly* 3 (1930), 136–45; Robert Bostock to James Cleveland, January 20, 1790, Robert Bostock Letterbooks, 387 MD 54-55, LRO; "William Grice's Statement of Facts," King's Bench Prison, July 2, 1804, "Miscellaneous Tracts, 1804–1863," 748F13, BL.

7. Letter of Instructions from David Tuohy (on behalf of Ingram & Co.) to Captain Henry Moore of the Ship *Blayds*, 25 July 1782, Tuohy papers, 380 TUO, (4/9). Another reason Tuohy advised circumspection was that Moore had never been to Cape Coast Castle or Lagos. See *TSTD*, #80578. For a study of the planning and coordination required of merchants and captains in the slave trade, see Stephen D. Behrendt, "Markets, Transaction Cycles, and Profits: Merchant Decision Making in the British Slave Trade," *William and Mary Quarterly* 3rd ser. 58 (2001), 171–204. For an account of business practices, see Kenneth Morgan, "Remittance Procedures in the Eighteenth-Century British Slave Trade," *Business History Review* 79 (2005), 715–49.

8. Jacob Rivera and Aaron Lopez to Captain William English, Newport, November 27, 1772, in Donnan III, 264; Thomas Leyland to Captain Charles Watt of the *Fortune*, April 23, 1805, 387 MD 44, Thomas Leyland & Co., ships' accounts 1793–1811, LRO. See also Samuel Hartley to James Penny, September 20, 1783, *Baillie v. Hartley*, exhibits regarding the Slave Ship Comte du Nord and Slave Trade; schedule, correspondence, accounts, E 219/377, NA.

9. Letters of instruction exist for the full range of years under study, 1700–1808, and for each major area of the slave trade: Senegambia, Sierra Leone/Windward Coast, the Gold Coast, the Bights of Benin and Biafra, and Kongo-Angola. For examples early and late in the period, see Thomas Starke to James Westmore, October 20, 1700, in Donnan IV, 76; William Boyd to Captain John Connolly, Charleston, July 24, 1807, in ibid., 568–69. See also Humphry Morice to William Snelgrave, October 20, 1722, "Book Containing Orders & Instructions to William Snelgrave Commander of the *Henry* for the Coast of Africa with an Invoice of his Cargoe and Journal of Trade &c. on the said Coast. 2d Voyage. Anno 1721"; Humphry Morice to William Snelgrave, October 20, 1722, "Book Containing Orders & Instructions for William Snelgrave Commander of the *Henry* for the Coast of Africa with an Invoice of his Cargoe and Journal of Trade &c. on the said Coast. 3d Voyage. Anno 1722"; Humphry Morice to William Snelgrave, September 22, 1729, "Book Containing Orders & Instructions for William Snelgrave Com-

mander of the *Katharine Galley* for the Coast of Africa with an Invoice of his Cargoe and Journal of Trade &c. on the said Coast. 5th Voyage. Anno 1729"; the Humphry Morice Papers, Bank of England Archives, London.

10. Morice to Clinch, September 13, 1722, Morice Papers; Thomas Leyland to Captain Caesar Lawson of the *Enterprize,* 18 July 1803, 387 MD 43, Leyland & Co., ships' accounts; Owners' Instructions to Captain Young, 24 March 1794, Account Book of Slave Ship *Enterprize,* DX/1732, MMM. See *TSTD,* #81302.

11. Humphry Morice to Edmund Weedon, March 25, 1725, "Book Containing Orders & Instructions for Edmund Weedon Commander of the *Anne Galley* for the Coast of Africa with an Invoice of his Cargoe and Journal of Trade &c. on the said Coast. 4th Voyage. March the 25th: Anno 1722"; Morice Papers; Jonathan Belcher, Peter Pusulton, William Foy, Ebenezer Hough, William Bant, and Andrew Janvill to Captain William Atkinson, Boston, December 28, 1728, in Donnan III, 38.

12. Isaac Hobhouse, No. Ruddock, Wm. Baker to Captain William Barry, Bristol, October 7, 1725, in Donnan II, 329; Joseph and Joshua Grafton to Captain——, November 12, 1785, in Donnan III, 80.

13. Humphry Morice to William Clinch, September 13, 1722, "Book Containing Orders & Instructions for William Clinch Commander of the *Judith Snow* for the Coast of Africa with an Invoice of his Cargoe and Journal of Trade &c. on the said Coast. Voyage 1. Anno 1722," Morice Papers; Thomas Leyland to Captain Charles Kneal of the *Lottery,* 21 May 1802, 387 MD 42, Leyland & Co., ships' accounts; James Laroche to Captain Richard Prankard, Bristol, January 29, 1733, Jeffries Collection of Manuscripts, vol. XIII, Bristol Central Library; Owners' Instructions to Captain William Young, March 24, 1794, Account Book of Slave Ship *Enterprize* Owned by Thomas Leyland & Co., Liverpool, DX/1732, MMM; the South Sea Company: Minutes of the Committee of Correspondence, October 10, 1717, in Donnan II, 215; Boyd to Connolly, July 24, 1807, in Donnan IV, 568.

14. John Chilcot, P. Protheroe, T. Lucas & Son, Jams. Rogers to Captain Thos. Baker, Bristol, August 1, 1776, Account Book of the *Africa,* 1774–1776, BCL. For an account of a voyage of the *Africa,* see W. E. Minchinton, "Voyage of the Snow *Africa,*" *Mariner's Mirror* 37 (1951), 187–96.

15. Behrendt, "Captains in the British Slave Trade," 93; "Sales of 338 Slaves received per the Squirrel Captain Chadwick on the proper Account of William Boats Esq. & Co Owners of Liverpool, Owners," Case & Southworth Papers, 1754–1761, 380 MD 36, LRO.

16. Ball, Jennings, & Co. to Samuel Hartley, September 6, 1784, *Baillie v. Hartley,* E 219/377. The breakdown was £1,221.1.3 for commission, £634.19.0 for privilege, £84 for wages.

17. The handling of privilege changed over time. In the early eighteenth century, the captain and other officers picked out the slaves they wanted to carry as privilege (reserving to themselves those who would bring the highest prices), but when these slaves died, they frequently switched their choices in order to shift the loss to the owner's account. In order to prevent this, merchants instructed captains to select—and brand—their slaves on the coast, in full view of other officers. Yet even this was not satisfactory, because all the officers had a community of interest on this issue and might cover for each other. So merchants began to take a different approach, specifying that a privilege slave would not be an individual but an average value of all slaves after they had been sold in the New World port. This created an incentive to take care of all slaves, but it also created

an incentive to kill the sickest, weakest slaves once near port, for these would have brought down the average and hence the value of the captain's privilege. See also Christopher, *Slave Trade Sailors,* 34–35.

18. Mathew Strong to Captain Richard Smyth, January 19, 1771, Tuohy papers, 380 TUO (4/4). It seems that relatively few captains actually owned shares of their vessels or cargo. Of forty-one captains (on forty-five ships) to whom letters of instruction were written, we know the investors and shipowners in thirty-nine cases. Only four of the thirty-nine captains owned shares: Williams Speers was listed as the "third owner" of the *Ranger* in 1767. David Tuohy was the "fourth owner" of the *Sally* in the same year. Thomas Baker and Henry Moore were the seventh and sixth owners, respectively, of their vessels in 1776 and 1782; *TSTD,* #91273, #91327, #17886, #80578. See also Madge Dresser, *Slavery Obscured: The Social History of the Slave Trade in an English Provincial Port* (London and New York: Continuum, 2001), 29; Behrendt, "Captains in the British Slave Trade," 107; Coughtry, *The Notorious Triangle,* 49–50.

19. Instructions to Captain Pollipus Hammond, Newport, January 7, 1746, Donnan III, 138.

20. Letter of Instruction from James Clemens to Captain William Speers of the ship *Ranger,* 3 June 1767, Tuohy papers, (4/2). For Clemens's voyages, see *TSTD,* #90408, #90613, and #90684.

21. Leyland to Kneal, 21 May 1802, 387 MD 42, Leyland & Co., ships' accounts; Henry Wafford to Captain Alexander Speers of the Brig *Nelly,* September 28, 1772, Tuohy papers, 380 TUO (4/6).

22. James Clemens, Folliott Powell, Henry Hardware, and Mathew Strong to Captain David Tuohy of the ship *Sally,* 3 June 1767, Tuohy papers, 380 TUO (4/2). See also Robert Bostock to Captain Peter Bowie of the *Jemmy,* July 2, 1787, Robert Bostock Letter-books, 1779–1790 and 1789–1792, 387 MD 54–55, LRO. For a discussion of sailors' mutiny, see chapter 8.

23. Hobhouse, Ruddock, and Baker to Barry, October 7, 1725, in Donnan II, 327–28; Humphry Morice to Jeremiah Pearce, March 17, 1730, "Book Containing Orders & Instructions for Jere[miah] Pearce Commander of the *Judith Snow* for the Coast of Africa with an Invoice of his Cargoe and Journal of Trade &c. on the said Coast. 7th Voyage. Anno 1730," Morice Papers; Unnamed Owner to Captain William Ellery, January 14, 1759, in Donnan III, 69.

24. Humphry Morice to Stephen Bull, October 30, 1722, "Book Containing Orders & Instructions for Stephen Bull Commander of the *Sarah* for the Coast of Africa with an Invoice of his Cargoe and Journal of Trade &c. on the said Coast. 2d Voyage. Anno 1722," Morice Papers; *Memoirs of Crow,* 22.

25. John Chilcott, John Anderson, T. Lucas, and James Rogers to Captain George Merrick, Bristol, 13th October 1774, Account Book of the *Africa,* 1774–1776, BCL; Boyd to Connolly, July 24, 1807, in Donnan IV, 568.

26. Robert Bostock to Captain James Fryer of the *Bess,* no date (but 1791), Bostock Letter-books, 387 MD 54–55. See *TSTD,* #80502. I have come across no other such threat in merchants' letters of instruction.

27. Chilcott et al. to Merrick, October 13, 1774, Account Book of the *Africa,* 1774–1776, BCL; Stephen D. Behrendt, "Crew Mortality in the Transatlantic Slave Trade in the Eighteenth Century," *Slavery and Abolition* 18 (1997), 49–71.

28. Ibid. See also K. G. Davies, "The Living and the Dead: White Mortality in West Africa, 1684–1732," in Stanley L. Engerman and Eugene D. Genovese, eds., *Race and*

Slavery in the Western Hemisphere: Quantitative Studies (Princeton: Princeton University Press, 1975), 83–98.

29. Starke to Westmore, in Donnan IV, 76; Joseph and Joshua Grafton to Captain ———, November 12, 1785, in Donnan III, 78– 79; Chilcott et al. to Merrick, October 13, 1774, Account Book of the *Africa;* Robert Bostock to Captain Samuel Gamble, November 16, 1790, Bostock Letter-books 387 MD 54–55; Chilcott et al. to Baker, August 1, 1776, Account Book of the *Africa.*

30. Joseph and Joshua Grafton to Captain ———, November 12, 1785, in Donnan III, 80. William Snelgrave to Humphry Morice, Jaqueen, April 16, 1727, Morice Papers.

31. Thomas Boulton, *The Sailor's Farewell; Or, the Guinea Outfit, a Comedy in Three Acts* (Liverpool, 1768); *Newport Mercury,* July 9, 1770. When Boulton later wrote *The Voyage, a Poem in Seven Parts* (Boston, 1773), he erased what must have been a painful memory (if he was writing about the same voyage). He did not mention the slaves or their uprising. See *TSTD,* #91564.

32. *An Account of the Life,* 19; *Three Years Adventures,* 6. Boulton failed to mention one of the most important means of recruitment: the crimp, a labor agent who used all kinds of nefarious means to get sailors aboard the slavers.

33. For a good and thorough example of how a slave ship was prepared to sail, see Account Book of the *Africa,* 1774–1776, BCL.

34. Joseph Hawkins, *A History of a Voyage to the Coast of Africa, and Travels into the Interior of that Country; containing Particular Descriptions of the Climate and Inhabitants, particulars concerning the Slave Trade* (Troy, N.Y.: Luther Pratt, 2nd edition, 1797), 150.

35. "Dicky Sam," *Liverpool and Slavery: An Historical Account of the Liverpool-African Slave Trade* (Liverpool: A. Bowker & Son, 1884), 21–22.

36. Interview of Mr. Thompson in *Substance,* 24; Testimony of James Towne, in 1791, in *HCSP,* 82: 27.

37. See, for example, *Times,* January 12, 1808; *Newport Mercury,* June 15, 1767; *An Account of the Life,* 26; *Enquirer,* September 12, 1806. See also the printed broadside *Unparalleled Cruelty in a Guinea Captain* (H. Forshaw, printer, no place, no date, but c. 1805), Holt and Gregson Papers, 942 HOL 10, LRO.

38. *Connecticut Courant,* August 10, 1789. See also *American Minerva,* May 15, 1794. For a case in which a slave-ship captain punched and kicked a member of his crew but whose treatment of him might still be called "very mild," see *Macnamera and Worsdale v. Barry,* August 26, 1729, Records of the South Carolina Court of Admiralty, 1716–1732, f. 729, National Archives, Washington, D.C.

39. Anecdote XI (about the *Othello,* Captain James McGauley), in *Substance,* 134; *TSTD,* #82978. For instances of captains commanding slaves to lash or abuse sailors, see *Seamen v. John Ebsworthy* (1738), "Minutes of the Vice-Admiralty Court of Charles Town, South Carolina," 1716–1763, Manuscripts Department, Library of Congress, Washington, D.C.; Robert Barker, *The Unfortunate Shipwright, or, Cruel Captain, being a Faithful Narrative of the Unparalleled Sufferings of Robert Barker, Late Carpenter on board the Thetis Snow of Bristol; on a Voyage from thence to the Coast of Guinea and Antigua* (orig. publ. 1760; new edition, London, "printed for the SUFFERER for his own Benefit; and by no one else," 1775), 26.

40. *Macnamera and Worsdale v. Barry,* South Carolina Admiralty, ff. 713, 729. On the use of the gun barrel, see Testimony of James Towne, 1791, *HCSP,* 82:29.

41. Wage Books for the *Swift* (1775–76), *Dreadnought* (1776), *Dalrymple* (1776), *Hawk* (1780–81), *Hawk* (1781–82), *Essex* (1783–84), *Essex* (1785–86), all in the William Davenport Archives, D/DAV/3/1-6, MMM. See *TSTD,* #91793, #91839, #91988, #81753, #81754, #81311, #81312. On the *African Galley* Captain James Westmore made more money selling items to the crew (£89.1.3) than he did through his wages of £6 per month. See "Accompts submitted by the Plaintiff in the Court of Chancery suit Capt. James Westmore, commander, v. Thomas Starke, owner of the slaver 'Affrican Galley' concerning expenses incurred by Westmore on a voyage from London to Virginia via St. Thomas' Island, Gulf of Guinea, and back, 20 Apr. 1701–4 Dec. 1702," Add. Ms. 45123, BL.

42. Testimony of Henry Ellison, 1790, *HCSP,* 73:371; Law Report, *Tarlton v. McGawley, Times,* December 24, 1793. For other examples of threatened or actual force, see Captain Baillie to the Owners of the *Carter,* Bonny, January 31, 1757, Donnan II, 512; Thomas Starke to James Westmore, no date, in Donnan IV, 80; Testimony of Alexander Falconbridge, 1790, *HCSP,* 72:321.

43. "Account Book of the *Molly,* Snow, Slave Ship, dated 1759–1760," Manuscripts Department, MSS/76/027.0, NMM. I have identified the voyage as *TSTD,* #17741, even though there is a discrepancy in the date. The *Molly* left Bristol on December 4, 1758, sold its slaves in Virginia on July 15, 1759, and arrived back in Bristol on November 22, 1759, but the account book of the *Molly* is dated 1759–60. (The account book could not have belonged to the vessel's next voyage, which began in Bristol on April 4, 1760, because the sale of slaves in this instance took place not in Virginia, as the account book states, but in Jamaica.) Other evidence supporting this identification includes the number of slaves delivered. The slave-trade database, based on other sources, shows that the vessel sold 238 slaves and imputes that it would have gathered an original number of 292. The actual number listed in the account book is 286 purchased. The notation of 1760 is apparently based on a final approval of the account book, on April 14, 1760, by someone with the initials PFW, perhaps a merchant or a clerk but not the owner of the vessel, who was Henry Bright. For other, less detailed trade books, see "Slave Trader's Accompt Book," compiled on board the schooner 'Mongovo George' of Liverpool, 1785–1787," Add. Ms. 43841, BL; George A. Plimpton, ed., "The Journal of an African Slaver, 1789–1792," *Proceedings of the American Antiquarian Society* 39 (1929), 379–465.

44. For an analysis of how African demand shaped the trade, see David Richardson, "West African Consumption Patterns and their Influence on the Eighteenth-Century Slave Trade," in Henry A. Gemery and Jan S. Hogendorn, eds., *The Uncommon Market: Essays in the Economic History of the Atlantic Slave Trade* (New York: Academic Press, 1979), 303–30.

45. For the nature of trade in nearby Old Calabar in this period, see Paul E. Lovejoy and David Richardson, "Trust, Pawnship, and Atlantic History: The Institutional Foundations of the Old Calabar Slave Trade," *American Historical Review* 104 (1999), 333–55. Captain Jenkins did indeed return to Bonny, on six more voyages between 1760 and 1769. See *TSTD,* #17493, #17531, #17599, #17626, #17635, #17722. For a shorter but comparable list of Windward Coast traders with whom Captain Paul Cross did business, see Trade book, 1773, Paul Cross Papers, 1768–1803, South Caroliniana Library, Columbia.

46. William Smith, *A New Voyage to Guinea: Describing the Customs, Manners, Soil, Climate, Habits, Buildings, Education, Manual Arts, Agriculture, Trade, Employments, Languages, Ranks of Distinction, Habitations, Diversions, Marriages, and whatever else is*

memorable among the Inhabitants (London, 1744; rpt. London: Frank Cass & Co., 1967), 34; [John Wells], "Journal of a Voyage to the Coast of Guinea, 1802," Add. Ms. 3,871, f. 10, Cambridge University Library; Captain Thomas Earle to Mrs. Anne Winstanley, Calabar, August 30, 1751, Earle Family Papers, MMM.

47. *City Gazette and Daily Advertiser,* December 10, 1807. For the *Hind* and *Byam,* see *TSTD,* #81862, #80722.

48. *Three Years Adventures,* 27.

49. For examples of captains denouncing their surgeons, see Viscountess Knutsford, ed., *Life and Letters of Zachary Macaulay* (London: Edward Arnold, 1900), 86; Captain Japhet Bird to ?, Montserrat, February 24, 1723, in Donnan II, 298; "Barque Eliza's Journal, Robert Hall, Commander, from Liverpool to Cruize 31 Days & then to Africa & to Demarary; mounts 14 Nine & Six Pounders, with 31 Men & boys," T70/1220, NA.

50. Testimony of Thomas Trotter, 1790, *HCSP,* 73:88–89.

51. Captain William Snelgrave, *A New Account of Some Parts of Guinea and the Slave Trade* (London, 1734; rpt. London: Frank Cass & Co., 1971), 181–85; *Memoirs of Crow,* 148–49.

52. Bruce Mouser writes, "A special camaraderie existed among the European captains who visited the coast." See Bruce Mouser, ed., *A Slaving Voyage to Africa and Jamaica: The Log of the* Sandown, *1793–1794* (Bloomington: Indiana University Press, 2002), 78.

53. Snelgrave, *A New Account,* 185–91. Robert Norris explained to a parliamentary committee in 1789 that he did not go belowdecks into the slave apartments because it was not his duty. See his Testimony of Robert Norris, *HCSP,* 68:8. For a captain who was extremely attentive to the mood of the enslaved, see Log of the Brig *Ranger,* Captain John Corran, Master, 1789–1790, 387 MD 56, LRO.

54. Testimony of George Malcolm, 1799, in *HLSP,* 3:219.

55. T. Aubrey, *The Sea-Surgeon, or the Guinea Man's Vade Mecum. In which is laid down, The Method of curing such Diseases as usually happen Abroad, especially on the Coast of Guinea: with the best way of treating Negroes, both in Health and in Sickness. Written for the Use of young Sea Surgeons* (London, 1729), 129–30.

56. Snelgrave, *A New Account,* 103–6.

57. *Providence Gazette; and Country Journal,* December 27, 1766; see also *An Account of the Life,* 26; Testimony of Zachary Macaulay, 1799, in *HLSP,* 3:339; *Three Years Adventures,* 85; Boulton, *The Voyage,* 27. Boulton himself may have had an amorous interest in Dizia, for it was she, he writes, "who did my peace of mind destroy."

58. Crow, *Memoirs,* 102; Snelgrave, *A New Account,* 165–68.

59. *Connecticut Journal,* January 1, 1768.

60. *Evening Post,* March 16, 1809.

61. Newton to Phillips, in Mary Phillips, *Memoir of the Life of Richard Phillips,* 29–31.

62. This section is based on the archival and primary sources cited in chapter 6, notes 1, 2, and 3.

63. Interview of Captain Bowen, *Substance,* 47. For a comment about the captain of a West India ship who had taken command of a slaver and had not yet been socialized into the customary brutality, see Interview of Mr. Thompson, ibid., 208–9.

64. *Three Years Adventures,* 41; *An Account of the Life,* 84; Africanus, *Remarks on the Slave Trade,* 47–48.

Chapter 8: The Sailor's Vast Machine

1. "Anonymous Account of the Society and Trade of the Canary Islands and West Africa, with Observations on the Slave Trade" (n.d., but 1779–84), Add. Ms. 59777B, BL. The author treated illness on the voyage, which suggests that he was a physician.

2. The recruiting is dated by the author's comment that it took place "about the commencement of the late disturbances," which would have been late summer 1775 (rather than April as he noted some years later when he actually wrote the account). See R. Barrie Rose, "A Liverpool Sailors' Strike in the Eighteenth Century," *Transactions of the Lancashire and Cheshire Antiquarian Society* 68 (1958), 85–92; "Extract of a Letter from Liverpool, September 1, 1775," *Morning Chronicle and London Advertiser,* September 5, 1775, republished in Richard Brooke, *Liverpool as it was during the Last Quarter of the Eighteenth Century, 1775–1800* (Liverpool, 1853), 332.

3. I would like to emphasize my indebtedness throughout this chapter to Emma Christopher's excellent study, *Slave Ship Sailors and Their Captive Cargoes, 1730–1807* (New York: Cambridge University Press, 2005).

4. "Anonymous Account of the Society and Trade of the Canary Islands and West Africa, with Observations on the Slave Trade" (n.d., but 1779–84), Add. Ms. 59777A, 3–5, BL. That sailors disliked the slave trade is a primary conclusion of Christopher, *Slave Trade Sailors,* 26–27.

5. *Three Years Adventures,* 6–10. Isaac Parker explained, "I had taken a fancy to go upon the coast of Guinea," while Nicholas Owen added, "I was one who had a desire to see what I had never seen before." See Testimony of Isaac Parker, 1790, *HCSP,* 73:137; Nicholas Owen, *Journal of a Slave-Dealer: A View of Some Remarkable Axedents in the Life of Nics. Owen on the Coast of Africa and America from the Year 1746 to the Year 1757,* ed. Eveline Martin (Boston: Houghton Mifflin, 1930), 43.

6. Colonel Spencer Childers, ed., *A Mariner of England: An Account of the Career of William Richardson from Cabin Boy in the Merchant Service to Warrant Officer in the Royal Navy [1780 to 1819] as Told by Himself* (Greenwich: Conway Maritime Press, 1970), 41–42. On the voyage of the *Spy,* see *TSTD,* #83598.

7. Robert Barker, *The Unfortunate Shipwright & Cruel Captain* (London, 1756); Robert Barker, *The Unfortunate Shipwright, or, Cruel Captain, being a Faithful Narrative of the Unparalleled Sufferings of Robert Barker, Late Carpenter on boar the Thetis Snow of Bristol; on a Voyage from thence to the Coast of Guinea and Antigua* (orig. publ. 1760; new edition, London, "printed for the SUFFERER for his own Benefit; and by no one else," 1775), 5–6, 8. Richardson would later be promoted to third mate before being busted back for mutiny. He died during the voyage.

8. *An Account of the Life,* 2–3, 10, 19. See *TSTD,* #16490. Nicholas Owen also went to sea on a slaver after a spendthrift father squandered a family fortune. See Owen, *Journal of a Slave-Dealer,* 1.

9. Interview of Mr. Thompson, in *Substance,* 24. For an account of an entire crew, out of Boston, deceived about a slave ship's destination, see *Commercial Advertiser,* September 24, 1799.

10. Ibid. Aboard the *Benson* in 1787, thirteen of the seamen were there because they had fallen into debt in port. See Anecdote X, *Substance,* 133.

11. Interview of Henry Ellison, *Substance,* 38.

12. John Newton Letter-book ("A Series of Letters from Mr.——— to Dr. J——— [Dr. David Jennings]," 1750–1760, 920 MD 409, LRO. Common sailors ranked low in the class

structure of eighteenth-century Britain, as the political arithmetic of Gregory King (1688), Joseph Massie (1760), and Patrick Colquhoun (1803) made clear; see Peter Mathias, "The Social Structure in the Eighteenth Century: A Calculation by Joseph Massie," *Economic History Review,* New Series, 10 (1957), 30–45. On seamen in eighteenth-century America, see Billy G. Smith, "The Vicissitudes of Fortune: The Careers of Laboring Men in Philadelphia, 1750–1800," in Stephen Innes, ed., *Work and Labor in Early America* (Chapel Hill: University of North Carolina Press, 1988), 221–51.

13. *Memoirs of Crow,* 169.

14. Testimony of James Penny, 1789, *HCSP,* 69:118.

15. [Robert Norris], *A Short Account of the African Slave Trade, Collected from Local Knowledge* (Liverpool, 1788), 14; Testimony of John Knox, 1789, *HCSP,* 68:150; Testimony of Thomas King, 1789, ibid., 68:321. Lord Sheffield suggested that two-thirds were landsmen. See his *Observations on the Project for Abolishing the Slave Trade, and on the Reasonableness of attempting some Practicable Mode of Relieving the Negroes* (orig. publ. London, 1790; 2nd edition, London, 1791), 18.

16. "Wage Book for the voyage of the ship *Hawk* from Liverpool to Africa, John Small Master," 1780–1781, William Davenport Archives, Maritime Archives & Library, D/DAV/3/4, MMM. See *TSTD,* #91793, #81753.

17. "Wage Book for the Voyage of the Ship *Essex* from Liverpool to Africa and the West Indies, Captain Peter Potter," 1783–1784, "Wage Book for the Voyage of the Ship *Essex* from Liverpool to Africa and Dominica, Captain Peter Potter," 1785–1786, William Davenport Archives, Maritime Archives & Library, D/DAV/3/5, D/DAV/3/6, MMM.

18. There has been no systematic study of wage rates for slave-trade sailors, so these remarks are impressionistic. For wage rates for sailors in all trades in the early eighteenth century, see Ralph Davis, *The Rise of the English Shipping Industry in the Seventeenth and Eighteenth Centuries* (London: Macmillan, 1962), 135–37; Marcus Rediker, *Between the Devil and the Deep Blue Sea: Merchant Seamen, Pirates, and the Anglo-American Maritime World, 1700–1750* (Cambridge: Cambridge University Press, 1987), Appendix C, 304–5. For a comment that appears to refer to lucrative private trading by seamen, see "Diary and Accounts, Commenda Fort, in Charge of William Brainie, 1714–1718," in Donnan II, 190.

19. "Answers from the Collector and the Comptroller," 1788, *HCSP,* 69:161. For examples of arrangements made by sailors to have part of their pay given to their wives while they were at sea, see Receipts for wages paid to Ellen Hornby on account of her husband, 1785–1786, D/DAV/15/5/4, and Receipts for wages paid to Mary Loundes on behalf of Her husband, 1786, D/DAV/15/2/13, Miscellaneous Items from the William Davenport Archives, Maritime Archives & Library, MMM.

20. *An Account of the Life,* 58; Testimony of Henry Ellison, 1790, *HCSP* 73:381–82.

21. [John Wells], "Journal of a Voyage to the Coast of Guinea, 1802," Add. Ms. 3,871, Cambridge University Library, f. 1; Samuel Robinson, *A Sailor Boy's Experience aboard a Slave Ship in the Beginning of the Present Century* (orig. publ. Hamilton, Scotland: William Naismith, 1867; rpt. Wigtown, Scotland: G.C. Book Publishers Ltd., 1996), 14; Case of the *Tartar,* 1808, Donnan IV, 585; Christopher, *Slave Trade Sailors and their Captive Cargoes,* ch. 2, "The Multiracial Crews of Slave Ships," 52–89. See also three appendices, "Black Sailors on Liverpool Slave Ships, 1794–1805," "Black Sailors on Bristol Slave Ships, 1748–1795," and "Black Sailors on Rhode Island Slave Ships, 1803–1807," 231–38.

22. Wage Book of *Hawk,* 1780–1781, D/DAV/3/4; *TSTD,* #81753. It appears that Abey belonged to second mate Hugh Lancelot, perhaps as his privilege slave. On black sailors, see Christopher, *Slave Trade Sailors,* 57–58, 70–73; Julius Sherrard Scott III, "The Common Wind: Currents of Afro-American Communication in the Era of the Haitian Revolution," Ph.D. dissertation, Duke University, 1986; W. Jeffrey Bolster, *Black Jacks: African American Seamen in the Age of Sail* (Cambridge, Mass.: Harvard University Press, 1997).

23. This and the next four paragraphs draw upon Robinson, *A Sailor Boy's Experience,* 24, 32–33, and Rediker, *Between the Devil and the Deep Blue Sea,* ch. 2.

24. Robinson, *A Sailor Boy's Experience,* 15; *Three Years Adventures,* 24.

25. *Daniel Macnamera and Nicholas Worsdale of the Snow* William *v.* Thomas Barry, August 26, 1729, "Records of the South Carolina Court of Admiralty, 1716–1732," f. 745, National Archives, Washington, D.C. See *TSTD,* #16546.

26. "A Journal of an Intended Voyage to the Gold Coast in the Black Prince her 8th Commencing the 5th of Septem'r 1764," BCL; Robinson, *A Sailor Boy's Experience,* 39; *TSTD,* #17573.

27. Captain William Snelgrave, *A New Account of Some Parts of Guinea and the Slave Trade* (London, 1734; rpt. London: Frank Cass & Co., 1971), 165–67, 170.

28. Testimony of John Knox, 1789, *HCSP,* 68:179.

29. Testimony of William James, 1789, *HCSP,* 69:137; Robinson, *A Sailor Boy's Experience,* 54–55; "Memorandum of the Mortality of Slaves on Board the 'Othello' while on the Coast of Africa and On her Passage to the West Indies," Accounts of the *Othello,* 1768–1769, in Donnan III, 235; *TSTD,* #36371.

30. Interview of Mr. James, *Substance,* 14; Testimony of Ellison, Noble, Trotter, and Millar, all 1790, *HCSP,* 375, 119, 85, 394.

31. Testimony of Ecroyde Claxton, 1791, *HCSP,* 82:33; Testimony of William Littleton, 1789, *HCSP,* 68:294, 309; Snelgrave, *A New Account,* 163–64; Robinson, *A Sailor Boy's Experience,* 55.

32. *Three Years Adventures,* 113–26. Robert Norris noted that on each ship, below-decks, "there are two White People to attend to the [men] Negroes, and Two Lights." See also Testimony of Isaac Wilson, 1790, *HCSP,* 72:289. It was also observed that seamen were not allowed into the women's apartment at night.

33. Reverend John Riland, *Memoirs of a West-India Planter, Published from an Original MS. With a Preface and Additional Details* (London: Hamilton, Adams & Co., 1827), 60–61.

34. Norris, *HCSP,* 68:4–5; Interview of Mr. Bowen, *Substance,* 44. I have drawn here on the testimony of slave trader and Liverpool representative John Matthews, who presented to Parliament "the History of Journal of One Day" in the life of the slaves aboard the slave ship. See *HCSP,* 68:19.

35. Testimony of Alexander Falconbridge, 1790, *HCSP,* 72:323; Testimony of James Arnold, 1789, *HCSP,* 69:125–26; Testimony of Henry Ellison, 1790, *HCSP,* 73:375; Testimony of James Towne, 1791, *HCSP,* 82:20.

36. Christopher, *Slave Ship Sailors and Their Captive Cargoes, 1730–1807,* ch. 5; Interview of Ellison, *Substance,* 36; *Three Years Adventures,* 133.

37. "Dicky Sam," *Liverpool and Slavery: An Historical Account of the Liverpool-African Slave Trade* (Liverpool: A. Bowker & Son, 1884), 36.

38. Testimony of Ecroyde Claxton, 1791, *HCSP,* 82:33–34.

39. "Documents Related to the Case of the *Zong* of 1783," REC/19, Manuscripts Department, NMM. The court ruled that the insurance company was not liable for payment

for the murdered slaves. See also Ian Baucom, *Specters of the Atlantic: Finance Capital, Slavery, and the Philosophy of History* (Durham, N.C.: Duke University Press, 2005).

40. Thomas Boulton, *The Sailor's Farewell, or the Guinea Outfit* (Liverpool 1768); *TSTD*, #36127; Herbert Klein, "African Women in the Atlantic Slave Trade," in Claire Robinson and Martin A. Klein, eds., *Women and Slavery in Africa* (Madison: University of Wisconsin Press, 1983), 29–38.

41. Robert Norris, 1789, *HCSP*, 68:9, 12; John Knox, 1789, *HCSP*, 68:171.

42. For a wage dispute in which sexual predation emerged as an issue, see *Desbrough v. Christian* (1720), HCA 24/132, 24/133.

43. Africanus, *Remarks on the Slave Trade, and the Slavery of Negroes, in a Series of Letters* (London, J. Phillips and Norwich: Chase and Co., 1788), 46; Alexander Falconbridge, *An Account of the Slave Trade on the Coast of Africa* (London, 1788), 30.

44. Snelgrave, *A New Account,* 162; Testimony of John Samuel Smith., 1791, *HCSP*, 82:140.

45. Richard H. Steckel and Richard A. Jensen, "New Evidence on the Causes of Slave and Crew Mortality in the Atlantic Slave Trade," *Journal of Economic History* 46 (1986), 57–77; Stephen D. Behrendt, "Crew Mortality in the Transatlantic Slave Trade in the Eighteenth Century," *Slavery and Abolition* 18 (1997), 49–71. Steckel and Jensen estimate that 60 percent of sailors died of fevers, while Behrendt puts the figure higher, at 80 percent. Behrendt also notes that the crew mortality was falling in the late eighteenth and early nineteenth centuries.

46. William Snelgrave to Humphry Morice, October 23, 1727, "Trading Accounts and Personal Papers of Humphry Morice," vol. 2, The Humphry Morice Papers, Bank of England Archives, London; Bruce Mouser, ed., *A Slaving Voyage to Africa and Jamaica: The Log of the* Sandown, *1793–1794* (Bloomington: Indiana University Press, 2002), 60; *Providence Gazette; and Country Journal,* December 8, 1770; *Federal Gazette & Baltimore Daily Advertiser,* March 12, 1796; *Courier,* March 25, 1801.

47. Riland, *Memoirs of a West-India Planter,* 37; *Three Years Adventures,* 40.

48. Petitions of Seamen, 1765–1774 and "Accounts of money for the relief of seamen and those disabled in the Merchant Service" (1747–1787), both in Society of Merchant Venturers Archive, Bristol Record Office. The Venturers traded to many parts of the world, and offered charity to their sailors regardless of route. The examples are sailors who worked in the slave trade. Their health was apparently worse than that of seamen who worked in other trades. See also Jonathan Press, *The Merchant Seamen of Bristol, 1747–1789* (Bristol, 1976).

49. *An Account of the Life,* 26; Wells, "Journal of a Voyage," f. 19; Interview of Ellison, *Substance,* 40.

50. "Voyage to Guinea, Antego, Bay of Campeachy, Cuba, Barbadoes, &c." (1714–1723), Add. Ms. 39946, BL, ff. 12–13; Robinson, *A Sailor Boy's Experience,* 97.

51. For a description of a burial ceremony, see Robinson, *A Sailor Boy's Experience,* 92.

52. "Inventory of the Cloths belonging to George Glover taken at his disease [decease] by Thos. Postlethwayt on board the Essex the 12 day of Novr 1783 viz and Sould," in "Wage Book for the Voyage of the Ship *Essex* from Liverpool to Africa and the West Indies, Captain Peter Potter," 1783–1784, William Davenport Archives, Maritime Archives & Library, D/DAV/3/5, MMM. See similar listings in the wage book for the *Essex* on its next voyage, 1785–86, in D/DAV/3/6. See *TSTD,* #81311, #81312.

53. The *Times,* March 15, 1788. For examples of the dead list, one kept by a surgeon, the other by a captain, see James Hoskins, "List of Mortality of the Ship's Company,"

1792–1793, "Certificates of Slaves Taken Aboard Ships," 1794, HL/PO/JO/10/7/982, HLRO, Westminster; Peter Potter to William Davenport, February 21, 1784, Letters from Captain Peter Potter to William Davenport & Co., 1783–1784, D/DAV/13/1/3, MMM.

54. This section draws upon the Information of Thomas Sanderson and William Steele (1750), HCA 1/58, ff. 1–10. The outcome of the case is unknown, but executions of the mutineers would not have been unlikely. See *TSTD,* #17198.

55. Sanderson had been sued a few years earlier, while working as a mate in the slave trade, for beating a sailor with a two-inch rope. See *Thomas Powell v. Eustace Hardwicke,* 1739, HCA 24/139.

56. Mutineers sometimes sent the captain and other officers ashore, as the men of the *Antelope* did. A few put them in the ship's boat on the high seas (which meant almost-certain death), and a substantial minority killed one or more outright. The observations in this section are based on a sample of thirty-seven mutinies that took place between 1719 and 1802.

57. *American Weekly Mercury,* December 7, 1721. See *TSTD,* #75419.

58. Information of John Bicknor, Meeting of the Grand Court of Jamaica, January 19, 1720, HCA 137/14, f. 9. This voyage of the *Abington* is not listed in the *TSTD* but the following one is. See #16257.

59. Examination of Thomas Williams (1734), HCA 1/56, f. 90; *Powell v. Hardwicke* (1738), HCA 24/139. The first report of the mutiny aboard the *Buxton* appeared in the *American Weekly Mercury* on September 26, 1734. See also *Boston News-Letter,* October 31, 1734. See also *TSTD,* #16758, and for the *Pearl Galley,* #16870. For an account of multiple ax killings aboard the *William* of Bristol in 1767, see *Boston News-Letter and New-England Chronicle,* April 10, 1767. See *TSTD,* #17634.

60. On the *Tewkesbury,* see *The Tryals of Seven Pyrates, viz. James Sweetland, John Kennelly, John Reardon, James Burdet, William Buckley, Joseph Noble, and Samuel Rhodes, for the Murder of Capt. Edw. Bryan of the Tewksbury of Bristol; and Running Away with the said Ship, November 2, 1737* (Bristol, 1738); *Boston Gazette,* March 13, 1738; "Proceedings of a Court of Admiralty held at Cape Coast in Africa the 19th November 1737 for the Trials of James Sweetland and other for Murder & Piracy," HCA 1/99, ff. 1–4. On other occasions, a captain or mate was killed by a sailor in a more-or-less spontaneous act of revenge, without a supporting bid to capture the ship. On the *Lovely Lass* of Bristol in 1792, "A black man, called *Joe or Cudjo,* together with *John Dickson* and *John Owens*" killed mate Robert Millagan. See the *Times,* November 8, 1794.

61. *Maryland Gazette and News Letter,* October 16, 1766, reprinted in Donnan II, 528–29; *Connecticut Journal,* November 17, 1769; *New London Gazette,* December 15, 1769. See *TSTD,* #17691 (*Black Prince*). For a mutiny in which sailors killed their captain and tried to blame his death on a slave insurrection, see *New-York Gazette,* March 11, 1765.

62. Christopher, *Slave Ship Sailors and Their Captive Cargoes, 1730–1807,* 127–32; Interview of James Towne, *Substance,* 56; Information of Hector McNeal (November 1731), HCA 1/56, f. 44.

63. Seamen sometimes deserted with a plan to recoup their wages, working "by the run" from a labor-scarce West Indian or American port back to England, at considerably higher wages. See Rediker, *Between the Devil and the Deep Blue Sea,* 136–38.

64. Testimony of Lord Rodney, 1790, *HCSP,* 72:182–83. For similar comments see Testimony of Sir George Young, *HCSP,* 69:155; Testimony of Sir George Young, 1790, *HCSP,* 73:211–12; Testimony of Thomas Clappeson, 1791, *HCSP,* 82:214.

65. Lord Sheffield, *Observations,* 18; Captain Francis Pope to Abraham Redwood, Antigua, May 24, 1740, in Donnan III, 135; Miles Barber to James Penny, March 11,

1784, *Baillie v. Hartley,* exhibits regarding the Slave Ship Comte du Nord and Slave Trade, E 219/377, NA. See also Samuel and William Vernon to Captain John Duncan, Newport, April 8, 1771: "If you have more hands than is necessary and can discharge them upon good Terms its best to do it and avoid all expenses upon your Vessel that you can." See Donnan III, 248. For lawsuits brought by sailors dumped by slavers in the West Indies, see *Soudin v. Demmerez* (1720), HCA 24/133, and *Fernando v. Moore* (1733), HCA 24/138.

66. Interview of Ellison, *Substance,* 41; Interview of Towne, *Substance,* 60. See also William James, 1789, *HCSP,* 68:139; Testimony of John Ashley Hall, *HCSP,* 72:233; Testimony of James Morley, *HCSP,* 73:164, 168.

67. Testimony of John Simpson, *HCSP,* 82:44 (Barbados); Testimony of Robert Forster, 1791, *HCSP,* 82:134 (Dominica, Grenada); *Connecticut Journal,* December 22, 1784 (Charleston); Hercules Ross, 1791, *HCSP,* 82:260; and Testimony of Mark Cook, 1791, *HCSP,* 82:199 (Jamaica).

68. *Three Years Adventures,* 137; Testimony of James Towne, *HCSP,* 82:30.

69. The first study of the event was Brooke, *Liverpool as it was,* which usefully includes the London newspaper articles. The best study of the strike remains, after almost half a century, Rose, "A Liverpool Sailors' Strike in the Eighteenth Century," 85–92. The other owners of the *Derby* were John Yates, Sam Parker, and Thomas Dunn. See *TSTD,* #92523.

70. This paragraph and the previous one draw upon two articles in London newspapers: *Gazetteer and New Daily Advertiser,* September 4, 1775, and *Morning Chronicle and London Advertiser,* September 4, 1775. Both Brooke and Rose (cited above) repeat the mistake that appeared in a couple of the newspaper articles that Yates was the captain of the *Derby* rather than one of its owners. Rose also says a sailors' protest march took place on Saturday morning, August 26, but the preponderance of the evidence suggests that it took place on Monday.

71. *Gazetteer and New Daily Advertiser,* September 4, 1775.

72. Information of James Waring, September 4, 1775, Records of the County Palantine of Lancaster, PL 27/5, NA; *Morning Chronicle,* September 4, 1775. The information about Thomas Staniforth was collected as oral history from his son Samuel by Brooke; see *Liverpool as it was,* 339.

73. The estimates of the number of cannon used by the sailors ranged from two to six.

74. Information of Richard Downward the Younger, September 2, 1775, PL27/5; *Gazetteer,* September 4 and 6, 1775. Whether these were sailors or people trying to defend the exchange, source does not say.

75. Information of William Sefton, September 3, 1775, PL 27/5; *Morning Chronicle,* September 8, 1775; *Gazetteer,* September 8, 1775.

76. *Morning Chronicle,* September 8, 1775, and September 11, 1775; *Gazetteer and New Daily Advertiser,* September 6, 1775. Many years later Richard Brooke talked with someone who "had taken part in the attack on Mr. Radcliffe's house." This person told him of the discovery of the chaff, "which the lower classes used as a by-word against Mr. Radcliffe for a long period of time afterwards." Mr. Radcliffe's son later confirmed the story. See Brooke, *Liverpool as it was,* 341.

77. *Morning Chronicle,* September 4, 1775, September 8, 1775; *Gazetteer,* September 6, 1775; Information of John Huddleston, September 1, 1775, and Information of John Adams, September 2, 1775, PL 27/5; Brooke, *Liverpool as it was,* 341. Gomer Williams, *History of the Liverpool Privateers and Letters of Marque: With An Account Of The Liverpool*

Slave Trade, 1744–1812 (London, 1897; rpt. Montreal: McGill-Queen's University Press, 2004), 557.

78. *Morning Chronicle,* September 4, 1775; *Daily Advertiser,* September 5, 1775; Information of Thomas Middleton, September 28, 1775, PL 27/5; *Chester Chronicle,* September 4, 1775.

79. Information of Thomas Blundell, September 2, 1775; Information of Anthony Taylor, September 2, 1775; Information of Henry Billinge, September 27, 1775, all in PL 27/5; the *Morning Chronicle,* September 8, 1775.

80. Information of Cuthbert Bisbronney, September 2, 1775; Information of William Stanistreet, September 2, 1775.

81. *Morning Chronicle,* September 11, 1775; Council Book of the Corporation, 1775, vol. 2, 717–18, cited by Brooke, *Liverpool as it was,* 345.

82. Snelgrave, *A New Acccount,* 162–63. See Christopher, *Slave-Trade Sailors,* ch. 6.

83. Testimony of John Simpson, 1791, *HCSP,* 82:42; Interview of George Millar, *Substance,* 3; Testimony of Sir George Young, *HCSP,* 73:136; *Three Years Adventures,* 41; Robinson, *A Sailor Boy's Experience,* 56; Testimony of Richard Story, 1791, *HCSP,* 82:13; Interview of Thompson, *Substance,* 24. It was alleged in court in 1701 that John Babb allowed fellow sailors to take food from the slaves, after which many died. See *John Babb v. Bernard Chalkley* (1701), HCA 24/127.

84. The wage reduction in Liverpool in August 1775 was the second one in a short period of time. As recently as mid-June 1775, slave-trade sailors shipping out of Liverpool were still getting the customary rate of forty shillings per month. See "Wage Book for the voyage of the ship *Dalrymple* from Dominica to Liverpool, Patrick Fairweather, Master," 1776, William Davenport Archives, Maritime Archives & Library, D/DAV/3/3, MMM. See also *TSTD,* #91988.

85. *Newport Mercury,* July 18, 1763.

Chapter 9: From Captives to Shipmates

1. *An Account of the Life,* 22–24. For the voyage of the *Loyal George,* see *TSTD,* #16490.

2. William D. Piersen, "White Cannibals, Black Martyrs: Fear, Depression, and Religious Faith as Causes of Suicide Among New Slaves," *Journal of Negro History* 62 (1977), 147–59.

3. Sidney W. Mintz and Richard Price, *The Birth of African-American Culture: An Anthropological Perspective* (orig. publ. 1976; rpt. Boston: Beacon Press, 1992); Michael A. Gomez, *Exchanging Our Country Marks: The Transformation of African Identities in the Colonial and Antebellum South* (Chapel Hill: University of North Carolina Press, 1998); Stephanie E. Smallwood, *Saltwater Slavery: A Middle Passage from Africa to American Diaspora* (Cambridge, Mass.: Harvard University Press, 2006).

4. Testimony of George Millar, 1790, *HCSP,* 73:394; Testimony of William Littleton, 1789, *HCSP,* 68:299; Samuel Robinson, *A Sailor Boy's Experience aboard a Slave Ship in the Beginning of the Present Century* (orig. publ. Hamilton, Scotland: William Naismith, 1867; rpt. Wigtown, Scotland: G.C. Book Publishers Ltd., 1996), 55; John Atkins, *A Voyage to Guinea, Brasil, and the West Indies; In His Majesty's Ships, the Swallow and Weymouth* (London, 1735; rpt. London: Frank Cass & Co., 1970), 180.

5. *Three Years Adventures,* 84; John Matthews, *A Voyage to the River Sierra Leone, on the Coast of Africa, containing an Account of the Trade and Productions of the Country, and*

of the Civil and Religious Customs and Manners of the People; in a Series of Letters to a Friend in England (London: B. White and Son, 1788), 151–52.

6. Testimony of Thomas Poplett, 1789, *HCSP*, 69:26; Robinson, *A Sailor Boy's Experience,* 78; Testimony of Thomas King, 1789, *HCSP,* 68:333; Captain William Snelgrave, *A New Account of Some Parts of Guinea and the Slave Trade* (London, 1734; rpt. London: Frank Cass & Co., 1971), 171–72; *Three Years Adventures,* 95–96, 125; Testimony of James Fraser, 1790, *HCSP,* 71:34. See also Alan J. Rice, *Radical Narratives of the Black Atlantic* (London: Continuum, 2003), 120–46.

7. Snelgrave, *A New Account,* 163; Testimony of Fraser, 1790, *HCSP,* 71:34.

8. Reverend John Riland, *Memoirs of a West-India Planter, Published from an Original MS. With a Preface and Additional Details* (London: Hamilton, Adams & Co., 1827), 20–24; Testimony of Ecroyde Claxton, 1791, *HCSP,* 82:34. Slave trader John Fountain testified in 1789, "It depends upon what nations they are of.—Duncoes are never put in irons—they supply a great number of the Slaves.—Fantees are always put in irons—the Ashantees and other nations as it may be necessary, and according to the offence they have committed." See *HCSP,* 69:269.

9. Roderick Terry, "Some Old Papers Relating to the Newport Slave Trade," Newport Historical Society, *Bulletin* 62 (1927), 23.

10. "Medical Log of Slaver the 'Lord Stanley,' 1792, by Christopher Bowes, MS. 129. d.27., Royal College of Surgeons, London. On the reduction of bodies to numbers, see Smallwood, *Saltwater Slavery,* 178.

11. Journal of the Ship *Mary,* 1795–96, in Donnan III, 375. See also *Three Years Adventures,* 39; *Memoirs of Crow,* 38, 40; Testimony of Fraser, 1790, *HCSP,* 71:45; Testimony of Alexander Falconbridge, 1790, *HCSP,* 72:294.

12. *Boston Weekly News-Letter,* September 1, 1737; *Boston Gazette,* November 22, 1762; Mungo Park, *Travels into the Interior of Africa, Performed under the Direction and Patronage of the African Association, in the Years 1795, 1796, and 1797,* ed. Kate Ferguson Marsters (orig. publ. 1799; rpt. Durham and London: Duke University Press, 2000), 305.

13. *Pennsylvania Gazette,* July 30, 1741; *Royal Georgia Gazette,* June 14, 1781; Testimony of Peter Whitfield Branker, in *HLSP,* 3:190. See also the testimony of Captains Richard Pearson and John Olderman, in ibid., 121, 151. For other instances of the enslaved fighting against privateers, see *Boston Weekly News-Letter,* July 31, 1760; *Massachusetts Spy: Or, the Worcester Gazette,* April 4, 1798; *Commercial Advertiser,* July 19, 1805; *American Mercury,* October 2, 1806; Testimony of James Penny, 1789, *HCSP,* 69:117; *Memoirs of Crow,* 102.

14. *Enquirer,* September 26, 1804; Robert Barker, *The Unfortunate Shipwright, or, Cruel Captain, being a Faithful Narrative of the Unparalleled Sufferings of Robert Barker, Late Carpenter on board the Thetis Snow of Bristol; on a Voyage from thence to the Coast of Guinea and Antigua* (orig. publ. 1760; new edition, London, "printed for the SUFFERER for his own Benefit; and by no one else," 1775), 20; Testimony of John Olderman, *HLSP,* 3:150; Captain James Penny to Miles Barber, July 24, 1784, *Baillie v. Hartley,* exhibits regarding the Slave Ship *Comte du Nord* and Slave Trade; schedule, correspondence, accounts, E 219/377, NA; *Newport Mercury,* November 18, 1765.

15. "Barque Eliza's Journal, Robert Hall, Commander, from Liverpool to Cruize 31 Days & then to Africa & to Demarary; mounts 14 Nine & Six Pounders; with 31 Men & boys," Royal African Company Records, T70/1220, NA; Testimony of Peter Whitfield Branker, *HLSP,* 2:119; Testimony of John Ashley Hall, *HCSP,* 72:233, 273.

16. Testimony of Falconbridge, 1790, in *HCSP,* 72:303; Testimony of Fraser, 1790, *HCSP,* 71:28.

17. *Three Years Adventures,* 116-17; Testimony of John Ashley Hall, 1790, *HCSP,* 72:230.

18. Falconbridge, *An Account of the Slave Trade,* 26.

19. Testimony of James Bowen, 1789, *HCSP,* 69:125; Testimony of John Knox, 1789, *HCSP,* 68:158.

20. Captain John Adams, *Sketches taken during Ten Voyages to Africa, Between the Years 1786 and 1800; including Observations on the Country between Cape Palmas and the River Congo; and Cursory Remarks on the Physical and Moral Character of the Inhabitants* (London, 1823; rpt. New York: Johnson Reprint Corporation, 1970), 9.

21. "Voyage to Guinea, Antego, Bay of Campeachy, Cuba, Barbadoes, &c." (1714–1723), Add. Ms. 39946, ff. 9–10, BL; Mouser, ed., *The Log of the* Sandown, 103; "The Slave Trade at Calabar, 1700–1705," in Donnan II, 15; Information of James Towne, in *Substance,* 236.

22. Falconbridge, *An Account of the Slave Trade,* 28; Examination of Rice Harris (1733), HCA 1/56, ff. 73–74; Testimony of James Arnold, 1789, *HCSP,* 69:126.

23. T. Aubrey, *The Sea-Surgeon, or the Guinea Man's Vade Mecum. In which is laid down, The Method of curing such Diseases as usually happen Abroad, especially on the Coast of Guinea: with the best way of treating Negroes, both in Health and in Sickness. Written for the Use of young Sea-Surgeons* (London, 1729), 129–32; Atkins, *A Voyage to Guinea,* 60; Testimony of Trotter, 1790, *HCSP,* 73: 84–85. The many meanings of death in the Black Atlantic will be explored with great insight by Vincent Brown, *The Reaper's Garden: Death and Power in the World of Atlantic Slavery* (Cambridge, Mass.: Harvard University Press, forthcoming). Essential background here is Kenneth F. Kiple, *The Caribbean Slave: A Biological History* (Cambridge: Cambridge University Press, 1984), 1–75. A useful summary of the extensive research on mortality in the slave trade is Herbert S. Klein, *The Atlantic Slave Trade* (Cambridge: Cambridge University Press, 1999), 130–42.

24. Testimony of Fraser, 1790, *HCSP,* 71:58; Falconbridge, *An Account of the Slave Trade,* 32; Testimony of Falconbridge, 1790, *HCSP,* 72:303.

25. "Extracts of such Journals of the Surgeons employed in Ships trading to the Coast of Africa, since the first of August 1788, as have been transmitted to the Custom House in London, and which relate to the State of the Slaves during the Time they were on Board the Ships," Slave Trade Papers, 3 May 1792, HL/PO/JO/10/7/920; "Log-books, etc. of slave ships, 1791–7," Main Papers, 17–19 June 1799, HL/PO/JO/10/7/1104; "Certificates of Slaves Taken Aboard Ships," 1794, HL/PO/JO/10/7/982, all in the HLRO. It should be noted that not all surgeons listed causes of death; therefore these archives contain more than the eighty-six journals analyzed here. Some of these journals (though not all) formed the empirical base of a study by Richard H. Steckel and Richard A. Jensen, "New Evidence on the Causes of Slave and Crew Mortality in the Atlantic Slave Trade," *Journal of Economic History* 46 (1986), 57–77.

26. Thomas Trotter, *Observations on the Scurvy, with a Review of the Theories lately advanced on that Disease; and the Theories of Dr. Milman refuted from Practice* (London, 1785; Philadelphia, 1793), 14; Captain James Penny to Miles Barber, July 1, 1784, *Baillie v. Hartley,* E 219/377, NA; Case of the *Mermaid,* July 10, 1739, Donnan III, 51–52; J. Philmore, *Two Dialogues on the Man-Trade* (London, 1760), 34–35; Zachary B. Friedenberg, *Medicine Under Sail* (Annapolis, Md.: Naval Institute Press, 2002). For a medical log in which a ship's surgeon, Christopher Bowes, tended to the sickness of the enslaved aboard the *Lord Stanley* in 1792, see "Medical Log of Slaver the 'Lord Stanley,' 1792." Bowes treated 33 people: 24 men, 3 "man-boys," 3 women, and 3 girls for a variety of

ailments—diarrhea, tremors, dysentery, fever, pain (bowels, chest, knee, ankle, head)—of whom 16 died, 3 on the coast and 13 in the Middle Passage (of the 392 on board). This ship had a comparatively low death rate of just over 4 percent. See *TSTD*, #82365.

27. "Anonymous Account," Add. Ms. 59777B, f. 39v; Nicholas Owen, *Journal of a Slave-Dealer: A View of Some Remarkable Axedents in the Life of Nics. Owen on the Coast of Africa and America from the Year 1746 to the Year 1757*, ed. Eveline Martin (Boston: Houghton Mifflin, 1930), 90; Thomas Winterbottom, *An Account of the Native Africans in the Neighbourhood of Sierra Leone, to which is added An Account of the Present State of Medicine among them* (London, 1803; rpt. London: Frank Cass & Co., 1969), vol. I, 236. See also Atkins, *A Voyage to Guinea*, 79, 101; Matthews, *A Voyage to the River Sierra Leone*, 123; Philip Curtin, "Epidemiology and the Slave Trade," *Political Science Quarterly* 83 (1968), 190–216; Kenneth Kiple and Brian Higgins, "Mortality Caused by Dehydration during the Middle Passage," in Joseph Inikori and Stanley Engerman, eds., *The Atlantic Slave Trade: Effects on Economies, Societies, and Peoples in Africa, the Americas, and Europe* (Durham, N.C.: Duke University Press, 1992), 322–31; Richard B. Sheridan, "The Guinea Surgeons on the Middle Passage: The Provision of Medical Services in the British Slave Trade," *International Journal of African Historical Studies* 14 (1981), 601–25; Sharla Fett, *Working Cures: Healing, Health, and Power on Southern Slave Plantations* (Chapel Hill: University of North Carolina Press, 2002).

28. "Richard Simsons Voyage to the Straits of Magellan & S. Seas in the Year 1689," Sloane 86, BL, f. 57; William Smith, *A New Voyage to Guinea: Describing the Customs, Manners, Soil, Climate, Habits, Buildings, Education, Manual Arts, Agriculture, Trade, Employments, Languages, Ranks of Distinction, Habitations, Diversions, Marriages, and whatever else is memorable among the Inhabitants* (London, 1744; rpt. London: Frank Cass & Co., 1967), 28; Snelgrave, *A New Account*, 187–88; Atkins, *A Voyage to Guinea*, 72. John Adams also used the "Tower of Babel" analogy when discussing the variety of West African languages. See Adams, *Sketches taken during Ten Voyages to Africa*, 64. See also John Thornton, *Africa and Africans in the Making of the Atlantic World, 1400–1800* (Cambridge: Cambridge University Press, 1992; 2nd edition, 1998), 19–20, 183–205.

29. Snelgrave, *A New Account*, 177–80; Testimony of Claxton, *HCSP*, 82:36; Testimony of Fraser, *HCSP*, 71:13; Testimony of Falconbridge, *HCSP*, 69:48.

30. [Thomas Thompson], *Memoirs of an English Missionary to the Coast of Guinea* (London, 1788), 28–29.

31. Testimony of James Rigby, 1799, *HSLP*, 3:88; [Thompson], *Memoirs*, 28–29; Testimony of William McIntosh, 1789, *HCSP*, 68:194; Winterbottom, *An Account of the Native Africans*, 1:11; Thornton, *Africa and Africans*, ch. 7. See also Okon Edet Uya, "The Middle Passage and Personality Change Among Diaspora Africans," in Joseph E. Harris, ed., *Global Dimensions of the African Diaspora* (Washington, D.C.: Howard University Press, 1993, 2nd edition), 87.

32. Falconbridge, *HCSP*, 72:294; Peter Linebaugh, "All the Atlantic Mountains Shook," *Labour/Le Travail* 10 (1982), 87–121.

33. Robinson, *A Sailor Boy's Experience*, 78; *Three Years Adventures*, 136. See also Testimony of Olderman, *HLSP*, 3:175; Matthews, *A Voyage to the River Sierra Leone*, 99; Testimony of Trotter, *HCSP*, 73:84.

34. *Three Years Adventures*, 111–12, 120, 93–94.

35. Testimony of Robert Norris, 1789, *HCSP*, 68:7.

36. Interview of Mr. Janverin, *Substance*, 249.

37. Testimony of Arnold, *HCSP*, 69:126; Testimony of Claxton, *HCSP*, 82:36.

38. Snelgrave, *A New Account*, introduction; *Three Years Adventures*, 131–32; Testimony of Robert Heatley, 1789, *HCSP*, 69:123.

39. Riland, *Memoirs of a West-India Planter*, 58–59; Thomas Clarkson to Comte de Mirabeau, November 8, 1789, ff. 1–2, Papers of Thomas Clarkson, Huntington Library, San Marino, California. See also Falconbridge, *An Account of the Slave Trade*, 30; Testimony of Falconbridge, 1790, *HCSP*, 72:307; Testimony of Ellison, *HCSP*, 73:376; Testimony of James Towne, 1791, *HCSP*, 82:22; Testimony of Claxton, *HCSP*, 82:36.

40. Testimony of David Henderson, 1789, *HCSP*, 69:139; Testimony of Arnold, *HCSP*, 69:127.

41. Antonio T. Bly, "Crossing the Lake of Fire: Slave Resistance During the Middle Passage, 1720–1842," *Journal of Negro History* 83 (1998), 178–86; Richard Rathbone, "Resistance to Enslavement in West Africa," in *De la traite a l'esclavage: actes du colloque international sur la traite des noirs*, ed. Serge Daget (Nantes, 1988), 173–84.

42. Riland, *Memoirs of a West-India Planter*, 52; Testimony of James Morley, 1790, *HCSP*, 73:160–61.

43. Testimony of Isaac Parker, 1790, *HCSP*, 73:124–25, 130; *TSTD*, #91135.

44. *Edward Fentiman v. James Kettle* (1730), HCA 24/136; *TSTD*, #76618. For other evidence that the enslaved would stop eating if they were mistreated, see Testimony of James Towne, 1791, *HCSP*, 82:21. For an instance in which the enslaved resorted to a collective—and successful—hunger strike in support of a mistreated African translator aboard their ship, see "The Deposition of John Dawson, Mate of the Snow *Rainbow*," 1758, in Donnan IV, 371–72.

45. Aubrey, *The Sea-Surgeon*, 128. For another judgment that violence did not work against the will of the enslaved, see Interview of Janverin, *Substance*, 249.

46. Snelgrave, *A New Account*, 190; "Anecdote IX" (author unnamed), in *Substance*, 315–16; *Jones v. Small*, Law Report, the *Times*, July 1, 1785.

47. "Voyage to Guinea," Add. Ms. 39946, f. 8 (*TSTD*, #75489); *Memoirs of Crow*, 44; James Hogg to Humphry Morice, March 6, 1732, Humphry Morice Papers, Bank of England Archives, London.

48. *Connecticut Journal*, February 2, 1786; Testimony of Falconbridge, 1790, *HCSP*, 72:307–8; "Extract from a Letter on Board the Prince of Orange," April 7, 1737, *Boston News-Letter*, September 15, 1737.

49. Testimony of Isaac Wilson, 1790, *HCSP*, 72:281; Testimony of Claxton, *HCSP*, 82:35–36; *Pennsylvania Gazette*, May 21, 1788 (article by Gandy, but not identified as such). Clarkson retold his story in a letter to Mirabeau, December 9, 1789, Papers of Clarkson, Huntington Library. On the *Zong*, see Granville Sharp to the Lords Commissioners of the Admiralty, London, July 2, 1783, "Documents Related to the Case of the *Zong* of 1783," Manuscripts Department, REC/19, f. 96, NMM.

50. Testimony of Wilson and Falconbridge, both in *HCSP*, 72:279, 300; Log of the Brig *Ranger*, Captain John Corran, Master, 1789–1790, 387 MD 56, LRO; [John Wells], "Journal of a Voyage to the Coast of Guinea, 1802," Add. Ms. 3,871, f. 15, Cambridge University Library; Testimony of Mr. Thompson, *Substance*, 207.

51. Extract of a letter to Mr. Thomas Gatherer, in Lombard Street; dated Fort-James, River Gambia, April 12, 1773, *Newport Mercury*, December 27, 1773; *Independent Journal*, April 29, 1786. For an example of a similar explosion on a French slave ship, see *Newport Mercury*, March 3, 1792. For other examples of mass suicides after failed insurrections, see *Newport Mercury*, November 25, 1765; *Connecticut Journal*, January 1, 1768; "The

Log of the *Unity*, 1769–1771," Earle Family Papers, D/EARLE/1/4, MMM; *Providence Gazette; and Country Journal*, September 10, 1791.

52. See citations in note 25 above.

53. For the legal ruling, see *Jones v. Small*, Law Report, the *Times*, July 1, 1785. Like other forms of resistance, the action of jumping overboard circulated from the Atlantic back to the metropolis, where various writers immortalized the decision of death before dishonorable slavery in poetry. A well-known abolitionist poem, "The Negroe's Complaint," jointly but anonymously written by Liverpool patricians William Roscoe and Dr. James Currie, said of African protagonist Maratan, "Tomorrow the white-man in vain / Shall proudly account me his slave! / My shackles, I plunge in the main— / And rush to the realms of the brave." See Dr. James Currie to Admiral Sir Graham Moore, 16 March 1788, 920 CUR 106, Papers of Dr. James Currie, LRO. The poem was originally published in the *World* and was later republished in the United States. See the *Federal Gazette, and Philadelphia Evening Post*, April 8, 1790. The same conceit appears in Roscoe's *The Wrongs of Africa* (London, 1788). See James G. Basker, *Amazing Grace: An Anthology of Poems About Slavery, 1660–1810* (New Haven, Conn.: Yale University Press, 2002).

54. Testimony of Ellison, *HCSP*, 73:374. The classic article on this subject is Lorenzo Greene, "Mutiny on the Slave Ships," *Phylon* 5 (1944), 346–54. See also the valuable work by Eric Robert Taylor, *If We Must Die: Shipboard Insurrections in the Era of the Atlantic Slave Trade* (Baton Rouge: Louisiana State University Press, 2006).

55. Testimony of Arnold, *HCSP*, 69:130. Snelgrave (*A New Account*, 167) was surprised to learn that a mere twenty men had made an insurrection aboard the *Eagle Galley* in 1704. Indeed the number was sometimes smaller. The rebels also wagered wrong in some instances, as others did not join them once the insurrection was under way.

56. The *Times*, July 1, 1785; "Log of the *Unity*," Earle Family Papers, D/EARLE/1/4; *Connecticut Journal*, February 2, 1786; Testimony of Robert Hume, 1799, *HLSP*, 3:110; Testimony of Trotter, *HCSP*, 73:87; Atkins, *A Voyage to Guinea*, 72–73. For boys, see Extract of a letter to Mr. Thomas Gatherer, April 12, 1773, *Newport Mercury*, December 27, 1773. See also Uya, "The Middle Passage and Personality Change," 91.

57. *Three Years Adventures*, 96; Snelgrave, *A New Account*, 77; Testimony of Fountain, *HCSP*, 68:273; Thornton, *Warfare in Atlantic Africa*, 140.

58. *Pennsylvania Gazette*, May 16, 1754. For other instances in which the enslaved used European weapons in the course of insurrection, see Lieutenant Governor Thomas Handasyd to the Board of Trade and Plantations, from Jamaica, October 5, 1703, Donnan II, 4; *Boston News-Letter*, May 6, 1731 (also *Boston Gazette*, April 26, 1731); *Bath Journal*, December 18, 1749; *Boston Gazette*, October 4, 1756; *Pennsylvania Gazette*, May 31, 1764; *New London Gazette*, December 18, 1772; *Newport Mercury*, December 27, 1773; William Fairfield to Rebecca Fairfield, Cayenne, April 23, 1789, Donnan III: 83; *Providence Gazette; and Country Journal*, September 10, 1791; *Massachusetts Spy: Or, the Worcester Gazette*, April 4, 1798; *Federal Gazette & Baltimore Daily Advertiser*, July 30, 1800; *Newburyport Herald*, March 22, 1808. Inikori estimates that 150,000 to 200,000 guns were imported per year into West Africa between 1750 and 1807, while Richards puts the number at 283,000 to 394,000. See Inikori, "The Import of Firearms into West Africa 1750–1807," 348, and Richards, "The Import of Firearms into West Africa in the Eighteenth Century," 43–44.

59. Smith, *A New Voyage to Guinea*, 28. On the Coromantee, see Trotter, *Observations on the Scurvy*, 23; Falconbridge, *An Account of the Slave Trade*, 70. See also Snelgrave, *A*

New Account, 168–69, 177–78. On the Ibibio, see *Memoirs of Crow,* 98–99, 200–1. David Richardson has suggested that the enslaved from the Senegambian region (along with those from Sierra Leone and the Windward Coast) were the most rebellious, with Gold Coast captives not far behind. See his "Shipboard Revolts, African Authority, and the Atlantic Slave Trade," *William and Mary Quarterly,* 3rd ser., 58 (2001), 76–77.

60. *Felix Farley's Bristol Journal,* March 24, 1753.

61. Smallwood, *Saltwater Slavery,* 123.

62. *Newburyport Herald,* December 4, 1801.

63. *Boston Post Boy,* August 13, 1750.

64. *Pennsylvania Gazette,* November 9, 1732; Atkins, *A Voyage to Guinea,* 175–76; see also *Three Years Adventures,* 103.

65. *Boston News-Letter,* September 18, 1729; *TSTD,* #77058; *Bath Journal,* December 18, 1749; *TSTD,* #90233.

66. *American Mercury,* January 31, 1785.

67. Testimony of Ellison, *HCSP,* 73:375; Snelgrave, *A New Account,* 167, 173; "Anecdote I" (author unnamed), in *Substance,* 311; Testimony of Arnold, *HCSP,* 69:134.

68. Testimony of Towne, 1791, *HCSP,* 82:21; Richardson, "Shipboard Revolts," 82–90.

69. *Boston News-Letter,* September 9, 1731; Richardson, "Shipboard Revolts," 74–75.

70. Thomas Clarkson, *An Essay on the Slavery and Commerce of the Human Species, particularly The African, translated from a Latin Dissertation, which was honoured with the First Prize in the University of Cambridge for the Year 1785, with Additions* (London, 1786; rpt. Miami, Fla.: Mnemosyne Publishing Co., 1969), 88–89.

71. *Newburyport Herald,* December 4, 1801; Clarkson to Mirabeau, December 9, 1789, ff. 1–2, Papers of Clarkson, Huntington Library.

72. Piersen, "White Cannibals, Black Martyrs," 147–59.

73. "Anonymous Account," Add. Ms. 59777B, ff. 40–41v; Testimony of John Douglas, 1791, *HCSP,* 82:125; Michael Mullin, *Africa in America: Slave Acculturation and Resistance in the American South and British Caribbean, 1736–1831* (Urbana and Chicago: University of Illinois Press, 1992), 66–69; Smallwood, *Saltwater Slavery,* 147. See also the interesting observations by Elisabeth Isichei in "Transformations: Enslavement and the Middle Passage in African American Memory," in her *Voices of the Poor in Africa* (Rochester, N.Y.: University of Rochester Press, 2002), 77–85.

74. "Voyage to Guinea," Add. Ms. 39946, ff. 9–10; Testimony of Millar, *HCSP,* 73:394; Hawkins, *A History of a Voyage to the Coast of Africa,* 108; Clarkson, *An Essay on the Slavery and Commerce of the Human Species,* 143–44. For other references to the belief, see the *Times,* February 2, 1790; Atkins, *A Voyage to Guinea,* 175–76.

75. "Anonymous Account," Add. Ms. 59777B, ff. 40–41v.

76. Testimony of Claxton, 1791, *HCSP,* 82:35; Snelgrave, *A New Account,* 183–84; *Memoirs of Crow,* 26. Snelgrave added that neither the man who was executed nor any of the other Coromantee (from the Gold Coast) believed in the return after death but that "many I had on board from other Countries had that Opinion."

77. Clarkson to Mirabeau, December 9, 1789, f. 1, Papers of Clarkson, Huntington Library.

78. Thornton, *Africa and Africans,* 195.

79. *Three Years Adventures,* 80–82; Testimony of William James, *HCSP,* 69:49; Testimony of Wilson, *HCSP,* 72:281–82; Testimony of Arnold, *HCSP,* 69, 50, 137–38; Testimony of Trotter, *HCSP,* 73:97, 99–100. For a case of a woman who exited a slave ship

and found her husband, from whom she had been torn two years earlier, see the *Sun,* November 18, 1805.

80. Matthews, *A Voyage to the River Sierra Leone,* 153; Interview of Bowen, *Substance,* 230. Note John Thornton's comment about the widespread West African cultural skill in incorporating "foreigners": *Africa and Africans,* 218.

81. Winterbottom, *An Account of the Native Africans,* 1:212; *Three Years Adventures,* 126. Winterbottom also relayed a story from a friend in Jamaica who met an African man who was going home late one evening, "carrying a box upon his head." In it was "the heart of a *ship-mate,* which he was carrying to an estate a few miles off, where a number of the friends of the deceased lived, in order that they might *cry* over it. He said he had already cried over the body the night before in committing it to the ground, and now he meant to join his friends, who were more remote, in the same ceremony" (1:212–13). See also Uya, "The Middle Passage and Personality Change," 93. I would like to thank my colleagues Jerome Branche and Shelome Gooden for valuable discussion of this theme.

82. Testimony of Falconbridge, *HCSP,* 72:308; Testimony of Ellison, *HCSP,* 73:381.

83. Testimony of Trotter, *HCSP,* 73:88; Interview of Bowen, *Substance,* 230; "Extract of a letter from Charleston to the Editor of the Repertory, dated March 8th," *Massachusetts Spy, or Worcester Gazette,* April 4, 1804. The author thought the three might have been sisters but seems to have changed his judgment to "friends."

84. Testimony of Thomas King, 1789, *HCSP,* 68:333; Testimony of Arnold, *HCSP,* 69:50. For examples of Adam and Eve, see Mouser, *The Log of the* Sandown, 64; *An Account of the Life,* 29. See also Doudou Diene, ed., *From Chains to Bonds: The Slave Trade Revisited* (Oxford: Berghahn, 2001).

Chapter 10: The Long Voyage of the Slave Ship Brooks

1. During the years 1788 and 1789, slave ships began 197 voyages from British ports, 19 voyages from American ports. Data drawn from *TSTD.*

2. Clarkson, *History,* vol. II, 111.

3. Thomas Cooper, Esq., *Letters on the Slave Trade: First Published in Wheeler's Manchester Chronicle and since re-printed with Additions and Alterations* (Manchester, 1787), 3–5. For a powerful new account of the origins and early history of the movement, see Christopher Brown, *Moral Capital: Foundations of British Abolitionism* (Chapel Hill: University of North Carolina Press, 2006).

4. Excellent recent work on the image of the slave ship includes J. R. Oldfield, *Popular Politics and British Anti-Slavery: The Mobilisation of Public Opinion against the Slave Trade, 1787–1807* (London: Frank Cass & Co., 1998), 99–100, 163–66; Philip Lapsansky, "Graphic Discord: Abolitionist and Antiabolitionist Images," in Jean Yellin Fagan and John C. Van Horne, eds., *The Abolitionist Sisterhood: Women's Political Culture in Antebellum America* (Ithaca and London: Cornell University Press, 1994), 201–30; Cheryl Finley, "Committed to Memory: The Slave-Ship Icon and the Black-Atlantic Imagination," *Chicago Art Journal* (1999), 2–21; Marcus Wood, "Imagining the Unspeakable and Speaking the Unimaginable: The 'Description' of the Slave Ship *Brooks* and the Visual Interpretation of the Middle Passage," in Katherine Quinsey, Nicole E. Didicher, and Walter S. Skakoon, eds., *Lumen: Selected Proceedings from the Canadian Society for Eighteenth-Century Studies* (Edmonton: Academic Printing and Publishing), 211–45; and Marcus Wood, *Blind Memory: Visual Representation of Slavery in England and*

America, 1780–1865 (Manchester and New York: Manchester University Press, 2000), 14–77.

5. "Admeasurement of the Ships at Liverpool from Captain Parrey's Account," no date (1788), Liverpool Papers, Add. Ms. 38416, f. 209, BL; "Dimensions of the following Ships in the Port of Liverpool, employed in the African Slave Trade," in *HCSP,* 67.

6. *Plan of an AFRICAN SHIP'S Lower Deck with NEGROES in the proportion of only One to a Ton* (Plymouth, 1788). It appears that the reproduction by T. Deeble of Bristol (17562/1, BRO) is identical to the Plymouth broadside. See also *Plan and Sections of a Slave Ship* (London: James Phillips, 1789); Clarkson, *History,* 111. It should be noted that there was an abolitionist agenda behind sending Parrey to Liverpool in the first place. Pitt opposed the trade, and his own purpose in gathering the measurements of the slave ships was to allow abolitionists and their allies in the House of Commons "to detect any misrepresentations" the Liverpool representatives might make during the hearings on the slave trade that had been ordered by King George III in early 1788. See Clarkson, *History,* vol. I, 535–36; Meeting of April 22, 1788, Minutes of the Abolition Committee, Add. Ms. 21255, BL.

7. "Dimensions of the following Ships in the Port of Liverpool," *HCSP,* 67. Information on the voyages of the *Brooks* appears in *TSTD,* #80663–80673.

8. *Plan of an AFRICAN SHIP'S Lower Deck.*

9. Oldfield notes that Elford was a friend of Pitt's. See *Popular Politics and British Anti-Slavery,* 99.

10. *Plan of an African Ship's Lower Deck, with Negroes in the proportion of not quite one to a Ton* (Philadelphia: Mathew Carey, 1789); *Plan of an African Ship's Lower Deck, with Negroes in the proportion of not quite one to a Ton* (New York: Samuel Wood, n.d.).

11. Philip Lapsansky writes: "The famous 1789 representation of the cross section of a slave ship packed with chained black bodies lying in every available inch of the vessel was reprinted countless times throughout the age of American slavery." Versions appeared, for example, in Charles Crawford's expanded edition of his pamphlet *Observations on Negro Slavery* (Philadelphia, 1790); Thomas Branagan, *The Penitential Tyrant* (New York, 1807); the various editions of Clarkson's *History;* and three editions of Samuel Wood's pamphlet *Mirror of Misery* (1807, 1811, 1814). See Lapsansky's "Graphic Discord," 204.

12. Clarkson, *History,* 111; *Plan and Sections of a Slave Ship.*

13. Captain Parrey's note of 609 was the number of captives carried before the passage of the Dolben Act.

14. See Wood, *Blind Memory,* 29–32. For publications of the Society for the Improvement of Naval Architecture, see chapter 2, note 32, on page 372. For changes in the ship-building industry, see Peter Linebaugh, *The London Hanged: Crime and Civil Society in the Eighteenth Century* (London: Allen Lane, 1991), ch. 11.

15. The former slave-ship captain and now merchant James Penny testified in June 1788 that there existed "an Average of Breadth of Fourteen Inches" for the adults, twelve inches for boys and girls. Testimony of James Penny, June 13 and 16, 1788, in *HCSP,* 68:39.

16. The quotation is drawn from Alexander Falconbridge, *An Account of the Slave Trade on the Coast of Africa* (London, 1788), a pamphlet that had been recently published by the London committee.

17. There is evidence of a dispute between the Plymouth and London committees over the image of the ship, but its nature is unclear. William Elford noted the London committee's "strictures on the plan of the slave's deck published by us," to which he responded with "strong" expressions for which he later apologized. See William Elford to

James Phillips, March 18, 1789, Thompson-Clarkson MSS, vol. II, 93, Friends House Library, London.

18. Meeting of June 12, 1787, Minutes of the Abolition Committee, Add. Ms. 21254.

19. Clarkson, *History,* vol. I, 293–94, 367. Most of the quotes in the remainder of this section come from this two-volume history.

20. Ibid., vol. I, 322, 344, 364.

21. Clarkson's Journal of his Trip to the West Country, June 25–July 25, 1787, in Correspondence and Papers of Thomas Clarkson, St. John's College Library, Cambridge University. See *TSTD,* #17982 (*Africa*), #17985 (*Brothers*).

22. Clarkson, *History,* vol. I, 316, 323, 330, 359, 361, 365. Many sailors were afraid of the slave-trade merchants and did not want to testify before Parliament.

23. Clarkson's Journal of his Trip to the West Country; Thomas Clarkson, *The Impolicy of the Slave Trade* (London, 1788), 44–45; Clarkson, *History,* vol. I, 301, 310–18.

24. Clarkson, *History,* vol. I, 385–88, 409. Clarkson did later rent a second room away from the King's Arms, where he could interview sailors and write.

25. Clarkson, *History,* vol. I, 407, 410; Ellen Gibson Wilson, *Thomas Clarkson: A Biography* (New York: St. Martin's Press, 1990), 35.

26. Clarkson, *History,* vol. I, 392, 395, 300, 408, 438.

27. Clarkson, *An Essay on the Impolicy of the Slave Trade,* iii.

28. It is important to note that Clarkson undertook a second tour to gather evidence from sailors beginning in August 1788, and that the interviews found in *Substance* reflect this knowledge, which was drawn from visits to ports other than Bristol and Liverpool.

29. Clarkson, *History,* vol. I, 329; *Sherborne Mercury,* December 8, 1788, and February 1, 1790, as quoted in Oldfield, *Popular Politics and British Anti-Slavery,* 100. Oldfield notes that "it is not at all clear who was responsible for the original design" of the image of the slave ship (182). Yet Clarkson certainly played a leading role. He had visited Plymouth in November 1788 and later wrote, "I laid the foundation of another committee," a part of which would have been his research on the slave ship and his interviews among the sailors, which were cited in the text of the Plymouth broadside featuring the *Brooks.* He also tracked down and interviewed William Dove, a seaman who had sailed out of Liverpool, but now lived in Plymouth and worked as a cooper. Clarkson encouraged the Plymouth committee to conduct similar research on their own, which they did. When the enemies of abolition later claimed that Clarkson had exaggerated the abuses and cruelties practiced in the slave trade, William Elford drew upon local research to rebut the charges: "the whole tenor of the extensive evidence which their situation had enabled them to collect on the subject, corroborates and supports Mr. Clarkson's accounts in the most positive and ample manner." Two of their informants, mentioned in the local newspaper, the *Sherborne Mercury,* were James Brown and Thomas Bell, both masters in the Royal Navy and both thanked for the "very important intelligence they have already communicated, and for the offers of future intelligence." Clarkson interviewed Bell, a sailor "bred to the sea," and looked at some of his personal papers in preparing *The Substance of the Evidence* for publication in 1789. Bell had told him about the cruelties perpetrated against both sailors and slaves aboard the slave ship *Nelly,* including a gruesome account of how the hogs on board the ship tore at the flesh of slaves both dead and alive.

30. "Extract of a letter received from England," *Pennsylvania Gazette,* April 13, 1791; Testimony of Isaac Parker, 1791, *HCSP,* 73:123–39.

31. Thomas Clarkson, *An Essay on the Comparative Efficiency of Regulation or Abolition as applied to the Slave Trade* (London: James Phillips, 1789), 32.

32. *Newport Mercury,* February 22, 1790, *Providence Gazette; and Country Journal,* March 6, 1790. For a South Carolina minister's sympathetic response to the image of the *Brooks,* and a prescient remark that "this state will be the last to acquiesce in the annihilation of so inhuman a traffic," see *Dunlap's American Daily Advertiser,* February 2, 1792. See also Seymour Drescher, *Capitalism and Anti-Slavery: British Mobilization in Comparative Perspective* (New York: Oxford University Press, 1987), 24.

33. William Wilberforce's speech to the House of Commons, "On the Horrors of the Slave Trade," May 12, 1789, in William Cobbett, ed., *The Parliamentary History of England, From the Norman Conquest in 1066 to the year 1803* (London: T. Curson Hansard, 1806–20), 28 (1789–91). See also Seymour Drescher, "People and Parliament: The Rhetoric of the British Slave Trade," *Journal of Interdisciplinary History* 20 (1990), 561–80.

34. Testimony of Robert Norris, *HCSP,* 73:4–5, 8, 10; 69:203.

35. Roger Anstey, *The Atlantic Slave Trade and Abolition, 1760–1810* (London, 1975), 293; Drescher, *Capitalism and Anti-Slavery,* 20; Hugh Thomas, *The Slave Trade: The Story of the African Slave Trade, 1440–1870* (New York: Simon and Schuster, 1999), 513–15; Adam Hochschild, *Bury the Chains: Prophets and Rebels in the Fight to Free an Empire's Slaves* (Boston: Houghton Mifflin, 2005), 153–58.

36. *Parliamentary Register* (London, 1788), vol. 23, 606–7; Fox and Windham quoted in Clarkson, *History,* 1:111, 187; 2:326, 457. See also James W. LoGerfo, "Sir William Dolben and the 'Cause of Humanity,'" *Eighteenth-Century Studies* 6 (1973), 431–51. The Dolben Act was renewed in 1789, with new clauses to protect seamen, amended in 1794 and 1797, and made permanent in 1799 by 39 George III, c. 80.

37. Clarkson, *History,* 151–55; Clarkson's Journal of his Visit to France, 1789, Thomas Clarkson Collection, Robert W. Woodruff Library, Atlanta University Center, Atlanta. Some years later, in June 1814, Clarkson presented the emperor of Russia, Alexander I, a copy of the slave ship at a congress in Calais. The emperor explained that he had grown violently seasick in his passage to the gathering but that the image of the *Brooks* "made me more sick than the sea." See Wilson, *Thomas Clarkson,* 125.

38. Thomas Clarkson to Comte de Mirabeau, December 9, 1789, Papers of Thomas Clarkson, Huntington Library, San Marino, California. See also Thomas Clarkson, *The True State of the Case, respecting the Insurrection at St. Domingo* (Ipswich, 1792), 8.

39. Testimony of Thomas Trotter, 1790, *HCSP,* 73:81–101. Trotter also produced other testimony about his experience on the ship: he had, in 1785, before the rise of the abolitionist movement, published a pamphlet in which he compared the shipboard experiences of naval sailors and enslaved Africans. See his *Observations on the Scurvy, with a Review of the Theories lately advanced on that Disease; and the Theories of Dr. Milman refuted from Practice* (London, 1785; Philadelphia, 1793).

40. Testimony of Clement Noble, 1790, *HCSP,* 73:109–21. The Noble family was prominent in the trade. William Noble, likely Clement's father or uncle, was captain of the *Corsican Hero* on a voyage of 1769–70; Clement himself was almost surely on board (as mate), because he would eventually gain command of the vessel. He would then do as his father or uncle had done, taking relatives, probably his own sons, aboard the *Brooks* a few years later. Muster rolls reveal that Joseph Noble sailed with him on the voyage of 1783–84 and that he and a William Noble sailed on the ship in 1784–85. Joseph apparently got his own ship a few years later, as he appears in 1790 as captain of the *Abigail* bound from Liverpool to the Gold Coast. A James Noble captained the slave

ship *Tamazin* out of Liverpool in 1792. Some of the knowledge and lore of the slave trade was apparently passed on in a "trade book" kept by the elder Captain Noble. See "A Muster Roll for the Brooks, Clement Noble, from Africa and Jamaica," Port of Liverpool, October 6, 1784, Board of Trade 98/44, NA; "A Muster Roll for the Brooks, Clement Noble, from Africa and Jamaica," Port of Liverpool, April 29, 1786, BT 98/46; Letter of Instructions from Mathew Strong to Captain Richard Smyth of the ship *Corsican Hero*, January 19, 1771 380 TUO 4/4, David Tuohy papers, LRO (for the trade book). For the voyages of William, Joseph, and James, see *TSTD*, #90589, #90655, #80008, #83702.

41. Trotter, *Observations on the Scurvy*, 19–20; Testimony of Trotter, *HCSP*, 85, 87.

42. Ibid., 119, 117, 120.

43. Testimony of Trotter, *HCSP*, 88–89. Noble was sure that this "very troublesome turbulent man" wanted to kill him, and he might have been right. See Testimony of Noble, *HCSP*, 113.

44. Testimony of Noble, *HCSP*, 110, 112.

45. Noble commanded 162 men; 118 sailed on the first two voyages, but 11 of them died, leaving 107 who could have sailed with Noble on another voyage. Those who sailed on the first voyage (1781–83) had two opportunities to re-sign with Noble, making for 168 chances altogether. Of this number only thirteen names recur on the muster rolls, and even this modest number overstates crew persistence. Two men (John Davis and John Shaw) were apparently mates; Joseph Noble was probably the captain's son; and four others appear to have been "boys" apprenticed by parents. Of the remaining six, three had such common names—John Jones, Edward Jones, and John Smith—we cannot be sure they were the same person voyage to voyage. That leaves a total of three sailors who can be identified with certainty as having signed on a second time with Captain Noble: Peter Cummins and Robert Hartshorn sailed on the second voyage and again on the third. The third, Pat Clarke, sailed on the first voyage and again on the second, but he apparently thought better of it and deserted Noble in Kingston, Jamaica. See Testimony of Noble, *HCSP*, 112; "A Muster Roll for the Brooks, Clement Noble, from Africa and Jamaica," Port of Liverpool, April 15, 1783, Board of Trade 98/43; "A Muster Roll for the Brooks," October 6, 1784, BT 98/44; "A Muster Roll for the Brooks," April 29, 1786, BT 98/46.

46. Captain John Adams, *Sketches taken during Ten Voyages to Africa, Between the Years 1786 and 1800; including Observations on the Country between Cape Palmas and the River Congo; and Cursory Remarks on the Physical and Moral Character of the Inhabitants* (London, 1823; rpt. New York: Johnson Reprint Corporation, 1970), 9.

47. Clarkson, *History*, vol. II, 187; Lapsansky, "Graphic Discord," 202; Oldfield, *Popular Politics and British Anti-Slavery*, 163.

48. Clarkson, *History*, vol. II, 115. In the late eighteenth century, terms like "savage," "barbarian," and "civilized" invoked an entire theory of social progress and development—a stadial theory of history in which European civilization stood at the pinnacle, representing the highest stage of human evolution. Cries of "savagery" and "barbarism" had long been weapons as Europeans built their empires and subdued the peoples of the world. Within this understanding, trade was considered a source of virtue and a means of civilizing the non-European world. The more that other parts of the world traded with Europe, the less "savage" and "barbarian"—and the more like Europe—they would become. See Philip Gould, *Barbaric Traffic: Commerce and Antislavery in the Eighteenth-Century Atlantic World* (Cambridge, Mass.: Harvard University Press, 2003).

49. Clarkson, *An Essay on the Comparative Efficiency,* 58.

50. Ibid., 48.

51. John Wesley had made the point as he addressed the slave-trade merchant in 1774: "It is you that induce the African villain, to sell his countrymen; and in order thereto, to steal, rob, murder men, women and children without number: By enabling the English villain to pay him for so doing; whom you over pay for his execrable labour. It is your money, that is the spring of all, that impowers him to go on: So that whatever he or the African does in this matter, it is all your act and deed. And is your conscience quite reconciled to this? Does it never reproach you at all? Has gold entirely blinded your eyes, and stupefied your heart?" See his *Thoughts upon Slavery* (London, 1774; rpt. Philadelphia, 1778), 52.

52. Emma Christopher, *Slave Trade Sailors and their Captive Cargoes, 1730–1807* (Cambridge: Cambridge University Press, 2006), 164–168.

53. This quotation appeared with the image of the *Brooks* and commentary in *Address to the Inhabitants of Glasgow, Paisley, and the Neighbourhood, concerning the African Slave Trade, by a Society in Glasgow* (Glasgow, 1790), 8. Marcus Wood writes, "There is an awful rigor to the design." See his *Blind Memory,* 29. See also Oldfield, *Popular Politics and British Anti-Slavery,* 165; E. P. Thompson, "The Moral Economy of the English Crowd in the Eighteenth Century," *Past and Present* 50 (1971), 76–136.

54. Finley, "Committed to Memory," 16; Wood, "Imagining the Unspeakable," 216–17.

55. The phrase "diabolical calculations" was Clarkson's. See *History,* vol. II, 556. "Calculated inches" comes from William Roscoe's poem *The Wrongs of Africa* (London, 1788). See also Ottobah Cugoano, *Thoughts and Sentiments on the Evil of Slavery* (orig. publ. London, 1787, rpt. London: Penguin, 1999), 46, 85; J. Philmore, *Two Dialogues on the Man-Trade* (London: J. Waugh, 1760), 36, 37, 41.

56. Anstey, *Atlantic Slave Trade and Abolition,* 293, 315, 375–76, 398, 412.

57. W. E. B. DuBois, *The Suppression of the African Slave-Trade in the United States of America, 1638–1870* (orig. publ. 1896; Mineola, N.Y.: Dover Publications, Inc, 1970), 41, 43–45, 48, 51, 52, 56, 60–62, 68, 73, 85–86, 104, 108–9.

58. *TSTD,* #80673.

Epilogue: Endless Passage

1. "John Cranston's testimony to the Grand Jury, June 15, 1791," Newport Historical Society, Newport, Rhode Island, Box 43, folder 24. All quotations of Cranston and the grand jury foreman come from this document. More information about the *Polly* can be found in *TSTD,* #36560. The *Litchfield Monitor* reported on June 8, 1791, that Caleb Gardiner, another leading slave trader, was part owner of the vessel. The original number of captives, 142, appears in the Deposition of Isaac Stockman and Henry Clannen taken before Joannes Runnels, Governor of the Island of Saint Eustatius, October 2, 1794, Rhode Island Historical Society, Newport, Rhode Island.

2. A "young Lady" who wrote about the incident aboard the *Polly* in the *American Mercury* (June 6, 1791) raised the possibility that Cranston had accused D'Wolf in retaliation for "bad usage" aboard the ship. This is unlikely for two reasons: first, had this been the case, Cranston would have brought a different charge against D'Wolf, probably suing him for excessive violence, bilked wages, or pinched provisions, from which he might have gotten some personal benefit; second, and more important, if this had been

an issue, Stockman and Clannen would certainly have mentioned Cranston's bias against the captain in their own deposition. They did not.

3. Cranston added that the woman was "about middle aged" and had been fed while in the foretop. He said he did not know whether she would have recovered had she not been thrown overboard.

4. The "young Lady" wrote to her brother, using the case to remonstrate with him against his own involvement in the slave trade, but did not express a principled opposition. A second writer gave no self-description and offered no opinion on the case. A third, a "gentleman from Rhode Island," was clearly an abolitionist. All three had heard the same story, although two of them did not name Captain D'Wolf, while the third called him "Captain Wolf." Even though two of the letters were published before Cranston was questioned by the grand jury, they all told the same story: the enslaved woman came down with the smallpox; Captain D'Wolf asked the crew to help him throw her overboard (two of the three actually said he "ordered" them) and was refused; the captain then performed the act himself. See extract of a letter from a young Lady, Rhode Island, to her Brother, in this State, date May 24, 1791, *American Mercury,* June 6, 1791; Extract of a letter from Newport (Rhode-Island) dated the 5th month 9th, 1791, *Litchfield Monitor,* June 8, 1791; Extract of a letter from a gentleman in Rhode-Island, *Connecticut Courant*, July 18, 1791.

5. The gentleman abolitionist seemed to know the most about the case and may have played a role in getting Cranston before the grand jury. He recounted that Captain D'Wolf had been heard to say of the sick woman, "Damn her, she must go overboard." He added that "both mates" had died on the voyage, perhaps hinting at the spread of disease, and that "the people" (meaning several members of the crew, not only Cranston) had reported the atrocity, which caused a public outcry, and the collecting of affidavits by public authorities. See the *Connecticut Courant,* July 18, 1791. D'Wolf's evasive voyage, whether in the *Polly* or some other ship he or his family members owned, is not listed with him as captain in the *TSTD.* It is possible that he sailed with another family member.

6. Deposition of Isaac Stockman and Henry Clannen, 1794. The *TSTD* notes that the number of crew was twelve, but Stockman and Clannen say they were fifteen in number. It should also be noted that Cranston had everything to lose and nothing to gain by taking on a powerful figure like D'Wolf and that Stockman and Clannen, on the other hand, had everything to gain and nothing to lose. Indeed they might have been paid to make the testimony, as captains frequently bribed sailors to defend themselves against legal accusations of wrongdoing. Clannen, it should be remembered, had been implicated by Cranston in the murder. Moreover, the timing of their deposition, more than three years after the event in question, suggests the guiding hand of Captain D'Wolf.

7. George Howe, *Mount Hope; A New England Chronicle* (New York: Viking Press, 1959), 105, 106.

8. In the larger history of the slave trade, this was a most unusual event. As far as can be told from surviving evidence, living captives were not thrown overboard often. The reasons for this were not moral but largely economic. Moreover, captains did not often seek the opinions of their crews, nor did sailors often refuse their masters' wishes. To do so was to risk a charge of insubordination, punishable by flogging, and even mutiny, punishable by death. A voyage to compare to that of the *Polly* is treated by Mitra Sharafi in "The Slave Ship Manuscripts of Captain Joseph B. Cook: A Narrative Reconstruction of the Brig *Nancy*'s Voyage of 1793," *Slavery and Abolition* 24 (2003), 71–100.

9. Isaac Manchester, who brought the charges against D'Wolf in St. Thomas, was not present on the *Polly* when the event in question took place, but he had "heard" about it. It is not accidental that five months after the judge's favorable ruling for D'Wolf, Manchester was made captain of a Bristol, Rhode Island, slaver named the *Sally,* which was owned by the D'Wolf family. Manchester would remain an employee of the D'Wolf family for three and a half years (three voyages) and then became a slave-ship owner, and eventually a merchant, in his own right. See Rufus King Papers, box 6, folder 2, New-York Historical Society; *TSTD,* #36616, #36668, #36680.

10. *No Rum!—No Sugar! or, The Voice of Blood, being Half an Hour's Conversation, between a Negro and an English Gentleman, shewing the Horrible Nature of the Slave-Trade, and Pointing Out an Easy and Effectual Method of Terminating It, by an Act of the People* (London, 1792).

11. Howe, *Mount Hope,* 130–31.

12. Elizabeth Boody Schumpeter, ed., *English Overseas Trade Statistics, 1697–1808* (Oxford: Clarendon Press, 1960), 60–62; Susan B. Carter, ed, *Historical Statistics of the United States: Earliest Times to the Present* (New York: Cambridge University Press, 2006); Robin Blackburn, *The Making of New World Slavery: From the Baroque to the Modern, 1492–1800* (London: Verso, 1997), 581. This paragraph draws on Seymour Drescher, *Econocide: British Slavery in the Era of Abolition* (Pittsburgh: University of Pittsburgh Press, 1977). See his estimate that 92.3 percent of the cotton imported between 1801 and 1805 was slave-dependent (86).

13. *Memoirs of Crow,* 22, 32.

14. Three quotations: Testimony of Thomas Wilson, 1790, in *HCSP,* 73:12; Interview of Mr. James, *Substance,* 17; Testimony of Captain John Ashley Hall, 1790, *HCSP,* 72:233. For more general information, see Testimony of James Morley, 1790, *HCSP,* 73:164, 168; Testimony of Thomas Bolton Thompson, 1790, *HCSP,* 73:173; Testimony of Ninian Jeffreys, 1790, *HCSP,* 73:240; Testimony of James Towne, 1791, *HCSP,* 82:30; Testimony of John Simpson, 1791, *HCSP,* 82:44; Testimony of Dr. Harrison, 1791, *HCSP,* 82:53; Testimony of Robert Forster, 1791, *HCSP,* 82:133–34; Testimony of Mark Cook, 1791 *HCSP,* 82:199; Testimony of Hercules Ross, 1791, *HCSP,* 82:260.

15. Interview of Thompson, *Substance,* 25; Interview of Mr. James, *Substance,* 17; Interview of Ellison, *Substance,* 41. Thomas Clarkson apparently found out about these diseased, destitute sailors and the acts of compassion by the enslaved in his interviews with sailors in 1787–88. Afterward he and other abolitionists apparently made it a point to ask other sailors and seafaring people about these matters, and hence they accumulated testimony on the subject from twenty-three people for parliamentary hearings and *Substance of the Evidence.*

16. Interview of Mr. James, *Substance,* 17; Interview of Ellison, *Substance,* 41; Interview of Jeffreys, *Substance,* 92. For examples of the use of the concept "shipmate" by a captain and sailor (referring to enslaved Africans), see *Memoirs of Crow,* 159, 129; *Three Years Adventures,* 144, 425–27. On the close relations between the enslaved and slave-trade sailors in the "Masterless Caribbean" in the late 1780s and 1790s, the time of abolitionist ferment, see Julius Sherrard Scott III, "The Common Wind: Currents of Afro-American Communication in the Era of the Haitian Revolution," Ph.D. dissertation, Duke University, 1986, 134–46.

17. Historical archaeologists of the Caribbean are not yet able to confirm that European sailors were buried in African graveyards, but the leading figure in the field for Jamaica, Roderick Ebanks, considers the proposition to be likely: "Based on what I know

about enslaved persons, what you relate would not be unusual" (personal communication to the author, July 31, 2006). Future excavations in urban cemeteries will likely address the question.

18. *Memoirs of Crow,* 291.

19. The centrality of violence and terror was argued in Peter Linebaugh and Marcus Rediker, *The Many-Headed Hydra: Sailors, Slaves, Commoners, and the Hidden History of the Revolutionary Atlantic* (Boston: Beacon Press, 2000).

20. My thinking here has been influenced by Paul Gilroy, *The Black Atlantic: Modernity and Double Consciousness* (Cambridge: Harvard University Press, 1993), and Ruth Gilmore, *Golden Gulag: Prisons, Surplus, Crisis, and Opposition in Globalizing California* (Berkeley: University of California Press; 2006).

INDEX

———⊗∞⊗———